To the Texas Health Student,

You learn many skills in school. To excel in your studies, you need particular academic skills. The health information you will learn in *Health and Wellness* will provide you with life skills. These life skills will help you look and feel your best today and in the future.

Health and Wellness gives you the tools to apply ten important life skills. You'll learn how to set health goals and use guidelines to make responsible decisions. You'll learn skills for managing stress. You'll learn how to analyze what influences your health; how to access valid health information, products, and services; how to advocate for healthful behaviors; and how to practice healthful behaviors. You'll also learn how to communicate in healthful, effective ways with peers and family members and how to resolve conflicts. Finally, you'll learn resistance skills, such as how to say "no" to alcohol, tobacco, and other drugs.

You'll also learn the importance of asking your parents or guardian for help in developing these life skills. These responsible adults are your most important partners in learning how to care for yourself and how to use the life skills you'll learn in this book.

Macmillan/McGraw-Hill

Health & Wellness

TEXAS

Linda Meeks
The Ohio State University

Philip Heit
The Ohio State University

Macmillan
McGraw-Hill

About the Authors

Professor Linda Meeks and Dr. Philip Heit

Linda Meeks and Philip Heit are emeritus professors of Health Education in the College of Education at The Ohio State University. As faculty members, Linda and Philip held joint appointments in Health Education in the College of Education and in Allied Medicine in the College of Medicine. Linda and Philip are America's most widely published health education co-authors. They have collaborated for more than 25 years, co-authoring more than 300 health books that are used by millions of students from preschool through college. They are co-authors of an organized, sequential K–12 health education program, *Health and Wellness*, available from Macmillan/McGraw-Hill. Together, they have helped state departments of education as well as thousands of school districts develop comprehensive school health education curricula. Their books and curricula are used throughout the United States, as well as in Canada, Japan, Mexico, England, Puerto Rico, Spain, Egypt, Jordan, Saudi Arabia, Bermuda, and the Virgin Islands. Linda and Philip train professors as well as educators in state departments of education and school districts. Their book *Comprehensive School Health Education: Totally Awesome® Strategies for Teaching Health* is the most widely used book for teacher training in colleges, universities, state departments of education, and school districts. Thousands of teachers around the world have participated in their *Totally Awesome® Teacher Training Workshops*. Linda and Philip have been the keynote speakers for many teacher institutes and wellness conferences. They are personally and professionally committed to the health and well-being of youth.

Chapter 6 outlines emergency care procedures that reflect the standard of knowledge and accepted practices in the United States at the time this book was published. It is the teacher's responsibility to stay informed of changes in emergency care procedures in order to teach current accepted practices. The teacher also can recommend that students gain complete, comprehensive training from courses offered by the American Red Cross.

The McGraw-Hill Companies

Macmillan McGraw-Hill

Published by Macmillan/McGraw-Hill, of McGraw-Hill Education, a division of The McGraw-Hill Companies, Inc., Two Penn Plaza, New York, New York 10121.

Foldables™ and Guidelines for Making Responsible Decisions™ are trademarks of The McGraw-Hill Companies, Inc.

Printed in the United States of America

ISBN 0-02-280377-7/6

7 8 9 027 09 08

RFB&D
learning through listening

Students with print disabilities may be eligible to obtain an accessible, audio version of the pupil edition of this textbook. Please call Recording for the Blind and Dyslexic at 1-800-221-4792 for complete information.

Contributors

Celan Alo, M.D., MPH
Medical Epidemiologist
Bureau of Chronic Disease and Tobacco
    Prevention
Texas Department of Health
Austin, Texas

Danny Ballard, Ed.D.
Associate Professor, Health
Texas A&M University
College of Education
College Station, Texas

Lucille Villegas Barrera, M.E.D.
Elementary Science Specialist
Houston Independent School District
Houston, Texas

Gus T. Dalis, Ed.D.
Consultant of Health Education
Torrance, California

Alisa Evans-Debnam, MPH
Dean of Health Programs
Fayetteville Technical Community College
Fayetteville, North Carolina

**Susan C. Giarratano-Russell, MSPH,
    Ed.D., CHES**
Health Education, Evaluation and Media
    Consultant
National Center for Chronic Disease
    Prevention and Health Promotion
Centers for Disease Control and Prevention
Glendale, California

Donna Lloyd-Kolkin, Ph.D.
Principal Associate
Public Health Applications and Research
Abt Associates, Inc.
Bethesda, Maryland

Mulugheta Teferi, M.A.
Principal
Gateway Middle School
Center for Math, Science and
    Technology
St. Louis, Missouri

Roberto P. Treviño, M.D.
Director, Social and Health
    Research Center
Bienestar School-Based Diabetes
    Prevention Program
San Antonio, Texas

Dinah Zike, M.Ed.
Dinah Might Adventures LP
San Antonio, Texas

Content Reviewers

Mark Anderson
Supervisor, Health Physical
    Education
Cobb County Public Schools
Marietta, Georgia

Ken Ascoli
Assistant Principal
Our Lady of Fatima High
    School
Warren, Rhode Island

Jane Beougher, Ph.D.
Professor Emeritus of Health
    Education, Physical
    Education, and Education
Capital University
Westerville, Ohio

Lillie Burns
HIV/AIDS Prevention
    Education
Education Program
    Coordinator
Louisiana Department of
    Education
Baton Rouge, Louisiana

Jill English, Ph.D., CHES
Professor, Soka University
Aliso Viejo, California

Elizabeth Gallun, M.A.
Specialist, Comprehensive
    Health Education
Maryland State Department
    of Education
Baltimore, Maryland

Brenda Garza
Health Communications
    Specialist
Centers for Disease Control
    and Prevention
Atlanta, Georgia

Sheryl Gotts, M.S.
Consultant, Retired from
    Milwaukee Schools
Milwaukee, Wisconsin

Russell Henke, M.Ed.
Coordinator of Health
Montgomery County Public
    Schools
Rockville, Maryland

Kathy Kent
Health and Physical
    Education Teacher
Simpsonville Elementary
    School at Morton Place
Simpsonville, South Carolina

Bill Moser, M.S.
Program Specialist for Health
    and Character Education
Winston-Salem Forsyth City
    Schools
Winston-Salem, North
    Carolina

Debra Ogden
Curriculum Coordinator
District School Board of
    Collier County
Naples, Florida

Thurman Robins
Chair/Professor
Health and Kinesiology
    Department
Texas Southern University
Houston, Texas

**Sherman Sowby, Ph.D.,
    CHES**
Professor, Department of
    Health Science
California State University,
    Fresno
Fresno, California

Greg Stockton
Health and Safety Expert
American Red Cross
Washington, D.C.

**Deitra Wengert, Ph.D.,
    CHES**
Professor, Department of
    Health Science
Towson University
Towson, Maryland

**Susan Wooley-Goekler,
    Ph.D., CHES**
Adjunct Faculty
Kent State University
Kent, Ohio

Medical Reviewers

Celan Alo, M.D., MPH
Medical Epidemiologist
Bureau of Chronic Disease
    and Tobacco Prevention
Texas Department of Health
Austin, Texas

Donna Bacchi, M.D., MPH
Associate Professor of
    Pediatrics
Director, Division of
    Community Pediatrics
Texas Tech University
Health Science Center
Lubbock, Texas

**Olga Dominguez
    Satterwhite, R.D., L.D.**
Registered Dietitian and
    Diabetes Educator
Baylor College of Medicine
Houston, Texas

Roberto P. Treviño, M.D.
Director, Social and Health
    Research Center
Bienestar School-Based
    Diabetes Prevention
    Program
San Antonio, Texas

Contents

UNIT A Mental, Emotional, Family, and Social Health

CHAPTER 1

Mental and Emotional Health

LESSON **1** **Health and Wellness** **A4**
LIFE SKILLS ACTIVITY: Set Health Goals, **A7**
ON YOUR OWN: Finding Valid Information, **A8**

LESSON **2** **Character and Personality** **A10**
WRITE ABOUT IT!: Assess Myself, **A11**
CAREERS: Camp Counselor, **A12**
LIFE SKILLS ACTIVITY: Analyze What Influences Your Health, **A13**
BUILD CHARACTER: Responsibility: Role-Play Character, **A15**
LEARNING LIFE SKILLS: Set Health Goals, **A16**

LESSON **3** **Making Responsible Decisions** **A18**
ON YOUR OWN: Chart Your Chores, **A19**
CONSUMER WISE: Sole Searching, **A20**
LIFE SKILLS ACTIVITY: Make Responsible Decisions, **A20**

LESSON **4** **Emotions and Stress** **A22**
LINK: Science, **A23**
ON YOUR OWN: Anxiety and Boredom, **A25**
HEALTH ONLINE: Stress, **A26**
LIFE SKILLS ACTIVITY: Set Health Goals, **A27**
LINK: Science, **A28**

CHAPTER REVIEW **A30**

CHAPTER 2

Family and Social Health

LESSON 1 Healthful Relationships **A34**
LINK: Music, **A36**
ON YOUR OWN: Mediating a Conflict, **A38**
LIFE SKILLS ACTIVITY: Be a Health Advocate, **A39**

LESSON 2 Express Yourself **A40**
LINK: Science, **A41**
WRITE ABOUT IT!: Write a Letter, **A42**
MAKE A DIFFERENCE: Brainstorm for the Greater Good, **A42**
BUILD CHARACTER: Respect: Round Table, **A43**
LINK: Art, **A44**
LIFE SKILLS ACTIVITY: Resolve Conflicts, **A45**
LEARNING LIFE SKILLS: Use Communication Skills, **A46**

LESSON 3 Family Life **A48**
LIFE SKILLS ACTIVITY: Access Valid Health Information, Products,
                                   and Services, **A49**
CAREERS: Grief Counselor, **A51**
LIFE SKILLS ACTIVITY: Set Health Goals, **A51**
CONSUMER WISE: Find Help, **A52**
BUILD CHARACTER: Responsibility: Write a Notebook Entry, **A53**

LESSON 4 Making and Keeping Friends **A54**
LINK: Art, **A55**
WRITE ABOUT IT!: A Play About Friends, **A56**
LIFE SKILLS ACTIVITY: Make Responsible Decisions, **A59**
BUILD CHARACTER: Responsibility: Write a Skit, **A60**
LIFE SKILLS ACTIVITY: Use Resistance Skills, **A61**

LESSON 5 Practicing Abstinence **A62**
BUILD CHARACTER: Respect, **A63**; Caring, **A65**
LINK: Math, **A65**; WRITE ABOUT IT!: Showing Affection, **A67**
HEALTH ONLINE: Resisting Risk Behaviors, **A68**
LIFE SKILLS ACTIVITY: Use Resistance Skills, **A69**

CHAPTER REVIEW **A70**

UNIT A ACTIVITIES AND PROJECTS **A72**

LOG ON

www.mmhhealth.com
For more on Unit A
Mental, Emotional, Family,
and Social Health.

CHAPTER 3

Growth and Development

LESSON 1 Support and Control Systems **B4**
LINK: Science, **B5**
LINK: Art, **B6**
LINK: Math, **B8**
LIFE SKILLS ACTIVITY: Practice Healthful Behaviors, **B8**

LESSON 2 Transport Systems **B10**
MAKE A DIFFERENCE: Respiratory Rights, **B12**
LIFE SKILLS ACTIVITY: Set Health Goals, **B13**
WRITE ABOUT IT!: Function Flash Cards, **B14**
LIFE SKILLS ACTIVITY: Make Responsible Decisions, **B14**

LESSON 3 Growing and Changing **B16**
BUILD CHARACTER: Honesty/Respect/Responsibility/Fairness/
        Caring/Citizenship: Make a Time Line, **B17**
HEALTH ONLINE: Write the News on Body Systems, **B18**
CAREERS: Endocrinologist, **B19**
LIFE SKILLS ACTIVITY: Be a Health Advocate, **B19**
CONSUMER WISE: Decide to Buy or Not to Buy, **B22**
LIFE SKILLS ACTIVITY: Use Communication Skills, **B23**
LEARNING LIFE SKILLS: Manage Stress, **B24**

LESSON 4 Pregnancy and Childbirth **B26**
LINK: Science, **B27**
ON YOUR OWN: Make a Time Line, **B29**
LIFE SKILLS ACTIVITY: Use Resistance Skills, **B30**
LINK: Social Studies, **B31**

CHAPTER REVIEW **B32**

CHAPTER 4
Nutrition

LOG
ON

www.mmhhealth.com
For more on Unit B
Growth and Nutrition.

LESSON 1 Following Dietary Guidelines **B36**
CAREERS: Farmer, **B39**
LIFE SKILLS ACTIVITY: Practice Healthful Behaviors, **B39**
LINK: Science, **B40**
CONSUMER WISE: Choose Healthful Foods, **B41**

LESSON 2 Healthful Eating Habits **B42**
CONSUMER WISE: Choosing Foods at School, **B43**
LIFE SKILLS ACTIVITY: Set Health Goals, **B45**
WRITE ABOUT IT!: Set a Goal, **B46**
LIFE SKILLS ACTIVITY: Make Responsible Decisions, **B48**
LINK: Social Studies, **B49**

LESSON 3 Choosing Foods Carefully **B50**
LINK: Science, **B51**
HEALTH ONLINE: Compare Fast-Food Meals, **B52**
LIFE SKILLS ACTIVITY: Access Valid Health Information, Products,
                and Services, **B53**
BUILD CHARACTER: Caring: Helping People Who Have Food Allergies, **B54**
LINK: Math, **B55**
LEARNING LIFE SKILLS: Analyze What Influences Your Health, **B56**

LESSON 4 Healthful Weight **B58**
LINK: Math, **B60**
LIFE SKILLS ACTIVITY: Practice Healthful Behaviors, **B61**
BUILD CHARACTER: Respect: Accepting Differences, **B62**

LESSON 5 Body Image **B64**
ON YOUR OWN: Looking Into Body Image, **B65**
LIFE SKILLS ACTIVITY: Be a Health Advocate, **B66**
ON YOUR OWN: Make a List, **B68**
BUILD CHARACTER: Responsibility: Develop a Positive Body Image, **B69**

CHAPTER REVIEW **B70**

UNIT B ACTIVITIES AND PROJECTS **B72**

CHAPTER 5

Personal Health and Physical Activity

LESSON 1 Personal Health Care **C4**
BUILD CHARACTER: Caring: Brainstorm Better Behaviors, **C5**
LINK: Science, **C6**
LIFE SKILLS ACTIVITY: Practice Healthful Behaviors, **C7**
CONSUMER WISE: Make a Hair Care Brochure, **C8**
LIFE SKILLS ACTIVITY: Set Health Goals, **C9**

LESSON 2 Keeping Healthy and Getting Checkups **C10**
LINK: Science, **C12**
LIFE SKILLS ACTIVITY: Access Valid Health Information, Products,
and Services, **C13**
LINK: Music, **C14**
ON YOUR OWN: Make a Safety List, **C15**
LINK: Math, **C16**
LIFE SKILLS ACTIVITY: Access Valid Health Information, Products,
and Services, **C16**
LEARNING LIFE SKILLS: Be a Health Advocate, **C18**

LESSON 3 Caring for Your Teeth **C20**
CONSUMER WISE: Smile Bright, **C21**
LIFE SKILLS ACTIVITY: Make Responsible Decisions, **C23**
WRITE ABOUT IT!: A World of Dental Care, **C24**

LESSON 4 Physical Activity and Fitness **C26**
CAREERS: Aerobics Instructor, **C29**
LINK: Math, **C30**
LIFE SKILLS ACTIVITY: Analyze What Influences Your Health, **C31**

LESSON 5 Developing a Physical Fitness Plan **C32**
LINK: Physical Education, **C33**
LINK: Math, **C36**
LIFE SKILLS ACTIVITY: Set Health Goals, **C37**

LESSON 6 Staying Safe During Physical Activity **C38**
HEALTH ONLINE: Safety Equipment, **C40**
LINK: Physical Education, **C41**
LIFE SKILLS ACTIVITY: Make Responsible Decisions, **C41**
LINK: Art, **C42**
BUILD CHARACTER: Responsibility: Be Prepared, **C43**

CHAPTER REVIEW **C44**

CHAPTER 6

Violence and Injury Prevention

LESSON 1 Reducing the Risk of Violence **C48**
- **BUILD CHARACTER:** Responsibility: Responsible Responses, **C50**
- **LIFE SKILLS ACTIVITY:** Analyze What Influences Your Health, **C51**
- **LINK:** Social Studies, **C52**

LESSON 2 Being Safe at School and in the Community **C54**
- **LINK:** Art, **C58**
- **LIFE SKILLS ACTIVITY:** Set Health Goals, **C58**
- **LEARNING LIFE SKILLS:** Resolve Conflicts, **C60**

LESSON 3 Being Safe at Home and Outdoors **C62**
- **CONSUMER WISE:** Microwave Demo, **C63**
- **LINK:** Physical Education, **C65**
- **ON YOUR OWN:** Safety Tour, **C66**
- **LIFE SKILLS ACTIVITY:** Make Responsible Decisions, **C67**

LESSON 4 Severe Weather and Natural Disasters **C68**
- **LINK:** Science, **C70**
- **LIFE SKILLS ACTIVITY:** Set Health Goals, **C71**
- **HEALTH ONLINE:** Moving Disasters, **C72**
- **MAKE A DIFFERENCE:** Help Those in Need, **C73**

LESSON 5 The Rules of First Aid **C74**
- **WRITE ABOUT IT!:** Publish Emergency Guidelines, **C75**
- **BUILD CHARACTER:** Citizenship: Learn Lifesaving Skills, **C76**
- **LIFE SKILLS ACTIVITY:** Manage Stress, **C77**

LESSON 6 Basic First Aid Skills **C78**
- **CAREERS:** Disaster Relief Worker, **C80**
- **LIFE SKILLS ACTIVITY:** Be a Health Advocate, **C81**
- **LINK:** Math, **C82**
- **ON YOUR OWN:** Gather First Aid Supplies, **C85**

CHAPTER REVIEW **C86**

UNIT C ACTIVITIES AND PROJECTS **C88**

LOG ON

www.mmhhealth.com
For more on Unit C
Personal Health and
Safety.

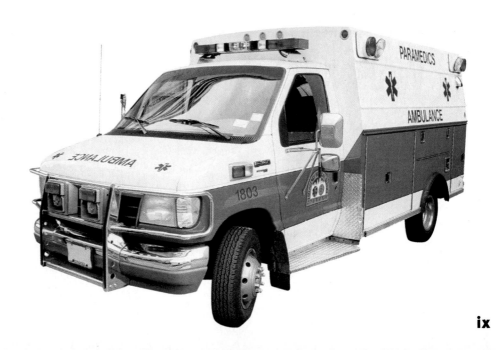

UNIT D Drugs and Disease Prevention

CHAPTER 7

Alcohol, Tobacco, and Other Drugs

LESSON 1 Drugs and Medicines **D4**
CONSUMER WISE: Know Your Medicine, **D5**
HEALTH ONLINE: Study Side Effects, **D7**
ON YOUR OWN: OTC Labels, **D8**
LINK: Math, **D9**
LIKE SKILLS ACTIVITY: Make Responsible Decisions, **D10**

LESSON 2 Living a Drug-Free Lifestyle **D12**
LIFE SKILLS ACTIVITY: Manage Stress, **D15**
BUILD CHARACTER: Responsibility: Show Your Support, **D16**
LINK: Art, **D17**
WRITE ABOUT IT!: Living Drug-Free, **D18**
ON YOUR OWN: Dialogue on Drugs, **D19**

LESSON 3 Tobacco **D20**
CONSUMER WISE: An Expensive Habit, **D22**
LINK: Science, **D23**
ON YOUR OWN: Learn the Law, **D24**
BUILD CHARACTER: Responsibility: Sing a Smoke-Free Song, **D25**
LIFE SKILLS ACTIVITY: Analyze What Influences Your Health, **D26**
LEARNING LIFE SKILLS: Use Resistance Skills, **D28**

LESSON 4 Alcohol **D30**
ON YOUR OWN: Alcohol Model, **D32**
LINK: Physical Education, **D34**
MAKE A DIFFERENCE: Maintaining a Drug-Free Lifestyle, **D36**
LIFE SKILLS ACTIVITY: Set Health Goals, **D37**

LESSON 5 Illegal Drug Use **D38**
BUILD CHARACTER: Honesty: Inform Others, **D39**
LINK: Science, **D40**
LIFE SKILLS ACTIVITY: Set Health Goals, **D41**
ON YOUR OWN: Make a Harmful/Healthful Card, **D43**
CAREERS: DEA Agent, **D44**

CHAPTER REVIEW **D46**

CHAPTER 8

Communicable and Chronic Diseases

LESSON 1 Communicable Diseases **D50**
    LINK: Science, **D52**
    CAREERS: Microbiologist, **D53**
    LIFE SKILLS ACTIVITY: Practice Healthful Behaviors, **D55**

LESSON 2 Sexually Transmitted Diseases, HIV Infection, and AIDS **D56**
    LINK: Social Studies, **D58**
    LIFE SKILLS ACTIVITY: Analyze What Influences Your Health, **D59**
    CONSUMER WISE: The Fine Points of Needle Safety, **D60**
    LIFE SKILLS ACTIVITY: Be a Health Advocate, **D61**

LESSON 3 Noncommunicable Diseases **D62**
    LINK: Art, **D64**
    LIFE SKILLS ACTIVITY: Use Communication Skills, **D65**
    LIFE SKILLS ACTIVITY: Set Health Goals, **D66**
    LINK: Science, **D67**
    BUILD CHARACTER: Responsibility: Plan for Emergencies, **D69**

LESSON 4 Managing Chronic Illnesses **D70**
    ON YOUR OWN: Allergen Checklist, **D72**
    HEALTH ONLINE: Treating Asthma, **D72**
    WRITE ABOUT IT!: Managing Illness, **D74**
    LINK: Science, **D74**
    LIFE SKILLS ACTIVITY: Be a Health Advocate, **D75**
    LEARNING LIFE SKILLS: Access Valid Health Information, Products, and Services, **D76**

CHAPTER REVIEW **D78**

UNIT D ACTIVITIES AND PROJECTS **D80**

LOG ON

www.mmhhealth.com
For more on Unit D Drugs and Disease Prevention.

CHAPTER 9

Consumer and Community Health

LESSON 1 Managing Your Time and Money **E4**
ON YOUR OWN: Track Your Time, **E5**
LINK: Math, **E6**
BUILD CHARACTER: Responsibility: Choose Entertainment Responsibly, **E8**
LIFE SKILLS ACTIVITY: Set Health Goals, **E8**
LEARNING LIFE SKILLS: Make Responsible Decisions, **E10**

LESSON 2 Finding Valid Health Information **E12**
ON YOUR OWN: Valid Sources, **E13**
HEALTH ONLINE: Find Valid Health Information, **E14**
LIFE SKILLS ACTIVITY: Use Resistance Skills, **E14**

LESSON 3 Evaluating Media and Advertising Influences **E16**
CONSUMER WISE: Let the Buyer Beware, **E17**
BUILD CHARACTER: Citizenship: Exercise Your Rights, **E18**
LIFE SKILLS ACTIVITY: Access Valid Health Information, Products,
                          and Services, **E19**
LINK: Music, **E20**
ON YOUR OWN: Compare Shampoos, **E21**

LESSON 4 Community Health Services **E22**
LINK: Math, **E23**
WRITE ABOUT IT!: The History of Health Care, **E24**
LIFE SKILLS ACTIVITY: Analyze What Influences Your Health, **E25**
MAKE A DIFFERENCE: Help Others, **E26**
LINK: Social Studies, **E27**
LINK: Art, **E28**
CAREERS: Health Inspector, **E29**

CHAPTER REVIEW **E30**

CHAPTER 10
Environmental Health

LOG ON

www.mmhhealth.com
For more on Unit E
Community and
Environmental Health.

LESSON 1 Your Environment **E34**
LINK: Science, **E35**
WRITE ABOUT IT!: Sports and Self-Esteem, **E36**
BUILD CHARACTER: Respect: Welcome a New Friend, **E37**
LINK: Math, **E38**
LIFE SKILLS ACTIVITY: Be a Health Advocate, **E39**
LEARNING LIFE SKILLS: Practice Healthful Behaviors, **E42**

LESSON 2 Social-Emotional Environment **E44**
BUILD CHARACTER: Caring: Pay Someone a Compliment, **E46**
LINK: Music, **E47**
LIFE SKILLS ACTIVITY: Resolve Conflicts, **E49**

LESSON 3 Clean Air **E50**
LINK: Science, **E51**
ON YOUR OWN: Home Safety, **E52**
LIFE SKILLS ACTIVITY: Analyze What Influences Your Health, **E53**
LINK: Science, **E54**
CAREERS: Climatologist, **E55**

LESSON 4 Clean Water **E56**
HEALTH ONLINE: Pollution and Conservation, **E58**
LINK: Science, **E59**
LIFE SKILLS ACTIVITY: Be a Health Advocate, **E61**
BUILD CHARACTER: Citizenship: Conserve at School, **E62**
LIFE SKILLS ACTIVITY: Set Health Goals, **E63**

LESSON 5 Clean Planet **E64**
LINK: Social Studies, **E66**
LIFE SKILLS ACTIVITY: Be a Health Advocate, **E67**
ON YOUR OWN: Saving Energy at Home, **E70**
LIFE SKILLS ACTIVITY: Set Health Goals, **E70**
CONSUMER WISE: Going Organic, **E71**

LESSON 6 Enjoying Your Environment **E72**
LINK: Social Studies, **E74**
LINK: Art, **E76**
LIFE SKILLS ACTIVITY: Practice Healthful Behaviors, **E77**

CHAPTER REVIEW **E78**

UNIT E ACTIVITIES AND PROJECTS **E80**

GLOSSARY **R1**

GLOSARIO **R9**

INDEX **R17**

Features and Activities

Unit A — Mental, Emotional, Family, and Social Health

Learning Life Skills
Set Health Goals, **A16**
Use Communication Skills, **A46**

Life Skills Activities
Set Health Goals, **A7, A27, A51**
Analyze What Influences Your Health, **A13**
Make Responsible Decisions, **A20, A59**
Be a Health Advocate, **A39**
Resolve Conflicts, **A45**
Access Valid Health Information, Products, and Services, **A49**
Use Resistance Skills, **A61, A69**

Build Character
Responsibility: Role-Play Character, **A15**
Respect: Round Table, **A43**
Responsibility: Write a Notebook Entry, **A53**
Responsibility: Write a Skit, **A60**
Respect: Choosing Friends, **A63**
Caring: Showing Empathy, **A65**

Cross-Curricular Links
Write About It!, **A11, A42, A56, A67**
Science, **A23, A28, A41**
Math, **A65**
Art, **A44, A55**
Music, **A36**

On Your Own for School or Home
Finding Valid Information, **A8**
Chart Your Chores, **A19**
Anxiety and Boredom, **A25**
Mediating a Conflict, **A38**

Consumer Wise
Sole Searching, **A20**
Find Help, **A52**

Health Online
Stress, **A26**
Resisting Risk Behaviors, **A68**

Unit B — Growth and Nutrition

Learning Life Skills
Manage Stress, **B24**
Analyze What Influences Your Health, **B56**

Life Skills Activities
Practice Healthful Behaviors, **B8, B39, B61**
Set Health Goals, **B13, B45**
Make Responsible Decisions, **B14, B48**
Be a Health Advocate, **B19, B66**
Use Communication Skills, **B23**
Use Resistance Skills, **B30**
Access Valid Health Information, Products, and Services, **B53**

Build Character
Honesty/Respect/Responsibility/Fairness/Caring/
  Citizenship: Make a Time Line, **B17**
Caring: Helping People Who Have Food Allergies, **B54**
Respect: Accepting Differences, **B62**
Responsibility: Develop a Positive Body Image, **B69**

Cross-Curricular Links
Science, **B5, B27, B40, B51**
Art, **B6**
Math, **B8, B55, B60**
Write About It!, **B14, B46**
Social Studies, **B31, B49**

On Your Own for School or Home
Make a Time Line, **B29**
Looking Into Body Image, **B65**
Make a List, **B68**

Consumer Wise
Decide to Buy or Not to Buy, **B22**
Choose Healthful Foods, **B41**
Choosing Foods at School, **B43**

Health Online
Write the News on Body Systems, **B18**
Compare Fast-Food Meals, **B52**

Unit C Personal Health and Safety

Learning Life Skills
Be a Health Advocate, **C18**
Resolve Conflicts, **C60**

Life Skill Activities
Practice Healthful Behaviors, **C7**
Set Health Goals, **C9, C37, C58, C71**
Access Valid Health Information, Products,
    and Services, **C13, C16**
Be a Health Advocate, **C18, C81**
Make Responsible Decisions, **C23, C41, C67**
Analyze What Influences Your Health, **C31, C51**
Manage Stress, **C77**

Build Character
Caring: Brainstorm Better Behaviors, **C5**
Responsibility: Be Prepared, **C43**
Responsibility: Responsible Responses, **C50**
Citizenship: Learn Lifesaving Skills, **C76**

Cross-Curricular Links
Science, **C6, C12, C70**
Music, **C14**
Math, **C16, C30, C36, C82**
Write About It!, **C24, C75**
Physical Education, **C33, C41, C65**
Art, **C42, C58**
Social Studies, **C52**

On Your Own for School or Home
Make a Safety List, **C15**
Safety Tour, **C66**
Gather First Aid Supplies, **C85**

Consumer Wise
Make a Hair Care Brochure, **C8**
Smile Bright, **C21**
Microwave Demo, **C63**

Health Online
Safety Equipment, **C40**
Moving Disasters, **C72**

Unit D Drugs and Disease Prevention

Learning Life Skills
Use Resistance Skills, **D28**
Access Valid Health Information, Products,
    and Services, **D76**

Life Skill Activities
Make Responsible Decisions, **D10**
Manage Stress, **D15**
Analyze What Influences Your Health, **D26, D59**
Set Health Goals, **D37, D41, D66**
Practice Healthful Behaviors, **D55**
Be a Health Advocate, **D61, D75**
Use Communication Skills, **D65**

Build Character
Responsibility: Show Your Support, **D16**
Responsibility: Sing a Smoke-Free Song, **D25**
Honesty: Inform Others, **D39**
Responsibility: Plan for Emergencies, **D69**

Health Online
Study Side Effects, **D7**
Treating Asthma, **D72**

Cross-Curricular Links
Math, **D9**
Art, **D17, D64**
Write About It!, **D18, D74**
Science, **D23, D40, D52, D67, D74**
Physical Education, **D34**
Social Studies, **D58**

On Your Own for School or Home
OTC Labels, **D8**
Dialogue on Drugs, **D19**
Learn the Law, **D24**
Alcohol Model, **D32**
Make a Harmful/Healthful Card, **D43**
Allergen Checklist, **D72**

Consumer Wise
Know Your Medicine, **D5**
An Expensive Habit, **D22**
The Fine Points of Needle Safety, **D60**

Features and Activities

Unit E — Community and Environmental Health

Learning Life Skills
Make Responsible Decisions, **E10**
Practice Healthful Behaviors, **E42**

Life Skills Activities
Set Health Goals, **E8, E63, E70**
Use Resistance Skills, **E14**
Access Valid Health Information, Products,
  and Services, **E19**
Analyze What Influences Your Health, **E25, E53**
Be a Health Advocate, **E39, E61, E67**
Resolve Conflicts, **E49**
Practice Healthful Behaviors, **E77**

Build Character
Responsibility: Choose Entertainment Responsibly, **E8**
Citizenship: Exercise Your Rights, **E18**
Respect: Welcome a New Friend, **E37**
Caring: Pay Someone a Compliment, **E46**
Citizenship: Conserve at School, **E62**

Cross-Curricular Links
Math, **E6, E23, E38**
Music, **E20, E47**
Write About It, **E24, E36**
Social Studies, **E27, E66, E74**
Art, **E28, E76**
Science, **E35, E51, E54, E59**

On Your Own for School or Home
Track Your Time, **E5**
Valid Sources, **E13**
Compare Shampoos, **E21**
Home Safety, **E52**
Saving Energy at Home, **E70**

Consumer Wise
Let the Buyer Beware, **E17**
Going Organic, **E71**

Health Online
Find Valid Health Information, **E14**
Pollution and Conservation, **E58**

Life Skills

Life skills are abilities that help you maintain and improve health.
Below are the life skills taught in this text.

- Access Valid Health Information, Products, and Services. See page **D76**.
- Practice Healthful Behaviors. See page **E42**.
- Manage Stress. See page **B24**.
- Analyze What Influences Your Health. See page **B56**.
- Use Communication Skills. See page **A46**.
- Use Resistance Skills. See page **D28**.
- Resolve Conflicts. See page **C60**.

- Set Health Goals. See page **A16**.
- Make Responsible Decisions. See page **E10**.
- Be a Health Advocate. See page **C18**.

Using  To help you learn these
life skills, each of the Learning Life Skills features in this
book includes Foldables™. Foldables are three-dimensional
graphic organizers you will make. They will help you
understand the main points of each life skill.

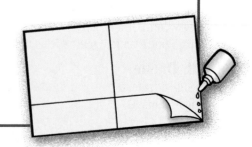

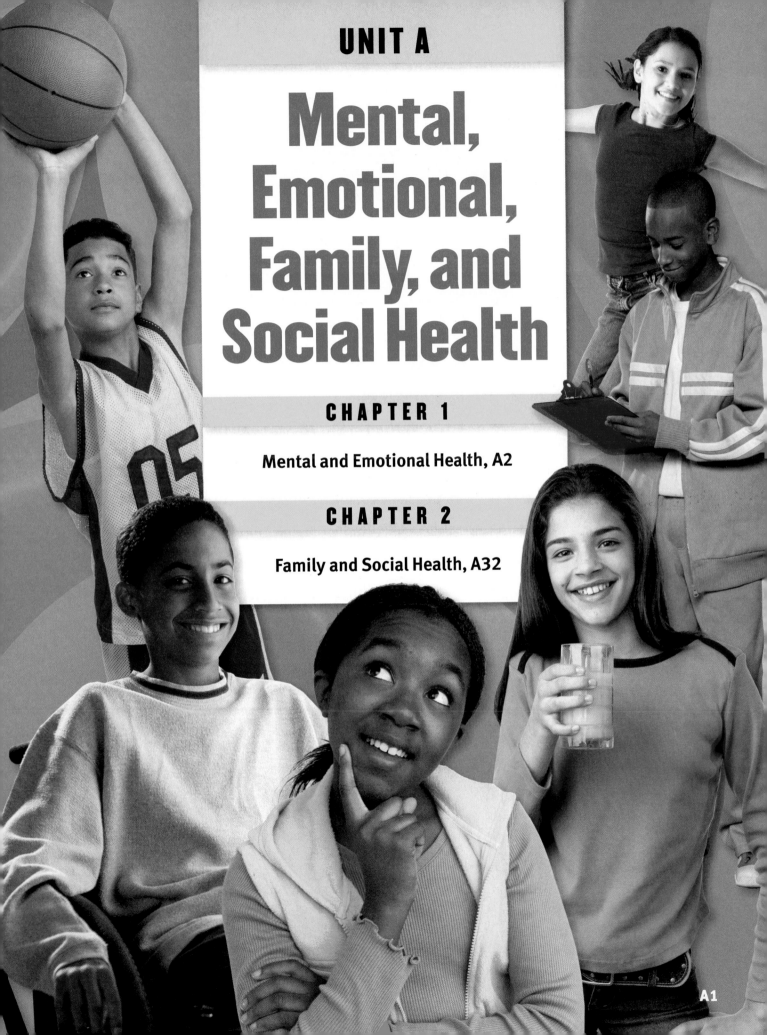

UNIT A

Mental, Emotional, Family, and Social Health

CHAPTER 1

Mental and Emotional Health, A2

CHAPTER 2

Family and Social Health, A32

A1

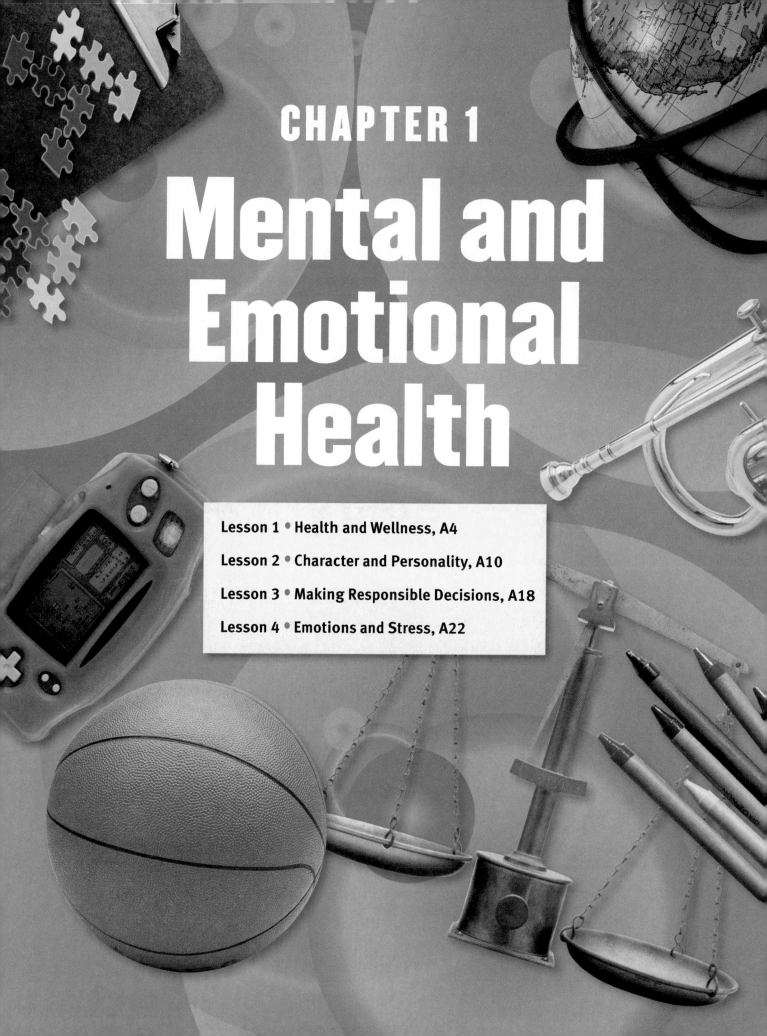

CHAPTER 1
Mental and Emotional Health

Lesson 1 • Health and Wellness, A4

Lesson 2 • Character and Personality, A10

Lesson 3 • Making Responsible Decisions, A18

Lesson 4 • Emotions and Stress, A22

What Do You Know About
Mental and Emotional Health?

1. What are the three parts of health?
2. Why is it important to set health goals?
3. How can you manage stress?

The Inside Story

A Riddle

What do you experience almost every day? There are a variety of things that cause it. Without it, your life would be very boring—maybe even dangerous. It helps you do your best in tough situations and rise to meet difficult challenges. It can increase your heart rate, make you tired, and increase your risk of disease. What is it? It is *stress*. While you cannot avoid stress, you can learn to reduce and manage it.

 LOG ON Visit **www.mmhhealth.com** for activities and information on mental and emotional health.

Health and Wellness

You will learn . . .

- the three parts of health.
- ways to take responsibility for your health.
- ten life skills to practice.
- steps to follow to set health goals and achieve them.
- steps to follow to access valid health information, products, and services.

Vocabulary

- health, A5
- physical health, A5
- mental and emotional health, A5
- family and social health, A5
- wellness, A5
- heredity, A5
- random events, A5
- lifestyle, A5
- life skill, A6
- risk behavior, A7
- abstinence, A7
- health goal, A7

You may have heard the saying "Anything worth having is worth working for." It is true of success in school, in sports, and in whatever else you do. It is also true for your health. Practicing healthful behaviors and staying healthy depend on how firmly you are committed to adopting healthful habits and practicing life skills.

What Is Health?

Health is the state of a person's body, mind, and feelings, and how he or she gets along with others.

There are three parts of health. **Physical health** is the condition of a person's body. **Mental and emotional health** is the condition of a person's mind and how he or she expresses feelings. **Family and social health** is the condition of a person's relationships with others.

The term *wellness* is another way of saying "good health." **Wellness** is a state of balanced health or well-being.

Wellness is not only about maintaining physical health. A person might have cancer, or even be confined to a wheelchair and still have a high level of wellness because their mental and emotional, and family and social health is positive. It's all about balance.

Factors That Affect Your Health

Several factors influence a person's health. One factor is **heredity**, the sum of the traits transmitted to a person by his or her biological parents, or inherited. You may inherit green eyes, or a health condition. Heredity is beyond your control.

Another factor that affects your health is the quality of health care you receive. People who get regular health care tend to enjoy better health than those who do not.

Random events are events over which a person has little or no control. Becoming a victim of a random event such as an unintentional injury or violence can be reduced by practicing preventive behavior. Some random events can even be prevented completely.

Finally, the decisions you make affect your health. If you do not make responsible decisions, your health will suffer. Your health will benefit if you choose a healthful lifestyle. **Lifestyle** means the way in which a person lives. For example, if you had an inherited risk of heart disease, you might reduce your risk by changing your lifestyle to include exercise.

▼ **To achieve wellness, you must keep all three parts of health in balance.**

Mental/ Emotional

Family/ Social

Physical

What three factors affect health?

A5

Do You Know

According to the Federal Communications Commission, on average children in the United States watch television for more than four hours each day.

▼ **Eating healthful foods is one way to take responsibility for your health.**

Taking Responsibility for Your Health

Some factors that affect your health are beyond your control. However, you can control many factors.

The fact that you have some control over your health means that you are responsible for much of your health. You can make responsible decisions and practice healthful habits. You can practice life skills to improve your health.

Ten Life Skills to Practice

A **life skill** is an ability that helps maintain and improve health. Practice the life skills below.

- Access valid health information, products, and services.
- Practice healthful behaviors.
- Manage stress.
- Analyze what influences your health.
- Use communication skills.
- Use resistance skills.
- Resolve conflicts.
- Set health goals.
- Make responsible decisions.
- Be a health advocate.

Practice Healthful Behaviors

One life skill involves practicing healthful behaviors, actions that increase the level of health. Examples are eating healthful foods, getting plenty of physical activity, getting enough rest and sleep, and getting regular physical examinations. To practice healthful behaviors:

1. Learn about a healthful behavior.
2. Practice the healthful behavior in the correct way.
3. Ask for help if you need it.
4. Make the healthful behavior a habit.

Avoiding Risk Behaviors

A **risk behavior** is an action that can harm people. There are many risk behaviors. Examples include using tobacco or riding a bike without a helmet.

Abstinence is the act of avoiding risk behaviors. You practice abstinence when you avoid situations where risk behaviors are likely. In Lesson 3, you will learn resistance skills to help you practice abstinence. Choosing friends who do not participate in risk behaviors also helps you practice abstinence.

Setting Health Goals

You can plan to achieve health. To help you it is useful to set health goals. A **health goal** is the healthful aim or purpose that a person can take steps to achieve through healthful actions over a lifetime.

To set goals, take four steps, as shown in the Life Skills Activity below. In step 3 you will make a plan. The plan must include a way to measure your progress.

▲ Setting health goals will help you avoid risk behaviors.

What is a risk behavior?

LIFE SKILLS

CRITICAL THINKING

Set Health Goals

1. **Write the health goal you want to set:** *I will take responsibility for my health.*

2. **Tell how the health goal will affect your health.** By taking responsibility for my health, I can reduce the risk of premature death and injuries from accidents.

3. **Describe a plan you will follow. Keep track of your progress.** Brainstorm some healthful behaviors, such as managing stress, that will help you take responsibility for your health. Record them in a notebook that you share with your family. On a calendar, record the days on which you do the healthful behaviors you listed.

4. **Evaluate how your plan worked.** After one week, review your calendar. Do you take responsibility for your health? What do you do? What do you need to do?

My Health Inventory
☑ I will take responsibility for my health.
☑ I will practice healthful behaviors.
☑ I will avoid risk behaviors.

Accessing Valid Health Information, Products, and Services

You need valid health information, products, and services to stay healthy. Valid information is accurate, based on actual research. Do you know if information is valid? How do you get health products and services? Follow these steps.

1. **Identify when you need health information, products, and services.** Suppose you are going to be in the sun and want to protect yourself against skin cancer. You need health information, products, and services.

2. **Identify where you can find health information, products, and services.** When you need health information, products, and services, you should turn to trusted sources. These include parents and guardians, health care professionals, such as your physician or dentist, and government and professional organizations such as the American Red Cross. Other sources include books, the World Wide Web, your health teacher, videos, and television programs. Are all of these sources valid?

3. **Locate health information, products, and services.** How do you check whether a source of information is valid? Is the researcher, author, speaker, or organization qualified? Is the information based on current research?

4. **Evaluate what you found.** Suppose you are not satisfied with health products or health services. You might write a letter of complaint or contact a federal agency.

◀ **Your school and local public libraries are good places to find valid health information.**

Being Health Literate

Being health literate means you have the knowledge and skill needed to protect all three parts of your health—physical, mental and emotional, and family and social. The four skills of health literacy include

Effective communication If you are health literate, you are able to communicate. You express your knowledge, beliefs, and ideas. You write, talk, draw, make a graph, or use technology.

Critical thinking If you are health literate, you investigate situations before you decide what to do. You use the Guidelines for Making Responsible Decisions™ (Lesson 3).

Self-directed learning If you are health literate, you are able to gather and use facts. You read books, contact organizations, or search the Internet for facts. You choose reliable and accurate sources.

Responsible citizenship If you are health literate, you consider how your behavior affects your community, nation, and world. Your behavior is healthful and safe. You obey laws and consider the guidelines of your family. You show respect to others.

 How would you define health literacy?

LESSON 1 REVIEW

Review Concepts

1. **Recall** the three parts of health.

2. **List** two examples of healthful behaviors that affect more than one part of health.

3. **Explain** steps you would follow if you needed valid health information.

Critical Thinking

4. **Evaluate** your actions and tell what you do to be health literate.

5. **Explain** why it is important for you to take responsibility for your health.

6. **LIFE SKILLS** **Set Health Goals** What is the first step in the process of setting health goals?

Character and Personality

You will learn . . .

- factors that influence your personality.
- ways to maintain positive self-esteem.
- the six traits of good character.

Vocabulary

- values, A11
- character, A11
- personality, A11
- environment, A11
- self-esteem, A12
- respect, A14

Who are you? What is it that makes you unique? How would you describe yourself? Many factors go into making up the unique person that you are. For one thing, the way you look is unique. You also have your own way of thinking. What else makes you who you are?

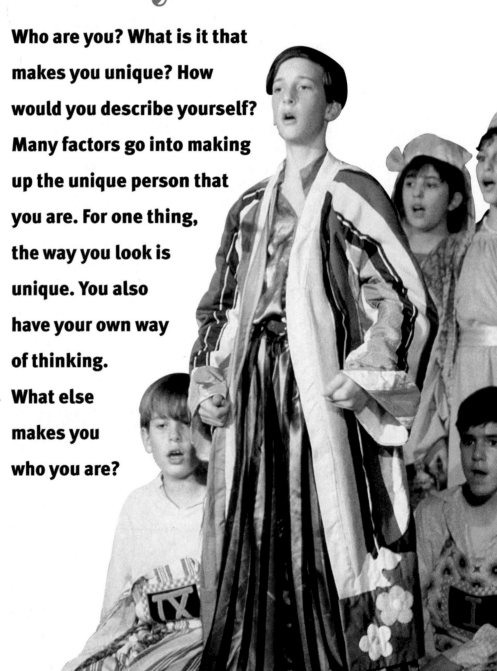

Personality

Several factors shape the person you will become. For example, you have a set of values. **Values** are the principles or standards that guide the way a person acts. Positive values include things such as family, health, or academic success. Another thing that sets you apart is your **character**, the effort a person uses to act on responsible values.

Personality is a person's unique blend of physical, mental, social, and emotional traits. It is what makes you act, think, and feel the way you do. While everyone has his or her own personality, many people share some common traits. For example, some people act quickly and take risks. Others are very careful in their actions.

Four factors influence your personality:

- Responsible adults influence your personality. They teach you their values, some of which you may adopt.

- The **environment** in which you live, everything that surrounds you, can affect your personality. Your environment includes the emotions, attitudes, and behaviors of people around you.

- Your heredity—the traits that have been transmitted to you by your biological parents—also shapes your personality. Your body type is inherited. You might be tall and muscular, or short and slim. Physical and mental traits can influence what you like to do and the way you perform tasks.

- Your behavior, or way of acting, also affects your personality. What you do will affect whether people think of you as outgoing or shy, friendly or withdrawn. Your self-concept—your mental view of who you are—may differ greatly from how others view you.

✔ **What factors influence your personality?**

write About It!

Assess Myself

Conduct an honest self-assessment to identify your strengths and weaknesses. What skills would you like to improve? Consider asking a trusted adult to help you. Then write down the results of your assessment. Include a plan for improving areas of weakness. Remember that everybody does something well. There's no shame in having weaknesses—if you strive to improve!

▲ **Your talents and hobbies help to shape your personality.**

Self-Esteem

Perhaps you wonder what other people think of you. However, what do you think of yourself? **Self-esteem** is what a person thinks about himself or herself. Your self-esteem can be positive or negative.

People with positive self-esteem tend to act responsibly. They are confident about reaching their goals. They are honest about evaluating their strengths and weaknesses and work to improve in all areas. They tend to learn from criticism. If they have a setback, they try to overcome it and focus on succeeding.

People with negative self-esteem, on the other hand, might take criticism as defeat. They might blame others for a mistake rather than correcting the situation. They might lack courage to try to reach their goals.

Ways to Maintain or Improve Self-Esteem

To maintain or improve self-esteem, work to develop new skills. Set goals to strengthen skills that need improvement. Join after-school programs to find

▲ **Positive self-esteem helps build confidence.**

CAREERS IN HEALTH

Camp Counselor

Do you like the out-of-doors and enjoy helping others? If so, you might consider becoming a camp counselor. Counselors work in all kinds of camps, from day camps to overnight camps, in cities and in the woods. Some camps focus on outdoor activities, while others highlight sports, drama, even health. Many camps have Counselor-in-Training programs for young people who want to become counselors. No matter what type of camp interests you, all camp counselors must be responsible.

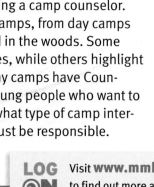

LOG ON Visit **www.mmhhealth.com** to find out more about this and other health careers.

new interests. Ask for help from parents, guardians, teachers, and other responsible adults. Learn to accept a mistake or failure by trying to correct the situation. Listen to criticism and use it to find ways you might improve. Show good character in all decisions and behaviors.

Analyze What Influences Your Health

As you set goals and make responsible decisions, it is important to analyze what influences your health. The following life skills activity lists the four steps that help you analyze what influences your health.

✔ **How can a person improve his or her self-esteem?**

Analyze What Influences Your Health

1. **Identify people and things that might influence you.** Make a list of people who have influenced your self-esteem.

2. **Evaluate how the influence might affect your health and decisions.** In what ways did these people influence your self-esteem?

3. **Choose positive influences on health.** If you feel someone is a positive influence, you might think of ways to include this person in your life more often.

4. **Protect yourself from negative influences on health.** If you feel that a friend has a negative influence on your self-esteem, you might want to end the friendship. Think of other ways you can protect yourself from negative influences.

▲ Family, friends, and teachers can influence your health.

Traits of Good Character

Character is the effort a person uses to act on responsible values. The chart describes six traits of good character.

SIX TRAITS OF GOOD CHARACTER

Honesty means telling the truth and acting on it. It also means not cheating.	**Fairness** means following the rules and caring about everyone's point of view.
Respect means treating others with dignity and consideration. It means not making fun of them.	**Caring** means sharing the pain and happiness of others. It means helping those in need.
Responsibility means making healthful decisions and honoring your promises.	**Citizenship** means doing your part as a member of the community. It means obeying laws and advocating for the health of others.

Being a Health Advocate

One way to show good character is to advocate for your own health and for the health of others. To be a health advocate:

1. Select a health-related concern to communicate.
2. Gather reliable information.
3. Identify your purpose and target audience.
4. Develop a convincing and appropriate message.

◀ Taking part in community service is a mark of good character.

A14

Breaking Harmful Habits

When you listed your strengths and weaknesses, you might have realized that you had some harmful habits. Harmful habits can be related to a lack of character. They may harm your physical health. For example, watching too much television could prevent you from getting enough exercise.

How do you break a harmful habit? Begin by admitting that you have one. If you have a harmful habit, the next step is to ask for help. Ask friends and trusted adults in your life for encouragement.

Another helpful step is to make a plan to break the harmful habit. Set a goal and make a plan for reaching it. Check on your progress regularly. Promise yourself a reward for achieving your goal.

What is the first step in breaking a harmful habit?

▶ **Keeping your room tidy is a sign that you are responsible.**

BUILD

Character

Role-Play Character

Responsibility Being responsible is hard work, but it is a skill you can develop. Follow these steps.

- Understand the benefits. Being more responsible will help you have higher self-esteem.

- Commit yourself. Sometimes it's hard to stick with a plan. You must commit yourself to being responsible, even when it is not easy. It will be worth it in the end.

- Be responsible to yourself and for yourself. You can show responsibility by avoiding risk behaviors and practicing healthful habits.

With a partner, role-play a situation in which both of you show responsibility. Perform your role play in front of others and have them evaluate how responsible you are.

LESSON 2 REVIEW

Review Concepts

1. **List** the factors that influence your personality.

2. **Recall** how you can improve your self-esteem.

3. **Identify** the six traits of good character.

Critical Thinking

4. **Evaluate** Why is good character an important part of having good health?

5. **LIFE SKILLS** **Analyze What Influences Your Health** Identify a harmful habit a teen might need to overcome. Suggest a plan for how a teen could overcome it. Include a regular system of checking on progress.

Set Health Goals

Dear Health Nut,

Here's the problem... A friend of mine keeps inviting me to play basketball with him and some other guys. I've watched them play. They are all very good. I'm not that good at basketball. I'm afraid to say "yes" and join them because I don't want to embarrass myself when they find out how badly I play. What can I do?

Sitting It Out in South Dakota

Dear Sitting It Out in South Dakota,

Here is how you might solve the problem . . . Your self-esteem is running on low. You are not being positive about your ability to take part in the basketball game. You can set a goal to improve your self-esteem. You can make a plan and track your progress. In time, you'll join your friends for fun.

Health Nut

Health Behavior Contract

Name _____ Date _____

Health Goal: _____
_____
_____

Effect on My Health: _____
_____
_____
_____

My Plan: _____
_____
_____
_____
_____
_____

My Calendar

Mon.	Tues.	Wed.	Thurs.	Fri.	Sat.	Sun.

How My Plan Worked: _____
_____
_____
_____

 **Foldables** To Learn Life Skills

Learn This Life Skill

Set Health Goals Follow these four steps to set health goals. You can use the Foldables to help organize your thoughts.

1 **Write the health goal you want to set.**

I will demonstrate good character.

2 **Tell how the goal will affect your health and decisions.**

If I have good character, other people will trust and respect me.

3 **Describe the plan you will follow. Keep track of your progress.**

Choose a way to improve your character, such as by being more honest or caring toward others. You can keep track of your progress by using a **health behavior contract**, which is a written plan to practice a life skill in order to reach a health goal. Share your plan with your parents or guardian.

4 **Evaluate how your plan worked.**

What were your results after one week? Did you improve? If not, what can you do to improve your plan?

Practice This Life Skill

Activity Think of a situation in your own life that requires you to set a health goal. Design a poster that describes your health goal. Share your poster with the class.

How to Make a Health Behavior Contract

- Write your name and the date.
- Write the healthful behavior you want to practice as a health goal.
- Write specific statements that describe how this healthful behavior reduces health risks.
- Make a plan to record your progress.
- Complete an evaluation of how the plan helped you accomplish the health goal.

1. Write the health goal you want to set.

2. Tell how the goal will affect your health and decisions.

3. Describe a plan you will follow. Keep track of your progress.

4. Evaluate how your plan worked.

You can work in a group to do this activity. Group members can write, fold, cut, or draw. Some may do a role play or comic strip as well.

Making Responsible Decisions

You will learn . . .

- steps to follow to make responsible decisions.
- steps to follow to resist negative peer pressure.

Vocabulary

- **priority,** A19
- **peer pressure,** A20
- **resistance skills,** A21

Many of the choices you make affect your health. You can choose to avoid risk behaviors and lessen your chances of illness and injury. Choosing to make responsible decisions keeps you and others healthy and safe.

How to Make Responsible Decisions

Making responsible decisions about your health has many benefits. Responsible decisions will help you avoid injury and illness and improve your self-esteem. Some decisions may have little effect in the short term, but others have long-term effects. For instance, the decision to avoid smoking cigarettes may have its biggest payoff years down the road.

When you make a decision, you reveal what you value most. You call something that you value a **priority**, something that deserves first attention. To make a responsible decision, clearly describe the situation. Then:

1. **Identify your choices.** That is, list the possible decisions you might make. Share the list with a parent or another trusted adult.

2. **Evaluate each choice. Use the Guidelines for Making Responsible Decisions™.** These are questions you ask about each of the choices. If any of the answers is "no," then that choice is not responsible.

   - Is it healthful?
   - Is it safe?
   - Is it legal?
   - Does it show respect for myself and others?
   - Does it follow my family's guidelines?
   - Does it demonstrate that I have good character?

3. **Tell what the responsible decision is. Check this out with your parent or another trusted adult.**

4. **Evaluate your decision.** Did your decision have the results that you expected?

 **What is a responsible decision?**

ACTIVITY

On Your Own
FOR SCHOOL OR HOME

Chart Your Chores

Ask a parent or guardian how you could contribute at home. Decide to assume some new responsibilities, such as washing the dishes without being asked. Design a chart of chores you could do. Try to help out with a new task each week.

Resisting Negative Peer Pressure

Peer pressure is influence or pressure that people of a similar age place on a person to behave in a certain way. Peer pressure can have positive results. For example, friendly competition with classmates may encourage you to work harder to do well on your math test.

Peer pressure can have negative results, too. It might tempt you to make wrong decisions. For example, you might be pressured to engage in risk behaviors such as smoking or riding a bicycle without a helmet.

Peer pressure can be hard to resist. You may worry that people will laugh at you if you do not join in the risk behavior. You may think your friends will get angry. You may feel that you have no choice. You *do* have a choice, though. You are responsible for the choices you make.

Consumer Wise

Sole Searching

You have been saving for new sneakers. You just found out that you can buy sneakers for half the price, but they are not name brand. It is your friend's birthday tomorrow. If you buy the name brand sneakers, you will not be able to afford to buy your friend a present. With two classmates, act out your response to this situation, using the Guidelines for Making Responsible Decisions™.

LIFE SKILLS

CRITICAL THINKING

Make Responsible Decisions

Suppose your friends plan to see a movie that you know your parents won't approve of. Your friends pressure you to go and you want to see the movie, but you don't want to break family guidelines. You need to make a responsible decision.

1 Identify your choices. What are your options? You could make up a story for your parents and go to the movie. You could tell your friends that you won't join them. Which choice will you make?

2 Evaluate each choice. Use the Guidelines for Making Responsible Decisions™. Ask yourself the following questions:

- Is it healthful?
- Is it legal?
- Will this decision result in actions that show respect for myself and others?

- Will this decision result in actions that follow the guidelines of responsible adults, such as my parents and other responsible adults?
- Will this decision result in actions that demonstrate good character?

3 Tell what the responsible decision is. Ask your parents or a trusted adult to help you make the right decision.

4 Evaluate your decision. What are the consequences of acting on this decision?

Resistance Skills

Resistance skills are skills that help a person say "no" to an action or leave a situation. The following demonstrates resistance skills for peer pressure.

1. **Say "no" in a firm voice.**

2. **Give reasons for saying "no."** You may need to repeat your "no" several times.

3. **Be certain your behavior matches your words.** Use nonverbal behavior to match your verbal behavior. Avoid situations in which there will be pressure to make wrong decisions. Avoid people who make wrong decisions. Resist pressure to engage in illegal behavior. Influence others to make responsible decisions.

4. **Ask an adult for help if you need help.**

Using resistance skills is not easy. Some people may laugh at you or argue with you. Practicing the skills can help. Work with a friend or a parent. And remember—your decisions reflect your character.

 **What is peer pressure?**

▲ **Make the responsible decision to wear proper safety equipment.**

LESSON **3** REVIEW

Review Concepts

1. **List** the steps to follow to make responsible decisions.

2. **Recall** the skills you can use to resist peer pressure.

Critical Thinking

3. **Compare and contrast** negative and positive peer pressure.

4. **Explain** How could using resistance skills help build character?

5. **LIFE SKILLS** **Make Responsible Decisions** Why is it not a responsible decision to drink alcohol?

Emotions and Stress

You will learn . . .

- healthful ways to express emotions.
- the causes and signs of stress.
- a plan to manage stress.
- healthful ways of dealing with depression and grief.

Vocabulary

- **stress**, A23
- **stressor**, A24
- **adrenaline**, A24
- **eustress**, A24
- **distress**, A24
- **depression**, A28
- **grief**, A29

It is normal to feel angry, happy, or sad. Learning healthful ways to manage emotions promotes mental and emotional health, family and social health, and physical health.

Expressing Emotions

Emotions are the feelings a person has. Familiar emotions might include anger, happiness, fear, love, and sadness. These are normal parts of life. In fact, emotions are part of what makes us human. Sometimes emotions can cause **stress**, the body's reaction to the demands of daily living.

At the same time, emotions can swing from one extreme to another. They can make a person feel confused and say things he or she will later regret. Remember that it is normal to experience a variety of emotions. It is the way in which a person expresses emotions that can be healthful or harmful.

Bottling emotions up inside is not healthful. For example, holding anger inside can prevent a person from facing problems. Losing control of one's emotions and reacting without thinking is not healthful either. Angry outbursts can harm relationships and cause physical harm to you and others. Follow these guidelines for healthful ways to express emotions.

1. **Admit** that you feel the emotions.
2. **Identify the emotions** you feel and the cause of your reaction.
3. **Calm down**—try not to act when your feelings are very strong.
4. **Tell others** what you feel by saying "I feel angry," or "I feel hurt." This helps keep others from feeling attacked.
5. **Walk away** if you feel you are losing control.
6. **Talk with a trusted adult** if you have problems with emotions.

Name at least four different emotions.

Science LINK
ACTIVITY
Detecting Lies

Draw a diagram of a person's body, labeling the body functions that a lie detector test measures. To do this, you need to know that the body changes when a person feels strong emotions. When a person becomes excited, his or her heart rate may increase. At the same time, the muscles may become tense and breathing becomes rapid. The ability to identify these changes—some of which are very small—is what makes a lie detector test work. Sensors placed on a person's body note even the smallest change in breathing, heart rate, or muscle tension. Increases in these readings are a sign that a person feels stress, and possibly that he or she is lying.

▶ **You can reduce stress by sharing emotions with friends.**

The Causes and Signs of Stress

Stress is the body's reaction to the demands of daily living. A **stressor** is a cause of stress.

Like emotions, stress is a natural part of people's lives. People encounter many stressors every day—traffic, long lines, tests, even growling dogs. When people experience such stressors, the body reacts by producing hormones. **Adrenaline** (uh·DRE·nuhl·uhn) is a hormone that prepares the body for quick action. We feel stress. We can recognize it by some of its signs. Muscles tense, and heart rate increases. Sugar is released into the bloodstream. **Eustress** (YOO-stres), is positive stress which prompts a healthful response. Eustress helps you ace that test or hit that home run. After meeting the challenge, you calm down.

In some cases, reactions to stressors are harmful. You overreact and feel overwhelmed. You might experience a stomachache. Stress that is negative, prompting a harmful response, is called **distress**.

When distress happens often, it can harm the body and the mind. Distress causes the heart and lungs to work too hard. It reduces the number of white blood cells that help your body fight germs.

People can manage stress by using four steps:

1. Identify the signs of stress.
2. Identify the cause of stress.
3. Do something about the cause of stress.
4. Take action to lessen the harmful effects of stress.

How the Body Reacts to Stress

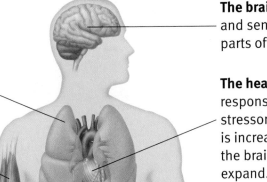

Breathing becomes faster. Air passages in the lungs become larger to provide the body with more oxygen.

To prepare for action, the **muscles** tense and tighten.

The adrenal (uh·DRE·nuhl) glands send **adrenaline** out to the body so it can respond to a stressor.

Perspiration increases to help the body remain cool.

The brain identifies a stressor and sends out signals to other parts of the body.

The heart beats faster in response to the message that a stressor is present. Blood flow is increased to the muscles and the brain as blood vessels expand.

The stomach and intestines, organs that digest food, slow down to save energy. Other organs in the body also slow down or constrict in size.

Reducing Stress

Suppose you feel anxious. You're finding it hard to focus on your schoolwork. You have difficulty falling asleep at night. These are common signs of stress. Once you recognize signs of stress, identify the causes of your stress so that you can do something about them.

These may include school, after-school activities, and the actions of certain people. You can avoid some stressors, but some you cannot avoid. Try to reduce them. Perhaps dropping one after-school activity will make life easier. If you have one less place to rush to, you will have less stress. Look at the chart below. It contains ideas on how to reduce stress in your life.

 **What are two ways to reduce stress?**

On Your Own
FOR SCHOOL OR HOME

Anxiety and Boredom

The guidelines below can also help a person cope with anxiety and boredom. Anxiety is a feeling of worry or uneasiness about something harmful that might happen. Boredom is a feeling of having nothing interesting to do. Work at home with a family member to discuss how to deal with anxiety – such as trying to achieve a positive outcome about what might happen. Work with a parent to set up a weekly schedule of interesting things to do at home, on your own, and together.

WAYS TO REDUCE STRESS

Identify the stressors.
Knowing the stressors in a person's life makes it easier to deal with them. Understanding the body's signals, such as faster breathing and tense muscles, will help manage stress.

Learn to manage time.
Set aside time each day to perform chores and homework. A schedule will help avoid rushing to do things at the last minute.

Use the energy that comes with stress.
Do something positive with the increased energy that comes with stress.
Help around the house, pick up a new hobby, or spend time with friends.

Talk to a friend or trusted adult.
Talking with a trusted person is a good way to reduce stress. Parents or trusted adults can offer good advice.

Learn to relax.
Relaxing helps put things in perspective. Remember that many people face difficult decisions or unpleasant tasks. When people are relaxed, problems don't seem bigger than they really are.

▶ **Relaxing with a hobby can reduce stress.**

Stress Management Skills

You may be able to reduce the number of stressors in your life. However, you cannot eliminate all stressors. You can practice these basic stress management skills.

- **Plan your day.** Decide what things you have to do.
- **Use the Guidelines for Making Responsible Decisions™** when you must make a hard decision.
- **Talk to a parent or guardian** about problems and decisions.
- **Get physical exercise.** Physical exercise uses up extra sugar in the bloodstream.
- **Get plenty of rest and sleep.** Plan to get 8 hours of sleep a day. During the day, rest after physical activity by taking a nap, reading a book, or listening to relaxing music.
- **Eat healthful foods** to keep the immune system strong. Eat plenty of whole grains, fruits, and vegetables. Some substances, such as sugar, may decrease the ability of the immune cells to fight infection.
- **Write in a notebook** that is your own or that you share with your family. Writing about problems and decisions is a way to express feelings.
- **Spend time with a pet.** A cat, dog, horse, or other pet can help you relax.
- **Plan something fun with friends.** Have something that you can look forward to.

◀ Spending time with a pet can help you manage stress.

Time Management

One of the best ways to reduce stress is to manage your time better. How well do you manage time? Do you always rush to complete tasks? Do you feel that you don't have time for the things that are really important to you? Tips for better time management include learning to say "no" to others, prioritizing your tasks, and combining several activities.

Reduce Your Stress with a Workout

Mental health experts suggest physical activity as a way to beat the blues. Running, biking, and other activities produce beta-endorphins (BAY•tuh•en•DOR•funz). These substances are released into the bloodstream and give you a sense of well-being. Next time you feel low, bounce back with a workout. Choose a physical activity that you enjoy. Make a schedule for the next week. You should set aside at least 30 minutes three times a week for your activity. Record how you feel before and after each workout.

▲ Find ways to manage your time so that you can have a healthful breakfast without rushing.

 What does it mean to manage stress?

ACTIVITY
LIFE SKILLS

CRITICAL THINKING

Set Health Goals

Use a health behavior contract to set a health goal.

1 **Write the health goal you want to set:** *I will follow a plan to manage stress.*

2 **Tell how the goal will affect your health.** If I manage stress, I will be less tired. I will perform better on tests. I will reduce the risk of stress-related injury and illness.

3 **Describe a plan you will follow. Keep track of your progress.** One way to reduce stress is to participate in regular physical activity. Develop ideas on how best to work physical activity into your daily routine. Write out a plan to exercise each day. Share it with your family.

4 **Evaluate how your plan worked.** Did regular physical activity help me to manage my stress?

Dealing with Depression and Grief

Certain times in your life may be more difficult than others. You might get a low grade on a test or perform poorly in a game. Maybe you did not get the part in the school play that you wanted, or you were not invited to a party.

Depression

Depression is a lasting feeling of being sad, unhappy, or discouraged. It's normal for young people to be depressed for short periods of time. However, if depression lasts for two weeks or more, seek an evaluation from a physician. Pay attention to the signs of depression.

- Loss of sleep
- Loss of appetite
- Loss of energy
- Loss of concentration
- Sloppy appearance
- Withdrawal from others
- Lack of enthusiasm
- Sadness
- Frequent crying
- Restlessness and anger

If these feelings last, talk to a parent or other responsible adult. They can listen and get you appropriate treatment. You can take action, too. Write in a notebook. Make a list of your strengths. Review them and remember that you do some things very well. Finally, get plenty of rest and exercise.

▶ All families must learn to cope with difficult times.

How People Express Grief

The death of a person can trigger great sadness. **Grief** is intense sadness caused by loss or death. Grief is not the same as depression, though it can lead to depression.

Grief is a normal reaction most people experience when someone close to them dies. This is true even if the death was expected. Signs that a person may be grieving include

- difficulty sleeping.
- inability to concentrate.
- sadness.
- depression.
- guilt.
- difficulty doing schoolwork.
- loss of appetite.
- crying.
- anger.

There are several things you can do to comfort someone who is grieving. First, do something thoughtful for him or her. Help the grieving person with his or her chores, prepare a favorite food for them, or bring them their school books. Express your concern and support. Send a card. Visit the family. Saying how you feel can be hard, but it helps. Be a good listener. Be available to your friend in person or by phone, so he or she can talk. Allow the person to express his or her feelings.

 **What is grief?**

▼ Communicating empathy can help a person who is grieving. *Empathy* means "sharing a feeling without having had the same experience." Doing helpful chores for a grieving person is a healthful way to communicate empathy.

LESSON 4 REVIEW

Review Concepts

1. **Recall** some healthful ways to express strong emotions.

2. **List** the causes of stress.

3. **Describe** the effect stress has on a person's body.

Critical Thinking

4. **Summarize** Describe healthful ways of dealing with grief.

5. **LIFE SKILLS** **Set Health Goals** What goals can a person set to reduce the harmful effects of stress?

CHAPTER 1 REVIEW

Chapter Summary

Lesson 1 • The three parts of health are physical, mental and emotional, and family and social health. Taking responsibility for one's health, making responsible decisions, avoiding risk behaviors, and achieving health literacy protects and promotes health.

Lesson 2 • Your personality and character affect the quality of your decisions. Making responsible decisions promotes good character.

Lesson 3 • Follow the Guidelines for Making Responsible Decisions™. Use resistance skills when you experience negative peer pressure.

Lesson 4 • How you express emotions can affect all three parts of health. You promote emotional health when you manage stress, get help for depression, and express grief in healthful ways.

Use Vocabulary

wellness, A5

lifestyle, A5

abstinence, A7

character, A11

self-esteem, A12

respect, A14

peer pressure, A20

resistance skills, A21

stress, A23

depression, A28

Choose the correct term from the list to complete each sentence.

1. Staying away from a risk behavior is known as _____?_____.

2. _____?_____, or how you feel about yourself, can play a role in the health decisions you make.

3. _____?_____ is a lasting feeling of sadness and unhappiness.

4. _____?_____ help a person say "no" in a tough situation.

5. _____?_____ is a state of balanced health or well-being.

6. _____?_____ means having a high regard for others.

7. _____?_____ is the body's reaction to the demands of daily living.

8. _____?_____ means the way in which a person lives.

9. _____?_____ is the effort a person uses to act on responsible values.

10. _____?_____ is influence or pressure that people of a similar age place on a person to behave in a certain way.

Review Concepts

Answer each question in complete sentences.

11. List four steps to access health information.

12. Discuss four factors that influence personality.

13. How does positive self-esteem promote good health?

14. How do resistance skills help you deal with negative peer pressure?

15. What are some ways that you can manage stress in your life?

Reading Comprehension

Answer each question in complete sentences.

Most people with positive self-esteem are positive about themselves. They are proud of their accomplishments. They set realistic goals and are confident in their ability to achieve them. Minor setbacks do not trouble them.

16. What are two attributes of people with positive self-esteem?

17. What kind of setbacks do not trouble people with positive self-esteem?

Critical Thinking/Problem Solving

Answer each question in complete sentences.

18. In addition to school, you play in the school band and are on the soccer team. Why should you make a time management plan?

19. What might you experience at a party where people engage in risk behaviors?

20. Compare the results you get from different methods you use to reduce the harmful effects of stress.

21. You decide to focus on your social life. You go to parties every weekend and stay up late at night to talk on the phone. How does the time you spend on social health affect the time you have for physical and mental and emotional health?

Practice Life Skills

22. **Set Health Goals** Use the four steps to set a goal to develop positive self-esteem.

23. **Make Responsible Decisions** A popular classmate whom you've been trying to impress invites you to go to the mall. You are supposed to go straight home to take care of your younger brother. "Come on, your mom won't mind," she says. What is the responsible decision to make in this situation? Use the Guidelines for Making Responsible Decisions™.

Read Graphics

Use the text in the visual below to answer the questions.

24. According to the bar graph, smoking among eighth graders decreased by what percent from 2001 to 2002?

25. What percent of eighth graders did not smoke in 2002?

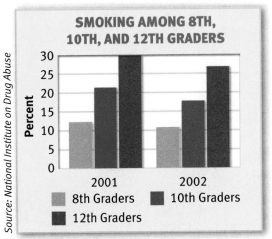

SMOKING AMONG 8TH, 10TH, AND 12TH GRADERS

Source: National Institute on Drug Abuse

■ 8th Graders ■ 10th Graders ■ 12th Graders

LOG ON Visit www.mmhhealth.com to find out how much you know about mental and emotional health.

CHAPTER 2
Family and Social Health

Lesson 1 • Healthful Relationships, A34

Lesson 2 • Express Yourself, A40

Lesson 3 • Family Life, A48

Lesson 4 • Making and Keeping Friends, A54

Lesson 5 • Practicing Abstinence, A62

What Do You Know About
Family and Social Health?

1. What is a relationship?
2. What is a conflict?
3. Why should young people practice abstinence?

Hi!
Back at...
I'm at
Trevor's
house

The Inside Story

Important Decisions

You will soon have to make decisions about dating and sex. The choices you make can affect the rest of your life. Some teens will choose to become sexually active. They risk disease and pregnancy. In the United States, there are more than 900,000 teen pregnancies each year. Teen pregnancies result in health risks for the mother and the baby. Teen parents have immense responsibilities. They miss out on opportunities that other teens will enjoy. Learn now to make responsible decisions about sex.

LOG ON Visit **www.mmhhealth.com** for activities and information on family and social health.

Healthful Relationships

You will learn . . .

- the effects that healthful relation-ships and harmful relationships can have on you.

- steps to take to improve relationships.

- how to use conflict resolution skills.

Vocabulary

- **relationship,** A35

- **conflict,** A38

- **conflict resolution skills,** A38

- **negotiate,** A38

- **mediation,** A39

Your family, the basic unit of society, is the first and most important group in your life. You probably spend a lot of time with your friends. You also get to know many other people—teachers, coaches, teammates, and others. You form a connection with each of these people or groups.

Your Relationships Affect You

A **relationship** is the connection a person has with other people. You have been in relationships from the day you were born. You may have relationships with parents, siblings, friends, teachers, classmates, and others. Your relationships help you learn about the world and how to treat others.

There are many types of relationships, and they can affect your life in many ways. A relationship can bring out the best or the worst in you. It may cause eustress, or positive stress. You need to be able to judge your relationships.

Healthful relationships How can you tell if a relationship is healthful? It is healthful if it involves honesty, trust, and communication. Each person cares about the other's best interests. The relationship makes you feel good about yourself; it also helps you make responsible decisions and practice healthful behaviors. You learn to communicate well and share your experiences. This type of relationship improves mental and emotional, family and social, and physical health.

Harmful relationships A harmful relationship, on the other hand, is marked by jealous and selfish acts. It may cause you to doubt or distrust the other person. Harmful relationships often involve risk behaviors and irresponsible decisions. Harmful relationships may cause distress, or negative stress.

Each day many teens face negative peer pressure, such as being offered cigarettes or alcohol. Healthful relationships help teens resist negative peer pressure.

▶ **Your relationship with your parent or guardian is very important.**

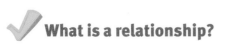
What is a relationship?

A35

ACTIVITY

Music
L I N K

Hear Relationships in Music

Relationships are a popular topic among songwriters. Listen to three songs in a row on the radio. Count how many of the songs deal with relationships. Evaluate the relationship as healthful or harmful. Compose your own song that deals with a healthful relationship theme.

Healthful Relationships

Think about how a relationship with a certain person affects you. It is important for you to be able to evaluate relationships. Is this relationship healthful or harmful? Use *The Relationship Scale* that follows to evaluate your relationships. Read the first statement from each list. Ask yourself which statement represents your experience with this person. It may be that both statements are true half the time. Or, one statement may be true most of the time. Continue this process for each statement on the lists. Write down your responses. You should consider making changes in or ending a harmful relationship.

THE RELATIONSHIP SCALE

Effects of Being in a Healthful Relationship	Effects of Being in a Harmful Relationship
1. I choose healthful behaviors.	1. I choose risk behaviors.
2. I make responsible decisions.	2. I make irresponsible decisions.
3. I obey my parents or guardians.	3. I disobey my parents or guardians.
4. I follow through on my responsibilities.	4. I do not follow through on my responsibilities, such as homework.
5. I settle disagreements without arguing or fighting.	5. I settle disagreements by arguing and fighting.
6. I have time for my family and friends.	6. I do not have time for my family and friends.
7. I respect myself.	7. I do not respect myself.
8. I feel encouraged.	8. I feel discouraged or depressed.
9. I do not feel pressured to do things I should not do.	9. I feel pressured to do things I should not do.
10. I set goals and work to improve myself.	10. I do not work to improve myself.

Taking Steps to Improve Relationships

You can take six steps to improve relationships.

- **Use the chart** on page A36 to evaluate your relationships. The Relationship Scale also will help you decide if your relationships are healthful or harmful.

- **Determine the value of the relationship.** You might need to end dangerous or abusive relationships right away. End the relationship if your parent or guardian tells you to do so.

- **Commit to making necessary changes to relationships you plan to continue.** Write down the changes that you decide to make: "I will not cut class with my friend anymore."

- **Talk to a respected adult.** Share your concerns about the relationship. Share your suggestions for changing it. Discuss ways to improve your relationship skills.

- **Talk to the person with whom you have the relationship.** Discuss how each of you can help improve the relationship.

- **Decide when to judge the relationship again.** Set a date to evaluate whether it has improved.

These steps will lead to relationships marked by respect. You acknowledge each other's views even when you disagree. You accept each other's differences. Respect means treating others the way you expect them to treat you.

Ending Harmful Relationships

What if you think a certain classmate is your friend. You share many good times after school. However, the classmate starts to argue with you and is jealous when you do well in school.

You might take the steps listed to improve a relationship. You set a date to evaluate whether or not the relationship has changed for the better. You find that the relationship is still causing you stress and has not improved. What can you do?

Sometimes the only solution may be to end the relationship. Ending a relationship may be a difficult step to take. However, you can always turn to a respected adult for help.

You should always end relationships that are dangerous. If a person asks you to participate in risk behaviors or to break the law, end the relationship. Talk to parents, guardians, or other respected adults about the relationship.

Why is it important to evaluate your relationships?

◀ **In a healthful relationship, you can settle disagreements without arguing.**

Resolving Conflicts

ACTIVITY

On Your Own
FOR SCHOOL OR HOME

Mediating a Conflict

If you had a conflict with a peer, which adults would mediate it? Make a list of respected adults from your school, neighborhood, or home whom you could ask to be a mediator. List the qualities each person has to enable him or her to do the job.

A **conflict** is a disagreement. A conflict can be between two or more people. You might have a conflict when you and your friend disagree about your weekend plans. A conflict can also be inside one person. A person may have an inner conflict about whether to do homework or watch television. Unresolved conflicts can lead to tension, even to violence. Your health depends on your ability to resolve conflicts.

Conflict resolution skills are steps that you take to settle a disagreement in a healthful way:

1. Stay calm.
2. Talk about the conflict.
3. Discuss possible ways to settle the conflict.
4. Agree on a way to settle the conflict.

When you use these steps you are learning to **negotiate**, or discuss a conflict to reach an agreement. When you negotiate, respect the other person's ideas, seek common interests, and avoid angry outbursts.

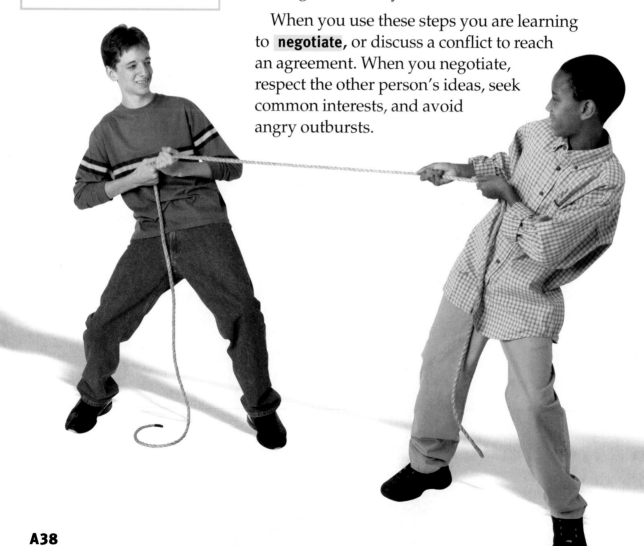

When you negotiate, you may not always reach a responsible solution. If it should fail, you might try **mediation**, a process in which a responsible adult helps settle a conflict. Each side should agree on a mediator who is fair. Then each side should describe the conflict to the mediator. The mediator will suggest possible solutions. The parties should then agree on a responsible solution that shows respect for each side.

✓ **Why are conflict resolution skills important?**

◄ **One way to resolve a conflict is to negotiate.**

Be a Health Advocate

Make it a practice to encourage friends with positive peer pressure. For example, you may have a friend who is tempted to try a risk behavior. Consider the steps you might take to help.

1 **Select a health-related concern to communicate.** Think of a healthful behavior to replace the risk behavior.

2 **Gather reliable information.** Learn what you can about the risk behavior and the healthful behavior.

3 **Identify your purpose and target audience.** Your purpose is to encourage friends with positive peer pressure. Your target is your friend.

4 **Develop a convincing and appropriate message.** Decide whether you will write to your friend or speak in person. Develop a convincing message that includes the information you gathered.

LESSON 1 REVIEW

Review Concepts

1. **Explain** how relationships affect your performance in school.

2. **List** five ways that you can try to improve a harmful relationship.

3. **Explain** the four steps for resolving conflicts and how respect is important in the process.

4. **Define** mediation.

Critical Thinking

5. **Predict** Suppose you become friends with a classmate at the start of the school year. You share several interests and have fun together. However, he or she tries to control you and does not respect your opinions. Write a paragraph predicting what might happen if you do nothing to improve the relationship.

6. **LIFE SKILLS** **Be a Health Advocate** Choose three important relationships in your life. For each relationship, describe one way in which you could be a positive influence in this person's life.

Express Yourself

You will learn . . .

- the four levels of verbal communication.
- how to use I-messages to express your feelings.
- how to use non-verbal communication.
- how to be an effective listener.

Vocabulary

- communication, A41
- I-message, A42
- you-message, A42
- nonverbal communication, A44
- gesture, A44
- active listening, A45

Healthful relationships depend on your ability to share thoughts, feelings, and ideas. The closer you are to someone, the more you tend to share with that person. Think about the people with whom you speak each day. Do you express yourself clearly?

Verbal Communication

Communication is the sharing of feelings, thoughts, and information with another person. One kind of communication is speaking. When you speak, you use verbal communication to share information. You can communicate verbally on four levels: using small talk; reporting facts; sharing ideas, opinions, and decisions; and expressing feelings.

Using small talk You may use small talk with people you do not know well. You might say "How are you?" or "Nice weather today." Small talk helps you break the ice with strangers. It may lead to a more meaningful conversation.

Reporting facts You report facts when you talk about an event or what someone has said or done. Statements such as "Joe scored three touchdowns in the football game" and "I went to the store" report facts. You give few personal comments when you report facts.

Sharing ideas, opinions, and decisions You help others get to know you when you share ideas, opinions, and decisions. Others often respond by sharing in return. As the conversation continues, you decide if you want to continue sharing. Your responses influence how much others choose to share with you.

Expressing feelings This is the deepest level of communication because it involves more risk. When you share personal feelings, there is a chance that others will not understand you. They may reject your feelings. Sharing feelings helps you get closer to other people. Letting them know the real you strengthens healthful relationships.

> **What are the four levels of communication?**

Science LINK ACTIVITY

Communicate With Technology

Advances in technology affect how people communicate with one another. Some teens have a personal cell phone. What if your friend just received a cell phone for her birthday? Draw a comic strip showing how the cell phone would change the way she communicates.

▼ **Sharing ideas is one of the four levels of communication.**

A41

Write About It!

Write a Letter

Suppose you are walking home from school with a friend who has had a difficult day. He or she is upset and complains about many things. Write a letter to communicate empathy to your friend. *Empathy* means "sharing another person's feelings without necessarily having had the same experiences." How might you communicate empathy to your friend without having had the same kind of difficult day?

Healthful Communication

Learning to communicate in healthful ways will help you develop healthful relationships. One of the skills you will use often is the ability to express feelings and respond to another person's feelings.

An **I-message** is a statement that refers to a specific behavior or event, describes the effect of the event on a person, and identifies the feelings that result. Use I-messages to talk about yourself, your feelings, and your needs. Suppose a friend forgot to e-mail you about meeting after school. The next time you see her, you might say: "When I didn't get an e-mail from you I was confused. I didn't know where the meeting would be held. I became angry." I-messages allow you to express feelings in a way that allows others to respond without feeling threatened.

A **you-message** is a statement that blames or shames someone. Think of the example of the friend who didn't send an e-mail. You might say: "You are thoughtless for not e-mailing me about the meeting after school." A you-message makes it hard for someone to respond calmly. Your friend may become angry and try to defend himself or herself. With you-messages, the conversation may turn into an argument.

MAKE a Difference

Brainstorm for the Greater Good

Nickole Evans lives in a small town in Washington State. Some young people, refugees from war-torn cities in other nations, beat and shot at Nickole several years ago. Nickole decided not to strike back but to reach out. She formed a group called Students Against Violence Everywhere (SAVE). The group uses conflict resolution skills and peer mediation to reduce the risk of violence and make schools safe. Brainstorm ways that you can help make a difference in your community.

Developing Verbal Communication Skills

You use communication skills every day. These skills will help you build healthful relationships. You will use them to resolve conflicts. Your success in school, and later at work, will depend in part on how well you learn these skills.

There are a few basic rules to follow to communicate well. Remember to let others talk. Do not interrupt. You can't listen to someone when you are talking. Keep an open mind. Respect the opinions of others. When you are in class, raise your hand before you speak. When you ask questions, you show that you are interested in the conversation.

When it is your turn to speak, think before you begin. Pay attention to your body language. Be aware of your listener. A hasty comment may offend someone and shut down the communication. Be honest. Few people will open up to those who are dishonest. In order to demonstrate good communication skills, speak in clear, direct sentences.

 What are the differences between I-messages and you-messages?

BUILD ACTIVITY
Character

Round Table

Respect With a small group of students, sit around a table or with desks arranged in a circle. Two other students sit outside the circle as "evaluators." The students in the circle talk about a topic from school or the news. Their objective is to follow all the basic rules of communicating well: *Use I-messages. Respect the opinions of others. Let others talk. Avoid hasty comments that might offend others.* The evaluators can interrupt the discussion at any point to advise the group that a rule has been broken and to help the situation.

Nonverbal Communication

People use more than words to share their thoughts, ideas, and feelings. **Nonverbal communication** is the use of actions rather than words to express oneself. How a person moves and the look on his or her face can tell as much as the words spoken.

A **gesture** is a movement of the body that communicates what a person is thinking. You might nod your head to indicate that you understand a plan. You might shrug your shoulders to show that you do not know the answer to a question. Facial expressions are similar to gestures. You might smile to show that you agree with someone. You might frown to indicate that you disagree with an idea.

Posture also expresses how you feel. Look at the two students in the photos on this page. The student who has correct posture shows that she is interested and attentive. The student who is slouching suggests that he is bored.

Your body language also sends out messages. Facing a person and leaning forward indicates that you are open to what he or she has to say. In some cultures, looking away or speaking with your back turned shows a lack of interest. A person who fidgets may be nervous. Someone who speaks with clenched fists might be angry.

Your posture can reflect the way you feel. Which of these two students do you think shows more interest?

Active listening is a way of responding that shows you hear and understand. It involves verbal and nonverbal communication. A friend who forgot to send an e-mail used active listening by responding, "I can understand why you feel angry. I'll try to remember to e-mail you next time." Gestures and facial expressions are part of active listening. I-messages and active listening make your message clear and avoid misunderstandings.

✓ **What are four types of nonverbal communication?**

LIFE SKILLS

ACTIVITY

CRITICAL THINKING

Resolve Conflicts

Use verbal and nonverbal communication to act out this scene with a partner. Suppose you have a friend who makes jokes about you in front of others. He or she may believe it is good fun, but the put-downs really hurt you.

1 **Stay calm.** Do not raise your voice or use threatening gestures such as shaking your fist.

2 **Talk about the conflict.** Identify I-messages you might use to express your feelings. Use active listening when your friend talks about the conflict.

3 **Discuss possible ways to settle the conflict.** Tell what you think is best and have your friend do so, too. For example, you might want your friend to agree to not put you down again.

4 **Agree on a way to settle the conflict. You may need to ask a trusted adult for help.** Find a solution to which you can both agree. If your friend will not agree to a responsible solution, ask a responsible adult to mediate the conflict.

◀ **Healthful communication enables you to send clear messages.**

LESSON 2 REVIEW

Review Concepts

1. **List** the four levels of verbal communication.

2. **Explain** the difference between I-messages and you-messages.

3. **Describe** how nonverbal communication can be used to express an emotion, such as happiness or sadness.

4. **Recall** ways to show you are actively listening.

Critical Thinking

5. **Classify** Write down all of the people you talk to during a single day. Recall the conversations you have with each person. Classify these conversations according to the four levels of communication. Which type of communication do you use most? Which level do you use least? Explain why you think your communication follows the pattern you observed.

6. **LIFE SKILLS** **Resolve Conflicts** Think about three conflicts you have had with others over the past year. Recall what caused each conflict. Describe how using I-messages and active listening could have improved the situation.

Use Communication Skills

Dear Health Nut,

Here's the problem ... I sit next to the same girl in three of my classes. We have many of the same friends and share many interests. We should be friends but we are not. It seems like all we ever do is argue. I don't understand why she does not like me. What can we do to get along with each other?

Frustrated in Phoenix

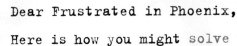

Dear Frustrated in Phoenix,

Here is how you might solve the problem . . . You don't get along with a classmate, a person you see every day. The constant lack of communication could possibly affect your schoolwork. However, you want to communicate but are not sure how to make this happen. In this case, use the steps on the next page to help you learn to communicate with your classmate.

Health Nut

Foldables To Learn Life Skills

Learn This Life Skill

The problem is due to a lack of communication. Neither person knows how the other feels. You can use the Foldables to help organize your thoughts.

1 **Choose the best way to communicate.**

Will you speak with your classmate after class? Send an e-mail? Call on the telephone?

2 **Send a clear message. Be polite**

Suppose you choose to meet with your classmate alone. Use I-messages to share your feelings. Avoid statements that blame. Use body language that conveys openness.

3 **Listen to the other person.**

Respond with active listening. Try to understand your classmate's viewpoint. Do not interrupt. Use nonverbal communication to further convey your interest in what your classmate is saying.

4 **Make sure you understand each other.**

Continue sharing until you both fully understand each other's feelings. Commit to using communication skills to improve your interaction.

1. Choose the best way to communicate.

2. Send a clear message. Be polite.

3. Listen to the other person.

4. Make sure you understand each other.

If you do this activity with a group of students, students can participate in different ways, such as writing, folding, or drawing. Some students may do the activity in other ways, such as by role-playing or drawing a comic strip.

Practice This Life Skill

Activity Think about a situation that involved a lack of communication. Write a short story based on this situation. Show the characters using communication skills to improve the situation.

Family Life

You will learn . . .

- how family members communicate in healthful ways.
- ways to adjust to family changes.
- ways to cope with abuse and violence.

Vocabulary

- **separation,** A50
- **divorce,** A50
- **family guideline,** A51
- **abuse,** A52
- **neglect,** A52
- **violence,** A52
- **domestic shelter,** A53

Healthful family relationships help you develop self-respect and build your self-esteem. They encourage you to make responsible decisions and to relate well to others. They also help you adjust to changes. Harmful family relationships have a negative influence.

Healthful Communication in a Family

A family is a group of people who are related to one another. It may include parents, stepparents, guardians, and siblings. Healthful family relationships depend on family members getting along with each other. Communication is a vital part of being a loving family member.

There are several ways you can promote healthful communication within your family. Share positive feelings with family members. Tell them what you like about them. Thank them when they do something for you. Spend time with family members. Support them during tough times.

You also can be a loving family member when disagreements arise. Practice healthful verbal and nonverbal communication when trying to use I-messages to promote open communication. Resolve conflicts in a responsible way.

▲ All members of a family should share chores and responsibilities.

✓ **How can you promote healthful communication in your family?**

LIFE SKILLS

CRITICAL THINKING

Access Valid Health Information, Products, and Services

You are asked to take care of your two-year-old brother while your mother is upstairs. How would you find information on how to childsit this child?

1 **Identify when you need health information, products, and services.** Because you might not know how to care for a toddler, you need information.

2 **Identify where you can find health information, products, and services.** What are likely sources of valid health information? Sources may be a trained professional, parents, guardians, and child care books.

3 **Locate health information, products, and services.** Visit the library or bookstore to find books recommended by the professional or relative. Search the Internet for Web sites that provide valid child care information. Attend a child care course.

4 **Evaluate what you found.** Are your sources reliable? Is the information valid?

Adjusting to Family Changes

Couple family—a husband and a wife who do not have children

Traditional family—a husband and a wife and their children

Foster family—an adult(s) who cares for a child or children who do not live with their birth parents

Single-parent family—one parent and a child or children

Joint-custody family—two parents living apart, sharing custody of their children

Single-custody family—two parents living apart and a child or children living with only one parent

Blended family—a husband and wife, one or both of whom have children from a previous relationship

Extended family—family members from three or more generations with other relatives who might live with them

Families change for many reasons. Separation is a situation in which a husband and wife remain married but live apart. Divorce is a legal end to a marriage. After a separation or divorce, a person might remarry.

Change can also occur when a family member becomes ill. The illness may require some family members to take on new responsibilities. Illness can cause severe stress for families.

The death of a loved one might cause great sorrow. Grief is the intense sadness caused by loss or the death of another person. Family members might talk to and support one another during these difficult times.

A person who is grieving may be in denial and not accept the death of the loved one. The person may become angry, depressed, or withdraw from others. In order to forget the pain, a grieving person may try to keep busy or may participate in risk behaviors.

One of the ways families can express love and affection is to comfort a family member who is grieving. Allow the grieving person to express his or her feelings. Encourage him or her to deal with grief through a healthful activity. This may include writing or making something to honor the person who has died. In some cases, a person might talk to a grief counselor.

◀ **Changes in the family can be difficult for young people.**

Family Guidelines

You can be a responsible family member. To be responsible is to be dependable. You do what is expected of you. Even when you are away from home, you follow your family's guidelines, such as cleaning up after yourself.

A **family guideline** is a rule a family makes to help members live in a responsible way. Your family sets these guidelines to direct your behavior. Guidelines about studying will help you succeed in school. Guidelines about telling the truth will teach you the value of honesty. Guidelines about chores will help you learn the value of hard work.

 Why is it important for you to follow family guidelines?

CAREERS IN HEALTH
Grief Counselor

Do you have a talent for comforting people who feel sad? If so, a career as a grief counselor might interest you. Grief counselors work in a variety of settings to help people deal with loss. They might work with grieving families in schools, hospitals, or a private practice. You may wish to talk to a grief counselor in your area about his or her training and experience. Volunteer work may help you learn if grief counseling is of interest to you.

LOG ON Visit **www.mmhhealth.com** to find out more about this and other health careers.

ACTIVITY • LIFE SKILLS

CRITICAL THINKING

Set Health Goals

Use a health behavior contract to set a health goal.

1 **Write the health goal you want to set:** *I will communicate with my family in healthful ways.*

2 **Tell how the goal will affect your health.** Communicating in healthful ways, especially about family problems, protects health. You don't let problems keep you from sleeping and thinking clearly.

3 **Describe a plan you will follow. Keep track of your progress.** Use your health behavior contract and a calendar to plan time to communicate with family members. Indicate to whom you will communicate, what you will communicate about, and when you will do it.

4 **Evaluate how your plan worked.** Write a few sentences describing ways that the planned time to communicate helped you. Do you need to plan for additional time?

Facing Abuse and Violence

All families and family members experience times of hardship. For example, some married couples struggle at times to have a healthful and committed marriage. These struggles can strengthen a marriage. Sometimes couples cannot work things out and they separate. They may seek a divorce. Some young people whose parents divorce feel guilty. They believe they caused the divorce.

Other young people become angry or afraid. They might worry about not spending time with one of the parents anymore. They might have to move and change schools. One or both parents might remarry. There might be stepparents, stepbrothers, and stepsisters.

Some families have one or more members who are abusive or violent. **Abuse** is the harmful treatment of another person. This may take the form of physical abuse, emotional abuse, sexual abuse, or **neglect**. Neglect is the failure to provide proper care and guidance. Abuse in any form causes hardship among young people. Some young people are confused and blame themselves.

Violence is the use of force to harm someone or destroy property. A person who is violent usually wants to control others. Sometimes other family members ignore or keep the violent behavior a secret. Thus the violence continues.

Sometimes there is drug dependence in a family. Drug dependence is repeated drug use that harms the body, mind, and relationships. Family members who are dependent on drugs do not think clearly and can become abusive toward other family members. Their actions affect other family members. Other family members might deny the problem and hide their feelings about it.

◀ **Some problems might require help from outside the family.**

Finding Help for Families

Young people need to talk about their feelings when there are family problems. Parents and guardians can provide support. However, problems such as drug abuse and violence might require outside help. Some families rely on the two S's—secrecy and safety. They might try to keep the problem a secret from those outside the family. Trying to keep secrets often prevents the family from getting help. Family members might ignore their safety. Ignoring safety can lead to serious injuries. Family members who are abusive or violent need treatment. So do those who abuse drugs or alcohol. Other members of the family should seek help, too.

Families can turn to many types of services for help. Family counselors handle a wide variety of problems. They can help family members identify and deal with their feelings. Family members who are at risk of being harmed by violence should go to a safe place. A **domestic shelter** is a place where family members can stay safe.

 What are three types of problems that harm family relationships?

BUILD ACTIVITY

Character
Write a Notebook Entry

Responsibility Role-play a way to resolve the following conflict. You may have said something in the heat of the moment that you now regret. Use a notebook to record the incident and how you can better assume responsibility for your actions in the future.

LESSON 3 REVIEW

Review Concepts

1. **Describe** two ways that you can be a loving family member.

2. **List** four different ways that families can change.

3. **Describe** the kinds of abuse.

Critical Thinking

4. **Compare** Describe a fictional family whose members communicate in healthful ways. Next, describe a fictional family whose members do not communicate in healthful ways. Suppose each family had to adjust to family changes. Compare how each family might deal with the changes and the possible results.

5. **Decide** Suppose you have a friend who has bruises and other injuries that indicate violence. Your friend denies that violence exists. Why is it responsible for you to discuss your observation with your parents, guardian, or another responsible adult?

6. **LIFE SKILLS** **Access Valid Health Information** Where would you find information on caring for a toddler?

7. **LIFE SKILLS** **Set Health Goals** How might setting a goal to communicate in healthful ways benefit your health?

Making and Keeping Friends

You will learn . . .

- how you can make a new friend.
- how to maintain friendships.
- why you should choose friends who make responsible decisions.
- how to resist negative peer pressure.
- when and how you would end a friendship.

Vocabulary

- **loyalty,** A58
- **reliable,** A58
- **sympathetic,** A58

A friendship is a special relationship with someone you like. Some friendships promote health and build self-esteem. Other friendships harm health and lead to irresponsible decisions. You should work to make and keep healthful friendships.

Why Friends Are Important

Friendships are among your most significant relationships. Friends are unique people in your life. They are different from siblings and classmates. While you cannot choose your siblings or classmates, you can choose your friends. Friends can pick you up when you are down, and they will listen when you need to talk to someone. As you grow older and your interests change, you may grow apart from some of your friends. Other friendships last a lifetime. Some young people have many friends. Making friends is easy for them. Others have only a few friends. The number of friends you have is not as important as the types of friendships you have.

For some young people, making friends is difficult. They may fear that they will always be alone. Remember that there is a friend out there for everyone. We all have the ability to make friends. Making new friends takes skill and practice. In this lesson, you will learn about making and keeping friends.

When making friends, it is important to choose people who make responsible decisions. They should have good character. They should be respected and liked, especially by your parents or guardians.

As you continue reading, you will understand why it is important to follow these guidelines. Remembering these guidelines helps you choose healthful friendships and avoid harmful friendships.

 What guidelines should you follow when choosing friends?

Art LINK

The Benefit of Friends

Design a collage that would teach a younger child how to choose a friend responsibly. Include words that describe healthful ways friends can communicate consideration for one another, such as respect, loyalty, and reliability, and list examples of how each trait can be shown.

A Play About Friends

Friendships with people whose backgrounds differ from yours can be rewarding. You discover new ideas and learn more about yourself and other cultures. Write a short play about two friends who come from different backgrounds. Pay special attention to the new things each person discovers about himself or herself and each other.

▼ **What qualities do you look for in a friend?**

Making New Friends

To make a friend, you need to know yourself first. Make a list of the reasons why you would be a good friend. What are your interests and talents? What are your positive qualities?

Think about a person whom you admire and would like to get to know better. Does this person attend the same school that you do, or does he or she participate in the same after-school program? Have you walked past this person but for some reason have never said hello? Well, the next time you see him or her, walk right over and say hello: It's as simple as that! Making friends can often start with a simple smile: It is that easy. You might be scared at first, but don't worry, it gets easier.

You meet friends by

- joining after-school clubs.
- participating in sports and activities.
- working in classroom groups.

Different Friends for Different Needs

People become friends for many different reasons. They might choose friends to meet specific needs. There are several reasons why young people make friends with certain individuals. Friends may have similar backgrounds, interests, or values. People feel at ease when they share common interests, thoughts, and belief systems. Also, admirable qualities may draw friends together.

Friends support each other to practice healthful behavior and make responsible decisions. People may become friends due to nearness. It's often easier to make friends with peers who live in your neighborhood or who attend the same school.

Choosing Friends Who Are Responsible

Friends can have a positive or negative influence on your health and well-being. Healthful friendships promote your emotional and physical well-being. Harmful friendships can lower your self-esteem.

In order to choose friends responsibly, there are certain guidelines to follow.

- Choose friends who want to protect your health.
- Choose friends who want you to stay safe.
- Choose friends who want you to obey laws.
- Choose friends who want you to have self-respect and respect for others.
- Choose friends who want you to obey your parents or guardian.
- Choose friends who want you to demonstrate good character.

You may know classmates who engage in risk behaviors. If you spend time with them, they may influence you to behave as they do. Responsible friends, on the other hand, have a positive influence on you. They encourage you to engage in healthful behaviors. They are concerned about your health and safety, and they encourage you to make responsible decisions.

Your parents or guardians can help you make responsible decisions when choosing friends. These trusted adults are responsible for you. They are concerned about your health and safety. They notice the effects friends have on you, and they notice changes in your behavior. Your parents or guardians encourage you to find friends who help you.

✔ **What are three factors that you should look for when forming a friendship?**

Do You Know

Many people use the telephone to communicate with friends. More than 80 percent of households have a cordless telephone and almost as many have an answering machine. About two of every three families use cell phones.

▶ **Responsible friends care about your health and safety.**

Having things in common with a friend is important, but you should also have some differences as well. Being too alike may be boring. Your different interests can help you both discover new ideas.

▼ **A good friend is loyal, reliable, sympathetic, and caring.**

How to Keep a Friend

You will make many types of friends. Some you won't know that well and will see only rarely. Others will be regular companions—you will learn a great deal about them and be with them often. Strong friendships such as these are based on mutual sharing, honesty, and trust. To be a good friend, you will have to display four qualities. The first is **loyalty,** a strong and lasting affection and support. Second, you can trust and depend on a **reliable** person. The third quality is that a good friend is **sympathetic** —you feel or show sympathy toward your friends. The fourth quality is caring—an interest, liking, or concern about a person. Having these qualities will help you keep your good friends.

Following Family Guidelines

Your parents or guardians set guidelines for you to follow. They try to guide you in loving ways. They notice the effects that friends have on you. They encourage friendships that help you, and they discourage those that might harm you. Choose friends that your parents or guardians will like.

Always tell your parents or guardian with whom you spend time. Ask your parents or guardian for feedback about your friendships. Listen to their feedback about your friendship choices. They might not approve of some of your friends. You need to end friendships when trusted adults ask you to do so.

QUALITIES OF A GOOD FRIEND	
Loyalty	Good friends are loyal. They forgive your mistakes. They do not gossip about you.
Reliability	Good friends are reliable. They keep their commitments to each other.
Sympathy	Good friends offer sympathy when you experience loss. They celebrate your joys. They are there to help when you are down.
Caring	Good friends care about the details of your life. They remember your birthday. They know what concerns you and what makes you happy.

Keeping Friends Whom Others Respect

Have you ever heard the saying "Birds of a feather flock together"? It means that those who are alike stay together. Other people think you are like your friends. Suppose someone does not know you well, but they do know your friends. That person might assume that you are similar to your friends.

Now suppose your friends start to engage in risk behaviors. People might get the wrong idea about you and think that you do the same things as your friends.

For example, you are with friends who start drinking beer. They have never done it before. These friends are breaking the law. It might be difficult to convince others that you have not broken the law. It is easy to get into trouble if you keep friends who get into trouble.

▲ Friends often share similar interests.

✓ What are the four qualities of a good friend?

Make Responsible Decisions

One of the responsibilities you face is to choose friends who are responsible. Responsible decisions will boost your social health and your mental and emotional health.

1 **Identify your choices. Check them out with your parent or another trusted adult.** List three classmates with whom you might want to be friends.

2 **Evaluate each choice. Use the Guidelines for Making Responsible Decisions™.** Use the Guidelines to evaluate the behavior of each of the three classmates.

• Is it healthful?

• Is it safe?

• Is it legal?

• Do I show respect for myself and others?

• Do I follow the guidelines of responsible adults?

• Do I demonstrate good character?

3 **Tell what the responsible decision is. Check this out with your parent or another trusted adult.** Would one or more of these classmates make a responsible friend?

4 **Evaluate your decision.** Tell why it is important for you to use this process to make decisions about friends.

BUILD
Character

Write a Skit

Responsibility Suppose you have a classmate who has fallen behind in school due to illness. You have agreed to help this classmate with his homework after school. Later, several of your friends invite you to join them in an after-school activity. Your classmate is not very popular. Your friends will make fun of you if you still help him. Write a skit that demonstrates the responsible way to act in this situation.

How to Resist Negative Peer Pressure

Sometimes it's hard not to go along with the crowd. What if you don't take part in what your friends are doing? Will they still like you? You want to fit in, but it's important that you learn how to resist negative peer pressure.

When friends pressure you with harmful behaviors, remember who you are. Stay true to your values. Use resistance skills. Think about the consequences of risk behaviors. Be clear about your decision to resist peer pressure. Limit the time you spend with those who pressure you. Look to healthful friendships for support, choosing activities that build your self-esteem. You also can ask a responsible adult for advice.

▶ **Good friends will not pressure you to take part in risk behaviors.**

Ending a Friendship

Suppose you told a friend something personal and she shared your story with others. You expected her to keep the story private, and her actions hurt you. A good friend will apologize for a mistake and promise not to do it again.

Suppose your friend continues to repeat what you share. Your friend has broken the limits of friendship. All friendships need limits. You must be willing to set limits and stick to them.

To end a friendship, you should talk to the friend alone. Tell why you are ending the friendship. Behave in caring ways when a friendship ends. Do not talk about a former friend. Keep the conversations you have shared private. Always end a friendship when your parents or guardians tell you to do so.

 When should you end a friendship?

Use Resistance Skills

Suppose you are part of a group of five friends. Your friends are popular and you enjoy spending time with them. Recently they have all started smoking and they have offered cigarettes to you. Devise a strategy to resist this peer pressure.

1 **Say "no" in a firm voice.** Firmly tell your friends that you will not smoke.

2 **Give reasons for saying "no."** Tell your friends why you will not smoke. Give reasons such as "I want to protect my health" and "I want to follow family guidelines."

3 **Be certain your behavior matches your words.** Avoid situations in which there will be pressure to make harmful decisions. Avoid being with them if they choose to smoke. Resist pressure to do something illegal, such as buying cigarettes.

4 **Ask an adult for help if you need help.** If your friends continue to pressure you, tell a responsible adult who can support you.

LESSON 4 REVIEW

Review Concepts

1. **Recall** the three guidelines for choosing friends.

2. **Recall** the steps you should take to make a new friend.

3. **List** three things you can do to maintain a good friendship.

4. **Describe** two ways to resist negative peer pressure.

5. **Explain** when you should end a friendship.

Critical Thinking

6. **Analyze** Choose a friendship that you learned about in a short story, novel, play, television show, or movie. Write a paragraph analyzing the qualities that made the fictional friendship so strong.

7. **LIFE SKILLS** **Make Responsible Decisions** How can you use the Guidelines for Making Responsible Decisions™ when choosing friends?

8. **LIFE SKILLS** **Use Resistance Skills** Make a list of ten risk behaviors that young people are pressured to engage in. For each risk behavior, write a healthful behavior to do instead.

A61

Practicing Abstinence

You will learn . . .

- that abstinence is expected of you.
- ten reasons to practice abstinence.
- the importance of setting limits and making decisions.
- ways to use resistance skills to say "no" to sex.

When you choose healthful behaviors, you make a commitment to protect your health. An important commitment to make is to practice abstinence from sex. **Abstinence from sex** is voluntarily choosing not to be sexually active. Abstinence from sex is the expected standard for you and your peers.

Vocabulary

- **abstinence from sex,** A62
- **self-respect,** A64
- **human immuno-deficiency virus (HIV),** A64
- **sexually transmitted disease (STD),** A64
- **reputation,** A64
- **pregnancy,** A65
- **limit,** A66
- **affection,** A66

Living Up to Adult Expectations

Many responsible adults help shape your life. They include your parents and guardian, as well as other relatives, teachers, coaches, and government officials. These adults realize that you are growing and changing, and they want to help you make responsible decisions and develop healthful relationships. They expect you to practice abstinence from sex and follow your family's dating guidelines.

Parents and guardians will discuss and set family rules for the age at which you can begin dating. They may want you to put off dating to focus on schoolwork, sports, or other activities. They want you to be prepared to date, follow dating guidelines they have established, and practice abstinence from sex.

Dating and Opposite Sex Friendships

Whether or not you are permitted to date, you can still learn about the dating process. Dating is an opportunity for you to learn about yourself and others. It is a chance for you to learn and practice social skills. At first, it is normal to feel awkward. Remember, social skills take practice. You can practice having conversations and making decisions about where to go and what to do.

Some parents and guardians prefer that their teens ease into dating relationships. At your age, they permit you to go on group dates, where you are with several boys and girls. They might permit you to go to parties supervised by responsible adults.

They encourage you to practice social skills and responsible behavior. You can practice sharing with others the guidelines you follow for responsible behavior.

 **What is abstinence from sex?**

BUILD ACTIVITY
Character

Choosing Friends

Respect If you have chosen wisely, your friends will encourage you to live responsibly. You will participate in healthful activities at home, in school, and in your community that promote your well-being. However, sometimes things can still go wrong. A friend suddenly tries to encourage you to do something that you know is not in your best interest. Using the Guidelines for Making Responsible Decisions™, role-play with a partner how you would respect yourself by avoiding that situation.

▼ **Your parents or guardian may set family guidelines about dating.**

Ten Reasons to Practice Abstinence

Suppose someone asks why you choose abstinence. There are at least ten reasons you can give.

1. **I want to do what is expected of me.** Abstinence is the expected standard for you.

2. **I want to respect myself.** **Self-respect** is having high regard for oneself because one behaves in responsible ways. You know that being sexually active is risky. Your future would change if you became a parent. Your future would also change if you became infected with HIV or an STD that could not be cured. **Human immunodeficiency** (I•myuh•noh•di•FI•shuhn•see) **virus (HIV)** is a virus that destroys helper T cells. A **sexually transmitted disease (STD)** is a disease spread through sexual contact.

3. **I want to respect others.** Respect is having a high regard for others. When you respect a person, you want the best for that person. Your actions protect the person from harmful consequences. After all, you do not want this person to risk his or her future.

4. **I want to have a good reputation.** **Reputation** is the quality of a person's character as judged by others. Abstinence is the expected standard for you. To demonstrate good character, you must keep to this standard. Other teens will judge you as having high standards.

5. **I do not want to feel guilty.** Guilt is the feeling that you have done something wrong. You protect your health if you practice abstinence. If you become sexually active, you will know that you have made a wrong decision.

   Sexual activity with a minor is illegal. (Legal age varies from state to state.) By practicing abstinence from sex, a teen avoids situations that could lead to being prosecuted for having sex with a minor.

6. **I am not ready for marriage.** Marriage provides a structure for the way a family lives in society. Before you marry, you need to finish your education. You need to be able to support yourself. And you need time to date and be involved in social activities.

◀ Erika Harold, voted Miss America in 2003, is a strong advocate for abstinence.

7. **I do not want to risk pregnancy.** **Pregnancy** is the time during which an unborn offspring develops within the female parent. Pregnancy places many demands on your emotions. Your emotions are not those of an adult yet. If you are male, you are not ready to support a female through pregnancy. If you are female, a pregnancy would also be physically difficult for you. Teens are the least likely of all mothers to receive proper health care when they are pregnant. Your body is not yet fully developed. You are still growing. Both male and female teens must consider the risk to the developing baby, too.

   Babies born to teens often have a low birth weight. A low birth weight is one that is less than 5.5 pounds. Babies with a low birth weight often have health problems. You have a better chance of having a healthy baby when you are older.

8. **I am not ready to be a parent.** You are not ready to be a mother or a father right now. You are still working on meeting your own needs. When you are a parent, you must be other-centered. To be other-centered is to focus on the needs of another person. It is easier for parents to put the needs of their baby first when they have reached adulthood and they are married.

9. **I do not want to be infected with an STD.** STDs can result in infertility. People who are infertile cannot have children. Some STDs cannot be cured. Genital warts and genital herpes are examples of STDs that have no cure. These two diseases also are linked to cancers in females.

10. **I do not want to be infected with HIV.** You cannot tell by looking at someone if the person is infected with HIV. HIV can be transmitted sexually. HIV causes AIDS. To date, there is no cure for AIDS. Practice abstinence to keep from becoming infected.

 **What are four reasons to practice abstinence from sex?**

Math LINK
Make a Graph

The birthrate among teens has fallen every year since 1991. Still, teen mothers account for about one out of every eight babies born in the United States. According to the Centers for Disease Control, teens gave birth to 453,725 babies in 2000. In 2001, teens gave birth to 447,509 babies. Calculate how many fewer teen births there were in 2001 than in 2000. Make a bar graph comparing the teen births in both years.

BUILD Character
Showing Empathy

Caring Role-play this situation with a partner. A friend has made a strong stand to practice abstinence from sex. However, your friend is being teased by others. How can you show empathy for your friend? In your role play you might discuss the reasons for practicing abstinence.

Setting Limits and Making Decisions

A **limit** is a boundary. It is a line that should not be crossed. A limit shows you the place to stay within. To prepare for the future, you must set limits for yourself. Your parents or guardians will help you. Some limits help you practice abstinence. Limits help keep you from being sexually active. They will protect your health and safety.

A Parent or Guardian Helps You Set Limits

Your parents or guardians can help you set limits on certain things relating to dating and sexual activity. They can decide when you are at an appropriate age to date, individually or in a group. Trusted adults can also choose the kinds of activities in which you can participate and with whom you can do those activities. They are able to explain appropriate ways to express **affection,** a warm feeling. Importantly, parents or a guardian can teach you appropriate actions to take when someone does not respect your limits.

Movies and TV Affect Decisions About Sex

Consider messages about sex in the movies and television programs you watch. Their messages feed your mind just as food feeds your body. Suppose you watch movies and TV programs in which young people are sexually active. These young people do not experience consequences. They might not experience unintended pregnancy or HIV infection. They might not become infected with other STDs. A steady diet of movies and TV programs can change your thinking. You might begin to believe that it is OK for you to be sexually active. You might forget the serious outcomes that can result.

◀ **Healthful activities support healthful decisions.**

Choosing Healthful Entertainment

In order to feed your mind in the most healthful way, be mindful of the entertainment that you watch. Choose movies and TV programs that are approved for your age group by your parents or guardians. Do not watch movies and TV programs that show drug use, violence, or teen sex as acceptable behaviors.

▲ Your parents or guardian can help you choose healthful entertainment.

Drinking Alcohol Affects Decisions About Sex

Alcohol is a drug. When a person drinks alcohol, alcohol enters the bloodstream. As the blood travels to the body's organs, it carries the alcohol with it. Alcohol affects these organs.

The cerebrum (suh•REE•bruhm) is the part of your brain that enables you to think and reason. It helps you make judgments. When alcohol affects a person's cerebrum, it keeps the person from making clear decisions. This includes decisions about sex. For example, a person may want to practice abstinence. However, if alcohol affects the person's judgment, he or she might not be able to stick with that decision. Alcohol also can prevent people from realizing that they are in risky situations.

Making Clear Decisions

To protect yourself and your health, it's important to commit to being drug free and abstaining from sex. This includes saying "no" if someone pressures you to drink. If people are drinking around you, you should stay away from them. Leave a situation if peers begin to drink. Call your parents or guardians for help.

 Write About It!

Showing Affection

Write a letter to a friend to show responsible affection by scheduling a time when you can both go for a walk together and share your feelings. While walking, share thoughts about favorite music, hobbies, or interesting books you have both read recently.

 Why are limits for expressing affection important?

▼ **Family guidelines help you spend time in healthful ways.**

How to Resist Pressure

Resistance skills help a person say "no" and teach you when to leave a potentially dangerous situation. You may be pressured to become sexually active. You may be pressured to choose behaviors such as watching movies and television programs that contain sexual activity. You may be pressured to drink alcohol. Use resistance skills in these situations.

Using Resistance Skills

Here are some resistance skills that you can use to practice abstinence.

1. **Say "no" to being sexually active.**
   - Use a firm voice.
   - Make eye contact.
   - Know that you are doing what is right.

2. **Give reasons for saying "no" to being sexually active.**
   - I want to do what is expected of me.
   - I want to respect myself and others.
   - I want to have a good reputation.
   - I do not want to feel guilty.
   - I am not ready for marriage.
   - I do not want to risk pregnancy.
   - I am not ready to be a parent.
   - I do not want to be infected with an STD.
   - I do not want to be infected with HIV.

3. **Be certain your behavior matches your words.**
   - Set limits for expressing affection.
   - Do not lead someone on.
   - Avoid situations in which there might be pressure to be sexually active.
   - Do not go to someone's house when a parent or guardian is not home.
   - Do not go to parties where young people are using drugs such as alcohol.

- Avoid being with peers who are sexually active.
- Make friends with peers who follow their families' guidelines.
- Influence peers to choose abstinence.
- Be proud that you have chosen abstinence.
- Share your decisions with friends.
- Set a good example for others.

4. **Tell an adult if you need help.**

- Call your parents, guardian, or another responsible adult for quick help in a pressure situation.
- Discuss difficult situations with your parents or guardian. They can give suggestions.

 What are resistance skills?

ACTIVITY LIFE SKILLS

CRITICAL THINKING

Use Resistance Skills

There are many ways to prepare for when your parents or guardian permits you to date. One way to get ready is to practice using resistance skills. Then, should someone pressure you to become sexually active, you are skilled in the use of resistance skills. For this Critical Thinking Activity, select a classmate and take turns role-playing. One of you will do the pressuring and the other the resisting.

1. **Say "no" in a firm voice.** Tell your classmate that you do not want to become sexually active.

2. **Give reasons for saying "no."** Use one or more of the ten reasons on pages A64–A65.

3. **Be certain your behavior matches your words.** Since you will not be able to demonstrate this in your role play, tell your classmate at least four behaviors you can do to match your words.

4. **Ask an adult for help if you need help.** Pretend you have a telephone. Call your parents or guardian and ask for help.

LESSON 5 REVIEW

Review Concepts

1. **Explain** why you should abstain from sex.

2. **Tell** why limits help you to plan for your future.

3. **Name** one way that TV and movies can affect your opinion about sexual activity.

Critical Thinking

4. **Assess** Find a magazine or newspaper article about the consequences of becoming sexually active at your age. Write a report assessing the effects of this behavior.

5. **Explain** Why does practicing abstinence from sex demonstrate to your parents or guardian that you are responsible?

6. **LIFE SKILLS** **Use Resistance Skills** You are at a classmate's home. The classmate turns on a television program that shows inappropriate sexual behavior. You suggest turning off the program and your friend pressures you. Write a dialogue showing the use of resistance skills.

7. **LIFE SKILLS** **Be a Health Advocate** How can you help others use resistance skills?

CHAPTER 2 REVIEW

Chapter Summary

Lesson 1 • Your relationships influence your health and well-being. Work to build healthful relationships and avoid harmful relationships.

Lesson 2 • Communication, both verbal and nonverbal, is how you express yourself to others. Developing communication skills is necessary to build relationships and avoid conflicts.

Lesson 3 • Your family is an influential part of your life. You should be a loving and responsible family member.

Lesson 4 • Good friendships with responsible peers promote health, self-esteem, and your ability to make responsible decisions.

Lesson 5 • Practice abstinence to protect your health, well-being, and future.

Use Vocabulary

relationship, A35
mediation, A39
I-message, A42
active listening, A45
family guideline, A51
reliable, A58
reputation, A64
self-respect, A64
limit, A66

Choose the correct term from the list to complete each sentence.

1. Timothy is a(n) _____?_____ friend if you can trust and depend on him.

2. A(n) _____?_____ is the connection a person has with other people.

3. Respond with _____?_____ to show another person that you hear and understand.

4. Your parents or guardian set a(n) _____?_____ to help you live in a responsible way.

5. A(n) _____?_____ is a boundary.

6. When negotiation does not lead to an appropriate solution, you may need to try _____?_____.

7. A person with _____?_____ will behave in responsible ways.

8. Mary made the decision to abstain from sexual activity in order to protect her _____?_____.

9. To communicate your personal feelings to others, you can use a(n) _____?_____ to strengthen your view.

Review Concepts

Answer each question in complete sentences.

10. What steps can you take to deal with a harmful relationship?

11. How can you cope with difficult family relationships?

12. Why should you practice abstinence?

13. What are the four types of nonverbal communication?

14. How can you maintain a friendship?

Reading Comprehension

Answer each question in complete sentences.

Dating can help young people learn social skills. It can teach teens how to develop healthful relationships. Dating can build self-esteem and enable young people to learn more about themselves.

15. How can dating help teens build social skills?

16. How can dating contribute to your social well-being?

Critical Thinking/Problem Solving

Answer each question in complete sentences.

Analyze Concepts

17. How do television shows and movies influence a person's attitudes about sex?

18. Compare healthful and harmful relationships.

19. What changes to your communication skills can improve your relationships?

20. Describe healthy ways to express affection and love to family members.

21. If negotiating fails to resolve a conflict, what else could you do to resolve conflict?

Practice Life Skills

22. Use Communication Skills Your brother has been acting strangely around you lately. He does not look at you or talk to you, and you don't know what is bothering him. How can you use communication skills to resolve this problem?

23. Make Responsible Decisions A boy who you have always wanted to be friends with invites you to a party. Once you get there, he offers you a drink of alcohol. He tells you that the drink will make things more fun. What should you do?

Read Graphics

Use the text in the visual below to answer the questions.

24. According to the table, what percentage of marriages among women age 17 or younger will end in divorce within 15 years? What about for women age 20 to 24?

25. Why do you think there is such a large difference between the two numbers?

Wife's Age at Marriage	Marriages Dissolved Within 15 Years
Under 18	60%
18–19	50%
20–24	37%

Source: Centers for Disease Control and Prevention

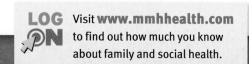

LOG ON Visit **www.mmhhealth.com** to find out how much you know about family and social health.

Effective Communication

Identify

Observe conversations between two classmates or a classmate and a teacher. Identify the types of nonverbal communication used by each person. Explain how nonverbal communication contributed to the conversation.

Self-Directed Learning

Discover

Go to the library or find information containing national statistics on sexually transmitted diseases. In the most recent year for which information is available, how many new STD cases were reported? What was the most common STD? How many people died from STDs?

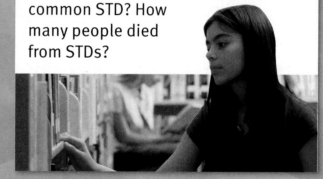

Critical Thinking and Problem Solving

Plan

Take note of the issues that cause conflict between your peers. Identify communication and conflict resolution skills that could be used to settle these disputes. Prepare a strategy list for reducing conflict. Explain how each strategy will help reduce conflict.

Cause of Conflict	Solution
1. _____	1. _____
2. _____	2. _____
3. _____	3. _____
4. _____	4. _____
5. _____	5. _____

Responsible Citizenship

Explain

Interview a grief counselor about the needs of a person who is grieving. Find out his or her recommendations for what to do for someone experiencing grief. Write a speech describing how to comfort a person who is grieving.

UNIT B

Growth and Nutrition

CHAPTER 3

Growth and Development, B2

CHAPTER 4

Nutrition, B34

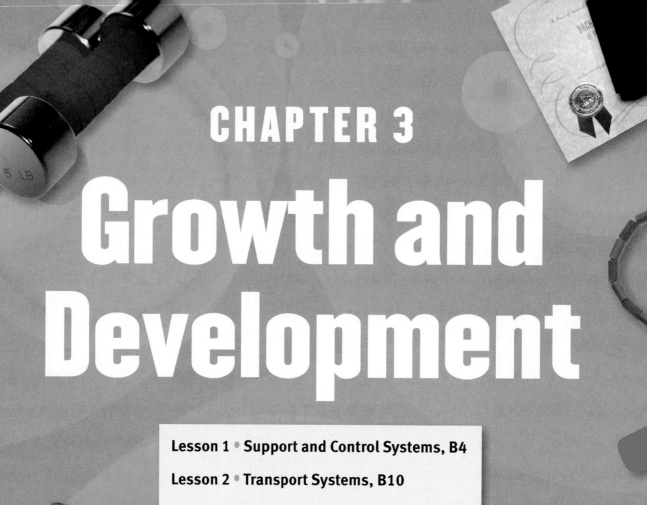

CHAPTER 3
Growth and Development

Lesson 1 • Support and Control Systems, B4

Lesson 2 • Transport Systems, B10

Lesson 3 • Growing and Changing, B16

Lesson 4 • Pregnancy and Childbirth, B26

What Do You Know About
Growth and Development?

1. Which body system is the body's control center?

2. What are the parts of a cell?

3. Why should you practice abstinence?

NO SMOKING

The Inside Story

It's Everywhere

Do you know how much air you inhale and exhale? The average person breathes about 15,000 liters of air each day! By comparison, you only drink about two liters of liquid on a daily basis. Breathing draws oxygen into your lungs. From there, your body systems send the oxygen to every part of your body. Without oxygen you could not survive.

 LOG ON Visit **www.mmhhealth.com** for activities and information on growth and development.

Support and Control Systems

You will learn . . .

- the function of skin.
- the function of the skeletal system.
- the function of the muscular system.
- the function of the nervous system.

Vocabulary

- **skeletal system,** B6
- **muscular system,** B6
- **muscle,** B6
- **joint,** B6
- **cartilage,** B6
- **tendon,** B7
- **nervous system,** B8
- **spinal cord,** B8
- **nerves,** B8

In order to race cars, a driver, a tire changer, a fuel pumper, and others work closely together as a team, a system. Your body works in a similar way: Many members or parts work together. The basic building blocks of your body are cells. There are blood cells, nerve cells, bone cells, and muscle cells, each with its own job. The cells are organized to form the body systems.

Cells, Tissues, Organs

Cells of the same kind work together in groups called tissues. For example, muscle tissue is made up of muscle cells. Different tissues are grouped into organs. For example, your heart contains blood tissue, nerve tissue, and other tissues. Different organs work together to make up organ systems. Together, all the cells, tissues, and organ systems make up an organism, a living being.

The Integumentary System

Skin, hair, and nails make up the integumentary (in•te•gyuh•MENT•uh•ree) system. Skin, the body's largest organ, contains melanin, which gives skin color that protects it from the sun's rays. Another part of this system is your hair and nails. Hair protects your skin from the sun and helps preserve body heat. Nails protect and support the tips of your fingers and toes.

 What is a body system?

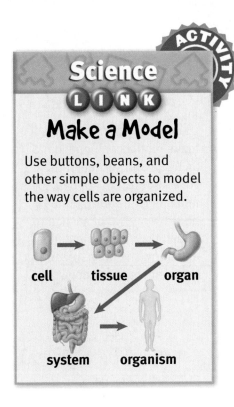

Science LINK
Make a Model

Use buttons, beans, and other simple objects to model the way cells are organized.

cell → tissue → organ → system → organism

Cells, Tissues, and Organs

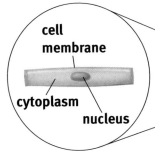

cell membrane
cytoplasm
nucleus

Your body contains many different kinds of cells, but all cells have three common parts. The **cell membrane**, a thin outer covering, holds the cell together, lets water and nutrients into the cell, and keeps out harmful items, such as germs. The **nucleus** controls the cell's activities. The **cytoplasm** surrounds the nucleus.

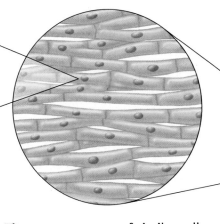

Tissues are groups of similar cells that work together. Tissue cells are shaped for the task they perform. For example, skin cells are thin and flat and fit tightly together. As a result, skin tissue is flat and thin. Clusters of nerve cells form the tissue of the brain.

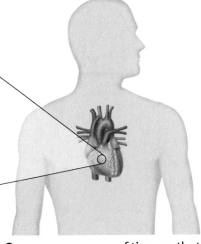

Organs are groups of tissues that work together. For example, nerve tissues make up most of your brain. Your heart is the organ that pumps blood to body cells. Some organs belong to more than one body system.

B5

The Skeletal and Muscular Systems

Do you play sports, dance, or jog? You could not do any of these activities without the support of bones and muscles. In fact, you could not even walk, stand, or sit without them.

The **skeletal system** is the body system that serves as a support framework. It holds the body together, protects inner body parts, and helps with movement. The **muscular system** is the body system that helps a person move and maintain posture. A **muscle** is a bundle of tissues that moves certain parts of the body.

The Skeletal System

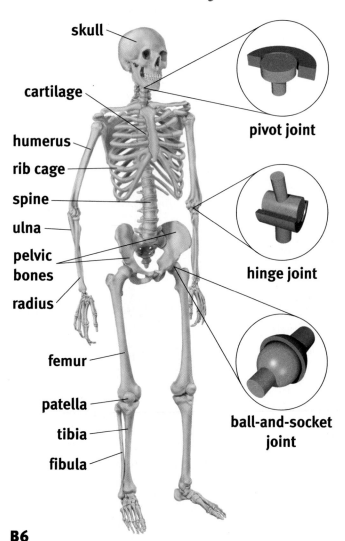

skull

cartilage

humerus

rib cage

spine

ulna

pelvic bones

radius

femur

patella

tibia

fibula

pivot joint

hinge joint

ball-and-socket joint

The Skeletal System

The 206 bones in the skeletal system support the entire body. Some bones protect specific organs. The skull, for example, protects the brain.

A **joint** is a point at which two bones meet. Joints enable the body to move. A hinge joint, such as your elbow or knee, lets bones move back and forth. A ball-and-socket joint, such as your shoulder, enables bones to move in a full circle. A fixed joint, such as your skull, allows no movement. A gliding joint allows back-and-forth and side-to-side movement. The vertebrae in your spine form gliding joints. Your neck has a pivot joint, which allows you to turn your head. **Cartilage** is soft material on the end of bones. It protects your bones by preventing them from rubbing together.

Skeletal System Health

In order to care for your skeletal system, you should exercise to make bones thicker and stronger. Be sure to wear shoes with good arches and use correct posture to support the spinal column. Eat many foods with calcium, phosphorus, and vitamin D.

The Muscular System

Your body contains different types of muscle. You use striated, or striped muscles for voluntary movements such as walking. Smooth muscles in your stomach and intestines squeeze food through the digestive system. Cardiac muscles help your heart beat.

Voluntary muscles are those that you can control. You use these muscles when you perform an action such as throwing a ball or standing up. You cannot control involuntary muscles, such as your heart.

Some muscles stretch across joints. A **tendon** (TEN•duhn) is a tough band of tissue that connects muscle to bone. Muscles work in pairs to move bones. One muscle contracts and shortens while another relaxes and lengthens.

Muscular System Health

In order to care for your muscular system, lift objects by bending your knees. Keep your back straight to prevent injury. When you exercise, warm up to prevent injury. Choose activities for different muscle groups. When deciding what to eat, pick foods rich in protein to help with muscle cell growth. Sleep on a firm mattress.

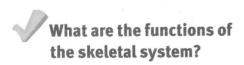

What are the functions of the skeletal system?

The Muscular System

trapezius

deltoid

triceps

biceps

abdominal muscles

Key:
muscles= red
tendon= white

quadriceps

gastrocnemius

HOW THE SKELETAL AND MUSCULAR SYSTEMS INTERACT

Body Part	System	Interaction
bones	skeletal	provide support framework for muscles
skeletal muscles	muscular	attached to bones; hold skeleton together; provide body shape; pull bones during movement
tendons	muscular	connect muscles to bone
joints	skeletal	allow bones to move as muscles pull them

B7

The Nervous System

The **nervous system** is the body system for communication and control. It is composed of neurons, which are masses of nerve cells. The nervous system has several parts.

The brain serves as the body's control center, and different parts of the brain perform different functions. Thinking takes place in the cerebrum. The cerebellum helps muscles work together. The brain stem passes messages between the brain and the body to control how your internal organs function. Critical life functions, such as maintaining heartbeat, take place in the brain stem.

The **spinal cord** is a thick band of nerves through which messages enter and leave the brain. It is soft, so a column of bones in the back called the spine surrounds and protects it. **Nerves** are bundles of fibers that carry messages from the brain to the spinal cord and other parts of the body.

The spinal cord connects the brain with nerves throughout the body. Nerves send messages to the brain by way of the spinal cord. Sometimes, the spinal cord works without the help of the brain. A reflex action is a quick movement that the brain does not direct. Quickly removing your hand after touching a hot stove is a reflex action.

ACTIVITY

Math LINK

Calci-yum

Calcium helps to maintain the health of your bones. The National Academy of Sciences recommends 1,300 mg of calcium each day for people age 9 to 18. Good sources of calcium include milk (1 cup) 300 mg; Swiss cheese (slice) 250 mg; broccoli (1 cup) 160 mg; yogurt (1 cup) 300 mg. Calculate how many cups of milk you would still need to drink to reach the recommended daily amount of calcium if you also ate a slice of Swiss cheese, a cup of broccoli, and a cup of yogurt.

ACTIVITY

LIFE SKILLS

CRITICAL THINKING

Practice Healthful Behaviors

Suppose a relative needs help moving. You have to load many heavy boxes onto a truck.

1. **Learn about a healthful behavior.** Find a Web site or book that describes, with diagrams, how to lift properly.

2. **Practice the healthful behavior in the correct way.** Use empty boxes or pillows to practice lifting with your legs. Perfect your technique before lifting anything heavy.

3. **Ask for help if you need it.** During the move, you may come across a box or an object that is too heavy for you to lift safely. Even if you can pick something up, it may be too heavy to carry for any distance. Ask someone to help you lift such items. This will prevent injury and save time in the long run.

4. **Make the healthful behavior a habit.** Always lift with your legs when moving boxes and furniture. Do this even when lifting light objects. Proper lifting technique will then become a habit.

Nervous System Health

The nervous system is the command center for all body systems, so it must be taken care of carefully. When riding in a car, wear a seat belt. Use a safety helmet when riding a bike or playing sports. Always follow safety rules. Avoid alcohol, other drugs, and poisons. Finally, get plenty of sleep.

How the Nervous System Interacts with Other Systems

Skeletal system The spine protects the spinal cord. The skull protects the brain.

Muscular system The brain sends messages through the spinal cord to the muscles. Motor neurons relay these messages, which control body movement.

 **What are nerves?**

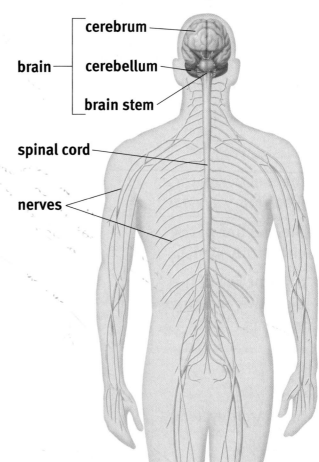

The Nervous System

- brain
  - cerebrum
  - cerebellum
  - brain stem
- spinal cord
- nerves

LESSON **1** REVIEW

Review Concepts

1. **Describe** the functions of the integumentary system. Give at least one function of each of three parts of the system.

2. **Recall** why you need both a skeletal system and a muscular system to move.

3. **List** the main parts of the nervous system. Explain how the two parts work together.

Critical Thinking

4. **Explain** Choose a sports event to watch. Select a specific play such as a basketball player taking a shot or a baseball player swinging at a pitch. Explain how the nervous system, muscular system, and skeletal system worked together during that play.

5. **LIFE SKILLS** **Practice Healthful Behaviors** Sometimes other people can be a source of healthful ideas. Talk to several people about how they care for their body systems. Identify one new way that you can care for your muscular system, skeletal system, and nervous system. Practice these behaviors.

Transport Systems

You will learn ...

- the function of the respiratory system.
- the function of the circulatory system.
- the function of the digestive and urinary systems.

Vocabulary

- **respiratory system,** B11
- **lungs,** B11
- **circulatory system,** B12
- **artery,** B12
- **vein,** B12
- **digestive system,** B14
- **esophagus,** B14
- **intestine,** B14
- **urinary system,** B15
- **kidney,** B15

Your body is very complex. At any given moment, several body systems are working together so that you can perform everyday tasks. In this lesson, you will learn about four body systems known as the transport systems. Each of them moves something through your body.

The Respiratory System

The **respiratory system** is the body system that helps the body use air that is inhaled. When you inhale, air enters the nose and mouth before traveling through the trachea. It then enters the lungs through two short tubes called the bronchial tubes. The **lungs** are the main organs of the respiratory system. Inside the lungs are millions of alveoli, small air sacs through which oxygen reaches your blood.

Your body has several defenses against air pollutants. The hairs in your nose trap particles in the air you breathe. Mucus in your nasal passages traps germs and particles. Tiny hairs called cilia line the air passages. They keep dirt out of your lungs. The quality of air you breathe is important to your health. Polluted air can get through your defenses to harm your lungs.

Caring for Your Respiratory System

To protect the health of your respiratory system:

1. **Stay** away from polluted air.
2. **Do not smoke** or breathe tobacco smoke.
3. **Exercise** to strengthen muscles needed for breathing.
4. **See a physician** if you have a respiratory problem.
5. **Use correct posture** to allow the lungs the space needed to breathe deeply.
6. **Wear a protective mask** to keep fumes from entering the lungs when you are around people working with chemicals.

Where does air go when you breathe?

The Respiratory System

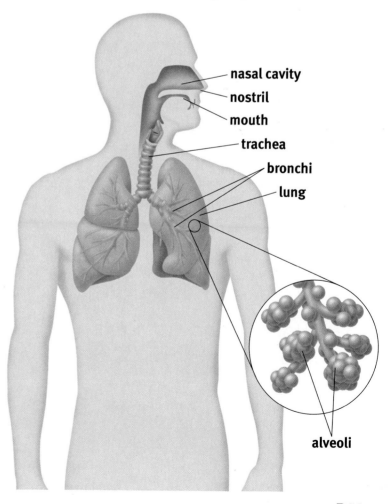

- nasal cavity
- nostril
- mouth
- trachea
- bronchi
- lung
- alveoli

The Circulatory System

The **circulatory system** is the body system that transports oxygen, food, and waste through the body. The circulatory system consists of blood, blood vessels, and the heart.

You have about one gallon of blood in your body. Plasma is the liquid part of blood. Blood contains three main kinds of cells. Red blood cells carry oxygen to body cells and carbon dioxide away from body cells. White blood cells fight germs that cause infection and illness. Platelets are blood cells that help blood to clot.

The heart is a muscular organ that pumps blood to the body through blood vessels. An **artery** (AR•tuh•ree) is a blood vessel that carries blood away from the heart. A **vein** (VAYN) is a blood vessel that returns blood to the heart. A capillary (KA•puh•lehr•ee) is a tiny blood vessel that connects arteries and veins.

MAKE a Difference

Respiratory Rights

Amit Bushan loves to bowl with his friends. However, cigarette smoke filled the bowling alleys in his Texas hometown. Amit started the Stop Tobacco in Restaurants (STIR) campaign. The group wrote more than 1,000 letters to its city council, which passed a law to ban smoking in public places. How can you improve your community?

The Circulatory System

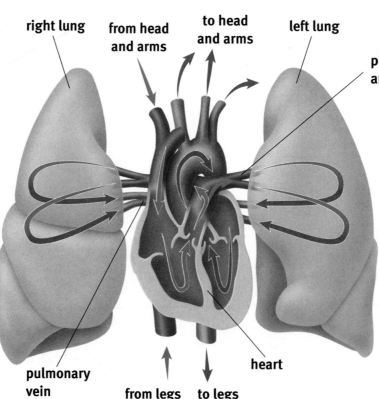

Blood passes into capillaries, releases oxygen to the cells, and picks up carbon dioxide. Blood then flows into the veins and back to the heart.

The pulmonary veins carry oxygen-rich blood from both lungs to the heart. There, the blood is pumped into arteries and then to all parts of the body.

The pulmonary artery carries oxygen-poor blood to the lungs. There, the blood gains oxygen and loses carbon dioxide.

Key:
blue= oxygen poor blood
red= oxygen rich blood

right lung
from head and arms
to head and arms
left lung
pulmonary artery
pulmonary vein
from legs and lower body
to legs and lower body
heart

Caring for Your Circulatory System

To protect the health of your circulatory system:

1. **Exercise** regularly to make your heart muscle strong.
2. **Keep your arteries clear** by reducing the amount of fatty food you eat.
3. **Don't smoke.**
4. **Maintain** a healthful weight.
5. **Keep stress low** to keep blood pressure normal.

How the Circulatory System Interacts with Other Systems

Skeletal system Bones contain red bone marrow that produces all three types of blood cells.

Respiratory system Oxygen enters the bloodstream through the capillaries that surround the alveoli. Red blood cells carry oxygen to the body cells and pick up carbon dioxide to be exhaled.

Muscular system The heart pumps blood through the body. Blood carries oxygen to the muscles.

Nervous system The brain maintains the heartbeat. Blood carries oxygen to the brain.

 What makes up your blood?

Set Health Goals

Use a health behavior contract to set a health goal.

1. **Write the health goal you want to set:** *I will adopt habits to care for my circulatory system.*

2. **Tell how the goal will affect your health.** Why is a healthy circulatory system important to your overall health?

3. **Describe a plan you will follow. Keep track of your progress.** Choose an exercise such as jogging or jumping rope, which will benefit your cardiovascular system. Eat healthful foods. Set daily and weekly goals to follow. Monitor your progress on a calendar.

4. **Evaluate how your plan worked.** Have your blood pressure checked. Are you in a healthy range? If not, consult with your physician about care for your circulatory system.

Write About It!

Function Flash Cards

Make flash cards for three organs from the digestive system and three organs from the urinary system. On one side of the card write the organ's name. On the other side write a sentence describing its function. Give your cards to a classmate. Ask your classmate to hold up a card with the organ name facing you. Write down the organ's function, and do the same for each card. Check your answers.

The Digestive and Urinary Systems

The **digestive system** is the body system that breaks food down so that it can be used by the body. A nutrient (NOO•tree•ent) is a substance that helps with growth, body processes, and the repair of cells.

Digestion begins in the mouth. The salivary glands produce saliva, a liquid that moistens and softens food. Chewing breaks food into smaller pieces, speeding the digestive process. Food exits the mouth to the **esophagus** (i•SAH•fuh•guhs), a tube through which food passes to the stomach. The stomach is the organ that releases digestive juices to break down food.

The **intestine** is a tube that digests food and moves remaining waste through the body. The small intestine is the organ in which most digestion takes place.

ACTIVITY
LIFE SKILLS

CRITICAL THINKING

Make Responsible Decisions

Decide what goes into a meal for your family that contributes to the health of the digestive and urinary systems.

1 Identify your choices. Check them out with a parent or another trusted adult. Review the items on this food list: chocolate; whole wheat bread; cinnamon rolls; rye crackers; lettuce; chicken broth; french fries; broccoli; pears (with skin); steak; peas; water; apple juice; coffee; skinless chicken breasts; hot dogs; blueberries; veal; celery.

2 Evaluate each choice. Use the Guidelines for Making Responsible Decisions™. For each item on the list, ask the following questions:
- Is it healthful?
- Is it safe?
- Do I show respect for myself and others?

- Does it follow the guidelines of my parents and of other responsible adults?

You may need to do some research to determine if the foods are healthful for the digestive and urinary systems.

3 Tell what the responsible decision is. Check this out with your parent, guardian, or another trusted adult. Choose foods from the food list that will contribute to the health of your digestive and urinary systems. Next, select foods from the list to plan a balanced meal for your family.

4 Evaluate your decision. Explain how eating the meal you prepared will affect a person's digestive and urinary systems. Should you have chosen other foods?

B14

Nutrients from the digested food enter the blood through capillaries. The remainder passes to the large intestine, an organ that stores undigested food until it leaves the body. A bowel movement passes undigested food out of the body.

The **urinary system** is the body system that removes liquid wastes from the body. Body cells produce waste as they use nutrients. The waste products pass into the blood. The **kidney** is an organ through which blood circulates as wastes are filtered.

Urine is the liquid waste that collects in the urinary bladder. When the bladder is full, the brain sends a message indicating that it is time to empty the bladder. The urethra is the tube through which urine leaves the body.

 How does the body eliminate waste products?

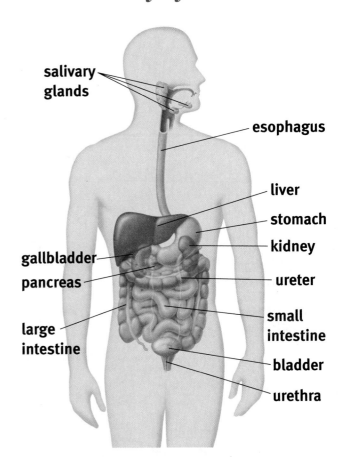

The Digestive and Urinary Systems

- salivary glands
- esophagus
- liver
- stomach
- kidney
- ureter
- small intestine
- bladder
- urethra
- gallbladder
- pancreas
- large intestine

LESSON 2 REVIEW

Review Concepts

1. **Name** the main parts of the respiratory system.

2. **Recall** how regular exercise helps your circulatory system.

3. **List** the parts of the body that food goes through as it passes through the digestive and urinary systems.

Critical Thinking

4. **Explain** Name something that you do each day. Tell why two or more body systems are necessary to perform that action.

5. **LIFE SKILLS** **Set Health Goals** What health goals might you set for yourself in order to improve and protect your respiratory health?

6. **LIFE SKILLS** **Make Responsible Decisions** Think about your weekly diet. What changes could you make to care for a body system? You might substitute celery for potato chips one snack each week. Make another small change each day. Record your progress for a week.

Growing and Changing

You will learn . . .

- the changes that occur throughout the life cycle.
- the function of the endocrine system.
- how to care for the changing adolescent body.
- emotional, intellectual, and social changes that occur during adolescence.

Vocabulary

- **life cycle,** B17
- **adolescence,** B17
- **endocrine system,** B18
- **hormone,** B18
- **pituitary gland,** B18
- **gonads,** B21
- **puberty,** B21
- **menstrual cycle,** B21

As you age, you go through a series of life stages. As a child, your body grows and you learn basic skills. During adolescence, you go through physical changes. You also develop emotionally, intellectually, and socially during this stage. You will soon enter adolescence. In this lesson, you will learn about the many changes that await you.

The Life Cycle

All living things grow, develop, age, and die. The **life cycle** is the different stages of growing, developing, aging, and dying. There are nine stages in the life cycle.

Stage 1: Infancy (birth to 1 year)

Stage 2: Early Childhood (1 to 3 years)

Stage 3: Middle Childhood (3 to 6 years)

Stage 4: Late Childhood (6 to 12 years)

Stage 5: Adolescence (12 to 18 years)

Stage 6: Transition to Adulthood (18 to 30 years)

Stage 7: First Adulthood (30 to 45 years)

Stage 8: Second Adulthood (45 to 70 years)

Stage 9: Late Adulthood (70+ years)

You grow and develop during the first five stages of the life cycle. As an infant, you learned to crawl and stand. In early childhood, you developed motor skills, mental abilities, and personality traits. In middle childhood, your speech skills improved and you continued to grow. In late childhood, you learned to read and write. Other mental skills soon followed.

Adolescence is the period between childhood and adulthood. During this stage, you develop a sense of your own identity.

Physical growth ends after the fifth stage. Aging occurs in the sixth through ninth stages. In the adult stages, a person often grows more concerned about family, career, and society. Health may become an increasing concern as a person ages. Death is the loss of life when vital organs no longer work. Sometimes a young person dies. Unintentional injuries, violence, and cancer are the most common causes of death among young people.

What are the five life stages during which physical growth occurs?

BUILD Character ACTIVITY

Make a Time Line

Honesty/Respect/Responsibility/Fairness/Caring/Citizenship Make a time line showing when you demonstrated each of these traits. For example, when was the first time you bought someone a gift? When was the first time you shared a toy with a friend?

▼ **How many stages of the life cycle are represented by this family?**

B17

The Endocrine System

The **endocrine system** is the body system made up of glands that produce hormones. A **hormone** is a chemical messenger that regulates body activities. Endocrine glands control many of the changes in the body. They are located throughout your body. Each gland produces a different hormone, and each hormone has a different function.

The **pituitary gland** secretes hormones that control the other glands. It is a small, pea-sized gland at the base of the brain. The pituitary is called the body's master gland. It also produces growth hormone, which makes your body grow.

▶ The glands in the endocrine system and the hormones that those glands produce affect almost all of the body's cells, organs, and functions. The effects produced by the endocrine system are not as fast acting as those produced by the nervous system, but in general they are more long lasting. The endocrine system regulates processes such as cell growth and metabolism.

The Endocrine System

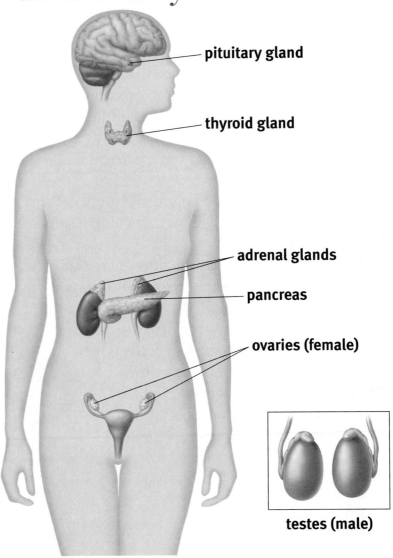

pituitary gland

thyroid gland

adrenal glands

pancreas

ovaries (female)

testes (male)

The thyroid is another major endocrine gland. It produces a substance called thyroid hormone that controls how fast your body burns nutrients to make energy. Your body has two adrenal glands. They produce adrenaline to increase your heart rate and blood pressure to prepare your body for stressful situations. The pancreas is a gland that produces a hormone to regulate your blood sugar level. The endocrine system also includes your reproductive glands.

Protecting Your Endocrine System

To make sure your endocrine system is working properly, it is important to have regular medical checkups. If you have any questions about your growth, you can ask your parents, guardians, or a physician.

 What is a hormone?

CAREERS IN HEALTH
Endocrinologist

An endocrinologist is a specialist in the diseases and disorders of the endocrine system. He or she is trained to recognize and treat hormone problems and to restore the natural balance of hormones. Some endocrinologists conduct research to learn more about glands. They also develop drugs and treatments for hormone disorders. To become an endocrinologist requires four years of medical school, then at least three years in an internship and residency program. An endocrinologist then spends two or three more years learning about the treatment and diagnosis of hormone conditions.

Diseases and disorders of the endocrine system include

- diabetes.
- Cushing's syndrome.
- Addison's disease.

LOG ON Visit **www.mmhhealth.com** to find out more about this and other health careers.

LIFE SKILLS

CRITICAL THINKING

Be a Health Advocate

Young people sometimes face pressure to engage in unhealthful practices, such as smoking cigarettes.

1 **Select a health-related concern to communicate.** Help a person who faces pressure to smoke.

2 **Gather reliable information.** Research some of the harmful effects of smoking.

3 **Identify your purpose and target audience.** Would it be best to talk face-to-face, call, or send an e-mail?

4 **Develop a convincing and appropriate message.** Write a monologue to let others know about your reasons to avoid smoking.

More than 30 different hormones regulate the activities of the human body. Since the 1940s, scientists have been able to design fake hormones, called synthetic hormones, which function like the body's real hormones. Physicians use these synthetic hormones for people who have a natural hormone deficiency.

Physical Changes of Adolescence

The endocrine system causes major physical changes during adolescence. For example, growth hormone produced by the pituitary gland affects how much and how fast you will grow. As the production of this hormone increases, you may experience a period of rapid growth called a growth spurt. It may seem like you are outgrowing your classmates. Or it may seem like all of them are growing faster than you. Either case is normal.

MALE BODY CHANGES

During puberty, the following body changes occur in males:

- Testes produce a hormone called testosterone.
- Testosterone produces secondary sex characteristics.
- Hair grows in pubic area, under arms, and on face and chest.
- Voice becomes deeper.
- Growth spurts.
- Production of male reproductive cells.
- Acne and perspiration.

CARING FOR THE CHANGING MALE BODY

Be sure to have regular medical checkups. Practice abstinence from sex. Wear protective gear when playing sports. Eat a variety of nutritious foods and engage in regular physical activity. Don't forget to receive sufficient rest and relaxation.

FEMALE BODY CHANGES

During puberty, the following body changes occur in females:

- Ovaries produce estrogen.
- Estrogen produces secondary sex characteristics.
- Hair grows in pubic area and under arms.
- Growth spurts.
- Fat deposits in breasts.
- Widening of hips.
- Beginning of menstrual cycle and formation of mature eggs. Egg cells are female reproductive cells.
- Acne and perspiration.

CARING FOR THE CHANGING FEMALE BODY

The adolescent female should engage in many of the same practices as the male. Have regular medical checkups. Practice abstinence from sex. Eat a variety of nutritious foods and engage in regular physical activity. Wear protective gear for sports and physical activity. Get sufficient rest and relaxation.

During adolescence, the pituitary gland makes hormones that affect the **gonads**, which are reproductive glands. In boys, the gonads are the testes and they produce sperm as well as hormones. In girls, the gonads are the ovaries and they produce egg cells. **Puberty** (PYOO•ber•tee) is the period in which gonads first begin to make hormones. These hormones cause the development of secondary sex characteristics, changes that make an adolescent's body like an adult's body. Puberty usually starts between the ages of 8 and 13 in girls. It occurs between 10 and 15 for boys. The physical changes of puberty enable males and females to reproduce.

The Menstrual Cycle

One sign that a female is approaching adulthood is the start of her **menstrual** (MEN•struhl) **cycle**, a monthly series of changes that occur in a female's body. During the menstrual cycle, an ovary first releases an egg. Next, a thick lining develops inside the uterus.

An egg cell may join with a sperm cell, as you will learn in Lesson 4. If the egg does not join with a sperm cell, this lining of the uterus breaks down. Finally, the lining of the uterus leaves the body during the menstrual period.

The menstrual period usually occurs every 28 days. Girls who are beginning to menstruate often have irregular periods. The cycle usually becomes regular after a few months. A woman who is pregnant does not have a menstrual period.

 **What is puberty?**

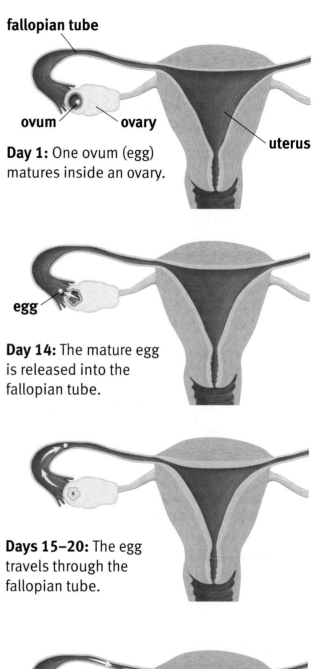

The Menstrual Cycle

fallopian tube

ovum   ovary

uterus

Day 1: One ovum (egg) matures inside an ovary.

egg

Day 14: The mature egg is released into the fallopian tube.

Days 15–20: The egg travels through the fallopian tube.

Days 21–28: The egg enters the uterus. If fertilization does not take place, menstruation begins after seven days.

Adolescent Changes

Puberty means more than just physical changes. The hormones produced by the endocrine system affect your emotions, learning skills, and ability to relate to others. All of these changes don't occur at the same time for everyone. Adolescents experience these changes at different ages.

Emotional and Intellectual Changes

Feelings are emotions such as excitement, sadness, happiness, and anger. Hormones influence the strength of your feelings. During puberty, the endocrine glands secrete hormones at an uneven rate. This can cause mood swings—changes in feelings caused by hormone levels. You might feel happy one moment and sad the next. You may be more sensitive than usual. Mood swings can be frustrating, but they are normal.

Puberty can be a confusing time. You might worry about how fast you're growing, or not growing. You may become self-conscious about your appearance. You may worry about pimples or a cracking in your voice as it changes. Rapid physical changes may make you feel clumsy. As your body develops, you may have new feelings about sex. So many changes happening so quickly can lead to anxiety.

Your mind also changes during puberty. Your thinking and analysis skills will develop. You will become able to understand more complex situations. You will become capable of evaluating another person's point of view. You will develop stronger values.

◀ Mood swings are a common part of adolescence.

Social Changes

Adolescence is also a time of great social change. You might want to become more independent from your parents or guardians. You will probably want to increase the time you spend with your peers. You will probably view the opposite sex in a new way. You may want to date.

Social changes are normal, but it is important to handle them responsibly. This is a sign of good character. Maintain healthful relationships with your family by communicating with them. They can provide an important, continuing source of support for you. Adolescence often brings increased peer pressure. Teens sometimes engage in risky new behaviors. You may have friends who want you to join them in such activities, but you need to learn to resist negative peer pressure.

 **What types of issues do adolescents worry about?**

ACTIVITY — LIFE SKILLS

CRITICAL THINKING

Use Communication Skills

Role-play this situation in a small group: You want to attend a party on Friday night. All of your friends will be at the party. How would you ask your parents or guardian respectfully for permission to attend the party?

1 **Choose the best way to communicate.** Write a letter or a short speech to deliver your message.

2 **Send a clear message. Be polite.** Use I-messages to convey your feelings. Convey to your family that you will act responsibly at the party. Assure your family that you will respect their decision, whatever it may be.

3 **Listen to the other person.** Realize that maintaining communication with family members is important. Your family members have a valid point of view. Try to understand it.

4 **Make sure you understand each other.** Repeat to your family members what you heard them say. Ask them to repeat what they heard you say. How can better communication prevent any problems in the future?

LESSON 3 REVIEW

Review Concepts

1. **Recall** the nine stages of the life cycle.

2. **Identify** the function of the endocrine system.

3. **List** the ways in which the body changes during adolescence.

4. **Discuss** the intellectual and social changes that adolescents experience.

Critical Thinking

5. **Compare and Contrast** Write an essay describing how the male and female bodies change during puberty. Explain in your essay how the changes are similar and how they are different.

6. **LIFE SKILLS** **Use Communication Skills** Review the types of emotional changes that adolescents experience. Make a list of how these changes can cause problems with family relationships. For each item on your list, write how communication skills could solve the problem.

Manage Stress

Dear Health Nut,

Here's the problem ... Lately my life seems to be out of control. I am often in a bad mood. The smallest things really irritate me. My parents make so many rules for me! I feel like a clown at school. My feet are enormous. I trip at least once a day. My clothes are all too small because I keep growing. What can I do to feel better about myself?

Stressed in St. Louis

CLOTHES FOR CHARITY

Dear Stressed in St. Louis,

Here is how you might solve the problem . . . You're experiencing puberty. It is normal that your body is going through dramatic changes. You feel self-conscious about your appearance. You have frequent mood swings. You have more conflicts with your parents. You feel stress. Talk about your feelings with your parents, other responsible adults, or friends. Everyone has encountered these emotions. Don't worry, things will get better.

Health Nut

Foldables To Learn Life Skills

Learn This Life Skill

What is happening to Stressed in St. Louis is normal. Follow these steps to help him deal with his stress. You can use the Foldables to help you organize your thoughts.

1 **Identify the signs of stress.**

Find a book in the library about stress. Learn the signs of stress.

2 **Identify the cause of stress.**

Read about the changes that occur during puberty. Physical and emotional changes during adolescence are normal.

3 **Do something about the cause of stress.**

Stressed in St. Louis can talk to his parents, guardians, or another responsible adult. They have likely experienced a similar situation and can help him sort out his feelings.

4 **Take action to lessen the harmful effects of stress.**

Stressed in St. Louis can stay active to help reduce stress and build self-esteem. He can cultivate his talents: play a sport, learn a musical instrument, join a drama club, or volunteer to help others.

> 1. Identify the signs of stress.
>
> 2. Identify the cause of stress.
>
> 3. Do something about the cause of stress.
>
> 4. Take action to lessen the harmful effects of stress.
>
> Manage Stress

If you do this activity with a group of students, students can participate in different ways, such as writing, folding, or drawing. Some students may do the activity in other ways, such as by role-playing or drawing a comic strip.

Practice This Life Skill

Activity Role-play with a partner to show an adolescent who faces stress caused by the changes of puberty. Show the problems and the steps taken to overcome stress. Include a member of the person's family.

Pregnancy and Childbirth

You will learn ...

- the function of the reproductive system.
- why health care is important during pregnancy.
- why teen pregnancy and parenthood are risky.

Vocabulary

- reproductive system, B27
- fertilization, B27
- uterus, B27
- chromosomes, B27
- gene, B27
- embryo, B28
- fetus, B28
- labor, B29

Do you ever think about becoming a parent? Do you wonder what your children will be like? Parenthood brings great responsibility. Young people are not ready to become parents, yet their bodies may be able to reproduce. Learning about pregnancy and childbirth will help you make responsible decisions that protect your future.

The Reproductive System

The **reproductive system** enables living beings to produce offspring. The reproductive system in males and females produces cells for reproduction. Males produce sperm cells. Females produce egg cells.

Each person begins as a single cell produced by fertilization. **Fertilization** (fuhr·tuh·luh·ZAY·shun) is the joining of a sperm cell and an egg cell to make a single cell called a fertilized egg. The fertilized egg divides and attaches itself to the uterus. The **uterus** (YOO·tuh·rus) is a muscular organ in a woman's body that supports the development of the fertilized egg during pregnancy.

Heredity

Heredity is the sum of traits that have been transmitted from a person's biological parents. You inherit traits through **chromosomes** (KROH•muh•sohmz), strands of matter found in the nucleus of a cell. Most human cells contain 46 chromosomes, but reproductive cells contain only half as many. An egg cell has 22 chromosomes plus an X chromosome. A sperm cell has 22 chromosomes plus an X or a Y chromosome. If a sperm cell with a Y chromosome fertilizes an egg cell, a male will develop. If the sperm cell has an X chromosome, then a female will develop.

A **gene** (JEEN) is a tiny piece of information found in a chromosome that controls heredity. DNA, an acid found in genes, carries this information. Each pair of genes contains information from both a mother and a father. A dominant gene produces an observable trait. A recessive gene produces an observable trait only if the other gene in the pair is the same.

How does fertilization occur?

▶ Your appearance is a trait you might inherit from your biological parents.

B27

Pregnancy

Pregnancy is the time between fertilization and birth, about nine months. After fertilization, the fertilized egg divides into a cluster of cells and attaches itself to the walls of the uterus. **Embryo** (EM·bree·oh) is the name of the developing baby from fertilization until the eighth week.

From the end of the eighth week until birth, the developing baby is called a **fetus** (FEE·tuhs). The mother-to-be provides the fetus in her uterus with food and oxygen through the umbilical cord. The mother's blood passes through the cord to the fetus and carries away wastes.

The Developing Baby

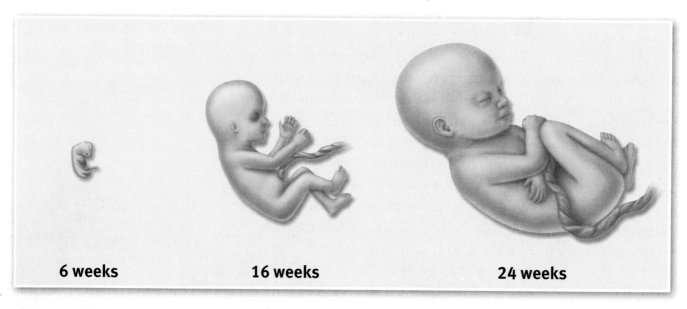

6 weeks

16 weeks

24 weeks

At fertilization, the embryo is a single cell that is invisible to the human eye. By the 6th week, the embryo is only about one sixth of an inch long. However, the heart has begun to beat and the respiratory and digestive systems are developing.

By the 16th week of pregnancy, the fetus has reached a length of about four inches. The fetus can now make voluntary muscle movements, and developing facial muscles allow for expressions such as squinting and frowning.

The fetus now weighs about one pound. Development of the inner ear enables the developing baby to sense his or her position in the uterus and to hear sounds. The hands can now feel the surroundings.

Prenatal Care

The health of a developing baby depends on the mother's health. Prenatal care is the health care given to an expectant mother and her unborn baby. During pregnancy, a woman should have regular examinations from a physician who specializes in prenatal care.

A mother-to-be should adopt healthful habits. Eating healthful foods provides vitamins, minerals, and other nutrients to the baby.

Doctors recommend that pregnant women avoid certain substances. The caffeine in coffee or some soft drinks, for example, can lower the mother's red blood cell count. Drinking alcohol during pregnancy can cause problems with the baby's heart or nervous system. If a pregnant woman smokes, she may have a premature birth. Babies born prematurely have more health problems than babies carried to a full term.

Expectant mothers should get a physician's permission before they start to exercise. They should get plenty of rest. They should be careful about the air they breathe. Pregnant women should avoid cigarette smoke. They should not inhale chemicals found in many household products, such as nail polish and cleaning agents.

Labor and Delivery

Expectant parents often take classes about labor and childbirth. **Labor** is a series of stages that result in the birth of a baby. Childbirth is the process by which the baby moves from the uterus out of the mother's body. A woman may choose to give birth at home, in a hospital, or in a birth center. A physician, certified nurse midwife, or other type of midwife assists with the delivery.

✔ **What should a woman avoid during her pregnancy?**

On Your Own
FOR SCHOOL OR HOME

ACTIVITY

Make a Time Line

The size of a newborn varies widely. Ask your parents or guardians how long you were and how much you weighed at birth. Make a time line showing your parents' and siblings' birth weights and heights in age order. Be sure to note if there is a trend in your family.

▼ **Childbirth classes can be an important part of prenatal care.**

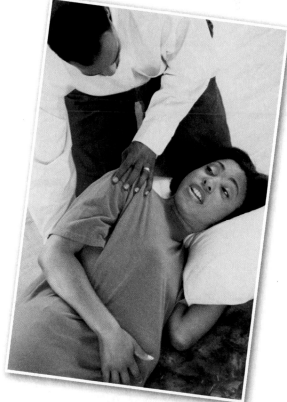

The Risks of Teen Pregnancy and Parenthood

Teen pregnancy is risky for many reasons. A teen's body is still developing. During these years, a girl needs extra nutrients, rest, and sleep. A pregnancy adds stress to her body. Pregnant teens have an increased risk for problems such as high blood pressure and miscarriage.

Some teens face pressure to smoke or drink alcohol. Even if a pregnant young woman stops these behaviors, it may be too late. The fertilized egg has divided many times before she knows that she is pregnant. Any drug use on her part can harm the developing baby.

Teen pregnancy leads to other problems. Teens often lack money for prenatal care. Pregnant teens may be depressed. They may not complete their education. They may have conflicts with their families because family guidelines discourage sexual activity in teens.

ACTIVITY

LIFE SKILLS

CRITICAL THINKING

Use Resistance Skills

Role-play this situation with a partner: You have joined an organization that has a goal to have members sign a pledge to practice abstinence. You like this idea. You tell a friend that you will sign this pledge but your friend says you shouldn't sign. Your friend says this pledge is ridiculous and pressures you to avoid signing. How would you respond to your friend?

1 Say "no" in a firm voice. Tell your friend that you will not give in to his or her pressure. Tell him or her that you intend to sign the pledge.

2 Give reasons for saying "no." Tell your friend that you want to sign the pledge, that your parents support your decision, and that you feel it demonstrates good character.

3 Be certain your behavior matches your words. Show your friend that you firmly believe in your decision to sign the pledge. Go to the organization's meetings. Take part in activities sponsored by the organization.

4 Ask an adult for help if you need help. Tell your parents or guardian that you face pressure not to sign the abstinence pledge. Ask them for their support.

Teen Parenting

Teen parenting also is risky. Even though teen fathers are legally responsible for their children, they usually are unable to provide support. As a result, many teen mothers lack the money or do not have a caring father for their child.

Pregnant teens are often not married. It is difficult to raise a child without emotional support from a committed partner. The demands of parenthood can frustrate some teen mothers. They are at a higher risk for abuse and neglect of their babies.

Teen parenthood is risky even when the parents marry. The divorce rate among teens is much higher than among adults. Married teens often drop out of school to work full time. Many must abandon their career goals.

Teen pregnancy and teen parenting also put society at risk. The risks include increased medical care costs, having more families living in poverty, and having a higher incidence of violence.

The Risks of Early Sexual Activity

Abstinence is the only way to remain safe from all of the risks of early sexual activity, such as pregnancy, sexually transmitted diseases, and a damaged reputation. Practicing it will protect your health, the health of others, and your future.

 Why is a teenage pregnancy risky?

Social Studies

L I N K

College Flow Chart

Work in a group to decide what steps you must take, including goals that you must set, if you wanted to attend college after high school. For example, decide what courses you should take in each grade level, what health behaviors you should practice to be sure you are at optimal health for college, and so on. Make a flow chart to show all the steps, in order, to reach the goal.

LESSON 4 REVIEW

Review Concepts

1. **Recall** the function of the reproductive system.

2. **Discuss** why it is important for a pregnant woman to remain healthy.

3. **List** reasons why teen pregnancy and parenthood are risky.

4. **Explain** the difference between an embryo and a fetus.

Critical Thinking

5. **Explain** How does practicing abstinence show respect for others?

6. **LIFE SKILLS** **Use Resistance Skills** Make a list of the risks involved with teen pregnancy and parenthood. Write each risk on a separate note card. How can you say "no" to the risks of teen pregnancy and parenthood?

Chapter Summary

Lesson 1 • Your skeletal and muscular systems enable you to move and provide support for your body. Your nervous system is the system for control and communication in your body.

Lesson 2 • The respiratory, circulatory, digestive, and urinary systems are your body's transport systems. They provide your body cells with what they need to function.

Lesson 3 • As an adolescent, your endocrine system initiates puberty, which brings about major physical, emotional, intellectual, and social changes.

Lesson 4 • Reproduction consists of fertilization, pregnancy, and childbirth. Teens are not yet ready for pregnancy and parenthood.

Use Vocabulary

muscular system, B6

spinal cord, B8

respiratory system, B11

esophagus, B14

adolescence, B17

puberty, B21

fertilization, B27

gene, B27

Choose the correct term from the list to complete each sentence.

1. The body system that helps a person move and maintain posture is called the _____?_____.

2. The period between childhood and adulthood is called _____?_____.

3. The body system that helps the body use air that is inhaled is the _____?_____.

4. The period in which gonads first begin to make hormones is called _____?_____.

5. A(n) _____?_____ is a tiny piece of information, found in a chromosome, that controls heredity.

6. An important part of the nervous system is the _____?_____, which connects the brain with the nerves throughout the body.

7. After food exits the mouth, it enters the _____?_____ in the next step of the digestive process.

8. When the egg cell and the sperm cell join, _____?_____ officially begins.

Answer each question in complete sentences.

9. What does the skeletal system do for your body?

10. How do the digestive and urinary systems work together to remove wastes?

11. Why is teen parenthood risky?

12. How does a male's body change during adolescence?

13. Why is prenatal care important for a woman during pregnancy?

Reading Comprehension

Answer each question in complete sentences.

Puberty means more than just physical changes. The hormones produced by the endocrine system affect your emotions, learning skills, and ability to relate to others. But all of these changes don't occur at the same time for everyone. Adolescents experience these changes at different ages.

14. What type of changes does puberty bring?

15. How have you dealt with these types of changes?

Critical Thinking/Problem Solving

Answer each question in complete sentences.

Analyze Concepts

16. Summarize how chromosomes and genes are involved in heredity.

17. Choose ways that you can take good care of your skeletal system.

18. Differentiate the many parts of the circulatory system.

19. Give an example of a situation in which the adrenal glands would have to work harder than usual.

20. Compare the behaviors of a responsible mother-to-be with an unhealthful expectant mother.

Practice Life Skills

21. **Set Health Goals** You just had an argument with your parents or guardian about how late you stayed up last night. Develop a plan that helps you to better follow family guidelines.

22. **Manage Stress** Your friend is having a hard time in math class. What advice can you give her to help her deal with her stress?

23. **Make Responsible Decisions** Your friend wants to ride bicycles together to a class picnic at a park a couple of miles away. You have lost your biking helmet. What is the responsible thing to do?

Read Graphics

Use the text in the visual below to answer the questions.

24. According to the chart, how much extra water should you drink if you exercise for one hour today?

25. How much water would you need to drink if you had a caffeinated beverage before and after a two-hour workout?

Activity	Amount of Water You Need to Drink to Remain Hydrated
Exercise	16 ounces two hours prior; 8 ounces every 20 minutes during exercise
Drinking caffeine or alcohol	8 ounces per drink

 LOG ON Visit **www.mmhhealth.com** to find out how much you know about growth and development.

CHAPTER 4
Nutrition

Lesson 1 • Following Dietary Guidelines, B36

Lesson 2 • Healthful Eating Habits, B42

Lesson 3 • Choosing Foods Carefully, B50

Lesson 4 • Healthful Weight, B58

Lesson 5 • Body Image, B64

What Do You Know About
Nutrition?

1. How do the Dietary Guidelines help you make responsible food choices?

2. Why should you read the Nutrition Facts panel on a food package?

3. What factors influence your food choices?

The Inside Story

Food on the Go

Almost everyone looks forward to vacation. Some people head for the beach, others go to the mountains, and still others stay close to home. No matter how you spend your vacation, food is likely to play a part in your plans. Food safety is an important consideration. It pays to plan ahead and to know the facts when it comes to preparing and handling food safely, especially when you are on the go.

LOG ON Visit **www.mmhhealth.com** for activities and information about nutrition.

Following Dietary Guidelines

You will learn . . .

- why you need the six nutrients.
- how to use the Food Guide Pyramid.
- how to follow the Dietary Guidelines.

Vocabulary

- **nutrients,** B37
- **proteins,** B37
- **fats,** B37
- **carbohydrates,** B37
- **vitamins,** B37
- **minerals,** B37
- **Food Guide Pyramid,** B38
- **food group,** B38
- **balanced diet,** B39
- **Dietary Guidelines for Americans,** B40
- **fiber,** B40

Nutrition is the study of what people eat and the effects of diet on health. What foods do you eat when you enjoy meals and snacks? Do you choose foods that promote health and reduce the risk of disease?

Your Need for Nutrients

When you hear the word *diet*, it often means a plan for losing weight. However, the word *diet* also refers to all the foods a person takes in each day. A *healthful diet* means taking in foods that provide all nutrients you need each day. **Nutrients** are substances in foods that the body needs for growth and repair of cells, for body processes, and for energy. There are six types of nutrients. Each provides for certain needs that your body has.

- **Proteins** are nutrients needed for growth and repair of body cells. They help make up muscles, organs, and other tissues. Foods that contain protein are meats, fish, eggs, milk, wheat germ, nuts, cheese, and beans.

- **Fats** are nutrients that provide energy and help the body store vitamins. There are fats in meats, butter, whole milk, ice cream, cheese, and many other foods.

- **Carbohydrates** (KAHR•boh•HY•drayts) are the body's main source of energy. Sugars and starches are types of carbohydrates. Many foods, such as cereal, rice, potatoes, bread, pasta, fruits, and vegetables, contain carbohydrates.

- **Vitamins** are nutrients that help the body use carbo-hydrates, proteins, and fats. There are many types—including vitamins A, B_1, B_2, B_{12}, D, E, and K. A variety of foods contains vitamins.

- **Minerals** are nutrients that are involved in many body processes. Calcium is a mineral that helps build bones and teeth. Other minerals include zinc, potassium, and iron. Many different foods contain minerals.

- **Water** is a nutrient that makes up blood and other body fluids. It carries nutrients and waste, cushions joints and the spinal cord, maintains body temperature, and helps digest food. Six to eight 8-ounce servings of water from beverages and foods are recommended daily.

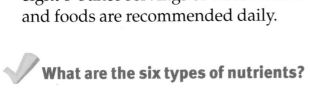

What are the six types of nutrients?

▲ **A healthful diet includes foods from each of the six kinds of nutrients.**

Using the Food Guide Pyramid

Healthful nutrition means eating healthful foods in amounts, called servings, that supply the nutrients you need daily. To help people make healthful food choices, the United States Department of Agriculture (USDA) prepared the **Food Guide Pyramid**, which shows how many servings you need to eat from each food group every day. A **food group** is made up of foods that provide similar nutrients.

The Food Guide Pyramid
A Daily Guide

▶ **Using the Food Guide Pyramid will help you make healthful choices.**

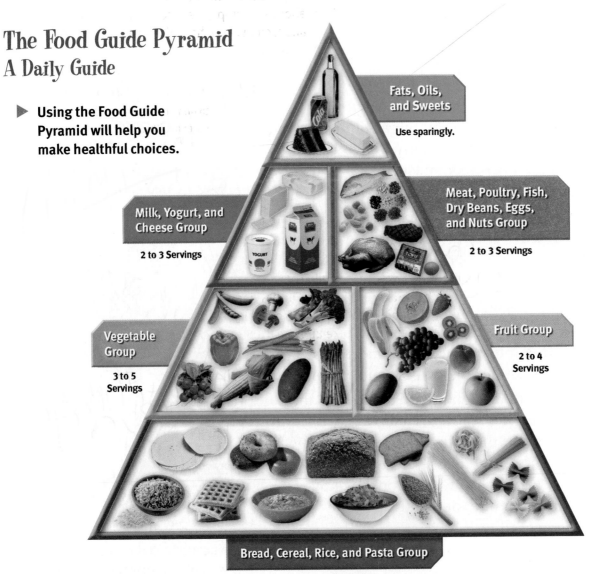

Fats, Oils, and Sweets
Use sparingly.

Milk, Yogurt, and Cheese Group
2 to 3 Servings

Meat, Poultry, Fish, Dry Beans, Eggs, and Nuts Group
2 to 3 Servings

Vegetable Group
3 to 5 Servings

Fruit Group
2 to 4 Servings

Bread, Cereal, Rice, and Pasta Group
6 to 11 Servings

Source: U.S. Department of Agriculture

Use the Food Guide Pyramid to plan a balanced diet. A **balanced diet** is made up of meals and snacks that provide the proper number of servings of foods from each group daily. The exact number of servings you need depends on your age, gender, body size, and your level of physical activity. Foods you should eat in greater amounts are at the bottom of the Food Guide Pyramid. The servings decrease as you go to upper levels of the pyramid. At the very top, Fats, Oils, and Sweets are not a food group, but rather foods to use sparingly.

 What factors affect how many servings you need each day from the different food groups?

CAREERS IN HEALTH
Farmer

You might have an interest in some aspect of farming. For example, you might be interested in producing crops that yield foods for people to eat, such as corn and wheat. Or you might be interested in raising animals that are sources of foods, such as cattle, pigs, and fowl. If so, there is much to learn. You might begin now by joining a 4-H club. You also might set a goal of getting a college degree in agriculture at a college or university, or taking courses at state extension programs. You might learn about soil, crops, diseases that affect crops, and those that affect animals.

LOG ON Visit **www.mmhhealth.com** to find out more about this and other health careers.

ACTIVITY
LIFE SKILLS

CRITICAL THINKING

Practice Healthful Behaviors

1 Learn about a healthful behavior. You know you should eat the recommended number of servings of each food group from the Food Guide Pyramid each day. How do you practice this healthful behavior? A good start is to review the types of foods that make up each food group in the Food Guide Pyramid.

2 Practice the healthful behavior in the correct way. Plan a menu listing what you will eat for one day. Include the recommended number of servings from each food group in your day's menu.

3 Ask for help if you need it. Check your menu choices with a parent or guardian.

4 Make the healthful behavior a habit. Refer to the Food Guide Pyramid when you decide what to eat each day. Quickly review whether you are eating the recommended number of servings from each food group. If not, make a plan to change your eating habits to follow the Food Guide Pyramid.

Science LINK

Baking Balloons

Bakers use yeast, a live, single-celled fungus, to make bread dough rise. You also can use yeast to make a balloon lift off. You will need a packet of active dry yeast, a cup of very warm water, two table-spoons of sugar, a large bal-loon, and an empty water bottle. Stir the yeast and sugar into the water. When they have dissolved, pour the mix-ture into the bottle. Attach the balloon to the mouth of the bottle. In a few minutes, the balloon will inflate. Why? The yeast feeds on the sugar and produces carbon dioxide. This gas has nowhere to go but up, so the balloon fills. It's the same idea bakers use to make light, airy loaves of bread.

The Dietary Guidelines

The **Dietary Guidelines for Americans** are a set of guide-lines for healthful eating and living for healthy Americans ages two and older. They were developed by the United States Department of Agriculture to help people stay healthy throughout their lives.

Aim for Fitness

1. **Maintain a healthful weight.** Being overweight can in-crease the risks of heart disease, diabetes, and some cancers.

2. **Be physically active each day.** Being physically active helps reduce the harmful effects of stress. It improves cardiorespiratory endurance. It helps you control your weight and have a lean body.

Build a Healthy Base

3. **Follow the Food Guide Pyramid.** The Food Guide Pyramid helps you get the recommended number of servings from each food group each day.

4. **Choose a variety of grains daily, especially whole grains.** Grains are low in fat, so a grain-rich diet helps you keep a healthful weight. Grains contain **fiber,** the part of grains and plant foods that cannot be digested. Fiber helps prevent colon cancer.

5. **Choose a variety of fruits and vegetables daily.** Like grains, these foods are low in fat and help you keep a healthful weight. They are rich in vitamins that help pre-vent heart disease and some cancers.

6. **Keep food safe to eat.** Germs can get into improperly prepared or stored foods and some make you ill. Wash your hands before you eat or prepare food.

◀ **Fresh vegetables are a good source of important nutrients.**

Choose Sensibly

7. **Choose a diet that is low in saturated fat and cholesterol and moderate in total fat.** Try to limit the foods you eat that contain saturated fats and cholesterol. Meats and dairy products contain saturated fat and cholesterol. Limiting foods that contain saturated fats and cholesterol helps you keep a healthful weight and reduces the risk of heart disease and some cancers.

8. **Choose beverages and foods to moderate your intake of sugars.** Cakes, cookies, candy, and some fruit drinks and colas are high in sugar and calories. They usually do not provide other nutrients. Limiting sugar helps you maintain a healthful weight and prevents tooth decay.

9. **Choose and prepare foods with less salt.** Sodium is a mineral found in salt. Cutting down on sodium by not salting foods and eating fewer chips, pretzels, and other salty foods helps keep your blood pressure normal. High blood pressure can cause heart disease, kidney disease, and stroke.

10. **Do not drink alcohol.** It is illegal and harmful for you to drink alcohol. It can harm mental and physical health. It can harm your relationships and increase the risk of unintentional injuries.

 What type of fat is it especially important to limit?

Consumer Wise — ACTIVITY

Choose Healthful Foods

Demonstrate these tips at home with your family. Never eat food from a package that was previously opened or damaged. Dispose of rusting, bulging, or dented canned goods. Follow the storage and preparation instructions on the package of foods you buy. Wash fruits and vegetables thoroughly before you eat them. Throw out foods that smell or look spoiled. When you eat out, order your food cooked thoroughly.

LESSON 1 REVIEW

Review Concepts

1. **Recall** why you need nutrients from the foods you eat.

2. **Describe** how your family could use the Food Guide Pyramid to plan meals.

3. **Explain** how following the Dietary Guidelines protects and promotes health.

Critical Thinking

4. **Compare and Contrast** the function of proteins with that of carbohydrates.

5. **LIFE SKILLS** **Practice Healthful Behaviors** Explain why it is healthful to choose foods and beverages that help you limit the amount of sugar you take in.

Healthful Eating Habits

You will learn...

- ways to follow the Dietary Guidelines when eating out.
- why you need to eat breakfast.
- ways to choose healthful snacks.
- ways healthful eating habits promote health.
- special dietary needs of teens.

Vocabulary

- **calorie,** B44
- **malnutrition,** B46
- **diabetes,** B46
- **osteoporosis,** B46
- **empty calories,** B47
- **anemia,** B48

With so many healthful foods to choose from, making a habit out of eating healthful foods is easy. Start with a healthful breakfast and make healthful food choices all day, even when you snack and eat out.

The Dietary Guidelines and Eating Out

When you eat out, you can make healthful food choices. Remember to use the Dietary Guidelines. Many popular menu items are high in fat, sugar, and salt. Portions are often huge. Even healthful foods can be served with dressings and sauces that add fat. The chart below provides some healthful alternatives when you eat out.

Choosing from the Menu

In addition to choosing healthful foods, there are some other things you can do to eat better on the go. If possible, ask for nutrition information on menu items. Many fast-food restaurants have pamphlets that provide nutrition information. Watch the portion sizes. Avoid jumbo sizes when possible. If you cannot avoid them, share them with a friend. Ask for any dressings or sauces on the side. Then you can limit the amount you use, because they usually are high in fat and cholesterol. Remember that fried foods are high in fat. Broiled foods contain less fat.

MAKING HEALTHFUL CHOICES

This Might Sound Tempting	This May Be More Healthful
Cheeseburger	Grilled chicken breast sandwich
Fries or potato chips	Salad and low-fat dressing or baked potato topped with broccoli or a little salsa (not butter or sour cream)
Bacon and eggs	Pancakes with fresh fruit
Ice cream or milkshake	Sherbet or sorbet
Pie or cookies	Fig bars or fresh fruit
Soda	Unsweetened fruit juice

 Why must you be on the alert to apply the Dietary Guidelines when eating out?

Healthful Breakfasts and Snacks

A **calorie** is a unit of energy available from food for use by the body. You get calories from the meals and snacks you eat throughout the day.

Healthful Breakfasts

Breakfast refuels your body after a night without food. You should follow the Food Guide Pyramid and Dietary Guidelines. Try to eat more whole grains, fruits, and vegetables, and limit sweets and fatty foods such as donuts and pastries. Choose cereals without a lot of added sugar. Start the day with some protein. Peanut butter, low-fat milk and cheese, and yogurt are all excellent sources of protein.

Healthful Snacking Habits

Choose snacks to get servings from the Food Guide Pyramid. Avoid potato chips and candy and choose instead

- **fruits and vegetables.** Try carrot and celery sticks, raisins, apples, bananas, oranges, even low-sugar canned fruit.
- **low-fat yogurt and cheese.**
- **grains.** Pasta, low-fat crackers, and popcorn without a lot of salt or butter make great snacks.

▼ **Eating a healthful breakfast provides energy throughout the morning.**

Have you ever evaluated your snacking habits? If not, you might want to ask yourself the following questions: Do I ask my parents or guardian to buy snacks that are low in sugar, salt, and calories, and high in vitamins and minerals? Do I eat snacks that help me get the servings I need from the Food Guide Pyramid? Do I eat too many sugary and salty snacks when I watch television? Do I eat sugary and salty snacks to cope with boredom, loneliness, stress, or sadness? It's okay to eat sugary and salty snacks sometimes. However, for good health, limit these snacks and eat snacks only when you are hungry.

 Why is it important to eat breakfast every day?

▲ **Make responsible decisions when you choose foods for snacks.**

CRITICAL THINKING

Set Health Goals

Use a health behavior contract to set a health goal. You are usually hungry after school. What is an appropriate health goal to set?

1 **Write the health goal you want to set:** *I will plan a healthful diet that reduces the risk of disease.* Focus on choosing snacks that reduce the risk of disease.

2 **Tell how the goal will affect your health.** If you eat snacks that are low in calories, sugar, and fat and contain vitamins and minerals, you will reduce the risk of weight gain, diabetes, and premature heart disease. You will reduce the risk of certain cancers that are associated with eating high-fat diets.

3 **Describe a plan you will follow. Keep track of your progress.** Keep your health behavior contract with you to write the healthful snack you eat each day after school for five days.

4 **Evaluate how your plan worked.** Did you eat a healthful snack each day? If not, why did you eat one or more snacks that were high in calories, sugar, and fat and low in vitamins and minerals? What can you change to reach your goal next week?

Set a Goal

Write a letter to a relative in which you discuss ways to have healthful eating habits. Include suggestions for making healthful food choices when eating out. Also include suggestions for making healthful food choices that reduce the risk of disease. Ask the relative to set a health goal and make a plan to follow one or more of your suggestions. Keep a copy of the letter and read it in three weeks and then again in six weeks. Are you following the suggestions you offered?

▶ A balanced diet provides nutrients and helps reduce your risk of certain health problems.

Ways Healthful Eating Habits Promote Health

The Food Guide Pyramid and the Dietary Guidelines for Americans help you plan and follow a balanced diet. Recall from Lesson 1, a balanced diet includes foods from all the food groups, providing the nutrients you need for good health. It also helps you avoid **malnutrition,** a harmful condition caused by not eating enough food or not eating the right kinds of food. Healthful eating also helps reduce your risk of developing health problems such as

- several types of cancer.
- stroke.
- **diabetes** (dy•uh•BEE•teez), a disease in which the body cannot use or does not produce enough of a necessary hormone called insulin.
- high blood pressure.
- **osteoporosis,** a disease in which bones are thin and break easily.
- being overweight, a risk factor for stroke, high blood pressure, heart disease, and some cancers.

Sugar, Salt, and Fat

Fat is a necessary part of your diet, but too much fat puts you at risk for heart disease, cancer, obesity, and other health problems. Saturated fats and trans-fatty acids are the fats that increase this risk the most. Follow these tips to reduce the amounts of these fats. Avoid foods that have the words *hydrogenated* or *partially hydrogenated* on their food labels. Instead, choose foods containing monounsaturated or polyunsaturated fats, such as olive oil or canola oil.

When you see *corn sugar, corn syrup, dextrose,* or *sucrose* on the food label, it means the food contains *sugar.* Sugary foods promote tooth decay. They are high in **empty calories,** which means they are high in fat or sugar and calories but low in other nutrients. Eating empty calories means you must eat more food to get the nutrients you need. This can cause you to gain unnecessary weight. Many people also eat much more salt than they need. Too much salt can contribute to high blood pressure. Look for low-salt ("low-sodium") foods or salt-free foods—like fresh carrot sticks or celery sticks.

Cholesterol

Cholesterol (kuh•LES•tuh•rawl) is a fatty substance that is made by the body and is found in dairy products and animal products. Your body makes all the cholesterol you need. However, many foods contain cholesterol, and some people's bodies make too much cholesterol. Having too much cholesterol in the bloodstream is a risk factor for heart disease. You should plan to eat no more than 300 mg of cholesterol each day.

 Why is it important to avoid empty calories?

Fats, Oils, and Sweets

Use sparingly.

▲ **Limit the servings you eat from the top of the Food Guide Pyramid.**

CHOLESTEROL IN COMMON FOODS	
6 oz sirloin steak	152 mg
Egg and sausage biscuit sandwich	302 mg
Scrambled egg	215 mg
Piece of chocolate cake, frosted	27 mg
American cheese (1 oz)	23 mg
Chicken breast, roasted	146 mg
Chicken breast, fried	238 mg
Fast-food cheeseburger (1 patty)	88 mg
Fast-food chicken fillet sandwich	60 mg
Hot dog	44 mg
Soft-serve vanilla ice cream (½ cup)	78 mg
Nonfat (skim) milk (1 cup)	5 mg
Whole milk (1 cup)	24 mg

Source: U.S. Department of Agriculture

Special Dietary Needs of Teens

The Dietary Guidelines are general rules that apply to healthy Americans ages two years and over. However, teens have special dietary needs. As you enter adolescence, your body changes rapidly. You will need more servings in each food group than younger children or older adults. Female teens need to get plenty of sources of iron. This helps prevent **anemia,** a condition in which the blood does not have enough red blood cells. Anemia is caused by poor diet or a loss of blood. Sources of calcium are important for male and female teens because their bodies are growing.

ACTIVITY LIFE SKILLS

CRITICAL THINKING

Make Responsible Decisions

Role-play this situation with a small group: Your family is going out to dinner to celebrate your sister's birthday. You are helping your family select a restaurant. You want to have foods you enjoy, but you want to make healthful food choices, too. What can you do?

1 Identify your choices. Check them out with a parent or another trusted adult. Make a list of the restaurants you are considering. Include ones that offer healthful foods that you and your family enjoy.

2 Evaluate each choice. Use the Guidelines for Making Responsible Decisions™. Ask yourself these questions about each of the restaurants you are considering. Will this decision result in actions that

- are healthful? Does the restaurant offer healthful food choices? Are the healthful food choices suitable for each member of your family?

- follow the guidelines of my parents and of other responsible adults? Do the food choices follow the Dietary Guidelines?

- demonstrate good character? Does your decision to recommend this restaurant show that you are considering each person's health and well-being?

3 Tell what the responsible decision is. Check this out with your parent, or another trusted adult. When you decide which restaurant you think the family should choose, discuss your decision with your parent or guardian.

4 Evaluate your decision. Did you and your family enjoy the meal? Did the restaurant offer food choices that allowed each person to follow the Dietary Guidelines and the Food Guide Pyramid?

Teens also make certain lifestyle choices, which may influence their nutritional needs. Teens may choose a very physically active lifestyle. In addition to being physically active each day, some teens may participate in one or more rigorous sports. These teens may require more servings of healthful foods.

Sometimes teens fall into a less physically active routine. They may spend lots of time each day in front of the computer or TV and less time being physically active. They may also develop unhealthful snacking habits. To maintain a healthful weight, they have to become more physically active and carefully follow healthful eating plans. They need to choose healthful snacks, such as fruits and vegetables. You will learn more about maintaining a healthful weight in Lesson 4.

 What are some special health concerns that a person might have?

Social Studies LINK

Salt—A Valuable Nutrient

Design a poster showing how people used salt in earlier times and how it is used today. Include any precautions based on the Dietary Guidelines. Salt is a nutrient we all need. It preserves and improves the taste of food. For many years, salt was a valuable trade item. In fact, soldiers of the Roman Empire sometimes received their pay in salt. This practice formed the root of our modern word *salary*.

◀ **You might need more nutrients if you play sports or are physically active.**

LESSON 2 REVIEW

Review Concepts

1. **Explain** how you can follow the Dietary Guidelines when you eat fast food.

2. **Recall** why eating breakfast is important.

3. **List** two ways that healthful eating habits promote health.

4. **Describe** the special dietary needs of teens.

Critical Thinking

5. **Recommend** Name four healthful foods to order at a fast-food restaurant. Explain your choices based on the Dietary Guidelines.

6. **LIFE SKILLS** **Make Responsible Decisions** What types of snacks should you limit in order to follow the Dietary Guidelines?

Choosing Foods Carefully

You will learn ...

- how to read a food label.
- how to compare the nutritional value and unit price of foods.
- ways to prevent foodborne illness.
- causes of food allergies and intolerances.

Vocabulary

- **food labels,** B51
- **Nutrition Facts,** B51
- **Daily Value,** B51
- **Percent Daily Value,** B51
- **unit price,** B52

Preparing a meal can be fun and challenging. You sharpen many skills—from shopping for healthful foods to preparing and storing foods to prevent illness. You can even find ways to prevent harmful reactions to foods.

Reading Food Labels

How do you go about making healthful food choices? You can start by reading **food labels,** panels of nutritional information that appear on food packages. The federal government requires food labels on most food packages. Wise consumers read them to make healthful decisions about food.

Where do you find food labels? The words **Nutrition Facts** make up the title of the food label. These words appear on every food label. Food labels all follow the same basic design and contain the same kind of information. They list serving size, calories per serving, and calories from fat. They also show how much of certain nutrients are in the food. You can see the number of grams or milligrams of each nutrient in a serving of the food.

You also can learn what this amount represents in your overall diet. This information is presented as the "percent daily value." The **Daily Value** is the amount of a nutrient that a person needs each day. The food label lists the **Percent Daily Value,** the percentage of the recommended daily amount of the nutrient that is found in a serving of the food. For example, if the food label shows that the percent daily value for fat is 5 percent, it means that a serving of that food has 5 percent of your recommended fat intake for the day.

▲ Comparing food labels helps you to make healthful choices.

 **What is a food label?**

Science
L I N K

The Danger of Bulging or Damaged Cans

Canned goods—especially foods canned at home—can be the source of botulism (BAH•chu•lizm). Botulism is a rare but dangerous disease caused by toxins produced by the *Clostridium botulinum* bacteria. These toxins can be produced inside a sealed can. Cooking the food might kill the bacteria, but the toxins may remain. What would you do if you saw a bulging can at the market?

Reading Food Labels to Compare Foods

Food labels make it very easy to compare the nutrition value of different foods. Each one contains the same categories of information.

Some food labels include information about trans-fatty acids, or trans fats, in the food. Eating trans fats increases the risk of heart disease. This information will be required on food labels in 2006. Reading food labels can also help you figure the **unit price,** the price of the food by weight, serving, or some other unit. For example, if a food label says a product has four servings and the product costs one dollar, the unit price is 25 cents per serving. You can use unit prices to compare the cost of products.

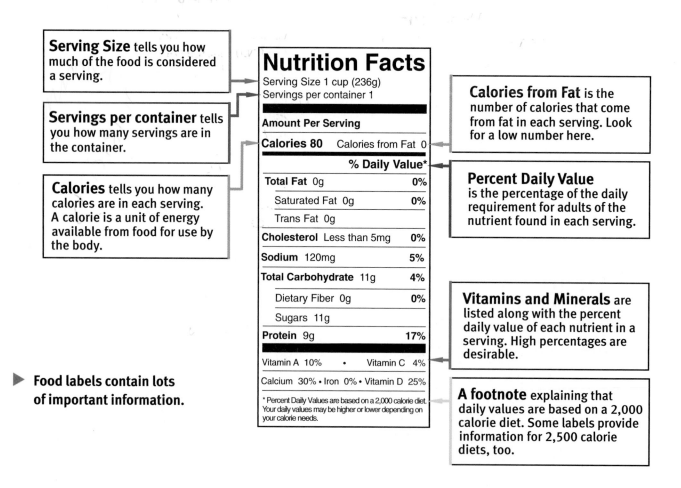

Serving Size tells you how much of the food is considered a serving.

Servings per container tells you how many servings are in the container.

Calories tells you how many calories are in each serving. A calorie is a unit of energy available from food for use by the body.

Calories from Fat is the number of calories that come from fat in each serving. Look for a low number here.

Percent Daily Value is the percentage of the daily requirement for adults of the nutrient found in each serving.

Vitamins and Minerals are listed along with the percent daily value of each nutrient in a serving. High percentages are desirable.

A footnote explaining that daily values are based on a 2,000 calorie diet. Some labels provide information for 2,500 calorie diets, too.

Nutrition Facts

Serving Size 1 cup (236g)
Servings per container 1

Amount Per Serving

Calories 80   Calories from Fat 0

% Daily Value*

Total Fat 0g	**0%**
Saturated Fat 0g	**0%**
Trans Fat 0g	
Cholesterol Less than 5mg	**0%**
Sodium 120mg	**5%**
Total Carbohydrate 11g	**4%**
Dietary Fiber 0g	**0%**
Sugars 11g	
Protein 9g	**17%**

Vitamin A 10%	•	Vitamin C 4%

Calcium 30% • Iron 0% • Vitamin D 25%

* Percent Daily Values are based on a 2,000 calorie diet. Your daily values may be higher or lower depending on your calorie needs.

▶ **Food labels contain lots of important information.**

Preventing Foodborne Illness

You have learned a reason to discard bulging, damaged cans. This is one way to help prevent *foodborne illness*, illness caused by eating food contaminated with germs. There are a number of foodborne illnesses. They can range from mild to life threatening. Here are some ways to prevent foodborne illness.

1. **Inspect the package.** Do not buy food if the package is torn open or a can is bulging. Tell a store clerk about the package or can.

2. **Inspect the food.** Do not eat food that looks, feels, or smells bad. Tell an adult about the food.

3. **Keep germs off food.** Wash your hands before handling food. Make sure all utensils, plates, and other surfaces are clean, too.

4. **Prepare and store raw and other foods separately.** Do not let raw foods, especially meats, touch each other. Use separate knives and cutting boards to prepare different foods.

5. **Check to see that food is cooked thoroughly.** Follow instructions for cooking foods. Meat and poultry should not be eaten when they are raw, red, or pink. Eggs should not be runny. Make sure you get an adult's help when you prepare food.

6. **Store and serve foods at the correct temperature.** Germs that can cause illness grow when food is between 40°F and 140°F. Keep hot foods hot and cold foods cold.

Access Valid Health Information, Products, and Services

You are having a picnic. Make a fact sheet of how to store, prepare, and serve foods safely.

1. **Identify when you need health information, products, and services.** You need information about how to keep germs out of the foods you will serve at the picnic.

2. **Identify where you can find health information, products, and services.** Make a list of possible sources of information about food safety. Tell the kind of information each source on your list contains. You may check cookbooks, culinary magazines, Internet sites, and the instructions on the food package. Responsible adults can answer questions.

3. **Locate health information, products, and services.** Gather information from at least two reliable sources from your list.

4. **Evaluate what you found.** Use the reliable sources to compile a fact sheet on food safety that you can share with the class.

7. **Don't share beverages or food that has been partially eaten.** Don't drink from the same glass or can as your friend. If you want to share food, cut off a piece before biting into it.

 **What is a unit price?**

BUILD
Character

Food Allergies

An allergy is a condition in which the body reacts to a food or other substance. Checking food labels for ingredients can help prevent allergic reactions in people who have a food allergy. For example, a person may have an allergy to peanuts. If that person eats a peanut, the body releases chemical substances that produce a range of symptoms. An allergic reaction can be life threatening.

Having a food allergy is not very common. Only about 3 percent of children have allergic reactions to a specific food; only about 1 percent of adults have food allergies. For young people, the most common foods that trigger allergic reactions are milk, eggs, and peanuts. For adults, shellfish—such as shrimp, crab, and lobster—nuts, fish, and eggs cause most food allergies. Children sometimes outgrow their allergies to foods such as soy and peanuts.

Although food allergies are rare, food intolerance is more common. *Food intolerance* is an unpleasant reaction to food. Some people have a food intolerance to milk and milk products. When they consume milk or milk products, they get an upset stomach or diarrhea. Some people have a food intolerance to wheat and other grains. People who have a food allergy or food intolerance should check food labels for the ingredients.

▲ Always tell a school nurse and teacher if you have a food allergy or intolerance to foods such as peanuts, shellfish, and milk.

Checking the Ingredients on a Food Label

Check food labels for the list of ingredients. The names of some ingredients in foods may be unfamiliar to you. For example, a common food additive called casein is made from milk. If you were allergic to or intolerant of milk, you might react to a food that contained casein. You would have to know to look for casein in the list of ingredients. The same could happen if you didn't know that many different sauces, such as soy sauce, contain wheat.

It is important to avoid the ingredients associated with a food allergy or intolerance. For example, some candies contain peanuts. If you were allergic to peanuts, you would know to avoid these candies. However, the food labels for some candies do not list peanuts among their ingredients but the candies may have come in contact with peanuts or peanut oil. If you have a food allergy, talk with your parent or guardian about how you can avoid foods that may cause you to have an allergic reaction.

 Why is reading food labels important for people who have food allergies?

Math LINK — ACTIVITY
Fast-Food Tips

Calculate how a typical fast-food item fits in with the Food Guide Pyramid.

Food Guide Pyramid Recommendation

- Eat two to three servings of lean meat, poultry, or fish each day.
- Each serving equals 2 to 3 ounces.

Fast-Food Menu Item

- Burger made with two quarter-pound patties.
- One pound equals 16 ounces.

How many double-patty hamburgers could you eat each day and stay within the recommended number of servings from the meat group in the Food Guide Pyramid?

LESSON 3 REVIEW

Review Concepts

1. **Describe** how information found on food labels helps you choose healthier foods.

2. **Recall** how unit prices help you compare the costs of different foods.

3. **Discuss** why it is important to handle, prepare, store, and serve foods safely.

4. **Describe** a food allergy.

Critical Thinking

5. **Compare** two foods that are similar, such as two boxes of bran cereal. Copy the Nutrition Facts found on their food labels. Write a paragraph comparing the two foods.

6. **Discuss** ways to reduce the risk of an allergic reaction in a person who has a food allergy.

7. **LIFE SKILLS** **Access Health Information** Summarize what kinds of useful information you can find on food packages. Explain why you think the government requires certain information on food labels.

Analyze What Influences Your Health

Dear Health Nut,

Here's the problem . . .

I have read restaurant reviews, seen ads, and heard friends talking about a variety of ethnic restaurants — Chinese, Mexican, Thai, Italian, Ethiopian, Lebanese, and Vietnamese. These reviews, ads, and people are influencing me to try more ethnic foods. Can I follow the Dietary Guidelines if I eat these ethnic foods?

Daring in Denver

Dear Daring in Denver,

Here is how you might solve the problem . . . There are a variety of influences that encourage you to eat ethnic foods. Be sure to analyze these influences to learn if the foods they want you to eat are healthful. Using the Dietary Guidelines will help you analyze the influences of these people and things.

Health Nut

Foldables To Learn Life Skills

Learn This Life Skill

You can analyze the influence that people and things might have on the ethnic foods you choose. Use this four-step process.

1 **Identify people and things that might influence you.**

Name one influence that encouraged you to eat an ethnic food. One restaurant review might encourage you to eat at a Japanese restaurant.

2 **Evaluate how the influence might affect your health and decisions.**

Consider what foods were recommended in the magazine review. If you ate these Japanese foods, would you follow the Dietary Guidelines?

3 **Choose positive influences on health.**

After analyzing the influence of this magazine article, you know it is positive. It encouraged you to eat healthful foods.

4 **Protect yourself from negative influences on health.**

If a review of any restaurant encourages you to eat at a restaurant that served fried, high-fat, high-calorie, or highly salted foods, do not allow the review to influence you. These foods do not follow the Dietary Guidelines.

1. Identify people and things that might influence you.

2. Evaluate how the influence might affect your health and decisions.

3. Choose positive influences on health.

4. Protect yourself from negative influences on health.

If you do this activity within a group of students, students can participate in different ways. Students can make an oral presentation of the final product. Some students may choose to do the activity in other ways, such as by role-playing, performing a skit, or drawing a comic strip to illustrate all four steps.

Practice This Life Skill

Activity Find an ad that influences people to eat at a fast-food restaurant. The ad should show photos of tasty foods. With a partner, use the Dietary Guidelines to analyze how this ad may influence you. Decide if the influence is positive or negative. Describe how you would protect yourselves from a negative influence.

Healthful Weight

You will learn . . .

- reasons to maintain a healthful weight.
- ways to maintain a healthful weight.
- how to determine what a healthful weight is.

Vocabulary

- **healthful weight,** B59
- **underweight,** B60
- **overweight,** B61
- **fad diet,** B61
- **body composition,** B62
- **obesity,** B62
- **Body Mass Index,** B62

What is your healthful weight? Healthful weight is not the same for everybody of the same age. To know if your weight is healthful, check with your family as well as a physician or nutritionist. Set a health goal to maintain it—to help reduce the risk of health problems now and in the future and to promote positive self-esteem.

Reasons to Maintain a Healthful Weight

Do You Know?

A **healthful weight** is a weight that is desirable for a person. Healthful weight varies from person to person. People have different body heights and body types. For example, one person may have broader shoulders than another. Even though a healthful weight is not the same for everyone, the reasons for maintaining it are the same.

Your body burns calories all the time, even when you sleep or read a book. However, you burn many more calories when you are physically active.

1. **You are more likely to have positive self-esteem.** At a healthful weight, you will look your best. This promotes positive self-esteem. In turn, positive self-esteem can influence total health and success in life.

2. **You will have more energy.** Your body works best at a healthful weight. You will have the fuel you need to do your best and you won't have any extra weight to slow you down.

3. **You reduce the risk of injury from accidents.** At a healthful weight, you will have better balance. This can help prevent falls that can lead to injuries.

4. **You reduce the risk of several diseases.** At a healthful weight, you are less likely to develop heart disease, certain cancers, diabetes, and stroke.

How does maintaining a healthful weight promote positive self-esteem?

◀ Maintaining a healthful weight will help you have better balance.

Ways to Maintain a Healthful Weight

The energy you get from food is measured in calories. A food that has 200 calories provides twice as much energy as a food that has 100 calories.

When you take in more calories than your body uses, you gain weight. You lose weight when your body uses more calories than you take in. To maintain a healthful weight, you need to balance the calories you take in with the calories your body uses (burns). You can find the number of calories you use for your daily activities. You also can find the total number of calories you take in from the foods you eat each day.

How to Gain Weight

Some people are **underweight,** or below a healthful weight. Being slightly underweight is not harmful. Sometimes this is the result of illness. A person who is underweight should be checked by a physician. The physician can treat the illness or simply help the person change his or her eating habits.

To gain weight, a person must take in more calories than he or she burns during the day. When gaining weight by increasing caloric intake, a person must continue to follow the Dietary Guidelines. A health professional will help determine how many more calories the person must take in each day.

Tips for Gaining Weight

To gain weight, a person should:

- Increase the number of servings from the food groups in the Food Guide Pyramid.
- Eat healthful snacks, but not before meals.
- Choose calorie-rich foods that contain nutrients needed for health, such as avocados, bread, pasta, and potatoes. Limit the amount of foods that contain saturated fats, trans fats, sugar, and cholesterol.

How to Lose Weight

A person who is **overweight** is above his or her healthful weight. To lose weight, a person must burn more calories than he or she takes in. This requires taking in fewer calories and increasing daily physical activity.

If you are overweight, it is important to discuss a weight management plan with your parents or guardian. They might acquire the assistance of a health care provider. Nutritionists, physicians, and nurses can help you make a plan to lose weight and still get the nutrients you need for good health.

Tips for Losing Weight

To lose weight, a person should:

- Increase the number of calories used by physical activity. This promotes weight loss and provides other health benefits.

- Do not lose weight quickly. Slow, steady progress is best.

- Continue to eat the correct number of servings from the Food Guide Pyramid. Choose lower-calorie foods and keep serving sizes small.

- Do not follow fad diets from magazines or TV shows. A **fad diet** is a weight-loss program based on popular trends rather than scientific evidence.

Remember to get help from a health care provider before trying to lose weight.

 How can you lose weight?

ACTIVITY · LIFE SKILLS

CRITICAL THINKING

Practice Healthful Behaviors

You want to maintain a healthful weight.

1 **Learn about a healthful behavior.** You know that regular physical activity helps you maintain a healthful weight.

2 **Practice the healthful behavior in the correct way.** Write out a weekly plan to get physical activity every day. Include a regular time to be physically active. If you need to, you can be physically active in several small periods of time. List the activities that you will do each day. Choose activities you like. That way, you won't be tempted to skip them.

3 **Ask for help if you need it.** Check with a responsible adult about suitable workout programs. Try joining with friends. It may be easier to work out together.

4 **Make the healthful behavior a habit.** Record your progress in a notebook. Evaluate your progress at regular intervals to learn if you have made getting regular physical activity a habit.

Accepting Differences

Respect What would you say if you saw classmates teasing a student who is overweight? Write and perform a monologue.

In any group of students, some will be overweight or underweight. Some face teasing or unfair treatment because of their weight. It's wrong and hurtful to make judgments about people based on their weight. Everyone deserves respect from others. This includes people who have not yet reached their healthful weight.

How to Determine What a Healthful Weight Is

Physicians often use **body composition,** the proportion of fat tissue to lean tissue in the body, to determine if a person's weight is healthful. Lean tissue includes muscle, bone, and organs. All people have some fat. A female teen with a healthful body composition may have about 15 percent body fat. A male teen with a healthful body composition, on the other hand, may have less than 10 percent. **Obesity** is the term for having too much body fat. People who are obese are usually overweight. There are several methods that can be used to measure body composition.

Some health professionals use another index to determine if a person's weight is healthful. **Body Mass Index** measures mass compared to height. The formula for figuring Body Mass Index is mass in kilograms divided by height in meters squared. (One inch is approximately 2.54 centimeters, and there are 100 centimeters in a meter. One pound of weight is equivalent to a mass of 0.45 kilograms.)

In adults, a Body Mass Index of 18.5 to 25 is considered healthful. Some people, such as very muscular people, may have high Body Mass Indexes. However, they may still have a healthful body composition. For young people, a healthful Body Mass Index varies by age and gender.

Remember that even if you have a healthful weight you still need healthful habits. You still need to get plenty of physical activity and eat healthful foods. If you have questions about the best weight for you, contact a health care provider.

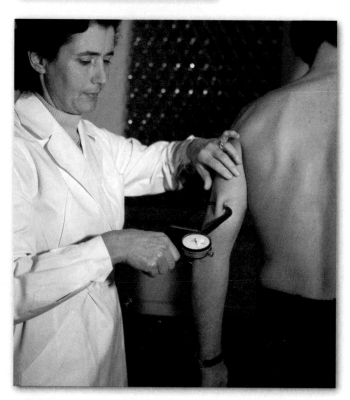

◄ Skinfold calipers are used to determine body composition.

Determining Body Type and Healthful Weight

Remember that each person—and each person's healthful weight—is different. In most cases, body type is determined by heredity. That does not mean that a child will have the same body type as either parent. A child may inherit a body type from earlier generations. There are three body types:

- **ectomorph**—thin and lean
- **endomorph**—round and thick
- **mesomorph**—strong and muscular

People of each body type can achieve a healthful weight and appearance. Some people have features of more than one body type.

Lifestyle choices have an effect on a person's weight. Children may or may not follow the same choices as a parent. An overweight parent may have children with healthful body weights.

▶ **People of the same age may have different body types.**

To determine your body type and healthful weight, check with a health care professional. A family physician can assess your body type and body composition. He or she can help you plan how to achieve and maintain a healthful weight.

 What is body composition?

LESSON **4** REVIEW

Review Concepts

1. **List** four reasons for maintaining a healthful weight.

2. **Describe** ways to maintain a healthful weight.

3. **Summarize** two ways to determine if a person has a healthful weight.

Critical Thinking

4. **Define** a healthful body composition.

5. **Explain** how to find the Body Mass Index of a person who is 5 feet tall and has a weight of 100 pounds.

6. **LIFE SKILLS** **Practice Healthful Behaviors** How can you use the Food Guide Pyramid to help maintain a healthful weight?

Body Image

You will learn ...

- factors that influence your body image.

- ways you can recognize eating disorders.

- treatments for eating disorders.

- ways to develop a positive body image.

Vocabulary

- **body image,** B65

- **eating disorder,** B66

- **anorexia nervosa,** B67

- **bulimia nervosa,** B67

- **binge eating disorder,** B67

Your feelings about your body influence your self-esteem and self-respect. When you accept your body, you feel more confident. You are more likely to choose healthful behaviors that protect your body. When you want to change things about your appearance, you make responsible decisions.

How Your Body Image Is Influenced

Your **body image** is the feeling you have about the way your body looks. It is the picture you see when you think of yourself. Your body image is determined by facts such as your height, weight, hair and eye color, and body type.

Factors That Influence Body Image

Your body image may be influenced by many factors:

- how you feel about yourself
- what you learn about your body from your parents or guardian
- how you feel about body changes that occur as you grow into an adult
- what peers say and how they act
- what you see and hear in the media

Analyze how these factors affect your body image. For example, when you look at people on TV and in movies, do you make comparisons?

After you analyze these influences, remember to choose positive influences. Protect yourself from negative influences on body image. For example, do not let movies convince you that attractive females all have skinny bodies. Do not let ads convince you that attractive males are always muscular. Develop a positive body image by accepting your body and keeping it in top condition.

 **What factors influence your body image?**

▶ **Choosing healthful behaviors helps develop a positive body image.**

B65

Do You Know?

Eating disorders are much more common among females than males. About 90 percent of those who have an eating disorder are female. However, eating disorders are harmful in males and females.

Recognizing and Treating Eating Disorders

A negative body image increases the risk that someone your age will develop an eating disorder. An **eating disorder** is an emotional problem that leads to harmful changes in eating habits. These habits may include eating little or no food, eating too much food, or eating food and then getting rid of it, such as by purging or throwing up. Eating disorders can harm a person's social and family relationships. They can cause serious health problems that can become life threatening.

There is no single cause of an eating disorder. People who have an eating disorder may have a negative body image. They may be underweight but believe they are overweight. They may be overweight and unable to control their eating. They may feel a strong need to control what is happening to their bodies and use food to gain this control. They may use food to deal with painful feelings.

ACTIVITY — LIFE SKILLS

CRITICAL THINKING

Be a Health Advocate

1 **Select a health-related concern to communicate.** Work with a small group to form a committee concerned about the number of teens who have developed an eating disorder. The committee believes a negative body image is a possible cause.

2 **Gather reliable information.** Use reference books in the library, articles on the Internet, and facts in this textbook to gather information on factors that influence body image.

3 **Identify your purpose and target audience.** The purpose of the committee is to promote positive body image. The target audience is teens.

4 **Develop a convincing and appropriate message.** Produce a "Positive Image" variety show. Using information that your committee collected, write songs, raps, poems, and skits offering tips to help teens develop a positive body image. Include resources that help teens who have a negative body image or who have signs of an eating disorder.

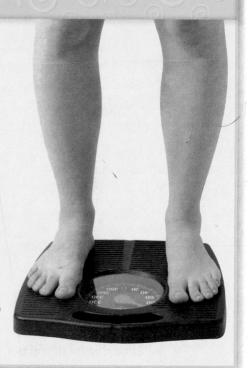

Common Eating Disorders

Anorexia nervosa (a•nuh•REK•see•uh nehr•VOH•suh) is an eating disorder in which a person starves himself or herself and has a low body weight. Anorexia, as it is often called, is life threatening.

People who have anorexia lose weight yet may still think of themselves as "fat." They are often very concerned about their appearance. They insist on avoiding certain foods or on avoiding food altogether. They may engage in compulsive physical activity to burn calories.

Bulimia nervosa (buh•LEE•mee•uh nehr•VOH•suh) is an eating disorder in which a person stuffs himself or herself and then tries to rid the body of food. Eating large amounts of food is called *bingeing*. Getting rid of the food is called *purging*. Purging may involve vomiting or exercising too much. Sometimes, people purge by taking diuretics and laxatives.

Binge eating disorder is an eating disorder in which a person frequently stuffs himself or herself with food but does not purge to get rid of the food. People who have binge eating disorder binge when they are stressed, depressed, or anxious. They are often overweight. People with this disorder do not binge when they are with others. They hide the amount of food they have eaten. They feel guilty and embarrassed after eating. They eat until they are so full that they feel uncomfortable.

▶ **The media and your peers might influence your body image.**

Treating Eating Disorders

People who have eating disorders need professional treatment. The sooner treatment begins, the more successful it is likely to be. Treatment may include medical care to overcome damage done from extreme weight loss, malnutrition, and purging. For binge eating disorder, treatment may include establishing a pattern of eating appropriate amounts of foods at designated intervals. Treatment for eating disorders often requires a stay in a hospital.

In addition to medical treatment, counseling is needed for negative body image and healthful expression of feelings.

✓ **What is an eating disorder?**

On Your Own

FOR SCHOOL OR HOME

Make a List

Make a list of your good qualities and the ones you would like to change. Be honest with yourself. Don't be afraid to give yourself some praise.

Developing a Positive Body Image

Developing a positive body image promotes and protects health. How can you develop a positive body image? A first step is to analyze negative influences on body image. Then you can find ways to protect yourself from negative influences. A second step is to practice healthful behaviors, such as eating healthful foods and getting plenty of exercise.

▼ Eating healthful foods will help you develop a positive body image.

BODY IMAGE INFLUENCES

Influence	Your Response
TV, Movies, and Magazines In the media, many people are thin or muscular. This might influence you to believe that this is what is required to be attractive.	Recognize that people in TV, movies, and magazines are not the norm. They are a select few, often chosen for their appearance. They use makeup and special effects to become more attractive. In real life, people come in a variety of shapes and sizes.
Friends and Classmates What people say might influence others' body image. For instance, sometimes people make fun of others because of how they look. Even when these comments are not directed at you, they might influence your body image, if you let them.	Do not let people who are critical of the appearance of others influence you. Don't put up with insults or jokes about people's appearance. Point out that all people have good qualities and features.
Your Self-Statements You might develop a negative body image if you have a habit of putting yourself down.	Develop new self-statements to remind yourself of your good qualities. Remember that beauty is not just about looks—it's about how you act. Dedicate yourself to living a healthful lifestyle. Eat nutritious foods, achieve a healthful weight, and exercise regularly.

Tips for Developing a Positive Body Image

- Practice healthful behaviors.
- Use positive self-statements.
- Discuss your feelings with a respected adult.
- Focus on what you like about your body.
- Don't compare yourself to others.

 **How do the media affect body image?**

Character

Develop a Positive Body Image

Responsibility Sometimes it may seem like the whole world is telling you how you should look, what you should wear, and who you should be. Guess what? Your body image is under your control. You must take responsibility for building a positive body image.

1. **Be honest about your body image.** Are you satisfied with your body?

2. **Identify why you feel this way.** Take a hard look at the influences on page B68.

3. **Make a plan to improve your body image.** Your plan should include one or more of the tips listed on this page. Talk over your plan with your family. If you do not need to improve your body image, make a plan for how you will identify and react to negative influences to body image in general.

◀ **Everyone can have a positive body image.**

LESSON 5 REVIEW

Review Concepts

1. **List** people and things that have a positive influence on your body image.

2. **Recall** signs that a person has an eating disorder.

3. **Discuss** the treatment for eating disorders.

4. **Identify** two ways teens can develop a positive body image.

Critical Thinking

5. **Analyze** people and things that might have a negative influence on a teen's body image. Suggest how teens can protect themselves from those influences.

6. **LIFE SKILLS** **Be a Health Advocate** Describe two ways to help classmates develop a positive body image.

Chapter Summary

Learning how to eat in a nutritious manner can benefit all aspects of your well-being, including your physical, family and social, and emotional and mental health.

Lesson 1 • The Dietary Guidelines and the Food Guide Pyramid help you plan a healthful diet.

Lesson 2 • Healthful eating can help your body grow and work properly. It can also help you prevent a variety of health problems, now and in the future.

Lesson 3 • Information on food labels and packages can help you choose healthful foods to buy.

Lesson 4 • Teens should strive for a healthful weight and body composition. This is a matter of each individual's size, shape, and body type.

Lesson 5 • Our body image is how we see and feel about our bodies. Having a positive body image helps protect you from developing an eating disorder.

Use Vocabulary

nutrients, B37

malnutrition, B46

empty calories, B47

food label, B51

calorie, B44

body composition, B62

obesity, B62

Body Mass Index, B62

body image, B65

eating disorder, B66

Choose the correct term from the list to complete each sentence.

1. You need to eat a variety of foods from the five food groups in order to get the proper balance of _____?_____.

2. Sugary foods have a lot of _____?_____ that do not provide healthful nutrients.

3. You can learn the daily values for certain nutrients by reading a(n) _____?_____.

4. When you eat food, you eat _____?_____(s), which must be burned off in order to maintain weight.

5. The proper balance of fat tissue and lean tissue is a healthful _____?_____.

6. Media messages may influence a person's _____?_____.

7. Having too much fatty tissue is called _____?_____.

8. _____?_____ measures weight compared to height.

9. A(n) _____?_____ is an emotional problem that leads to harmful changes in eating habits.

10. _____?_____ is a harmful condition caused by not eating enough food or not eating the right kinds of food.

Answer each question in complete sentences.

11. Give examples of positive and negative influences on a person's body image.

12. What are some ways to maintain a healthful weight?

13. How can you reduce the risk of foodborne illness?

14. What can you do in order to follow the Dietary Guidelines?

Reading Comprehension

Answer each question in complete sentences.

When you take in more calories than your body uses, you gain weight. You lose weight when your body uses more calories than you take in. To maintain a healthful weight, you need to balance the calories you take in with the calories your body uses (burns). You can find the number of calories you use for your daily activities. You can also find the total number of calories you take in from the foods you eat each day.

15. How can you gain weight?

16. How can you maintain a healthful weight?

Critical Thinking/Problem Solving

Answer each question in complete sentences.

Analyze Concepts

17. Contrast anorexia nervosa with bulimia nervosa.

18. Classify the six different types of nutrients, providing an example in each category.

19. Suggest healthful breakfast alternatives to your friend who eats a donut every morning.

20. Design a meal that contains foods from each of the five healthful food groups.

21. Discuss how television, magazines, and movies influence a teen's body image.

Practice Life Skills

22. Analyze What Influences Your Health You overhear some classmates teasing a friend who is very tall and thin. Analyze the influence their teasing might have. What might you do to change this influence?

23. Make Responsible Decisions After school, a few days a week, you go to the house of one of your friends to relax and start your homework together. Whenever you are there, she offers you some type of junk food as a snack. You're hungry, but you know that her snacks are not healthful. What is the responsible decision to make?

Read Graphics

Use the text in the visual below to answer the questions.

24. Why are fats, oils, and sweets placed at the top of the Food Guide Pyramid?

25. Why is the Grains Group at the bottom of the Food Guide Pyramid?

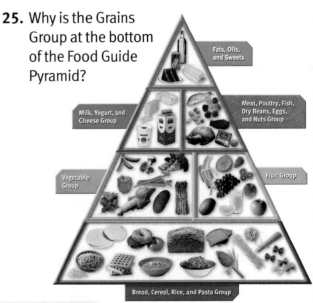

Fats, Oils, and Sweets

Milk, Yogurt, and Cheese Group

Meat, Poultry, Fish, Dry Beans, Eggs, and Nuts Group

Vegetable Group

Fruit Group

Bread, Cereal, Rice, and Pasta Group

Source: U.S. Department of Agriculture

LOG ON Visit **www.mmhhealth.com** to find out how much you know about nutrition.

Effective Communication

Compare Food Labels

As a class, build a model of the Food Guide Pyramid. Assemble five containers to represent the five healthful food groups. Into each group, students drop index cards with the names of favorite healthful foods. Students select cards from each group to plan daily meals and snacks based on the Dietary Guidelines. Post daily menus as a way of communicating balanced diets.

Self-Directed Learning

Caring for Your Joints

Without forcing or moving in any unusual way, find the kinds of motion your movable joints allow. For example, your knee is like a door hinge, enabling your lower leg to kick forward and back. Your wrist allows your hand to move in a way to trace a circle. Describe your findings and suggest how each of your joints needs care to avoid injury.

Critical Thinking and Problem Solving

Compare Calories

Make a list of all the foods and beverages you consume in one day. Use a reference book or Internet sources to find the number of calories in each of these foods and beverages. People your age should consume between 2,200 and 2,800 calories per day. Calculate how many calories you consume in one day. How does this number compare to the recommended calorie intake for people your age?

Responsible Citizenship

Analyze Food Labels

Interview class members to make a list of the top twenty foods that students eat. Then check food labels for as many of these foods as you can. Evaluate the fat and cholesterol content. Tabulate the information you find and suggest healthful alternatives when necessary. Present your findings as a classroom commercial for more healthful eating.

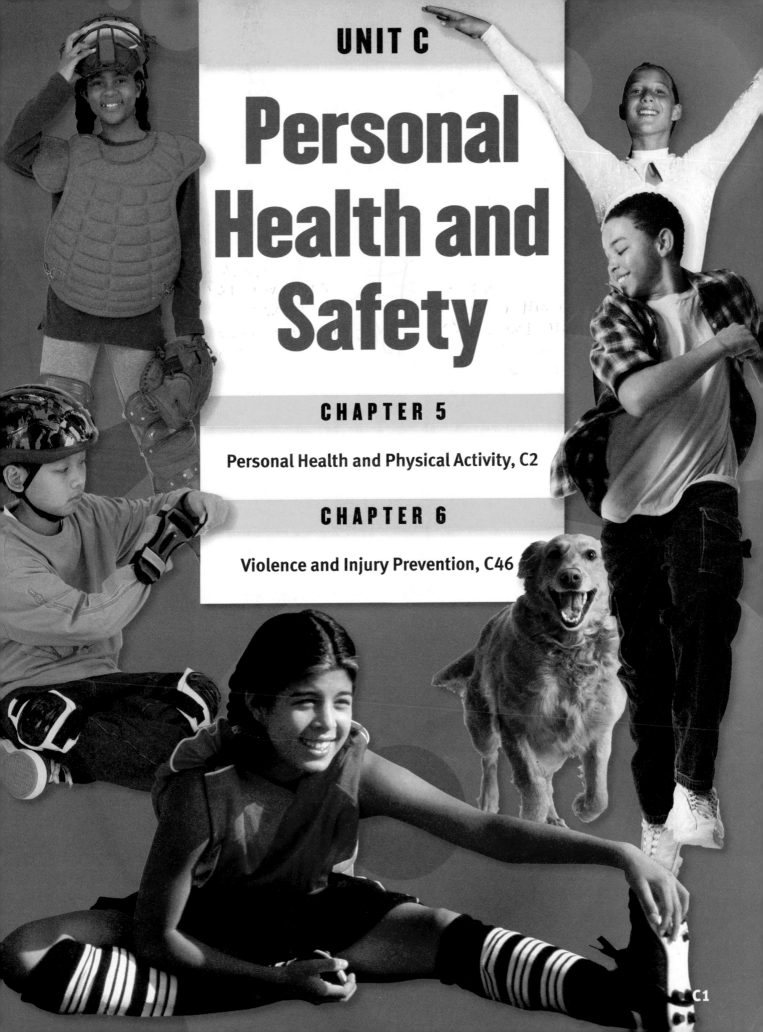

UNIT C

Personal Health and Safety

CHAPTER 5

Personal Health and Physical Activity, C2

CHAPTER 6

Violence and Injury Prevention, C46

CHAPTER 5

Personal Health and Physical Activity

Lesson 1 • Personal Health Care, C4

Lesson 2 • Keeping Healthy and Getting Checkups, C10

Lesson 3 • Caring for Your Teeth, C20

Lesson 4 • Physical Activity and Fitness, C26

Lesson 5 • Developing a Physical Fitness Plan, C32

Lesson 6 • Staying Safe During Physical Activity, C38

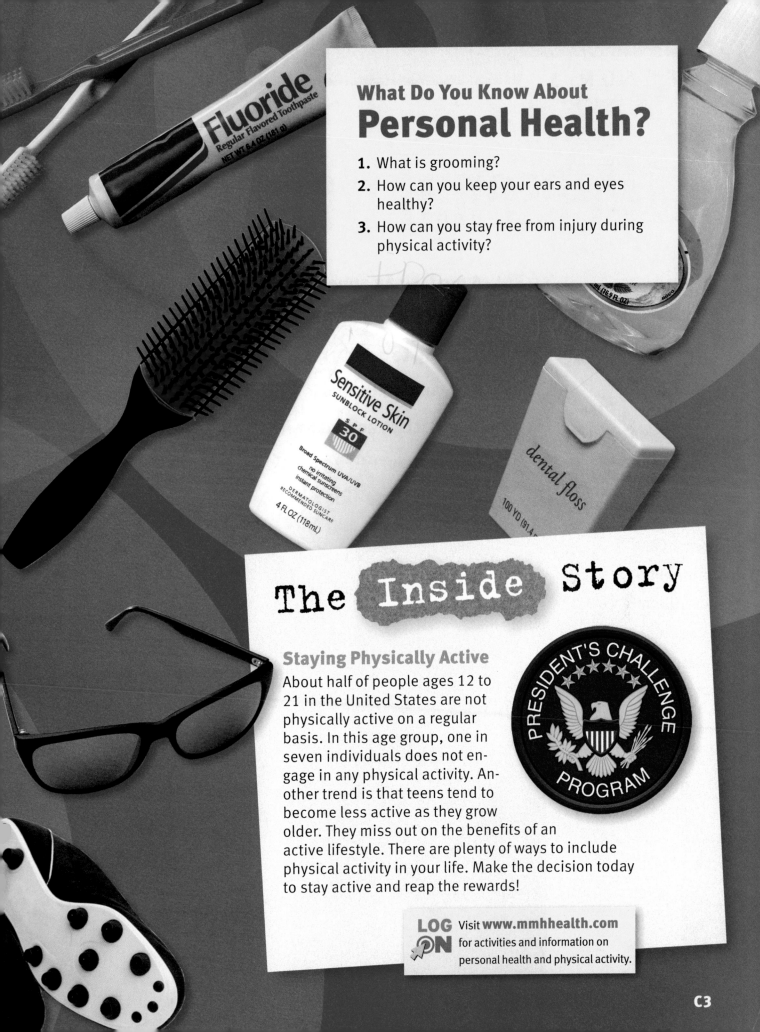

What Do You Know About
Personal Health?

1. What is grooming?
2. How can you keep your ears and eyes healthy?
3. How can you stay free from injury during physical activity?

The Inside Story

Staying Physically Active

About half of people ages 12 to 21 in the United States are not physically active on a regular basis. In this age group, one in seven individuals does not engage in any physical activity. Another trend is that teens tend to become less active as they grow older. They miss out on the benefits of an active lifestyle. There are plenty of ways to include physical activity in your life. Make the decision today to stay active and reap the rewards!

LOG ON Visit **www.mmhhealth.com** for activities and information on personal health and physical activity.

C3

Personal Health Care

You will learn . . .

- the benefits of being well groomed.
- the benefits of rest and sleep.
- ways to care for your skin.
- ways to care for your hair and nails.

Vocabulary

- **grooming,** C5
- **epidermis,** C6
- **dermis,** C6
- **acne,** C7
- **perspiration,** C7
- **dermatologist,** C7

A neat, clean appearance makes an immediate impression on everyone around you. However, sticking to a daily routine for caring for your skin, hair, and nails also is a healthful behavior that you can practice and make into a lifetime habit to protect yourself against disease. Your skin, after all, is the first-line defense against disease.

Being Well Groomed

Grooming is everything people do to stay clean and have a healthful appearance. There are many benefits to being well groomed. When you pay attention to being clean, you remove dirt and germs that cause illness. Staying clean also can help protect you from skin infections and rashes. During puberty, your body is changing. Your skin may become oilier, clogging your pores. You may perspire more, which may produce body odor. Washing, bathing, and showering help prevent acne and body odor.

Being well groomed improves your mental and emotional health. When you have a clean and neat appearance, you feel better about yourself. This promotes positive self-esteem and helps you keep self-respect. Being well groomed improves your social health. Others notice that you care enough about yourself to be well groomed. You earn their respect. They enjoy being with you because you have a pleasant and clean appearance.

Benefits of Rest and Sleep

Rest is a time of relaxation. Rest gives you a temporary break from activity. Balance mental and physical activity with rest. Re-energize your mind and body. Take a study break to return to homework alert. Rest after physical activity before doing more activity.

Sleep is a restful state in which there is no conscious thought. You may need eight to ten hours of sleep each night. Your heart rate slows down 10 to 15 beats per minute during sleep. Your blood pressure and breathing rate slow down. Your muscles are less tense. The body repairs cells and grows. The body fights infections during sleep.

How does being well groomed promote health?

BUILD ACTIVITY
Character

Brainstorm Better Behaviors

Caring Suppose you have a classmate who has body odor. You care about your classmate and do not want others to reject him or her. Brainstorm a few ideas about how you can tactfully tell your classmate that he or she needs to pay attention to being well groomed.

▼ Being well groomed promotes self-esteem.

Caring for Your Skin

The skin is the largest organ in your body. It protects your internal organs from injury and infection. The skin helps maintain body temperature. It also prevents the loss of needed body fluids.

The skin consists of two main layers. The **epidermis** is the thin outer layer of the skin. It provides a protective coating. The **dermis** is the thick inner layer of the skin. It contains sweat glands, nerves, and blood vessels.

Ways to Care for Your Skin

Each day you should take a shower or bath. Wash your body with soap and water. Drink plenty of water to flush impurities out of your skin. Wash sheets and pillowcases frequently to remove dirt and oil.

Your skin needs protection from the sun's harmful rays. Wear a sunscreen with a sun protective factor of at least 15 (SPF 15). Apply one ounce to exposed skin and be sure to remember areas that normally don't burn, such as your ears. Wear a hat and protective clothing. Avoid tanning booths. They expose people to ultraviolet rays and increase the risk of skin cancer.

ACTIVITY

Science
L I N K

Discuss Skin Repair

If a person injures a large area of skin, he or she may need a skin graft. In this procedure, doctors graft healthy skin from one part of the body and transfer it to the damaged area. The grafted skin grows new cells. In time, fresh skin covers the wounded area. With your classmates, hold a discussion about possible injuries that might require a person to have a skin graft.

Parts of the Skin

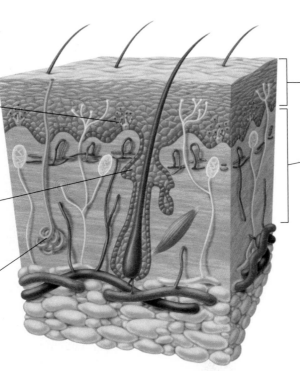

Melanin (MEHL•uh•nin) gives the skin its color. Freckles are spots of melanin.

Oil glands in the dermis help your skin repel water and remain soft.

Sweat glands enable perspiration to cool the surface of the skin. They also help eliminate water and salt from the body.

The epidermis is the thin outer layer of skin that replaces old skin cells with new ones.

The dermis is the thick inner layer of skin that contains hair roots, blood vessels, and nerve endings.

Skin Conditions to Look Out For

During puberty, the oil glands in your skin become active. Excess oil can produce **acne**, a skin disorder that results in pimples, whiteheads, and blackheads. It occurs when skin pores become clogged with oil and dead skin cells. Wash your face twice each day with a mild acne-preventing soap to help prevent acne. Wash after any physical activity that causes you to perspire.

Sweat glands in the skin produce **perspiration**, a mixture of water, salt, and waste products. Along with bacteria, perspiration can cause body odor. Some health care products can help with this condition. Antiperspirants help reduce perspiration. Deodorants can reduce body odor.

Have regular checkups for your skin and seek medical advice for rashes and acne. A **dermatologist** is a physician who screens for and treats skin disorders. Your dermatologist will help you keep your skin healthy.

What can you do to care for your skin?

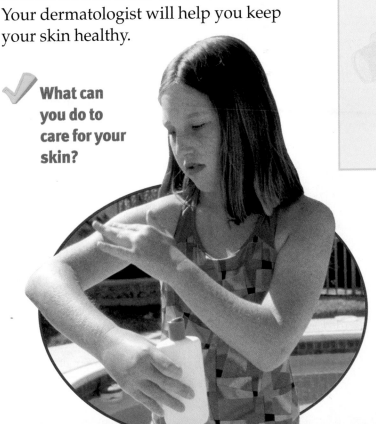

CRITICAL THINKING

Practice Healthful Behaviors

Practice a healthful behavior to care for your skin, hair, or nails.

1 Learn about a healthful behavior. Select a magazine or Web site that contains tips on personal grooming. Find an article or feature about caring for your skin, hair, or nails. From what you find, list two healthful behaviors that you might want to practice.

2 Practice the healthful behavior in the correct way. Read the article to find out how to practice the two healthful behaviors you listed. Write a plan for practicing each healthful behavior.

3 Ask for help if you need it. Share the two healthful behaviors with your parents or guardians. How might they help you practice the two healthful behaviors?

4 Make the healthful behavior a habit. Write a short paragraph that discusses how you will make the two healthful behaviors a habit.

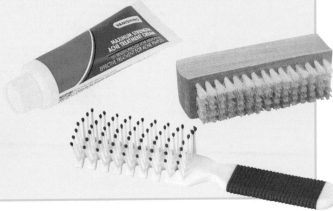

◀ Use sunscreen to protect your skin from the sun's harmful rays.

C7

Caring for Your Hair and Nails

Your hair and nails have several functions. Your hair preserves heat and protects your head and skin. Nails protect and support the tips of your fingers and toes. You use fingernails to scratch and to pick up small objects.

Proper hair and nail care helps you maintain a healthful appearance. Clean, well-groomed hair makes you more attractive. Clean, trimmed nails show others that you are well groomed.

Caring for Your Hair

Glands in your scalp produce oil, which can trap germs and dirt. You should wash your hair at least twice a week to remove the dirt, germs, and oil. You may need to wash hair daily if you have an oily scalp. Some people use a dandruff shampoo to remove flakes of dead skin from the scalp. Washing your hair more often than you need to can make it dry and dull. Using conditioner will make your hair shine and help with tangles.

Lice are small insects that can live in the human scalp. They lay eggs and can spread quickly on items that touch hair. Do not share combs, barrettes, or caps with anyone. If you become infected with lice, you need a special comb to remove their eggs. Wash your hair with anti-lice shampoo. Wash your clothing and bedding in hot, soapy water. Vacuum furniture and carpets to remove lice from your house.

◀ **Choose hair care products carefully.**

Caring for Your Nails

Keeping your nails healthy is easy. Remove any dirt from under the nails, and trim them. Use nail clippers to cut the nails straight across. Do not cut them too short. Never bite or pick your nails. Biting and picking can cause bleeding, irritation, and infection.

Use a nail file to smooth the edges of your nails. To care for your cuticles, the tough layer of skin around the nails, gently push the cuticles back after washing your hands or showering.

 Why should you care for your hair? Why should you care for your nails?

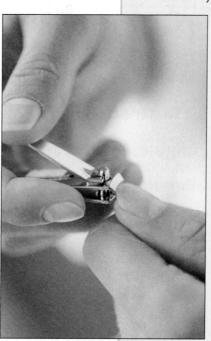

CRITICAL THINKING

Set Health Goals

Use a health behavior contract.

1 **Write the health goal you want to set:** *I will keep my hair and nails healthy.*

2 **Tell how the goal will affect your health.** Make a list of the functions of your hair and nails. Make a second list noting what might occur if you neglect your hair and nails.

3 **Describe a plan you will follow. Keep track of your progress.** Create a schedule for grooming your hair and nails. Include each grooming task and when you will do it. For example, you may want to wash your hair on Mondays, Wednesdays, and Fridays. You may decide to trim your fingernails every Thursday. Keep track of your progress.

4 **Evaluate how your plan worked.** After a week, check to see if you did everything on your calendar. If there is room for improvement, adjust your schedule.

LESSON 1 REVIEW

Review Concepts

1. **Tell** the benefits of being well groomed.

2. **Describe** three ways to take care of your skin.

3. **List** three ways to take care of your hair and three ways to take care of your nails.

Critical Thinking

4. **Predict** ways a person's mental and emotional, physical, and family and social health might be affected by not being well groomed.

5. **LIFE SKILLS** **Practice Healthful Behaviors** What are three healthful behaviors to practice to be well groomed?

6. **LIFE SKILLS** **Set Health Goals** Set a health goal and make a plan to take care of your skin.

Keeping Healthy and Getting Checkups

You will learn . . .

- what happens during a regular physical examination.
- ways to care for your eyes.
- ways to care for your ears.
- the causes of and treatment for vision and hearing problems.

Vocabulary

- **optometrist**, C12
- **ophthalmologist**, C12
- **farsightedness**, C16
- **nearsightedness**, C16
- **astigmatism**, C16
- **conjunctivitis**, C17
- **noise pollution**, C17

To keep a car running safely, the owner takes it to a mechanic. The mechanic checks the engine, brakes, and tires and makes repairs. Regular maintenance can prevent a car from breaking down. In much the same way, your body needs to be checked regularly.

Physical Examinations

You should have a physical examination once each year. During the examination, a licensed health care provider—a physician, nurse practitioner, nurse, or physician assistant—asks questions about your health and performs checks and tests. You should see a health care provider when you have any unusual symptoms. A *symptom* is a change in the way a person behaves or the body functions.

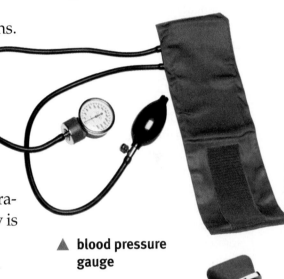

◀ thermometer

During your examination, a health care provider makes notes about your past health and habits. Your parents or guardian may be asked about your family's past and present health. This information becomes part of your health record.

A health care provider also measures your height, weight, and body temperature. He or she makes sure that these measurements fall within standard ranges. A temperature above 98.6°F is a fever and may indicate that the body is fighting an infection.

▲ blood pressure gauge

The health care provider checks your heartbeat, blood pressure, and pulse. These indicators tell whether your heart and blood vessels are healthy. Blood pressure is the force of the blood against the walls of blood vessels called arteries. A sample of your blood may be taken. A lab will test the sample to check your red and white blood cell counts. Your reflexes may be checked to see if your nerves are healthy.

▲ reflex tester

Checkups for Parts of the Body

The health care provider examines parts of your body. He or she shines light into your eyes to check blood vessels. He or she looks at your ear canal and eardrum and performs a hearing test to check hearing. The nostrils and mucous membranes are checked for irritation. Your mouth and throat are checked for infection. The size, location, and condition of your body organs are inspected. In addition, he or she uses a stethoscope on your chest and back to listen to body sounds.

▼ stethoscope

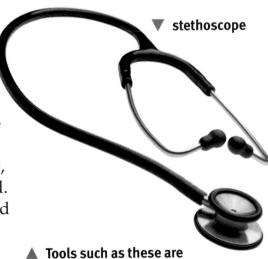

▲ Tools such as these are used during your physical examination.

What is checked during a physical examination?

Caring for Your Eyes

You use your eyes in many activities. You learn and remember information by seeing. Squinting and holding a textbook close to or far away from your eyes may indicate a vision problem. You can get help with eye care from an optometrist. An **optometrist** is a health care professional who is trained and licensed to examine people's eyes and prescribe eyeglasses or contact lenses. An **ophthalmologist** is a physician who treats diseases and injuries to the eye.

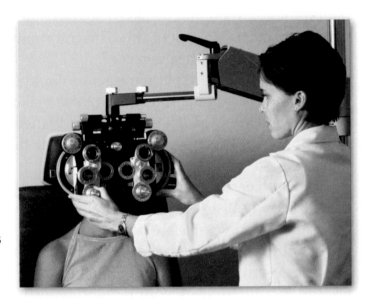

▶ Regular examinations are an important part of eye care.

Parts of the Eye

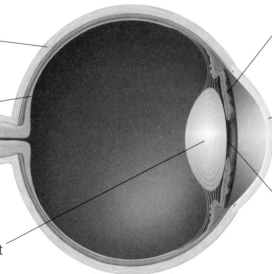

sclera
Tough, white material that covers most of the eyeball

retina
Membrane that receives the image formed by the lens and sends it as a signal to the optic nerve

optic nerve
Nerve that carries messages from the retina to the brain

lens
Transparent part of the eye that focuses light on the retina

iris
Round, colored portion of the front of the eye

cornea
Clear, outer layer that covers the front of the eye

pupil
Opening in the iris that allows light to enter the eye

Ways to Care for the Eyes

There are several things you can do to care for your eyes. When you spend time in the sun, never look directly at it. Wear sunglasses with ultraviolet (UV) ray protection. Wear protective eyewear when you play sports and when you work with chemicals or power tools. Keep a safe distance from fireworks.

Artificial tears can be used to soothe dry, irritated eyes. Avoid products intended to remove redness from your eyes because they may strain your eyes' blood vessels. Because you might touch your eyes from time to time, wash your hands often to keep germs from getting in your eyes. If you wear contact lenses, carefully follow an optometrist's instructions for using and cleaning them.

▲ Sunglasses help protect your eyes from the sun.

 What are three ways you can care for your eyes?

CRITICAL THINKING

Access Valid Health Information, Products, and Services

Suppose your parent or guardian just took you for an eye examination. You found out that you need corrective lenses.

1 **Identify when you need health information, products, and services.** You often hear about contact lenses but do not know much about them. Find out about them. For example, how do they compare with eyeglasses? What different kinds are available? What kind of care do they need?

2 **Identify where you can find health information, products, and services.** Ask an optometrist or ophthalmologist about contact lenses. He or she may guide you to a source where you can learn about them with a parent's or guardian's help. Make a list of people you know who wear contacts.

3 **Locate health information, products, and services.** Read books and visit Internet sites about contact lenses to find out about the different types that are available. Talk to people who wear contacts.

4 **Evaluate what you found.** Think about your sources. What are each source's qualifications? Is the source a company trying to sell a product? How would that affect the information you found? How can you be sure that the information is valid?

Caring for Your Ears

ACTIVITY

Music
LINK
Give Sound Advice

Most young people enjoy listening to music. However, loud noise can damage hearing. Sound is measured in decibels, and continued exposure to sounds above 85 decibels can cause hearing loss. Put a CD player with a headset on the table and turn up the volume. How far away from the sound do you have to stand in order not to hear it? Lower the volume and see how close you have to stand to hear it. Analyze your results.

Hearing is another important body sense that you need to protect. You use your hearing when you listen to other people. Hearing allows you to understand a teacher's directions. Hearing may warn you of a dangerous situation, such as an approaching car. You should take care of your ears so that you will always be able to hear.

Parts of the Ear

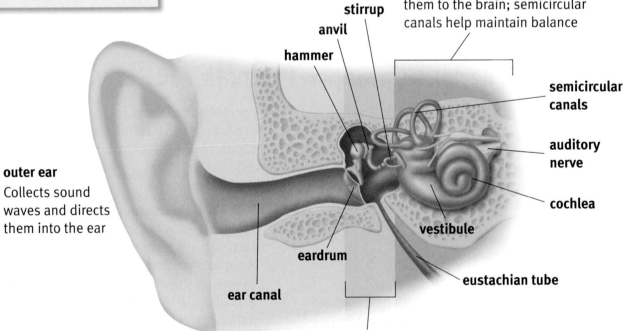

inner ear
Cochlea turns sound waves into signals and passes them to the auditory nerve, which transmits them to the brain; semicircular canals help maintain balance

stirrup

anvil

hammer

semicircular canals

auditory nerve

cochlea

vestibule

eustachian tube

outer ear
Collects sound waves and directs them into the ear

eardrum

ear canal

middle ear
Contains the eardrum and several tiny bones—hammer, anvil, stirrup—which transmit sound waves to the inner ear; eustachian tube helps equalize air pressure on both sides of eardrum

Ways to Care for Your Ears

To take good care of your ears, have your ears and hearing checked regularly. Every day, wash your outer ears with water and then shake the water out. After swimming, rinse your ears and dry them carefully. A parent or guardian can use a few drops of medicinal alcohol to help remove any water that gets trapped in your ear canals. Never place your finger or anything else inside your ears.

When you listen to music, keep the volume low, especially inside a car or when using headphones. The volume is too high if someone next to you can hear the music from your headphones. Wear protective ear equipment, such as earplugs, whenever you have to be exposed to loud noises. Avoid prolonged exposure to loud noises, such as noise from jet engines, sirens, and jackhammers.

On Your Own

FOR SCHOOL OR HOME

Make a Safety List

You can protect your hearing and eyesight at home. Make a list of items in your home that could damage your hearing or eyesight. For each item on your list, write how you can protect your eyes and ears. For example, if you use a lawn mower, you might write that you should wear eye and ear protection.

 What are three ways you can care for your ears?

Common Noise Levels, in Decibels

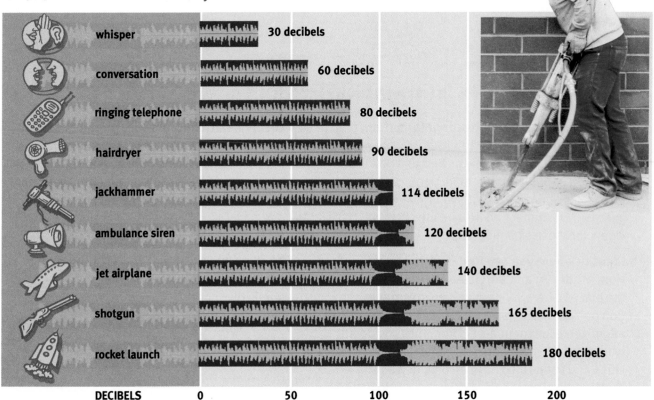

whisper	30 decibels
conversation	60 decibels
ringing telephone	80 decibels
hairdryer	90 decibels
jackhammer	114 decibels
ambulance siren	120 decibels
jet airplane	140 decibels
shotgun	165 decibels
rocket launch	180 decibels

DECIBELS   0   50   100   150   200

Exposure to noise over 85 decibels may cause hearing loss.

C15

Eye and Ear Problems

ACTIVITY

Math
L I N K
Chart Sight

Nearsightedness is called myopia. Find a journal or Web site that shows the percentage of people in the United States who are nearsighted. Then figure out what percentage of the students in your class have myopia. Make a chart to compare your class percentage to the national percentage.

Several health problems can affect your eyes and ears. Certain types of injuries can damage vision and hearing. Hearing and vision problems are sometimes due to heredity. Changes in the eyes during puberty can alter eyesight. Infections may cause hearing loss. Learning about vision and hearing problems and their causes can help you protect your vision and hearing.

Common Eye Problems

Farsightedness is a vision problem in which close objects appear blurred while distant objects are seen clearly. **Nearsightedness** is a vision problem in which distant objects appear blurred while close objects are seen clearly. **Astigmatism** (uh•STIG•muh•ti•zuhm) is a vision problem in which the cornea or the lens of the eye is curved unevenly, causing blurred vision.

Eyeglasses or contact lenses can correct vision. In some cases, reshaping the eye with laser surgery may correct vision.

ACTIVITY

LIFE SKILLS

CRITICAL THINKING

Access Valid Health Information, Products, and Services

1 **Identify when you need health information, products, and services.** Think about what might happen if your family moved to a new town. You should have regular eye, ear, and physical examinations. With your parents or guardian, you must find new health care providers for these examinations.

2 **Identify where you can find health information, products, and services.** Make a list of all the places where your family can get information on health care providers. For example, you might get recommendations from the providers who cared for you before you moved. Many cities and towns also have an official Web site that lists local providers.

3 **Locate health information, products, and services.** Make a list of health care providers in your local area who offer eye, ear, and overall health care. List any information that you can find, including your family's past providers.

4 **Evaluate what you found.** You may want to evaluate the health care providers based on what you have learned. Why is one provider better for you and your family than another?

Infections and injury may cause eye problems. **Conjunctivitis,** commonly called pinkeye, is a very contagious infection in which the tissue around the eye and inside the eyelid swells. A physician can prescribe medicine to treat and cure pinkeye. A scratched cornea is an injury that might occur while playing a sport or from a problem with a contact lens. The eye becomes red, irritated, and sensitive to light. To prevent permanent damage to the eye, talk to your ophthalmologist about any eye injury or infection.

Ear Problems

Nearly one of every ten people has a hearing problem. Some people are born deaf and cannot hear any sound. Others lose their hearing in the first few days after birth. Hearing loss can occur during childhood, adolescence, or adulthood.

There are many causes of hearing loss. **Noise pollution** is loud or constant noise that causes hearing loss. You should avoid noise pollution. Middle ear infection is the most common cause of hearing loss in children and teenagers. Medicines usually clear up the infection and restore hearing. Some people who have hearing loss wear a hearing aid, a small device that makes sounds louder and easier to hear.

✔ **What are four common vision problems?**

◀ **Hearing aids can benefit those who have some types of hearing loss.**

LESSON 2 REVIEW

Review Concepts

1. **Tell** why you should have regular physical examinations.

2. **Describe** two ways to care for the eyes and two ways to care for the ears.

3. **List** the major causes and treatments for vision and hearing problems.

Critical Thinking

4. **Plan** During the summer, you and your friends go for a swim in the neighborhood pool every afternoon. List ways you can protect yourself from getting ear infections.

5. **LIFE SKILLS** **Access Valid Health Information, Products, and Services** Suppose you have a hearing problem and a vision problem. Discuss health products and services you might need.

Be a Health Advocate

Dear Health Nut,

Here's my problem ... Our class recently learned how important it is to get regular physical examinations. Many of us know that checkups are necessary. However, some of my classmates still don't get the point. How can I help them understand the need to get regular checkups?

Concerned about Checkups

SEE FOR YOURSELF

An Eye Exam Could Give You a Whole New Outlook

Dear Concerned about Checkups,

Here's how you might solve the problem . . . You're learning how to care for your health. You know the value of regular examinations. You have checkups for your eyes, ears, and the rest of your body. Use the steps on the next page to be a health advocate.

Health Nut

Foldables To Learn Life Skills

Learn This Life Skill

Follow these four steps to be a health advocate. You can use the Foldables to help you organize your thoughts.

1 **Select a health-related concern to communicate.**

You want to encourage your peers to receive regular physical examinations.

2 **Gather reliable information.**

Search books, magazines, and Web sites for information about the value of regular checkups. Ask your family physician for information.

3 **Identify your purpose and target audience.**

Make a list of ways you can reach your classmates. For example, would they notice posters in the school hallway? How could you make your posters appealing to your classmates?

4 **Develop a convincing and appropriate message.**

Design posters that encourage your classmates to get regular physical examinations. Seek permission from your school administrators to hang the posters in a location where students will notice them.

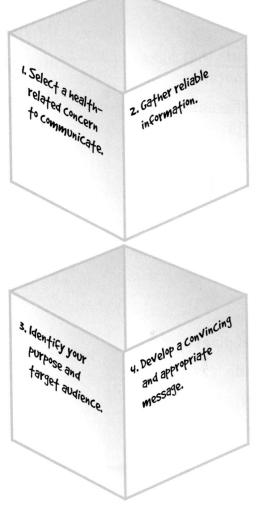

You can work in a group to participate in this activity by writing, cutting, folding, or drawing. You can do a role-play as well.

Practice This Life Skill

Activity You have noticed that some of your classmates do not protect their hearing. Write a short skit describing how you would advocate for hearing health. Act out your skit with a classmate.

Caring for Your Teeth

You will learn . . .

- the parts that make up a tooth.
- the different kinds of teeth.
- what is included in a dental health plan.
- how dental problems are prevented and treated.

Vocabulary

- **dental plaque,** C22
- **fluoride,** C23
- **cavity,** C24
- **periodontal disease,** C25
- **gingivitis,** C25
- **malocclusion,** C25
- **orthodontist,** C25

Do you realize the value of your teeth? They do more than just chew food. Teeth help you speak clearly and make a bright, pleasant smile. Proper oral hygiene and dental care can keep your teeth healthy for life.

The Structure of Teeth and Gums

The visible part of each tooth, called the crown, consists of several layers. The outer layer of the crown is the enamel. Enamel acts as a protective barrier for the tooth. Under the enamel is the dentin, which protects the pulp, the inner layer that contains nerve endings and blood vessels. The dentin and pulp extend below your gums where they make up the root of the tooth.

There are four types of permanent teeth: incisors, canines, premolars, and molars. The eight incisors are in the front of your mouth, four on the top and four on the bottom. They are used for biting and cutting food. The four canines, or cuspids, are next to your incisors. They help to tear food.

Beyond the canines are eight premolars, also called bicuspids. They are used to tear and grind food. At the very back of your mouth are eight wide molars that mash food and prepare it for swallowing. Four more will grow in as you get older.

 What are the four different types of teeth?

Types and Parts of Teeth

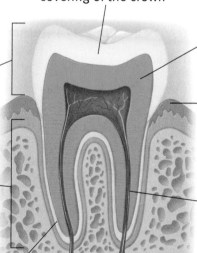

canines
Pointy, sharp teeth used for tearing

incisors
Flat, sharp teeth used to cut and chop

premolars
(bicuspids)
Large teeth used to crush and grind

molars
Large ridged teeth that prepare food for swallowing

enamel
Protective white covering of the crown

crown
Visible part of the tooth

root
Area below the gum

cementum
Holds the root of tooth to the jawbone

dentin
Bonelike matter surrounding the pulp

gum
Pink tissue that surrounds the tooth

pulp
Innermost part of tooth that contains nerve endings and blood vessels

Caring for Your Teeth and Gums

A dental health plan includes brushing, flossing, using toothpaste with fluoride, eating a healthful diet, wearing a mouth guard, wearing a seat belt, and having regular dental exams. Brushing removes **dental plaque,** a sticky substance containing bacteria that forms on teeth. Flossing removes dental plaque and food from between the teeth.

Brushing

The American Dental Association (ADA) suggests the following steps for brushing:

1. Place the toothbrush beside the teeth, with the bristle tips at an angle to the gums. (See #1 below.)
2. Move the toothbrush back and forth. Use short strokes about a half-tooth wide.
3. Brush the outer surface of each tooth.
4. Use the same action on the inside surface of each tooth.
5. Scrub the chewing surface of each tooth. (See #2 below.)
6. Brush behind the front teeth and over the gums. (See #3 below.)
7. Brush the tongue.

Flossing

The American Dental Association suggests the following steps for flossing:

1. Break off about 16 inches of floss. Wind one end around your finger.
2. Wind the rest of the floss around the same finger of the opposite hand.
3. Use the thumbs and forefingers to guide the floss between the teeth.
4. Hold the floss tightly and gently insert it between the teeth. Never push the floss into the gums. When the floss reaches the gumline, curve it into a gentle C-shape against one tooth. Gently slide it into the space between the gums and the tooth.
5. Hold the floss tightly against the tooth. Move the floss away from the gum by scraping the side of the tooth.
6. Do not remove the floss. Curve it around the other tooth and scrape it, too.
7. Repeat this procedure on the rest of your teeth.

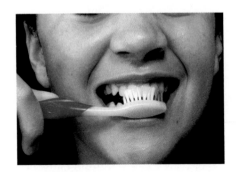

1. Gently brush the outer surface of the teeth, using a back-and-forth motion.

2. Place the brush against the chewing surface of teeth and use a back-and-forth motion.

3. Tilt the brush behind the front teeth and make several up-and-down strokes.

Fluoride

Fluoride (FLAW•ryd) is a mineral that helps prevent tooth decay. It hardens the enamel and makes it more resistant to acid. The ADA recommends that everyone have a source of fluoride. Fluoride is most effective during the early stages of tooth formation, so it is important for babies and young children to have fluoride. It is often available in drinking water, mouthwashes, and toothpastes. Dentists can apply fluoride to teeth.

Diet

You can care for your teeth and gums by reducing the amount of sugar in your diet. Sugar is a major cause of tooth decay. Sugar and bacteria in dental plaque form an acid that breaks down the enamel of the tooth and causes decay. Candies dissolve slowly in your mouth and contribute to tooth decay because the sugar stays near the teeth for a long time.

Choosing foods and beverages with calcium promotes dental health. Calcium is a mineral that strengthens teeth and the bones that support the teeth. Vitamin D also makes teeth strong. Dairy products are a source of calcium and vitamin D. Vitamin C, found in citrus fruits such as oranges, keeps gums healthy.

Preventing Injury

You can prevent injuries to your teeth by using a mouth guard when you participate in sports or engage in any physical activity. Always use seat belts when you ride in a car or school bus.

Make Responsible Decisions

You are on a committee to plan the menu for a party at school. What foods and beverages should you plan to serve? Which foods and beverages are healthful for teeth and gums?

1 **Identify your choices. Check them out with your parent or another responsible adult.** Make a list of all the types of foods that would be appropriate for the party.

2 **Evaluate each choice. Use the Guidelines for Making Responsible Decisions™.** For each food that you are considering, ask the following questions:

- Is it healthful?
- Is it safe?
- Does it show respect for myself and others?
- Does it follow the guidelines of responsible adults?

3 **Tell what the responsible decision is. Check this out with your parent or another trusted adult.** Use your answers to the above questions to select the foods for the class party.

4 **Evaluate your decision.** Were your selections tasty and inviting as well as healthful?

Dental Checkups

Dental checkups are needed every six months to prevent tooth decay and gum problems. The dentist examines your teeth and gums and treats any problems you might have. A dental hygienist cleans your teeth to remove hard plaque deposits.

 Why should you wear a mouth guard for contact sports and a seat belt when riding on a school bus?

A World of Dental Care

Dental care is not the same everywhere in the world. In some areas, fluoride is not available in drinking water. People are not always able to receive dental care. Choose two cultures that are different from your own and research their dental care. Write a newspaper article that describes how dental care varies across the world.

Preventing and Treating Tooth and Gum Problems

A number of problems can affect the teeth and gums. Learning and following a dental health plan will prevent problems and protect your teeth and gums.

Cavities

A common tooth problem that many people face is tooth decay. Tooth decay is a gradual wearing away of a tooth that can result in the loss of the tooth. The problem begins when dental plaque forms on teeth. If dental plaque is not removed, it may result in a **cavity,** a hole in the enamel of a tooth. When you eat sugary foods, the sugar mixes with the bacteria in dental plaque, producing acid. This acid can wear away the enamel of a tooth and form a cavity.

Your dentist will check your teeth for cavities. He or she will repair any cavities with fillings. Fillings keep bacteria from getting into the dentin. If bacteria do get into the dentin, they can destroy the tooth and cause disease.

Sealants, plastic material applied to the chewing surfaces of the back teeth, can help prevent cavities. Sealants fill in the grooves of the teeth, making it difficult for plaque and acids to cause tooth decay.

Stages of Tooth Decay

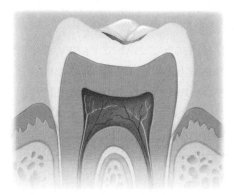

Stage 1. Sugar from food mixes with the bacteria in plaque to form an acid.

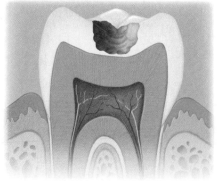

Stage 2. The acid eats through the tooth's enamel, creating a cavity.

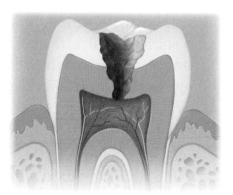

Stage 3. If the cavity is not filled it can reach the pulp, causing pain and further dental problems.

Periodontal Disease

Periodontal (pehr•ee•oh•DAHN•tuhl) **disease** is a disease of the gums and other tissues that support the teeth. The first stage of periodontal disease is **gingivitis** (jin•juh•VY•tuhs), a condition in which the gums are sore and bleed easily. Plaque around the gums causes gingivitis. Regular tooth brushing and flossing can prevent this condition. Your dentist can help treat your gums if gingivitis develops.

Untreated gingivitis leads to periodontal disease. If plaque is not removed, it forms *calculus*, hardened plaque. The buildup of calculus causes the gums to separate from the teeth and make spaces that fill with bacteria. The bacteria can destroy the bones that support the teeth. As a result, the teeth will loosen. A dentist treats periodontal disease by removing the calculus and dental plaque.

Malocclusion

Malocclusion (ma•luh•KLOO•zhuhn) is the abnormal fitting together of teeth in the jaw. An **orthodontist** is a dentist who treats malocclusion. Treatment may include braces, metal wires used to move the jaws and teeth. An orthodontist may wait for a patient's permanent teeth to come in before applying braces. This often happens between the ages of 12 and 14, but a person can get braces at any age. The length of time that a person has braces varies, but the average is two years.

If you get braces, your mouth may be sore for about a week. You also may experience soreness when you have your braces tightened. Most of the time, braces do not cause pain or discomfort. Wear a mouth guard while playing contact sports.

 What is malocclusion?

LESSON 3 REVIEW

Review Concepts

1. **Identify** the main parts of the tooth and each part's function.

2. **Describe** what is included in a dental health plan.

3. **Explain** how periodontal disease develops.

Critical Thinking

4. **Make Predictions** Your friend brushes her teeth every day, but she neglects to floss. How might this affect the health of her teeth and gums in the future? How might you help your friend?

5. **LIFE SKILLS** **Make Responsible Decisions** Why is having a dental checkup every six months part of a dental health plan?

Physical Activity and Fitness

You will learn . . .

- how regular physical activity benefits the three areas of health.
- how you can achieve health-related fitness.
- which lifestyle changes can increase physical fitness.

Vocabulary

- **health-related fitness,** C28
- **endurance,** C28
- **flexibility,** C28
- **anaerobic exercise,** C29
- **aerobic exercise,** C29

Do you enjoy playing sports? Regular physical activity can protect your health and help you stay fit. Regular physical activity can reduce stress and build your self-esteem. It also can increase your social circle and teach you about teamwork and setting goals.

Benefits of Physical Activity

Physical activity is movement of muscles using energy. Regular physical activity improves mental and emotional health, family and social health, and physical health. Physical activity improves the health and well-being of all age groups.

The Rewards of Physical Activity

Physical activity improves all three areas of health.

- **Mental and emotional health** Physical activity improves blood flow to the brain. This can make you feel alert and reduces stress. Physical activity also increases energy and causes the brain to secrete beta-endorphins. These are chemicals in your brain that produce feelings of pleasure. Participation in sports promotes positive self-esteem.

- **Family and social health** Physical activity provides opportunities to meet new people and enjoy friendships. It helps strengthen the bonds between friends and family. Group activities teach skills such as fairness and teamwork.

- **Physical health** Physical activity strengthens your bones and muscles, including your heart muscle. It helps your brain and body function. Physical activity can enhance your appearance because it uses calories, helps control appetite, and improves posture. Regular physical activity reduces the risk of certain diseases, such as diabetes, coronary heart disease, and colon cancer. You also are less likely to have an accident and be injured.

Physical activity helps you manage your weight. It helps balance your intake of calories with calories used. Regular physical activity affects the part of the brain that controls appetite. If you participate in regular physical activity, you are less likely to overeat.

How does physical activity benefit your family and social health?

Health-Related Fitness

Physical fitness is the condition of the body that results from regular physical activity. **Health-related fitness** is the ability of the heart, lungs, muscles, and joints to perform well.

Kinds of Health-Related Fitness

There are five kinds of health-related fitness. You can learn to develop all of the following five areas:

1. **Muscular strength** is the ability to lift, pull, push, kick, and throw with force. This kind of fitness can help you throw a baseball or carry heavy boxes.

2. **Muscular endurance** is the ability to use the same muscles for a long period of time. When you ride a bicycle up and down a hilly trail, you need muscular endurance to keep pedaling without stopping. Fitness helps boost your **endurance**, the ability to perform an extended activity without becoming overly tired.

3. **Flexibility** is the ability to bend and move the joints through a full range of motion. You need flexibility to serve a tennis ball or to touch your toes while standing up. You are less likely to be injured if your muscles are flexible.

4. **Cardiorespiratory endurance** is the ability to do activities that require increased oxygen for a period of time. This kind of fitness keeps you from tiring. It allows you to swim several laps in a pool or run a long distance without stopping to rest.

5. **Healthful body composition** is having a high ratio of lean tissue to fat tissue in the body. Fat tissue cushions and protects organs, but too much is not healthful. Lean tissue is firm and gives you tone. Blood flows easily through lean tissue.

Achieving Health-Related Fitness

You can work to achieve all five kinds of health-related fitness. You might try participating in exercises and physical activities that develop certain parts of the body or build specific skills.

To build muscular strength, a person must exercise muscle groups. Weight lifting, push-ups, and pull-ups are helpful for strengthening arm muscles. Sports such as gymnastics and golf also develop the upper body muscles. For the lower body muscles, try mountain biking or hiking. Even carrying groceries or climbing a tree can build muscular strength.

You can improve muscular strength and muscular endurance by doing anaerobic exercise. An **anaerobic exercise** is exercise in which the body's demand for oxygen is greater than the supply. This type of exercise requires short bursts of energy. Sprinting is an anaerobic activity.

Another way to improve your muscular endurance is by biking or running for long distances.

You can build flexibility by participating in activities that require you to stretch. Wrestling and gymnastics are such sports. Karate and ballet also improve flexibility. They help extend your range of motion.

You build cardiorespiratory endurance with **aerobic exercise**, exercise that requires oxygen use for a period of time. Swimming and jogging for long distances are popular aerobic exercises. Soccer and lacrosse are examples of aerobic sports.

Many forms of exercise, particularly those that build cardiorespiratory endurance, can improve body composition. They help keep body fat within a healthful range and build lean tissue. Engaging in aerobic exercise three to five times a week will produce results.

 What are the five kinds of health-related fitness?

CAREERS IN HEALTH

Aerobics Instructor

Participating in an aerobics class is a healthful way to exercise in a social setting. If you enjoy doing aerobics and teaching people, you might think about becoming an aerobics instructor. Aerobics instructors lead different types of classes, motivating their students to achieve exercise goals. Through teaching, they use leadership and social skills. To learn more about becoming certified to teach aerobics, talk to aerobics instructors about their training and experience.

 LOG ON Visit **www.mmhhealth.com** to find out more about this and other health careers.

Time for Fitness

Determine how many hours are in a week. Subtract from that total the number of hours you spend at school. Next, subtract the number of hours you spend sleeping, eating, and doing homework. Finally, subtract the number of hours you spend on chores and other activities. Calculate how many hours are left for you to participate in physical activities.

▼ **Physical activity provides many long-term health benefits.**

Fit for Life

If you've never included physical activity in your life, you should do so now. You will begin to reap the rewards immediately. You will enjoy many long-term health benefits. There are several ways to make fitness part of your life.

By Yourself

You can change your habits to lead a more physically active lifestyle. You don't need to play a sport with others. There are many things you can do by yourself to be active.

Instead of	I can
Riding in a car	Ride my bicycle
Taking an escalator	Walk up the stairs
Playing video games	Shoot baskets
Watching sports on television	Skateboard or in-line skate
Listening to the stereo at home	Jog while wearing headphones
Watching music videos	Dance

With Your Family and Friends

You can enjoy physical activity with friends and family as well. Explore activities that you like or have an interest in learning. Then invite a friend to try one with you, or suggest it to your family as an outing.

Many factors affect the physical activities a young person chooses. Personal interest is a major factor. You should select activities you enjoy. Your parents or guardian also may influence your activities.

Instead of	We can
Talking on the phone	Talk while hiking
Watching football on TV	Play catch with a football
Playing air hockey or foosball	Join a hockey or soccer team
Playing cards	Go bowling
Hanging out at the mall	Swim at the beach or in a pool

Your parents or guardian may encourage or discourage a certain activity. Social experience plays a role. People often like to do what their friends are doing. Environment makes a difference. For example, it is easier to take up skiing if you live near mountains. Finally, opportunity is a factor. You can participate only in those activities that you have the opportunity to learn.

 What factors might affect the physical activities you choose?

◀ **You can choose from many types of physical activity.**

ACTIVITY LIFE SKILLS
CRITICAL THINKING

Analyze What Influences Your Health

There are a number of influences on your physical fitness. Some factors encourage you to be active, while others do not. Make a plan to increase the positive influences in your life.

1 **Identify people and things that might influence you.** Think about people and things that influence whether or not you exercise. List these on a separate sheet of paper.

2 **Evaluate how the influence might affect your health and decisions.** Next to each person or thing, write whether its influence is positive or negative and explain why.

3 **Choose positive influences on health.** Note which people or things on your list influence you in a positive way and seek them out. For example, if spending time with a particular friend inspires you to be active, try joining a sports team with that friend.

4 **Protect yourself from negative influences on health.** Examine the people and things on your list that had a negative influence. Avoid those that limit your physical fitness.

LESSON **4** REVIEW

Review Concepts

1. **Name** ways that regular physical activity benefits each of the three areas of health.

2. **Explain** how you can achieve one of the five kinds of health-related fitness.

3. **Describe** three ways to include more physical activity in your daily life.

Critical Thinking

4. **Evaluate** Suppose you and a friend decide to enter a long-distance race for charity. To train for the race, your friend works on her muscular strength and you work on your muscular endurance. Based on training, who is more likely to do better in the race? Why?

5. **LIFE SKILLS** **Analyze What Influences Your Health** Who or what influences you to participate in regular physical activity?

Developing a Physical Fitness Plan

You will learn . . .

- resources to consider when making a physical fitness plan.
- tests to measure your level of physical fitness.
- how to develop a physical fitness plan.

Vocabulary

- physical fitness plan, C33
- skill-related fitness, C33
- President's Challenge, C34
- resting heart rate, C36
- target heart rate, C36
- warm-up, C37
- cool-down, C37

How fit are you? You may be neglecting certain areas of your body. A physical fitness plan will help you work different muscle groups. It also will help you establish a regular schedule for physical activity.

Physical Activity Resources

A **physical fitness plan** is a written schedule of physical activities to do to develop health-related fitness and **skill-related fitness,** the ability to perform well in sports and physical activities. Fitness skills include agility, balance, speed, power, coordination, and reaction time. Before making a plan, you must know the resources that are available. Then you must assess your current level of fitness.

To start, consider the following five resources:

1. **Time** Like most students, you probably have a busy schedule. After school, you have homework to do. You also might have club meetings to attend or chores to complete. Will you have enough time for the physical activities you choose?

2. **Facilities** Some physical activities require special facilities. You might need a tennis court, ski slope, swimming pool, or golf course for your activity. Does your community have the facility you need? Is the facility available when you need it?

3. **Equipment** Some physical activities require special equipment. You might need a bicycle and helmet, weights, or scuba gear. Do you have the equipment? Is it possible for you to rent or buy it?

4. **Money** Some physical activities cost money. You might need lessons to learn the skills you will need. Can you afford to participate in the activity you choose?

5. **Other people** For some activities, such as tennis and racquetball, you need a partner. Some people find participating with others to be helpful. Be sure to get your parent's or guardian's approval for any activity you choose.

What resources might you consider when making a physical fitness plan?

ACTIVITY

Physical Education
L I N K
Fitness Skills

Demonstrate a simple activity that you can do to develop each fitness skill.

Agility is the ability to move and change direction.

Balance is the ability to keep from falling.

Coordination is the ability to use body parts and senses together for movement.

Reaction time is the length of time it takes to move after a signal.

Speed is the ability to move quickly.

Power is the ability to combine strength and speed.

Tests to Measure Your Level of Fitness

Before starting any exercise program, it is important to determine your level of fitness. Visiting your physician for an examination is one way to assess your fitness. In fact, you must have a physical exam before you can play certain sports. Tests also measure your fitness level. You can compare your beginning fitness scores with improvement in each area. Physical fitness is judged on your personal improvement.

The President's Challenge

The **President's Challenge** is a physical fitness test that measures students' fitness in five areas. Schools, youth organizations, and Boys and Girls Clubs administer the test. Students win awards based on how their performance compares to national standards. Before taking the Presidential Challenge, you should know the correct techniques for each test.

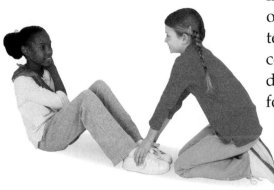

▲ Curl-ups test the strength of your abdominal muscles.

▲ Performing well on the shuttle run requires quickness and agility.

1. **Curl-ups** This test measures your abdominal strength and endurance. Lie on your back with your knees flexed. Place your feet about 12 inches from your buttocks. Cross your arms and place your hands on opposite shoulders. Your elbows should be close to your chest. Have a partner hold your feet. Begin the curl-up by raising your trunk so your elbows touch your thighs. Then lie back down to touch your shoulders to the floor. The test measures how many curl-ups you can do in one minute.

2. **Shuttle run** The shuttle run measures speed, quickness, and agility. It also measures the strength and endurance of your leg muscles. For this test you will need two parallel lines 30 feet apart. Place two blocks of wood behind one line. Stand behind the other line. At the signal, run to the opposite line and pick up a block. Carrying the block, run back and place it behind the starting line. Then run and pick up the second block and run back across the starting line.

3. **Endurance run/walk** This event is also called the one mile walk/run. It measures cardiorespiratory endurance. The endurance run/walk usually takes place on a track. The goal is to run a mile as quickly as possible. You may walk any part of the distance if you become tired. It is important to pace yourself during this event. To prepare, practice running at a steady pace for short distances.

4. **Pull-ups** This test measures strength and endurance of upper body muscles. You perform it using a horizontal bar. Begin by reaching up to grab the horizontal bar with an overhand or underhand grip. Hang from the bar with your arms fully extended. Your feet should not touch the floor. Then raise your body so that your chin clears the bar. Finish the pull-up by lowering your body to the starting position. Complete as many pull-ups as possible. You may not kick, bend your legs, or swing your body during a pull-up.

5. **V-sit reach or sit and reach** This event measures the flexibility of the lower back and calf muscles. For the V-sit reach, sit on the floor with your feet in front of you. Place your heels 8 to 12 inches apart. Have a partner hold your legs flat. With your palms down, slowly reach forward as far as possible along a measuring line. Your teacher will record your distance. The sit and reach is similar. You reach forward along a special box instead of along the floor.

Other Tests of Fitness

In addition to those used in the President's Challenge, other tests are also used to determine fitness. For example, the trunk lift measures strength and flexibility of trunk muscles. This test is done by lying flat on the abdomen and lifting the head and shoulders and legs. Regular push-ups measure the strength of upper body muscles. Body composition is measured by the skinfold test. This test requires a trained professional to measure a fold of skin on a person's upper arm and calf and add the two measurements.

After taking tests, you can evaluate the parts of your physical fitness. You can work with a physical education teacher or coach and your parents or guardian to set fitness goals and develop a plan to reach them. Consider your overall health. For example, a person who has asthma may need to take particular care to avoid getting short of breath while exercising.

✓ **What five tests are included in the President's Challenge?**

▼ **You must have flexible muscles to excel at the V-sit reach exercise.**

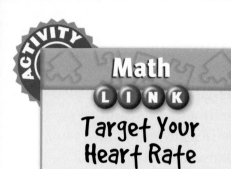
Developing a Physical Fitness Plan

The best way to stay in shape is to develop a physical fitness plan. As you design your plan, keep in mind your resources and your fitness needs. Then follow your plan closely. The key to success is staying focused on your goals.

Choose Your Activities

Use the results of your fitness tests to select activities for your physical fitness plan. The physical activities you choose should help you reach your fitness goals. You may use the results of the President's Challenge to set goals. Choose exercises that build performance in those events. For example, to improve at the V-sit reach you need to increase your flexibility. Activities such as ballet or karate will add to your flexibility.

You may also want to choose physical activities that will improve your heart rate. Regular physical activity helps reduce your blood pressure and your resting heart rate. Your **resting heart rate** is the number of times your heart beats each minute when you are standing still. Physical activities such as aerobics, jogging, and swimming build cardiorespiratory endurance.

Target Heart Rate

During physical activity, you should maintain a **target heart rate**, a heart rate of 60 percent to 75 percent of maximum heart rate. Your maximum heart rate is 220 beats per minute minus your age. You can find out whether you exercise at your target heart rate by checking your pulse during your workout. Even though you can check your pulse to estimate your heart rate, a heart rate monitor is the only accurate form of measurement. Try to exercise at, or close to, your target heart rate.

◀ **Many types of activities can increase your cardiorespiratory endurance.**

Warming Up and Cooling Down

To prevent injuries during physical activity, it's important to start and finish properly. A **warm-up** is a period of three to five minutes of easy physical activity. Warming up prepares the muscles to begin exercise. A **cool-down** is a period of three to five minutes of reduced physical activity. During a cool-down, the heart rate slows back to its resting rate.

✓ **Why should you warm up before physical activity?**

Set Health Goals

Design a physical fitness plan so that you can gain the benefits of physical activity.

1 **Write the health goal you want to set:** *I will follow a physical fitness plan.*

2 **Tell how the goal will affect your health.** Make a list of ways a physical fitness plan can benefit the three areas of health.

3 **Describe a plan you will follow. Keep track of your progress.** Include exercises that build up the areas tested in the President's Challenge. Share your plan with a parent, guardian, school coach, or family physician.

4 **Evaluate how your plan worked.** After three weeks, take the President's Challenge again. Have you improved your level of fitness?

LESSON 5 REVIEW

Review Concepts

1. **List** the resources you should consider before making a physical fitness plan.

2. **Describe** the tests included in the President's Challenge.

3. **Explain** how to use the results of a physical fitness test to choose physical activities.

Critical Thinking

4. **Modify** List the body areas tested by the President's Challenge. Modify the challenge by selecting five new events. Make sure that your modified challenge is balanced. Consider including the events you chose as part of your physical fitness plan.

5. **LIFE SKILLS** **Set Health Goals** Set a health goal to become physically fit. Make a plan to improve upper body strength, lower body strength, flexibility, and cardiorespiratory endurance. Record your progress in a daily log.

Staying Safe During Physical Activity

You will learn . . .

- ways to prevent injuries during physical activity.
- how to stay safe when you participate in physical activities and exercise outdoors.
- how to recognize and treat injuries.

Vocabulary

- **scrape,** C42
- **cut,** C42
- **dislocation,** C42
- **sprain,** C42
- **PRICE,** C43

Minor injuries can be a common part of participating in physical activities, but you can reduce the risks by following safety guidelines. If an injury does occur, you can take steps to help.

Preventing Injuries During Physical Activity

Injuries that occur during physical activities are often preventable. Before starting a physical activity, learn how to prevent injuries.

In order to prevent injuries:

- **Have a physical examination** before starting an exercise program.
- **Wear the proper safety equipment.**
- **Tape or strap** any joints that are prone to injury.
- **Warm up before physical activity.** Include slow stretches in your warm-up.
- **Do not bounce during stretches.** This will help avoid muscle tears.
- **Drink plenty of water** before, during, and after physical activity.
- **Use the correct grip** for handheld sports equipment.
- **Learn the proper techniques** for operating exercise machines.
- **Stop an activity if you feel pain,** become short of breath, develop an irregular heartbeat, or become tired.
- **Cool down after an activity.** Include slow stretches in your cool-down.
- **Allow yourself time to recover** between workouts.

Helmets are among the most important pieces of safety equipment. You should wear a helmet for activities such as bicycling and skating. Always wear a helmet designed for the activity you are doing. Goggles, face masks, and mouth guards provide protection from elbows and flying objects. Wrist, knee, and elbow guards prevent fractures, breaks, and cuts.

Set aside at least two days a week to recover from rigorous physical activity. Overworking your body can lead to injury. If you do have an injury, be sure to rest. Continued activity might cause further damage. Always get plenty of sleep.

✓ **What are three ways you can prevent injuries during physical activities?**

▼ **Keeping your equipment in top shape will help reduce the risk of injury.**

Avoiding Injuries Outdoors

Exercising outside can be fun and healthful. Yet outdoor activities bring added injury risks. You can take steps to prevent common outdoor injuries.

Prepare for the weather when you exercise outdoors. Hot weather puts an added strain on the body. Try to exercise during the cooler times of the day. If that's not possible, take precautions to prevent heatstroke, heat exhaustion, and sunburn.

Drink plenty of water to remain hydrated. Avoid caffeinated beverages, which dehydrate you. To protect your skin from sunburn, wear protective clothing and a cap. Apply sunscreen with a sun protection factor (SPF) of at least 15. Wear sunglasses to protect your eyes from the sun. Use insect repellent to prevent bug bites.

You also must prepare for physical activity in cold and snowy weather. Cold muscles are more easily injured than warm ones. Spend extra time warming up. Include plenty of stretching. Wear warm clothing in layers to retain body heat. Hats, boots, and gloves prevent loss of body heat. Drink plenty of water, as cold weather can cause fluid loss.

Outdoor Safety

Outdoor activities such as biking and jogging sometimes take place near traffic. Learn and follow traffic rules. Use proper hand signals while biking. Avoid areas of heavy traffic. Wear bright-colored clothing so motorists can see you. If you must walk on a road, walk on the left side, facing oncoming traffic.

Exercising outdoors at night requires special safety measures. Regardless of your activity, try to remain in well-lit areas. Exercise with a friend if possible. Place reflector discs on your clothes and your bike to ensure that motorists can see you.

Proper sports equipment is essential for outside activities. Find out what you need. Check your gear regularly to make sure it's in good condition. Shoes are especially important. The right footwear helps prevent injury and improves your performance. Wear footwear designed for the specific activity you are doing.

 What are three important factors to consider when exercising outdoors?

ACTIVITY

Physical Education
L I N K
It Must Be the Shoes

Have you noticed how many different types of athletic shoes are available? There are shoes for specific activities, including baseball, football, basketball, tennis, running, walking, skateboarding, and bicycling. Investigate the special athletic shoes for three different activities. Draw each type of shoe, labeling the features that make it suited to a particular form of exercise.

ACTIVITY

LIFE SKILLS

CRITICAL THINKING

Make Responsible Decisions

Your class is planning a trip during winter recess to participate in a mountain hike. You are on the trip planning committee.

1 **Identify your choices. Check them out with your parent or another trusted adult.** You have several decisions to make. What clothing should you wear on the trip? What equipment and supplies will you need? Make a list of the clothing, equipment, and supplies you will need.

2 **Evaluate each choice. Use the Guidelines for Making Responsible Decisions™.** For each item on your list, consider the following questions:
- Is it healthful?
- Is it safe?
- Is it legal?

- Does it show respect for myself and others?
- Does it follow the guidelines of responsible adults?
- Does it demonstrate good character?

3 **Tell what the responsible decision is. Check this out with your parent or another trusted adult.** Note which items follow the guidelines. Use these items to make a list of the clothing, equipment, and supplies you will take on the trip. Have a parent or trusted adult and your teacher review the list.

4 **Evaluate your decision.** After your trip, review your packing list. Did you pack the items needed for a safe winter hiking trip? If not, write down any additional items you should have included, and plan to take them next time you go hiking.

Treating Injuries

It's important to know how to treat injuries. You should always make sure that a parent, guardian, or other trusted adult knows when you have an injury.

A **scrape** is the wearing away of skin caused by rubbing against a rough surface. When skin is scraped, nerve cells are irritated. There is a small amount of bleeding.

When treating a scrape, first wash the area with soap and warm water. Be sure to use an antibiotic ointment to prevent infection. Place a bandage over the scrape. See a physician if pus collects in the scrape. You can prevent scrapes by wearing protection, such as gloves, knee and elbow pads, long sleeves, and long pants.

A **cut** is an opening caused by something sharp. Cuts are deeper than scrapes and can collect dirt. You must wash the area with soap and warm water. Next, use a clean cloth or bandage and place pressure on the cut to stop bleeding. Apply an antibiotic ointment to prevent infection. For deep cuts, you need to receive medical treatment. Cuts sometimes require stitches.

A **dislocation** is the movement of a bone away from its joint. Pain and swelling occur. Moving the joint worsens the pain. To treat a dislocation, it is important to get prompt medical attention. Apply cold packs to reduce swelling.

Muscle soreness is pain from overuse of muscles. You can prevent muscle soreness with warm-up and cool-down exercises. If you experience muscle soreness, you can use the PRICE treatment, described on the next page.

A **sprain** is an injury to the tissue that connects bones to a joint. A sprain can occur when a joint is twisted. The tissue stretches or tears. There is sharp pain, soreness, and swelling. To help someone with a sprain, use the PRICE treatment. If swelling and soreness continue, you should be checked by a physician.

▼ **Wearing proper safety gear will reduce the risk of injury.**

The PRICE Treatment

PRICE stands for protect, rest, ice, compression, and elevation. Use the PRICE treatment for muscle soreness, muscle spasms, strains, sprains, and bruises. The sooner you apply PRICE to an injury, the better. Apply the five steps together. Seek medical treatment if PRICE does not work after a day or two.

The PRICE treatment includes the following steps:

1. **Protect** the injured part from further injury by immobilizing it.

2. **Rest** the injured part.

3. **Ice** the injured part with a cold compress or ice pack.

4. **Compress** with an elastic bandage to stop bleeding. Be careful not to apply the bandage too tightly. Check the body part for pain, numbness, and change in color. After 30 minutes, remove the bandage and ice for 15 minutes. Then reapply the ice and bandage for 30 minutes. Repeat the procedure for three hours.

5. **Elevate** the injured part above the level of the heart. This drains the blood and fluid from the injured area.

 **For what injuries would you use the PRICE treatment?**

BUILD ACTIVITY

Character

Be Prepared

Responsibility With a partner, perform dialogue (only) to show how this situation is resolved. You are playing softball at the park with a group of friends and your younger brother. Your brother runs to catch a ball, trips, and scrapes his knee. The scrape is bleeding. Your brother wants to continue the game. What is the responsible action for you to take?

◀ **It is important to follow all five steps of the PRICE treatment.**

LESSON **6** REVIEW

Review Concepts

1. **List** the steps included in the PRICE treatment.

2. **Name** five ways to prevent injuries when you participate in outdoor sports.

3. **Explain** why it is important to set aside at least two days a week for recovery from vigorous physical activity.

Critical Thinking

4. **Determine** why experts recommend including slow stretches in your warm-up routine.

5. **LIFE SKILLS** **Make Responsible Decisions** Your friend wants you to ice skate in very cold weather. What can you do to prevent injuries?

CHAPTER 5 REVIEW

Chapter Summary

Lesson 1 • Being well groomed promotes health and well-being. You should adopt healthful habits to care for your skin, hair, and nails.

Lesson 2 • Regular physical examinations are important to maintaining your health. You should have regular exams to care for your eyes and ears.

Lesson 3 • To protect your teeth and gums, it is important to follow a dental health plan.

Lesson 4 • Regular physical activity benefits all three areas of health. You can change your lifestyle to become more physically active.

Lesson 5 • Before making a physical fitness plan, you should evaluate your resources and assess your level of fitness. Following a physical fitness plan has many health benefits.

Lesson 6 • You can learn to prevent and treat physical activity-related injuries.

Use Vocabulary

grooming, C5

acne, C7

astigmatism, C16

noise pollution, C17

dental plaque, C22

gingivitis, C25

aerobic exercise, C29

warm-up, C37

sprain, C42

Choose the correct term from the list to complete each sentence.

1. An exercise that helps the body take in and use more oxygen for a period of time is a(n) _____?_____.

2. An injury to the tissue that connects bones to a joint is called a(n) _____?_____.

3. A vision problem in which the cornea or the lens of the eye is curved unevenly, causing blurred vision, is called _____?_____.

4. A sticky substance containing bacteria that forms on teeth is called _____?_____.

5. Everything that a person does to stay clean and have a healthful appearance is _____?_____.

6. A skin disorder with pimples, whiteheads, and blackheads is called _____?_____.

7. A condition in which the gums are sore and bleed easily is _____?_____.

8. Before exercising, it is important to engage in a _____?_____, a period of three to five minutes of easy physical activity.

9. Loud or constant noise that causes hearing loss and stress is _____?_____.

Review Concepts

Answer each question in complete sentences.

10. How can you protect your ears when you're exposed to loud noise?

11. What function does the enamel of the tooth have?

12. How does physical activity benefit your mental and emotional health?

13. What should you keep in mind when developing a physical fitness plan?

14. How should you treat a cut?

Reading Comprehension

Answer each question in complete sentences.

You can care for your teeth and gums by reducing the amount of sugar in your diet. Sugar is a major cause of tooth decay. Sugar and bacteria in dental plaque form an acid that breaks down the enamel of the tooth and causes decay. Candies dissolve slowly in your mouth and contribute to tooth decay because the sugar stays near the teeth for a long time.

15. How does sugar cause tooth decay?

16. How might the habit of sucking on candy contribute to tooth decay?

Critical Thinking/Problem Solving

Answer each question in complete sentences.

17. Why is it important to practice good hygiene?

18. Distinguish between farsightedness, nearsightedness, and astigmatism.

19. Contrast the functions of the incisors and the canines.

20. Summarize the importance of warming up before activity and cooling down after activity.

21. Describe the three things you should consider when using a helmet for physical activities.

Practice Life Skills

22. Be a Health Advocate You want to encourage teens in your community to be physically active. How can you motivate them to participate in regular physical activity?

23. Make Responsible Decisions You are jogging with friends and have become short of breath. You also have a pain in your chest. What are your options? Use the Guidelines to explain what the responsible decision is.

Read Graphics

Use the text in the visual below to answer the questions.

24. According to the chart, if a 145-pound man walked for one hour, about how many calories could he burn?

25. What activity on the chart burns the most calories?

Activity	Calories Burned in 1 Hour for a 140 to 150-Pound Person
Walking	160–170
Jogging	512–544
Dancing	288–306

Source: Mayo Clinic

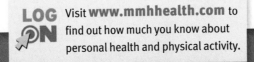

LOG ON Visit **www.mmhhealth.com** to find out how much you know about personal health and physical activity.

CHAPTER 6
Violence and Injury Prevention

Lesson 1 • Reducing the Risk of Violence, C48

Lesson 2 • Being Safe at School and in the Community, C54

Lesson 3 • Being Safe at Home and Outdoors, C62

Lesson 4 • Severe Weather and Natural Disasters, C68

Lesson 5 • The Rules of First Aid, C74

Lesson 6 • Basic First Aid Skills, C78

FIRST AID KIT

What Do You Know About
Violence and Injury Prevention?

1. What are some responsible ways to manage anger?

2. How can you keep safe during a tornado?

3. What is cardiopulmonary resuscitation?

NEIGHBORHOOD CRIME WATCH

We immediately report all SUSPICIOUS PERSONS activities to our Police

CAUTION

WET FLOOR

NO TRESPASS VIOLATO BE PRO

The Inside Story

Preventing Injuries

Injuries can occur in the blink of an eye. One moment, you and your friends are having fun playing baseball. The next moment, someone has fallen while running toward home plate and needs help right away. Injuries at home, at school, and outdoors are among the most common reasons for emergency care. However, you can protect yourself, your family, and your friends by learning to prevent the most common injuries.

LOG ON Visit **www.mmhhealth.com** to learn more about violence and injury prevention.

Reducing the Risk of Violence

You will learn . . .

- factors that promote the risk of violence.
- forms of violence.
- forms of and signs of abuse.
- warning signs of suicide.
- responsible ways to manage anger.

Violence is part of our world, but it does not need to be part of your life. Knowing the forms of violence and the factors that promote the risk of violence can help you recognize violence around you before it starts. That is the first step in reducing the risk of violence.

Vocabulary

- **weapon,** C49
- **prejudice,** C49
- **suicide,** C49
- **physical abuse,** C50
- **emotional abuse,** C50
- **sexual abuse,** C50
- **mediator,** C53

What Is Violence?

Violence is the use of force to harm someone or to destroy property. Violence can include name-calling, fighting, stealing, bullying, and using weapons. A **weapon** is any device used to inflict violence.

Factors that Promote the Risk of Violence

Violence is rooted in a person's mental and emotional health as well as social and family health. It also is rooted in a person's character and surroundings. Factors that promote the risk of violence (the chance that violence will occur) include

Being unable to handle emotions and stress Sometimes people keep emotions and stress locked inside until they "blow up," using angry words or actions.

Living with family violence Some people see violence in their homes. Parents may hurt each other or their children. Children who grow up in these homes are more likely to harm themselves and others.

Wanting material things Sometimes people steal to get what they want or need. Stealing is a crime. It can result in injury and death.

Negative self-esteem People who have negative self-esteem may give in to negative peer pressure, use harmful drugs, and join gangs.

Facing negative peer pressure To show loyalty to peers such as gang members or bullies, some teens act against their values and commit crimes.

Using alcohol and other harmful drugs More than half of all violent crimes are committed by people who are under the influence of alcohol and other drugs.

Using weapons Violent acts are more likely to occur when weapons are available.

Prejudice **Prejudice** is an opinion formed before all the facts are known. It involves making judgments about people because they belong to a particular race or religion. It can lead to acts of violence called hate crimes.

Depression Depression is a feeling of sadness, unhappiness, or discouragement that lasts for weeks or months. It can cause teens to attempt **suicide**, the taking of one's own life on purpose.

 **What are the causes of violence?**

Form of Violence	Description
Fighting	taking part in a physical struggle
Sexual harassment	unwanted sexual comments or touches
Domestic violence	violence within the family
Hate crimes	violence against people because they belong to a particular group, such as a race or religion
Rape	threatened or actual use of force to have sex with someone without consent or to have sex with a minor
Homicide	killing a person, either unintentionally or on purpose
Suicide	taking one's life on purpose

Character

Responsible Responses

Responsibility Write each of the following on a separate index card:

- put downs
- a challenge to a fight
- continued teasing

Shuffle the cards. Each student in a small group picks a card and replaces it. The student must describe one responsible way to respond to examples of abuse, using the Guidelines for Making Responsible Decisions™.

What Is Abuse?

Abuse is the harmful treatment of another person. Some kinds of abuse are physical, but people may also be abused in ways that do not leave bruises or scars. Put-downs, threats, and humiliating actions are all harmful, even if they do not involve physical force.

Forms of Abuse

Abuse takes many forms. It can affect anyone. Child abuse occurs when parents, guardians, or child care workers harm a minor. Parent abuse happens when a child harms a parent. Spouse abuse happens when one partner in a marriage harms the other. Abuse also is classified by the kind of harm involved.

Physical abuse is harmful treatment of a person that results in physical injury. Hitting, burning, and beating are all examples of physical abuse. Physical abuse also can occur when parents, guardians, or others use objects to discipline children.

Emotional abuse is harmful verbal or non-verbal treatment that lowers a person's self-esteem. This kind of abuse includes yelling, teasing, threats, harsh criticism, shunning or ignoring.

Sexual abuse is sexual behavior that is forced on a person. Sexual abuse can occur among people of any age. Rape and sexual harassment are common forms of sexual abuse.

Neglect is the failure to provide proper care and guidance. Neglect includes failing to provide educational and emotional needs, as well as physical needs such as medical care. Leaving a young child home alone is neglect. So is repeatedly ignoring a child or failing to feed him or her.

◀ **Talk to a responsible adult if you are threatened by abuse.**

Recognizing Abuse

People don't always realize that they are being abused. Even when they do, they may not tell others about the abuse. People who are being abused may be ashamed. They may feel as if the abuse is their fault. In addition, the person inflicting the abuse may have threatened to do more harm if the abused person tells anyone about the abuse.

Signs/effects of abuse People who are being abused often stay silent about the abuse but show signs of the abuse. They may cut themselves off from their peers. They may be depressed. They may fail to show up for planned activities. They also may have bruises or other injuries.

Students who are being abused may miss school, show a sudden drop in their grades, and show little interest in schoolwork and homework. They may show signs of neglect, such as poor hygiene or dirty clothes.

Responding to abuse If you are being abused or if you suspect someone else is being abused, you need to report it. Students can talk to teachers or counselors and other responsible adults at school. They can join support groups. Abuse is against the law. Someone in immediate danger of physical or sexual abuse should call the police or go to a shelter or crisis center.

What are some of the ways people can be abused?

Analyze What Influences Your Health

Relationships that you have seen portrayed in movies and on television may involve abuse. Work with a group of students to form a review committee.

1 Identify people and things that might influence you. Committee members can identify TV and film characters who treat each other with respect. Name any who do not. Explain your reasons. Members should get information from newspaper and magazine reviews without actually seeing the TV shows and movies.

2 Evaluate how the influence might affect your health and decisions. Committee members should summarize the effect movies and TV shows showing healthful relationships can have on health and decisions.

3 Choose positive influences on health. The committee can publish a "top ten/must see" list of films and TV shows that focus on healthful relationships. For each name on the list, the committee states qualities of the program that make it positive. Before sharing it with the class, the group members should check with parents, guardians, or other responsible adults.

4 Protect yourself from negative influences on health. The committee can also publish a "keep away" list of films and TV shows that focus on harmful relationships.

Preventing Violence

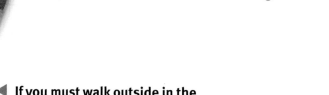

ACTIVITY
Social Studies
LINK
Community Map

Working in a group, make a map of places in the community where people can go for help if they become victims of violence or any form of abuse. Plot the locations of crisis centers, shelters, police stations, hospitals, youth organizations, and religious organizations that provide housing and counseling.

The best way to stop violence is to prevent it. If someone challenged you to fight, what would you do? Step back and think about your options. Walk away. The following ideas will help you prevent violence.

- **Don't carry a weapon.** Weapons increase the chance of serious injury.
- **Don't use alcohol or other drugs,** and never argue with someone who does.
- **Stay away from gangs.**
- **Don't go out alone** with someone you don't know well.
- **Don't walk alone** after dark.
- **Don't open the door** unless you know who is there. If you are alone, don't let a stranger in, no matter who it is.
- **Don't let a stranger know you are alone.**
- **Call the police or 9-1-1** (or whatever your local emergency number may be). Call the operator (0) if you need help.

Suicide Warning Signs

If you think someone plans to hurt himself, herself, or others, tell a teacher, counselor, or security guard right away. Also immediately tell a responsible adult if someone has a weapon in school.

Certain behaviors may indicate that someone is depressed or is considering suicide. A person who talks about death, suicide, or "going away," or who pulls away from friends may be considering suicide.

Major changes in appearance, such as extreme messiness, a loss of interest in activities, or sudden cheerfulness after a long period of sadness may also indicate suicidal thoughts.

◀ If you must walk outside in the evening, travel with a group.

Managing Anger

You let a friend borrow your math book. He calls to tell you that his little brother tore pages out of it. You get angry because you feel your friend should have taken care of your book. How can you get your anger out in a healthful way?

- **Do what you need to do to calm down.** Say goodbye, hang up, do something that helps you cool off. Write about your feelings. Share what you write with a parent or guardian.

- **Talk about your feelings with someone you trust.** Ask for help if needed.

- **Talk to the person who is making you angry.** Stay calm and think before you speak. Define the problem and how it makes you feel. Use I-messages, such as, "I'm angry because I trusted you with my book." Think of solutions to the problem that will make you less angry.

If these steps don't work, ask a **mediator**, a trusted adult, to help settle the conflict. A mediator does not take sides or solve the problem for you. He or she helps you define the problem and come up with possible solutions that appeal to everyone involved.

▲ Using I-messages can help resolve a conflict.

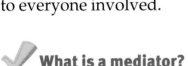 **What is a mediator?**

LESSON 1 REVIEW

Review Concepts

1. **List** three forms of violence.

2. **Describe** how a friend might act if his parents were abusing him.

3. **Identify** signs that might let you know a friend is thinking about suicide.

4. **Discuss** responsible ways of dealing with anger.

Critical Thinking

5. **Evaluate** Think about a recent disagreement you've had. Did you resolve your conflict in a healthful way? Describe how you would handle the problem if it occurred again.

6. **LIFE SKILLS** **Analyze What Influences Your Health** Make a list of people in your life who help improve your self-esteem. What do they do to boost your self-esteem? How does their positive influence contribute to your well-being?

Being Safe at School and in the Community

You will learn ...

- protective factors to reduce the risk of violence in schools and the community.

- ways to get help when harmed by violence.

- ways schools and communities promote safety.

Vocabulary

- protective factors, C55

- self-protection, C55

- street smart, C55

- bullying, C56

- gang, C57

You may have read stories about places where there were no gangs, no bullies, and no weapons, where everyone felt safe. You have learned that neighborhoods and even school may not be as safe as you may have thought. You can learn ways to be safe in your environment. You can work with other teens to make your environment safer.

Safety in the Community

Violence can affect any community. However, you can reduce your risk, or chance, of being involved in violence by practicing protective factors. **Protective factors** are ways a person behaves or characteristics of a person's surroundings that promote health and safety. For example, recognizing violent behavior is a protective factor. Another is practicing self-protection. **Self-protection** means taking steps to protect oneself.

Being Street Smart

You can practice protective factors by being street smart outside your home. **Street smart** means being aware of possible danger and knowing what to do. It also means being alert and making responsible decisions.

For example, always tell a parent or guardian where you are going, and call when you get there. Carry identification and money. Walk in groups if possible.

Be aware of your surroundings and avoid dangerous places. Do not walk close to parked cars, bushes, or doorways where someone can hide. If someone attacks you, make as much noise as you can. Blow a whistle, scream, or yell "Help!" If you feel threatened, find a phone and dial 9-1-1, or whatever your local emergency number may be. Give up personal belongings rather than risk being hurt.

Safety from Weapons

Weapons include not only guns and knives but anything used for violence. The most basic protective factor is to stay clear of weapons to avoid injury. Do not carry a weapon. Stay away from people who have weapons. Never pretend that you have a weapon.

If you find a weapon, or if someone shows you one, don't touch it. Leave immediately and tell a responsible adult. Always assume a gun is loaded and can go off. In addition, consider your safety if someone has an object such as a bat or razor that could be used as a weapon.

 What are some ways you can stay safe on the street?

▶ **Always let a responsible adult know where you are and when you will be home.**

Safety in School

School is usually one of the safest places you can be. Yet you should be alert to possible violence in school. Bullying, sexual harassment, and weapons are some dangers teens may face at school.

Bullying **Bullying** is hurting or threatening someone younger, weaker, or smaller. Some teens bully by teasing a person about something that makes him or her different. Others physically harm people. If you are bullied at school, don't fight back with violence. Walk away. If you need help, talk to a teacher or counselor.

Sexual Harassment Sexual harassment often takes the form of unwanted touching. However, it may also involve making sexual comments, jokes, or gestures about another person, or asking someone out on a date repeatedly when he or she has said "no."

If you are being sexually harassed, tell the other person to stop. Report what is happening to the proper authority. Tell your parents or guardians. Keep a log of each incident so you can make an official complaint, and include the date, time, what happened, and witnesses' names.

Weapons School shootings occur for many reasons. Sometimes they occur because students are frustrated about their own problems. These students take out their anger on their classmates and teachers. School shootings are rare. However, if you hear a student say that he or she has a gun, or if you see a student with a gun, tell a responsible adult immediately.

Protective Factors at School

Practice these behaviors to stay safe at school. Stay away from gangs and fights. Don't use, buy, or sell drugs, and keep away from those who participate in these actions. Don't carry a weapon or keep one at school. Tell an adult if someone threatens to harm you.

▲ Practice protective measures to increase your safety at school.

Avoiding Gangs

A **gang** is a group of people who usually are involved in dangerous or illegal activities. Gangs may adopt a particular name, symbol, color, or type of clothing to identify themselves. Gangs can be a dangerous force in communities and even in schools.

Gangs may appeal to teens by offering them excitement, protection, money, or a sense of belonging. They don't give a clear picture of the dangers of gang life. Gang members commit many of the serious violent crimes in the United States.

Many community groups try to get rid of gangs by working against violence. In Montgomery, Alabama, a group called Fathers Active in Children's Education planned a Stop the Violence rally and celebrity basketball game. They had students sign a "Stop the Violence" pledge.

Follow these guidelines to avoid gang-related problems.

- Stay away from gang members.
- Avoid places where gang members hang out.
- Do not dress in gang colors or clothes.
- Do not write the symbol for a gang on anything that belongs to you.
- Get involved in after-school activities, such as soccer or drama.
- Do not use drugs, including alcohol or tobacco products.
- Obey laws.
- Spend time with your family.
- Do not skip school.

 **What is a gang?**

Avoiding gangs and gang behavior is the objective of a nationwide program. The Gang Resistance Education and Training (G.R.E.A.T.) Program helps young people set goals, resist pressures, and resolve conflicts without violence.

▼ **Participating in after-school activities will help you avoid gang-related problems.**

Design a Mural

SHINE, an organization that helps teens build a better society, runs a project that uses artwork to promote peace. Known as Harmony Sidewalk Murals, the project allows teens to design murals to illustrate the positive aspects of their community. Try this activity with your class. Think about the positive aspects of your school. On a large sheet of brown wrapping paper, design a mural illustrating the best features of your school community.

Making a Difference

Students and staff at schools and community members can take two important steps to deal with violence. First, help must be made available for those who are affected by violence. Second, people of all ages must work together to promote safety and prevent violence.

Finding Help

A person who is harmed by violence or abuse needs help. First, the abuse must be reported to a responsible person. A physical exam may be needed to check for injuries and diseases. The person may need treatment for injuries or diseases. Counseling—for anger, fear, and inability to trust—may be needed. In addition, support from family and friends can help the individual recover.

Another source of information is an organization such as the National Center for Victims of Crime. Other local groups also can provide help.

Set Health Goals

Use a health behavior contract to set an important goal.

1 **Write the health goal you want to set:** *I will protect myself from people who might harm me.*

2 **Tell how the goal will affect your health.** Summarize how your mental and physical health may be affected if there is less violence at school.

3 **Describe a plan you will follow. Keep track of your progress.** Work with a group. Make a list of the steps your class can take to reduce the risk of violence in school. For example, how can you help others resolve conflicts? Put your plan into action and encourage your classmates to work with you.

4 **Evaluate how your plan worked.** Record how you put your plan into action each day. What are your results after one week? How might you adjust your plan to make it more effective?

STOP the VIOLENCE Before It Starts!

Promoting Safety in Schools

Schools all over the country are looking for the best ways to keep students safe. Some schools focus on changing the school environment or teaching students how to manage anger and conflict. Other approaches used by schools include

- suspension or expulsion.
- alternative programs for violent students.
- mediation and conflict-resolution programs.
- mentoring programs, in which a responsible older person guides a younger person.
- student photo identification and fingerprinting.
- work and volunteer opportunities.
- metal and explosives detectors.
- classroom telephones.
- safe havens.
- multicultural sensitivity training.

▶ **Young people who are troubled by abuse or violence can talk to a counselor or another responsible adult.**

In North Carolina, students, parents, teachers, and police worked together to organize a program called "Bullies Don't Belong." What are your ideas about how to stop school violence?

Promoting Safety in Communities

To promote safety, communities are putting more police on the streets—on horseback and on foot as well as in patrol cars. Tougher laws are being enforced. Neighborhood watches and safe havens are increasing. Lighting in public places is being improved to deter crime.

 How are schools promoting safety?

LESSON 2 REVIEW

Review Concepts

1. **List** people and resources that can help you if you have been affected by violence.

2. **Discuss** ways you can be safe at school.

3. **Identify** methods to avoid weapon-related violence.

Critical Thinking

4. **Recommend** One of your classmates has confided to you that she is being sexually harassed at school. Where can you suggest she get help?

5. **LIFE SKILLS** **Set Health Goals** What steps can you follow to achieve a goal of staying away from gangs?

Resolve Conflicts

Dear Health Nut,

Here's the problem . . . I keep a tiny stapler in my pencil case so I can staple my assignments. Other students know I have a stapler, and they often "borrow" it without asking. I don't like it when they go through my things, and I'm angry because I run out of staples quickly and have to buy more. How can I settle this problem?

Staple-less in Seattle

Dear Staple-less in Seattle,

Here is how you might solve the problem . . . You need to try to resolve the conflict with your classmates. This situation makes you angry because you are losing both your privacy and your staples. Use the steps on the next page to help you resolve the conflict in a healthful way.

Health Nut

C60

Learn This Life Skill

There are four steps to resolving conflicts. Follow these steps to help you work out the problem with your classmates.

1 **Stay calm.**

Yelling will just make people upset. Keep calm so you can explain the problem clearly. Make a list of five ways you can stay calm when things get tough.

2 **Talk about the conflict.**

Before you start, make a list of rules you will observe (no yelling, no name-calling, and so on). Use I-messages, such as "I don't like my stapler being borrowed without my knowing," to explain to your classmates how you feel.

3 **Discuss possible ways to settle the conflict.**

Check out each way to settle the conflict. Use the Guidelines for Making Responsible Decisions™.

- Is it healthful?
- Is it safe?
- Is it legal?
- Do I show respect for myself and others?
- Do I follow the guidelines of responsible adults, such as my parents or guardians?
- Do I demonstrate good character?

4 **Agree on a way to settle the conflict. You may need to ask a trusted adult for help.**

Decide together on a solution that all of you will follow. If it is too hard to reach a solution, you may need to ask a trusted adult for help or mediation.

Resolve Conflicts

1. Stay calm.

2. Talk about the conflict.

3. Discuss possible ways to settle the conflict.

4. Agree on a way to settle the conflict. You may need to ask a trusted adult for help.

You can work in a group to participate in this activity in many ways: writing, folding, drawing, or even role-playing.

Practice This Life Skill

Activity Two students argue over who should get the last locker at school. Write a short skit describing ways they might solve the conflict.

Being Safe at Home and Outdoors

You will learn . . .

- how to be safe in the kitchen.
- how to prevent falls, fires, electric shock, poisoning, and suffocation.
- how to be safe at home and outdoors.
- how to be safe in motor vehicles and when walking, biking, and skating.
- how to be safe while hiking and swimming.

Vocabulary

- **hazards,** C63
- **smoke alarm,** C64
- **flammable,** C64
- **burglary,** C66

Working around your home can be fun. However, be on the alert for possible injury. Unintentional injuries—that is, injuries caused by unexpected events—can be prevented if you follow safety guidelines at home.

Safety in the Kitchen

An unexpected event that can lead to an unintentional injury is called an *accident*. To prevent an unintentional injury, be on the lookout for habits or conditions that can cause an accident. For example, do not take unnecessary risks. A *risk* is a chance of loss or harm. Climbing on a countertop to reach a shelf, for example, is an unnecessary risk. Using a sturdy step stool is safer. Be aware of hazards. **Hazards** are possible sources of harm or danger in and around the home. When you spot a hazard, take steps to prevent injury. Start by looking for possible hazards in the kitchen.

Foodborne illness People can become ill if they eat food that contains certain pathogens, disease-causing organisms or particles. When you work in the kitchen, keep pathogens off food by washing your hands with soap and water before you start. After touching foods (such as raw meat, fish, eggs, and poultry) wash your hands, kitchen countertops, and cutting boards with soap and warm water. Many fruits and vegetables are sprayed with pesticides to protect them from insects. Wash these foods carefully before preparing or eating them. Prevent food illness by setting the temperature in the refrigerator at 40°F and the freezer at 0°F.

Unintentional injuries Do not run in the kitchen. Keep small children and pets out of the kitchen while you are working there. Clean up spills right away. Use knives with care, and only with your parents' or guardian's permission. When you are chopping or slicing, use a cutting board. Make sure the blade of the knife is pointed away from you and your fingers.

Burns Use potholders and oven mitts to handle pots and pans that have been in the oven or on the stove. Point pot handles toward the back of the stove to avoid spills and burns.

What steps should you take to avoid food-related illness?

▼ **Take care to prevent unintentional injuries in the kitchen.**

Safety in the Home and Outdoors

Unintentional injuries are the leading cause of death for people between the ages of 1 and 34. You can reduce the risk of these injuries by being aware of the hazards at home and while walking, biking, skating, and riding in cars.

HOW TO BE SAFE AT HOME

Hazard	Prevention	Response to Injury or Emergency
Fires	Install a **smoke alarm**, a device that alerts individuals to dangerous levels of smoke. Keep objects that are **flammable**, or able to catch fire easily, away from fireplaces, lamps, and stoves. Practice a fire escape plan. Know two exits from each room. Know where to meet at a given spot outside.	Drop a lid on small stove fires. For small electrical fires, unplug the appliance and smother the fire with a towel. Don't use water. If a large fire starts, get out! Drop to your knees and crawl to the nearest exit if a room is filled with smoke. Touch the door before opening it. If it is hot, find a different way out.
Falls	Keep rugs in place with pads. Keep objects off floors and stairs. Keep a sturdy step stool or ladder on hand for reaching shelves. Install handrails on staircases and grab bars in bathrooms. Use nightlights to make walking at night easier. If there is an infant or young child in the house, install safety gates at the top and bottom of stairs.	Call 9-1-1 (or whatever the local emergency number may be) if the person seems to have a head injury or broken bones.
Electric Shock	Cover unused outlets. Unplug any unused appliances. Place stereos and televisions against walls so infants and young children cannot reach cords.	Call the local emergency number. Disconnect the electrical source. Check to see if the person is breathing. If not, start rescue breathing. (See page C80.)
Poisoning	Keep medicines and cleaning supplies in locked cabinets. Keep purses out of children's reach. If you live in an old building, have the paint tested for lead.	Call poison control or the local emergency number. Try to figure out what substance the person swallowed.
Suffocation	Keep plastic bags out of children's reach. Never place an infant face down on soft bedding, pillows, or a mattress covered with plastic. Don't let infants play with large stuffed animals.	Call the local emergency number. Check the person's airway. Begin rescue breathing.

Safety in motor vehicles Wear a seat belt at all times. If you are 12 or younger, sit in the back seat. Do not ride with someone who has been drinking alcohol. Do not distract the driver. Do not stick your head or hands out of the vehicle.

Safety while walking Use sidewalks and crosswalks. If there is no sidewalk, walk on the left side of the road, facing traffic. Wear reflective clothing in the dark, and do not wear headphones in traffic. Do not cross when a traffic light is changing, and do not enter the street between parked cars. Do not hitchhike.

Safety while biking Wear a safety helmet and closed-toe shoes for riding. Do not wear pants that might get caught in the bicycle chain. At night, wear light-colored clothing. Keep your bike in good working order, and attach reflectors to it so it will be visible at night. Ride single file, obey traffic signs and signals, and use proper hand signals: extend left arm and hand out to the left for a *left turn;* bend left elbow and point left hand up for a *right turn;* point down for a *stop.* Follow the same rules of the road as for cars. Walk your bike through intersections.

Safety while hiking Get permission to camp or hike from a parent or guardian, and have an adult accompany you. Tell a responsible adult the trail you will take and stay on it. Take a first aid kit and fresh water, identification, and money. Check the weather report and dress for the weather. Choose a safe campsite. When you leave, put your campfire out with water and smother it with dirt or sand.

Safety while skating Wear a helmet, knee and elbow pads, gloves, and wrist guards. Do not skate in traffic. Learn how to stop quickly.

Safety in the water Know how to swim. Never swim alone. Swim only when a lifeguard is on duty. Get out of the water during a storm.

✓ **What are some ways to be safe while riding in a car?**

◀ **Follow safety guidelines when you hike or camp.**

Avoiding Danger at Home

Being safe in your home involves knowing what to do in the event of a stranger coming to the door as well as keeping your home secure.

Strangers Some of the dangers that affect people at home come from outside. For instance, you are looking out your window and see a stranger crouching in the bushes below. The stranger might be about to commit burglary. **Burglary** is a crime in which a person breaks into a shop, home, or other location to steal something. If you see a stranger lurking near your home, tell an adult. Know your local emergency number and your police station number, in case you need to call for help.

Not every burglar is easy to identify. Sometimes burglars knock on the front door and pretend to be someone they are not. Always ask visitors to identify themselves. Ask your parents if you may open the door. Be sure your parents know that you are opening the door. Do not open the door for strangers for any reason.

Locks It is also important to keep your home secure. Always lock the door. Use a deadbolt if your door has one. Make sure that ground-floor windows are secure, too.

Weapons Another danger that affects families is weapons. Some families choose to keep guns for hunting and for protection. Many injuries occur when children find loaded guns in their homes. Parents or guardians should keep guns and ammunition locked in separate cabinets. If you find a gun at home or at a friend's house, don't touch it. Leave the area, and tell an adult.

◀ Locking the door helps reduce the risk of burglary.

At Home with a Childsitter

Parents or guardians may need to leave their child with a childsitter while they go out on an errand. Childsitters and the children they watch need to follow the same household safety information noted on page C66. In addition, childsitters must

- never leave children alone.
- look in on sleeping children frequently.
- never invite friends over.
- never let a stranger know that the adults are away.
- have a list of emergency phone numbers and numbers where the adults can be reached.
- know ahead of time when the adults are returning.

 **What is burglary?**

Make Responsible Decisions

Role-play this situation with two partners: You are home with a childsitter but no adults. A friend calls, asking you to come over to work on a group project for school.

1. **Identify your choices. Check them out with a parent or another trusted adult.** List the choices you may need to make. Consider all the safety issues.

2. **Evaluate each choice. Use the Guidelines for Making Responsible Decisions™.** Decide which questions fit this situation and ask them about each of your choices.
   - Is it healthful?
   - Is it safe?
   - Is it legal?
   - Do I show respect for myself and others?
   - Do I follow the guidelines of responsible adults, such as my parents or guardian?
   - Do I demonstrate good character?

3. **Tell what the responsible decision is. Check this out with your parent or another trusted adult.** Based on the answers to the questions you asked about each choice, state the most responsible decision.

4. **Evaluate your decision.** Would the decision you make protect your safety?

LESSON 3 REVIEW

Review Concepts

1. **Discuss** how to prevent falls in your home.

2. **List** three ways to prevent electric shock in your home.

3. **Identify** ways to be safe in the kitchen.

Critical Thinking

4. **Prepare** You and your friend are going hiking. What can you take with you to keep you safe?

5. **LIFE SKILLS** **Make Responsible Decisions** You have noticed that your family does not have a smoke alarm in every room of your house. What is the responsible thing to tell your parents?

Severe Weather and Natural Disasters

You will learn . . .

- ways to stay safe during storms.
- ways to stay safe in hot and cold weather.
- ways to stay safe during natural disasters.

Vocabulary

- natural disaster, C69
- electrical storm, C69
- blizzard, C69
- whiteout, C69
- heat exhaustion, C70
- heatstroke, C70
- frostbite, C71
- hypothermia, C71
- flood, C73

What do you think of when you hear the word *severe?* Severe means harsh or brutal. Blistering heat, biting cold, and powerful storms are a few types of severe weather you might experience. You are not able to control the weather, but you can learn to respond appropriately and stay safe in severe conditions.

Safety During Storms

A **natural disaster** is an event caused by nature that results in heavy damage. It is important to be prepared and to follow safety guidelines during natural disasters.

In the summer, you may see an **electrical storm,** a storm with bolts of lightning. In the winter, you may see a **blizzard,** a heavy snowstorm with strong winds. Safety precautions can help you and your family avoid harm during storms.

Electrical Storms

You can take precautions to protect yourself from electrical storms. If you are outside and hear thunder, take shelter in a building or a car. Avoid tall objects such as trees, flagpoles, and metal fences, which attract lightning. Get out of and stay away from bodies of water. Water conducts electricity.

If your skin tingles or your hair stands on end, lightning may be about to strike near you. Roll your body into a ball. Making yourself smaller reduces your risk of getting hit by lightning.

If you are inside during a storm, unplug appliances and do not take a bath or shower. Use the telephone only in an emergency. Keep away from the fireplace in case the chimney is struck by lightning.

Blizzards

Blowing snow makes it hard to see, walk, and drive. The storm may cause power lines to fall. People can become electrocuted if they touch fallen power lines. A **whiteout** is a severe blizzard in which a person cannot see the horizon and can only make out dark shapes. People can get lost in whiteouts and freeze to death.

Prepare your home to stay safe during blizzards. Encourage your family to install storm windows. If you have a fireplace, keep a supply of wood nearby. A kerosene heater is a good alternate source of heat if the power goes out.

During a blizzard, don't go out until the storm lets up. When you go outside, dress warmly and cover your mouth.

 **What is a whiteout?**

▶ **Blizzards can cause many hazards.**

Science LINK

Temperature Graph

Use a household thermometer or listen to the weather report to find the temperature at four times during the day, such as 9 A.M., noon, 3 P.M., and 7 P.M. Repeat the observations for a week. Make a line graph with multiple lines in different colors to show the temperature readings for the different days. How did the days compare? Which days had the highest and lowest readings? On which days did the temperature change the most?

Weather Extremes and Health

Have you ever stepped outside into extremely hot weather? Have you taken a walk on a day when it was so cold that your face stung? Weather extremes are not just uncomfortable. They can also cause serious injuries unless you take safety precautions.

Hot Weather

A beautiful summer day can be filled with fun activities, but you must protect yourself in hot temperatures. Dress in light-colored, lightweight clothes and wear sunscreen to protect exposed skin, such as your face. Stay in the shade as much as possible. Try to stay indoors during the hottest parts of the day. You may perspire heavily in hot weather, so drink lots of water.

Not following these guidelines can result in heat exhaustion. **Heat exhaustion** is extreme tiredness from being in hot temperatures. The person experiences nausea and the pulse rate speeds up. The person becomes weak and dizzy. If someone develops heat exhaustion, call emergency services. Then have the person rest in a cool place with his or her feet elevated. Give the person water to drink. If possible, offer a salty snack. Loosen the person's clothing.

Watch for signs of heatstroke. **Heatstroke** is an overheating of the body that is life threatening. The person's body temperature increases. The pulse becomes rapid. The person may stop sweating and collapse. To help, call emergency services. Have the person rest in a cool place and remove any heavy clothing. Wrap the person in cool, wet towels or sheets. Place ice packs near the person's neck, armpits, and groin.

◀ **Drink plenty of fluids during hot weather.**

Cold Weather

If you live in or visit an area that has cold winters, you may enjoy skating, making snowballs, and sledding. Be sure to bundle up. Dress in multiple, thin, loose layers. Wear waterproof boots, gloves or mittens, and a hat. Keep as dry as possible. If your clothes get wet, change them.

If you do not dress properly in the cold, you could get **frostbite**, a condition in which a person's body tissues freeze. Frostbite can numb and discolor the fingers, toes, nose, and earlobes. To help a person with frostbite, call the local emergency number. Find a responsible adult to take the person to a medical facility. The medical professionals will warm the frostbitten body parts by soaking them in warm water. They will place moist cloths on the person's nose, ears, and face. Do not rub frostbitten body parts. It damages the skin.

Another hazard that can occur in cold weather is **hypothermia**, a condition in which a person's body temperature drops from exposure to cold. People with hypothermia may shiver uncontrollably, speak slowly, and seem drowsy. To help a person who has hypothermia, call emergency services. Find a responsible adult to take the person to a medical facility. Wrap the person in blankets and cover his or her head so heat does not escape.

 **What is heatstroke?**

▶ **Proper clothing protects you from the effects of cold weather.**

ACTIVITY
LIFE SKILLS
CRITICAL THINKING

Set Health Goals

Use a health behavior contract to set a health goal. Are you prepared for a natural disaster? Plan ahead so that you and your family members will stay safe.

1. **Write the health goal you want to set:** *I will follow safety guidelines for severe weather and natural disasters.*

2. **Tell how the goal will affect your health.** Write the name of any severe storms or natural disasters that might occur in your area and reasons why you need to be prepared for each.

3. **Describe a plan you will follow. Keep track of your progress.** List the steps you need to take to develop a plan to prepare for the condition listed in step 2. Prepare your emergency kit. Your parents or other trusted adults can help you. You might use a log to note the steps you need to take and when you have completed them.

4. **Evaluate how your plan worked.** Have you completed all your steps? What still needs to be done? Who can help you do it?

▼ **A tornado moves quickly through an area, leaving a well-defined path of destruction behind it.**

Moving Natural Disasters

Several natural disasters move from place to place—hurricanes, tornadoes, and floods—or involve strong motion in a particular place, such as earthquakes.

Hurricanes

A *hurricane* is a tropical storm with heavy rains and winds over 74 miles per hour. Some hurricanes are 400 miles across. The powerful winds circle around the middle, called the eye, which is calm.

Hurricane season lasts from June through November. If you live along the eastern or southern coastlines of the United States, be prepared for a hurricane. Know evacuation routes and where to find hurricane shelters. Prepare an emergency kit with a flashlight, batteries, a battery-operated radio, food, water, and first aid supplies. If a hurricane occurs, follow these safety guidelines. Listen to the radio to find out when the hurricane will arrive. Stay away from windows. Leave the area if you are told to do so. Bring your emergency supplies with you.

Tornadoes

A *tornado* is a violent, spinning windstorm with a funnel-shaped cloud. Its winds can blow faster than 250 miles per hour. Each year, tornadoes in the United States cause about 80 deaths and more than 1,500 injuries.

Prepare for tornadoes by knowing where to go if one strikes. The safest place is a basement or center hallway on the bottom floor of your house. Make sure the place you choose has no windows. Assemble a kit with first aid supplies, canned food, water, a flashlight, batteries, and a battery-operated radio. Keep it handy during the spring and summer, when most tornadoes occur. If a tornado strikes, go to the basement or the ground floor. Stay away from windows. If you are outside, lie flat in a ditch or low area.

Earthquakes

An *earthquake* is a violent shaking of Earth's surface. Earthquakes can cause damage by starting fires and making buildings and bridges collapse. Prepare yourself by knowing the safest places in your home. For example, staying under a sturdy desk or table can protect you from falling objects. If an earthquake occurs, position yourself under a piece of heavy furniture. Keep your head down. Be prepared to take cover again during aftershocks. In the United States, most earthquakes occur along the Pacific coast.

Floods

A **flood** is the overflowing of a body of water onto dry land. Floods occur when rainstorms fill a river or stream with more water than it can hold. A *flash flood* is a flood that occurs suddenly, lasting only a few minutes or hours.

To protect yourself from floods, prepare an emergency kit. Find out about shelters and evacuation routes in your area. If a flood occurs, follow these safety guidelines. Bring any outdoor possessions inside, and move valuables to your home's upper floor. If water rises in your house before you can leave, climb to the attic or roof and wait for help. If you go outside, don't walk or drive through flooded areas. Watch out for fallen power lines.

 **What is a flood?**

LESSON 4 REVIEW

Review Concepts

1. **Discuss** steps someone can take to prevent frostbite.

2. **List** ways to stay safe during an earthquake.

3. **Recommend** activities to avoid during an electrical storm.

Critical Thinking

4. **Apply** You are playing soccer on a hot day. Suddenly, one of your friends collapses on the field. Her skin is hot and dry. What's wrong? What should you do?

5. **LIFE SKILLS** **Set Health Goals** If you live in an area that floods frequently, how would you design a plan to meet the goal of being prepared?

The Rules of First Aid

You will learn . . .

- how to be prepared for any first aid emergency.
- how to take the initial steps of first aid for all emergencies.

Vocabulary

- **emergency,** C75
- **first aid,** C75
- **universal precautions,** C76
- **airway,** C77

"It's an emergency!" Many situations may *seem* like emergencies—such as missing the school bus and needing to get to practice on time—but they are not. A real emergency is a serious matter. Knowing what to do in an emergency will help you remain calm and take the most appropriate action.

Preparation

"Be prepared" is simple but important advice that will help you deal with emergencies. An **emergency** is a serious situation that calls for quick action. In some emergencies, a person needs first aid. **First aid** is the temporary and immediate care given to a person who has a sudden illness or injury. You can help if you are prepared—if you know what to do and have the necessary supplies and equipment.

Getting Help

In many areas, you can dial 9-1-1 to get help from emergency services. In other areas, you should keep numbers of the police station, fire station, and emergency medical services by the phone.

If you need to call for help, stay calm. Tell the operator your name and where the emergency occurred. Explain what happened and who is hurt. Follow the operator's instructions carefully. Stay on the phone until the operator tells you to hang up.

Getting Permission

If the injured person is conscious, you must get written or spoken permission from the person before beginning first aid. If the person is a minor, under 18 years of age, a parent, guardian, or supervising adult can give permission.

 **What is an emergency?**

 **write About It!**

Publish Emergency Guidelines

Write a set of emergency guidelines about how to call for help in your area. Give advice on when to call for help, and provide telephone numbers to use. Describe the local emergency services and the types of assistance they provide. Present your guidelines in a short booklet.

 **American Red Cross**

WHAT BELONGS IN A FIRST AID KIT?

- Activated charcoal
- Adhesive tape
- Antiseptic ointment
- Bandages (different sizes)
- Blanket

- Cold pack
- Disposable gloves and face mask
- Small flashlight and extra batteries
- Gauze pads and roller gauze
- Hand cleaner and bottled water

- Plastic bags
- Scissors and tweezers
- Triangular bandage

First Steps

What would you do if a person on the street collapsed in front of you? First try to get help. Follow basic rules: get help, get permission if the person is conscious, protect yourself, check the person, and be ready to do first aid until help arrives.

Following Universal Precautions

An injured person's body may carry pathogens, disease-causing organisms or particles such as bacteria or viruses. If you come into contact with the blood or bodily fluids of a person with a pathogen, the pathogen could be transferred to your body. To give first aid safely, practice **universal precautions**, the steps taken to keep people from having contact with pathogens in body fluids.

Universal precautions include

- Wear disposable gloves.
- Wash hands with soap and water after you remove gloves.
- Use a face mask or shield when you give first aid for breathing.
- Cover cuts or scrapes on your body and avoid contact with the person's blood.

INJURED PERSON CHECKLIST

Injured Person Check	• Ask the person what happened. If the person can talk, he or she is breathing and has circulation.
	• Tap the person and shout to see if he or she responds.
	• If the person doesn't respond, check for breathing. Place a finger under the nose or near the mouth to feel for air being exhaled. Listen for signs of breathing.
If there are no signs of breathing . . .	• Make a 5-second recheck for breathing signs. Put the person on his or her back and support the head and neck. Tilt the head back and lift the chin to open the mouth. Check for breathing.
If there are still no signs of breathing . . .	• Wear a face mask or shield for protection. Blow two breaths of air into the person's mouth.
	• Check for circulation.
	• Check the person's body for severe bleeding. Follow universal precautions.
	• Check for other illnesses and injuries.

- Dispose of the person's bodily fluids.
- Do not touch your mouth, eyes, or nose while caring for a person.

Checking the Ill or Injured Person

Before starting first aid, you need to check the ill or injured person to determine if the person

- is breathing and/or severely bleeding.
- has an open airway. An **airway** is a passage in the body that takes in air.
- has a heartbeat.
- has any illnesses or injuries.

 **What are universal precautions?**

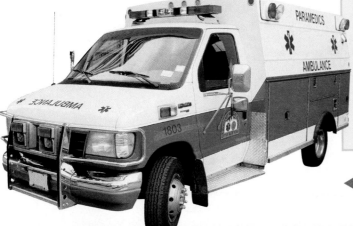

Manage Stress

Dealing with an emergency can be stressful. If you or someone you know has been injured, it is important to remain calm. Deliver a monologue to the class to describe how a person could manage stress in this situation. Think of what might happen if a person is with a friend who has fallen off his or her bicycle and is injured.

1. **Know the signs of stress.** Start your explanation by describing how the person might react upon seeing a friend injured.

2. **Identify the cause of stress.** The cause of the stress is the friend being injured. Describe any other events that might be occurring at the same time that might increase the stress.

3. **Do something about the cause of stress.** List the steps you should take in this situation, such as call for help or have someone nearby call for help. What other steps could you take?

4. **Take action to lessen the harmful effects of stress.** What can a person do in advance to manage his or her stress level in emergency situations? Should the person make a plan, such as a list of the most important things to do in a crisis? The person might review the plan with a parent or another responsible adult.

◀ Calling for help is an important first step.

LESSON 5 REVIEW

Review Concepts

1. **Name** four kinds of information you should tell an emergency services operator.

2. **Discuss** the initial steps you should take in all first aid emergencies.

3. **Describe** how to check for an injured person's breathing.

Critical Thinking

4. **Classify** Think about the items in a first aid kit. List categories to which the items belong. Then list some of the items in each category.

5. **LIFE SKILLS** **Manage Stress** One important skill in performing first aid is handling the stress of the situation. What are some ways to keep calm in an emergency?

Basic First Aid Skills

You will learn . . .

- how and when to perform abdominal thrusts.
- how to give rescue breathing and CPR.
- how to control bleeding and shock.
- how to give first aid for broken bones and sprains.
- how to recognize and treat first-, second-, and third-degree burns.

Vocabulary

- **abdominal thrust,** C79
- **rescue breathing,** C80
- **cardiopulmonary resuscitation (CPR),** C80
- **wound,** C82
- **shock,** C83

Emergencies can occur anywhere. As you eat your lunch in the cafeteria, you might see a student choking at the next table. Riding in the car with your family, you might come upon the scene of a crash. In these situations, every second counts. If you know what to do, you could help save a life.

Abdominal Thrusts

Choking occurs when something is caught in a person's airway. People who are choking cannot cough or speak. They might use the universal sign for choking. This is a warning shown by clutching the throat with one or both hands.

Do not slap a choking victim on the back. Call or have someone call for emergency help. Use **abdominal thrusts** to help dislodge an object.

For a Conscious Adult or Older Child

When a conscious adult or older child is choking, follow these steps to help.

1. Stand behind the person and wrap your arms around his or her waist.
2. Make a fist with one hand and place it just above the navel, with your thumb against the body.
3. Grab your fist with the other hand and thrust quickly, inward and upward.
4. Repeat until the object is forced out, the person can breathe on his or her own, or the person becomes unconscious.

For Yourself

If you are choking, you can perform abdominal thrusts on yourself. Follow these steps.

1. Get someone's attention so he or she can call for emergency help. Use the universal choking signal.
2. Make a fist and place the thumb side against your abdomen, above the navel.
3. Cover your fist with the other hand. Thrust quickly upward.

4. Repeat until the object is forced out.

If a chair or another firm object is available, you can use it to perform an abdominal thrust. Press your abdomen against the edge of the object to make the thrust.

For an Conscious Infant

When an infant is choking, use

1. **back blows** Place the infant face-down over your forearm, supporting the head with your hand. Lay this arm on your thigh, so that the infant's head is lower than his or her chest. Give 5 firm back blows between the infant's shoulder blades with the heel of your free hand.

2. **chest thrusts** If the infant is still choking, turn him or her face-up on your forearm, again supporting the head with your hand and resting your arm on your leg. Lay your middle and index fingers on the infant's breastbone, running along and one finger's-width below the center of an imaginary line running between the infant's nipples. Give 5 chest thrusts. Repeat back blows and chest thrusts until the object comes out, the infant can breathe on his or her own, or the infant becomes unconscious.

For unconscious infants, children, and adults

Follow the procedures outlined on pages C80–C81.

What is an abdominal thrust?

Rescue Breathing and CPR

Rescue breathing is breathing air into an unconscious person who has a pulse. **Cardiopulmonary resuscitation (CPR)** is a way to restore heartbeat and breathing. It should be performed only by those who are trained and certified in CPR. Always use universal precautions.

Rescue Breathing

Call for help, then:

1. Place the person on his or her back.
2. Tilt the head back and lift the chin up.
3. Pinch the nostrils shut.
4. Put a face mask on the victim. Give a slow, gentle breath for 2 seconds. Pause and give another breath.
5. Check to see if the person has circulation. Look for signs of movement or coughing.
6. Give one slow breath every 5 seconds if the person has circulation but is not breathing. Look for signs of breathing between your breaths.
7. Recheck for circulation (signs of movement or coughing) after a minute. Continue rescue breathing as long as the person is not breathing but has circulation.

How to Give CPR

If a person loses circulation during rescue breathing, or if you come upon someone who has no circulation, call emergency services immediately. Then a person who is trained and certified in CPR can begin CPR. Always use universal precautions.

CPR for Adults

1. Kneel next to the person's chest.
2. Feel along the bottom of the ribcage with the hand closer to the person's feet. Put your middle finger where the ribcage meets the breastbone. Place your index finger next to your middle finger. Put the heel of your other hand next to your index finger and your free hand on top of it.
3. Kneel forward, lock your elbows, and press down 5 times every 3 seconds.

CAREERS IN HEALTH

Disaster Relief Worker

Would you like to help people in crisis situations? If so, you might choose a career as a disaster relief worker. Organizations such as the American Red Cross respond to disasters by providing emergency workers, cleanup crews, health care, food, and shelter to people affected by natural or human-made disasters. Disaster relief workers possess a wide variety of skills, ranging from health care or firefighting experience to knowledge of sanitary engineering. For more information about becoming a disaster relief worker, contact your local American Red Cross chapter.

LOG ON Visit **www.mmhhealth.com** to find out more about this and other health careers.

4. After doing 15 compressions, give 2 rescue breaths. Repeat the cycle 4 times. Check for signs of movement or regular breathing.

5. Alternate compressions and breathing until help arrives or the person has circulation and can breathe.

CPR for Children over Age One

1. Kneel next to the person on a firm surface.

2. Find the bottom of the breastbone, as if giving CPR to an adult. Place the heel of your hand the width of two fingers above that spot.

3. Press down 5 times every 3 seconds with one hand.

4. Give 1 rescue breath after 5 compressions. Repeat until the child revives or help arrives.

CPR for Infants

1. Kneel next to the infant on a firm surface.

2. Place your third and fourth fingers on the center of the breastbone.

3. Compress the chest with your fingers 1/2 inch to 1 inch, at a pace of 5 times every 3 seconds.

4. Give 1 rescue breath after 5 compressions. Repeat until the infant revives or help arrives.

What is rescue breathing?

Be a Health Advocate

Performing CPR when it is needed can save someone's life. However, people can only perform the procedure if they have been trained to do so. What steps can you take to increase the number of people who are trained and certified in CPR?

1. **Select a health-related concern to communicate.** I will encourage people to sign up for CPR training and certification programs.

2. **Gather reliable information.** Contact health organizations such as the American Red Cross, American Heart Association, and local hospitals to find out about CPR classes available in your area.

3. **Identify your purpose and target audience.** Determine which groups of people in your community should be encouraged to get CPR training and certification. Write a statement summarizing the many benefits of having this skill.

4. **Develop a convincing and appropriate message.** Design a poster or flyer describing the features of the CPR programs offered in your area. Include information about the benefits of having as many people as possible prepared to perform CPR.

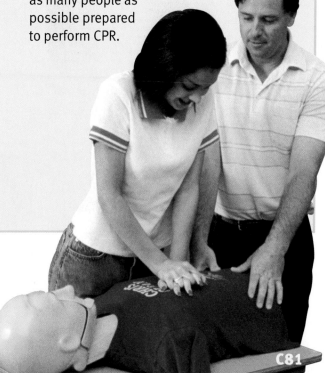

Bleeding and Shock

A **wound** is an injury to the body's soft tissues. How you care for a wound depends on what kind it is and how deep it is. Remember to follow universal precautions.

- **Minor wounds** To treat minor wounds, such as small cuts or scrapes, first wash the wound with soap and water. Apply an antibiotic ointment to kill pathogens and prevent infection. Cover the wound with a clean bandage. Look for signs of infection, such as redness, swelling, throbbing, pus, or red streaks. If infection occurs, keep the area clean and dry. Apply antibiotic ointment regularly, and see a physician if symptoms continue.

- **Nosebleeds** Tilt the person forward. Pinch the nostrils together below the bony part of the nose for ten minutes. Place an ice pack around the nose. Repeat these steps if necessary. If the bleeding does not stop, get medical attention.

- **Puncture wounds** Puncture wounds result when the skin is broken by a sharp object such as a nail. If left untreated, puncture wounds can result in tetanus, a condition that produces painful muscle spasms throughout the body. To treat a puncture wound, first wash your hands. Clean the wound with soap and running tap water. Apply a clean bandage. See a physician to find out if you need an antibiotic or a tetanus shot. Soak the wound four times a day in warm, soapy water. Apply a clean bandage after each soaking. Rest and elevate the wound as much as possible.

◀ Be sure to receive permission before administering first aid.

ACTIVITY

Math LINK

Be Prepared

Suppose you and your family are gathering some emergency supplies for your home. You need to decide how much drinking water to include. There are four people in your family, and you would like to have enough supplies for three days. Each person should have six to eight glasses of water each day. How many pints of water will each person need per day? How many total pints should you store? (Remember there are two cups in a pint.)

- **Heavy bleeding** First call emergency services. Then elevate the wound above the level of the heart, if the wound is on an arm or leg. Cover the wound with a clean cloth and apply direct pressure to the wound for 15 minutes or until the bleeding stops. Do not remove the cloth if the blood soaks through. Add another cloth and keep applying pressure. Tie the cloth in place if the bleeding slows. If the bleeding does not stop, apply pressure to the nearest pressure point, a place where there is a main artery sending blood to the affected part of the body. Pressure points are located along arteries in the wrists, upper arms, upper thighs, and the backs of the knees. Keep the injured area elevated, and apply pressure until the bleeding slows or help arrives.

- **Shock** **Shock** is a dangerous drop in blood flow. It can result from bleeding, heart attacks, infections, allergic reactions, dehydration, spinal injuries, or trauma. Shock is life threatening and must be treated promptly.

People in shock may feel anxious, confused, dizzy, restless, or faint. They may look pale, with bluish lips and fingernails and clammy skin. People in shock often breathe shallowly, have a rapid pulse, nausea, and vomiting.

If you see someone with symptoms of shock, you can help by following these steps. Call emergency medical services. Check to make sure the person is breathing. Perform rescue breathing and CPR if necessary. Lay the person down, elevating the feet. Loosen tight clothes and cover the person with a blanket. Turn the person's head to one side in case of vomiting. Give first aid for other injuries while you wait for help. Do not move the person. (There might be a spinal injury.) Cover the person with a blanket and wait for help to arrive.

What is shock?

▼ **Elevate the feet of a person in shock when possible.**

Breaks, Sprains, Burns

Three common kinds of injuries that require immediate care are broken bones, sprains, and burns.

Fractures A break in a bone is called a *fracture.* There are different kinds of fractures. In some, the sharp edge of the broken bone pokes through the skin, while in others, the broken part moves unnaturally. To find out if an injured person has a broken bone, ask questions. Did the person hear a snapping sound when the injury occurred? Is the injured part hard to move? Does touching it hurt? These are all signs of a broken bone.

If you think someone might have a broken bone, follow these guidelines. Call emergency services. Apply pressure with a clean cloth if there is bleeding. If the person must be moved, splint or stabilize the broken limb. Do not try to straighten the injured part. You can make a splint with a board or a long piece of cardboard. Pad the splint with towels or pillows. Place cold packs on the injured area. Keep the person lying down until help arrives.

Sprains A sprain is an injury to the tissue that connects bones to a joint. It happens when tissue stretches and partially tears. Sprains can be hard to distinguish from breaks. To make sure an injury is a sprain, call a doctor.

Treat sprains with the PRICE method (Protect–Rest–Ice–Compress–Elevate). Protect the body part by applying a splint or sling to immobilize it. Rest the body part. Apply ice every few hours for the first two days, for 10 to 15 minutes at a time. Compress the sprain to reduce swelling. Wrap it in an elastic bandage. Elevate the sprain as often as possible. Don't apply heat for at least 24 hours. A physician may recommend an over-the-counter pain reliever.

▼ **A physician uses X rays to determine if a bone is broken.**

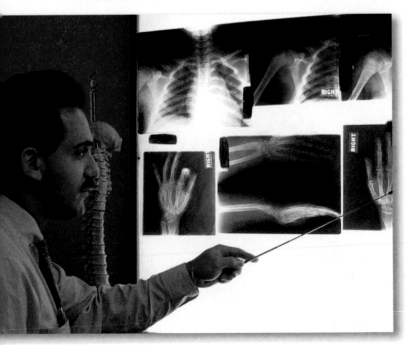

Burns

A burn is an injury caused by heat, electricity, chemicals, or radiation. A burn is described as first-, second-, or third-degree, depending on the seriousness.

First degree A first-degree burn affects the outer layer of skin. If the skin is not broken, soak the burn in cool water. After 5 minutes, cover it with a dry gauze bandage. Offer over-the-counter pain medicine to reduce pain and swelling. If you have a lotion with aloe vera, apply it to the burn.

Second degree A second-degree burn affects the outer layer of skin and the layer just beneath it. The burn may appear red, swollen, and blistered. Call the emergency number for medical help. Soak the burn in cool water for 15 minutes. Do not break the blisters. Cover the burn lightly with a bandage. Offer over-the-counter medicine for pain.

Third degree A third-degree burn involves all layers of skin and the tissues beneath them. The burned area may appear black or brown. If nerves have been damaged, there will be no pain. Contact emergency services immediately. Make sure the person is removed from the source of heat, but don't remove burnt clothing. Give rescue breathing and CPR if needed. Cover the burn with a moist bandage or a clean cloth. Treat the person for shock.

 What is a sprain?

On Your Own
FOR SCHOOL OR HOME

Gather First Aid Supplies

What would you do if someone broke a leg, sprained an ankle, or burned a hand? Use a plastic spoon as a model for a person's arm to demonstrate the basic procedures you would follow to treat an injury. As you do so, compile a list of all the items you would need to treat an actual injury. Use the list to assemble an emergency kit.

LESSON 6 REVIEW

Review Concepts

1. **Describe** how to perform abdominal thrusts on a conscious adult.

2. **Explain** what to do if you are giving rescue breathing to an adult who loses circulation.

3. **Identify** steps to take if a wound does not stop bleeding.

Critical Thinking

4. **Compare and Contrast** What are the similarities and differences among first-degree burns, second-degree burns, and third-degree burns?

5. **LIFE SKILLS Be a Health Advocate** Relate ways you can convey to others the importance of the first aid skills you have learned.

CHAPTER 6 REVIEW

Chapter Summary

Lesson 1 • Learning how to recognize violence and abusive relationships, manage anger, and identify signs that someone is considering suicide will help you protect your health and the health of others.

Lesson 2 • Learning protective behaviors lowers your risk of being affected by crime at school or in your community. Knowing resources for recovery will help you if you are affected by violence.

Lesson 3 • Guidelines for preventing falls, fires, electric shock, and kitchen accidents will help you stay safe at home.

Lesson 4 • Knowing what to do in severe weather or a disaster can mean the difference between life and death.

Lesson 5 • Knowing how to get help, use universal precautions, and check the person will enable you to offer assistance in a medical emergency.

Lesson 6 • Training in abdominal thrusts and first aid enables you to help others in need.

Use Vocabulary

prejudice, C49

physical abuse, C50

protective factors, C55

hazards, C63

burglary, C66

natural disaster, C69

emergency, C75

universal precautions, C76

cardiopulmonary resuscitation (CPR), C80

Choose the correct term from the list to complete each sentence.

1. An event caused by nature that results in extensive damage is a(n) _____?_____.

2. A crime in which a person breaks into a shop, house, or other indoor space to steal something is a(n) _____?_____.

3. _____?_____ is harmful treatment of a person that results in physical injury.

4. A sudden dangerous situation that calls for quick action is a(n) _____?_____.

5. A method of restoring heartbeat and breathing to an unconscious person is _____?_____.

6. Steps taken in an emergency situation to avoid contact with another person's body fluids are _____?_____.

7. An opinion that is formed before all the facts are known is _____?_____.

8. Things that increase the chance of a positive outcome, such as having a safe environment, are called _____?_____.

9. Possible sources of harm or danger in and around the home are known as _____?_____.

Answer each question in complete sentences.

10. How can you help make sure that you stay safe in school?

11. What are some ways to protect yourself when working in the kitchen?

12. What signs might show that a person is thinking about committing suicide?

13. How can you keep yourself away from harm in a hurricane?

14. What are the initial steps of performing first aid?

Reading Comprehension

Answer each question in complete sentences.

If you find a weapon, or if someone shows you one, don't touch it. Leave immediately and tell a responsible adult. Always assume a gun is loaded and can go off. In addition, consider your safety if someone has an object such as a bat or razor that could be used as a weapon.

15. What should you always assume about a gun?

16. What actions should you take if you find a weapon?

Critical Thinking/Problem Solving

Answer each question in complete sentences.

Analyze Concepts

17. Describe the steps to take when you suspect that someone has a broken bone.

18. Your friend is being bullied by someone who is physically stronger. What are some ways he can avoid violence and protect himself?

19. How can you be a responsible pedestrian?

20. Compare and contrast tornadoes and hurricanes.

21. Design a plan for yourself to manage your anger in a responsible way. What are some things you can do to stay calm?

Practice Life Skills

22. **Resolve Conflicts** Your brother and sister argue frequently. What steps can you take to resolve this conflict in a healthful way?

23. **Make Responsible Decisions** Your classmate tells you she is thinking about joining a gang. What advice could you offer to help her make the responsible decision?

Read Graphics

Use the text in the visual below to answer the questions.

24. During an automobile crash, you are four times more likely to die if you are thrown from the car. Look at the chart below. What conclusions can you draw from it about the importance of wearing a seat belt?

25. Do you think that wearing a seat belt might affect other crash statistics, such as the number of people who are injured? Why or why not?

SEAT BELT STATISTICS, 2000

Percent of people wearing seat belts who were thrown from the car in a crash.	1
Percent of people not wearing seat belts who were thrown from the car in a crash.	22

Source: U.S. Department of Transportation

LOG ON Visit **www.mmhhealth.com** to find out how much you know about violence and injury prevention.

Effective Communication

Give a Speech

Encourage good sportsmanship at a sports event. For example, spectators should congratulate players of both teams and avoid foul language. Players should accept decisions of judges. Add any other guidelines that are appropriate.

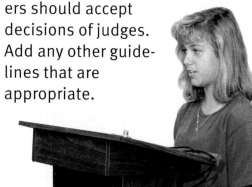

Self-Directed Learning

Personal Health Care Products

Pick any two kinds of personal health care products—for example, toothpaste and shampoo. Compare similar kinds of each product, such as brands of tartar control toothpaste or shampoo with conditioner. Compare information on labels and prices. Make a comparison chart to help shoppers make the best choice.

Critical Thinking and Problem Solving

Poisonous Plants

Make a presentation of first aid for a person who touches a poisonous plant. Symptoms can cause swelling, itching, and redness. Draw pictures of poison ivy (shown here with its recognizable three-leaf pattern), poison oak, and poison sumac to show characteristics of these plants.

Responsible Citizenship

Be Prepared

Choose a form of severe weather or a natural disaster and make a poster that shows ways for a person to stay safe from its danger. Display the poster in your classroom or school hallway so people can remember how to prepare for all types of conditions.

UNIT D

Drugs and Disease Prevention

CHAPTER 7

Alcohol, Tobacco, and Other Drugs, D2

CHAPTER 8

Communicable and Chronic Diseases, D48

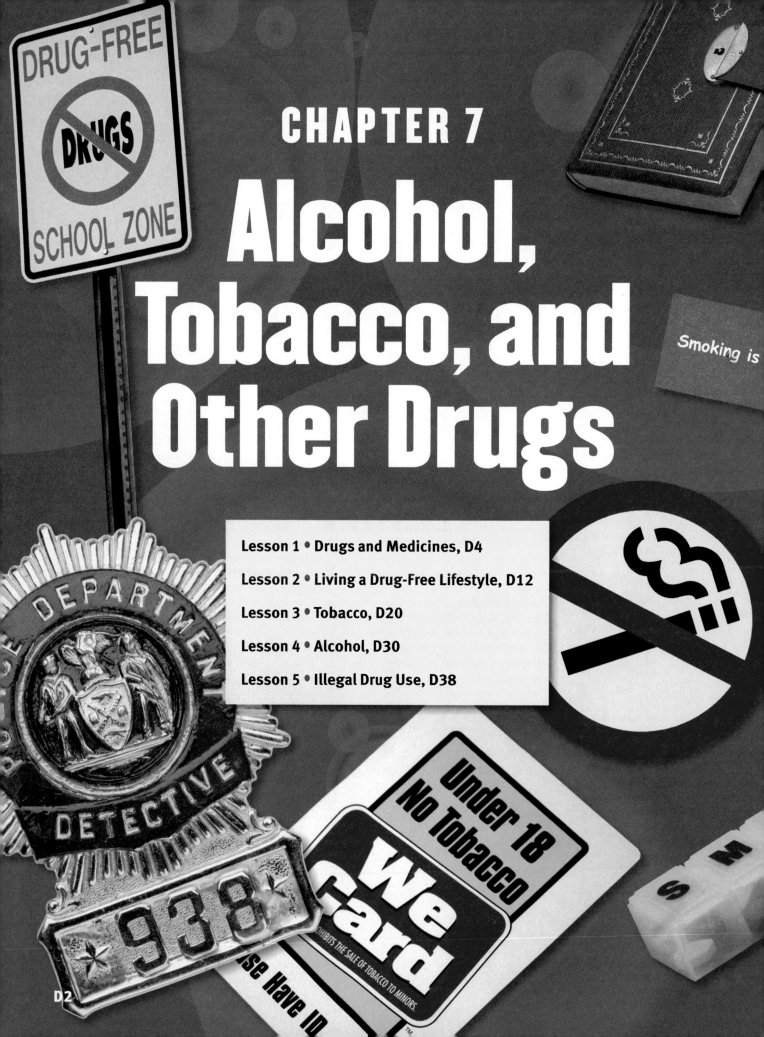

CHAPTER 7

Alcohol, Tobacco, and Other Drugs

Lesson 1 • Drugs and Medicines, D4

Lesson 2 • Living a Drug-Free Lifestyle, D12

Lesson 3 • Tobacco, D20

Lesson 4 • Alcohol, D30

Lesson 5 • Illegal Drug Use, D38

What Do You Know About
Alcohol, Tobacco, and Other Drugs?

1. Why is it important to follow instructions and safety guidelines for using prescription and over-the-counter drugs?
2. What skills do you need to resist pressure to use illegal drugs?
3. How does drinking alcohol affect the brain?

SURGEON GENERAL'S WARNING: Cigarette Smoke Contains Carbon Monoxide.

The Inside Story

What a Wonderful World

There is a diverse world of medicines, ranging from liquids to lotions to lozenges. Even as you read this, the number of medicines available is growing. In 2003, government agencies tested and approved about 70 new medicines for the American public. Because of this research, we can look forward to medical break-throughs to prevent, control, and cure illnesses.

Multi-Symptom
DAYTIME
COLD & FLU RELIEF

10 FL OZ (296 mL)

LOG ON Visit **www.mmhhealth.com** for activities and information on alcohol, tobacco, and other drugs.

Drugs and Medicines

You will learn . . .

- ways medicines promote health.
- how drugs enter and affect the body.
- the safe use of over-the-counter and prescription drugs.
- why drug abuse is dangerous.

Vocabulary

- **drug,** D5
- **medicine,** D5
- **prescription drug,** D5
- **over-the-counter (OTC) drug,** D5
- **dose,** D7
- **side effect,** D7
- **tolerance,** D7
- **pharmacist,** D8
- **drug misuse,** D10
- **drug abuse,** D10
- **physical dependence,** D11
- **psychological dependence,** D11

Medicines are drugs. You can find them on the shelves of drugstores and grocery stores. People store them in bathroom cabinets and carry them in purses and overnight bags. Medicines promote health when guidelines for their safe use are followed. You need accurate information about medicines to use them safely.

How Medicines Help You

A **drug** is a substance that changes the way the body or mind works. Some drugs produce healthful changes while others produce harmful changes. A **medicine** is a drug used to prevent or cure illness or disease, or to relieve pain. Pain relievers, allergy pills, eyedrops, cough syrups, and throat lozenges are all medicines.

Some medicines require a prescription to be purchased. A *prescription* is a written order from a physician. A **prescription drug** is a medicine that can be obtained only with a written order from a physician. A medicine that can be purchased without a prescription is called an **over-the-counter (OTC) drug**. When used properly, both kinds of medicine protect and promote health. The United States Food and Drug Administration (FDA) is the only government agency that decides which drugs require a prescription and which drugs may be sold over the counter.

Ways Drugs Are Used as Medicine

Some medicines help cure illness or disease. For example, medicines called antibiotics fight diseases by killing the bacteria that cause them. Other medicines, including vaccines, prevent illness. They prepare your body to fight off disease-causing germs.

Some medicines treat the symptoms that accompany sickness or injury. If you sprain your ankle, you might take the OTC drug acetaminophen. This pain reliever does not heal the sprain, but it will reduce pain.

Many people take medicines to treat a condition that lasts a long time. For example, a person with high blood pressure might take a medicine that decreases blood pressure. This medicine reduces the risk of stroke and heart attack.

 **What are four ways in which medicines can help you?**

▼ **Carefully follow the directions that accompany a prescription medicine.**

How Drugs Enter the Body

Drugs that are injected or inhaled begin working almost instantly. Drugs that are swallowed take longer to work because they must be digested first.

Drugs can enter the body in a variety of ways. Some drugs are swallowed. Others are injected into a muscle or vein, inhaled through the mouth or nose, or absorbed through the skin or mucous membranes. The way drugs enter the body is determined by how they work.

Five Ways Drugs Enter the Body

Drugs such as ointments, drops, and sprays can be applied directly to the linings of the eyes, nose, and mouth, where they are absorbed into the body.

Drugs inhaled through the mouth or nose enter the lungs and pass quickly into the bloodstream. Inhaled medicines work quickly.

Drugs dissolved in liquid can be injected by needle directly into veins or muscles.

Many drugs are swallowed. They pass through the stomach and are absorbed into the bloodstream.

Creams and ointments can be rubbed onto the skin for absorption. Patches containing medicines can be placed on the skin.

Multi-Symptom
DAYTIME
COLD & FLU RELIEF
NASAL DECONGESTANT, PAIN RELIEVER, COUGH SUPPRESSANT, FEVER REDUCER
ACETAMINOPHEN, DEXTROMETHORPHAN HBr, PSEUDOEPHEDRINE HCl
non-drowsy, alcohol-free, antihistamine-free
NEW LABEL INFORMATION
10 FL OZ (296 mL)

How Drugs Affect the Body

A 3-year-old child and a 33-year-old adult might take the same drug to reduce fever. Yet they would not take the same dose. A **dose** is the amount of a drug taken at one time. Doses differ to account for age, body weight, and other factors that determine a drug's effect on the body.

The factors that influence a drug's effect are

1. **the amount of the dose.** The larger the dose, the stronger the effect. An overdose is too large an amount of a drug.

2. **the age of a person.** A drug might affect a younger person differently than an older person.

3. **the body weight of a person.** The greater a person's body weight, the greater the dose that is needed.

4. **the health of a person.** A drug might affect a person who is in optimal health differently than a person who is in poor health.

5. **the state of mind of a person.** A person's mood might affect a drug's performance and a drug might affect a person's mood.

6. **the presence of other drugs in the body.** The presence of another drug can increase or decrease a drug's effect.

7. **the possible side effects of the drug.** A person might respond to the drug differently than another person. For example, a person might be allergic to the drug.

An unwanted reaction to a drug is called a **side effect.** Sometimes when a person takes a drug too frequently, his or her body becomes used to it. The body may develop a **tolerance,** a condition in which increasing amounts of a drug are needed to produce the desired effects. Not all drugs lead to tolerance, however.

 **What is a dose?**

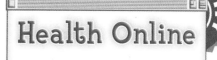

Health Online

Study Side Effects

ⓔ-Journal

Report on the responsible use of medicines, including how side effects are important in the use of medicines, by visiting **www.mmhhealth.com** and clicking on ⓔ-Journal.

▼ **It's important to take the correct dose of a medicine.**

Using Drugs Safely

Over-the-counter drugs are sold at pharmacies and grocery stores. Prescription drugs also can be purchased at pharmacies. A **pharmacist** is a licensed professional who distributes drugs that are prescribed.

Over-the-Counter Drugs

OTC drugs can be purchased and used without the help of a medical professional. Still, you should discuss your symptoms with a health care provider—a physician, pharmacist, nurse practitioner, or physician assistant—before starting to use OTC drugs. When you take OTC drugs, you are responsible for following guidelines for their safe use.

The most important guideline is that parents or guardians supervise the use of OTC drugs. Never take them on your own. Read the drug's label carefully and follow all its instructions. Use an OTC drug only for its stated purpose. If you have side effects, tell a parent or guardian and stop taking the drug. Do not buy an OTC drug if the seal on the package has been broken, or after the drug's expiration date. To make sure that you take the correct medication, keep all OTC drugs in their original containers. If you have any doubts about the drug, ask a health care provider.

OTC Drug Label

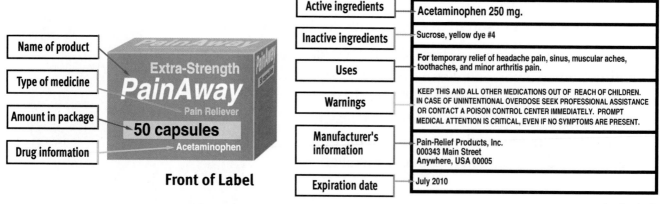

Active ingredients	Acetaminophen 250 mg.
Inactive ingredients	Sucrose, yellow dye #4
Uses	For temporary relief of headache pain, sinus, muscular aches, toothaches, and minor arthritis pain.
Warnings	KEEP THIS AND ALL OTHER MEDICATIONS OUT OF REACH OF CHILDREN. IN CASE OF UNINTENTIONAL OVERDOSE SEEK PROFESSIONAL ASSISTANCE OR CONTACT A POISON CONTROL CENTER IMMEDIATELY. PROMPT MEDICAL ATTENTION IS CRITICAL, EVEN IF NO SYMPTOMS ARE PRESENT.
Manufacturer's information	Pain-Relief Products, Inc. 000343 Main Street Anywhere, USA 00005
Expiration date	July 2010

Name of product

Type of medicine

Amount in package

Drug information

PainAway

Extra-Strength
PainAway
Pain Reliever
50 capsules
Acetaminophen

Front of Label

Back of Label

▲ Follow the guidelines printed on the label of an OTC drug.

Prescription Drugs

When your parents or guardian purchase a prescription drug, the pharmacist explains how to use and store it. You and your family must listen carefully to all directions.

Take a prescription drug only from a parent or guardian, a licensed health care provider, or an adult who has your parents' or guardian's permission. You should also know the name of the prescription drug, how much of it to take, and how often to take it. Be aware of the conditions under which the prescription drug should be taken, such as with or without a meal. Also, know what to do if you miss a dose of the drug. Never use a prescription drug prescribed for another person. As with OTC drugs, keep prescription drugs in their original containers. Always ask a health care provider if you have questions about the use of a prescription drug.

 What can you do to make sure you are using an OTC drug or a prescription drug correctly?

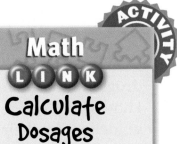

Math LINK

Calculate Dosages

Read the prescription drug label on this page. How often each day must the patient take a capsule? The label directs the patient to finish all of the drug. Draw a calendar to show the number of days the patient will be taking the drug.

Prescription Drug Label

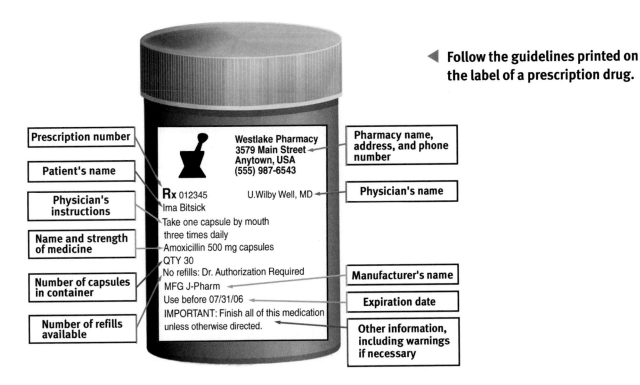

◀ **Follow the guidelines printed on the label of a prescription drug.**

| Prescription number |
| Patient's name |
| Physician's instructions |
| Name and strength of medicine |
| Number of capsules in container |
| Number of refills available |

Westlake Pharmacy
3579 Main Street
Anytown, USA
(555) 987-6543

Rx 012345   U.Wilby Well, MD
Ima Bitsick
Take one capsule by mouth three times daily
Amoxicillin 500 mg capsules
QTY 30
No refills: Dr. Authorization Required
MFG J-Pharm
Use before 07/31/06
IMPORTANT: Finish all of this medication unless otherwise directed.

| Pharmacy name, address, and phone number |
| Physician's name |
| Manufacturer's name |
| Expiration date |
| Other information, including warnings if necessary |

Drug Misuse and Drug Abuse

All medicines are drugs, but not all drugs are considered medicines. As you know, drugs can be healthful when guidelines for their safe use are followed. When guidelines are not followed, however, drugs can be harmful.

Drug misuse is the harmful use of a legal drug that is not done on purpose. Lack of knowledge might lead to drug misuse. If you do not follow the instructions for the proper use of a drug, you are misusing it. You might misread a medicine label in the middle of the night and take too big a dose. You might take an antibiotic after the expiration date. In each case, you would be misusing a drug.

Drug abuse is the harmful use of any drug on purpose. Taking a higher dose of a medicine than a physician prescribes is drug abuse. Using a prescription drug without a prescription or using a drug such as marijuana is illegal. The use of any illegal drug is drug abuse. The use of alcohol and tobacco by youth is also considered to be drug abuse.

A person who follows guidelines for the safe use of drugs is responsible and takes steps to protect his or her health. Taking drugs in a harmful way is called *drug use*. This term includes the harmful practices of both drug misuse and drug abuse.

ACTIVITY

LIFE SKILLS

CRITICAL THINKING

Make Responsible Decisions

Role-play this situation with a partner: You are at your friend's house after soccer practice. Both of you have sore muscles. Your friend says there is a prescription muscle relaxant in the medicine cabinet and says they are safe to use.

1 **Identify your choices. Check them out with your parent or another trusted adult.** With a group of classmates, brainstorm possible choices.

2 **Evaluate each choice. Use the Guidelines for Making Responsible Decisions™.** Use the questions below to evaluate each of the possible choices.

- Will this decision result in actions that promote health?

- Will this decision result in actions that protect safety?
- Will this decision result in actions that follow laws?
- Will this decision result in actions that show respect for myself and others?
- Will this decision result in actions that follow the guidelines of my parents and other responsible adults?
- Will this decision result in actions that demonstrate good character?

3 **Tell what the responsible decision is. Check this out with your parent or another trusted adult.** Use answers to the questions to make the most responsible decision in this situation.

4 **Evaluate your decision.** Weigh the possible benefits and drawbacks of your choice.

Drug Dependence

Misusing and abusing drugs can lead to drug dependence. When a person is drug dependent, he or she craves the drug and uses it repeatedly. Dependence can be physical, psychological, or both.

Physical dependence is repeated drug use that causes tolerance. For someone who is physically dependent on a drug, not taking it can cause problems such as headaches, chills, and nausea. These unwanted effects are called *withdrawal symptoms*.

Psychological (sy•kuh•LAH•juh•kuhl) **dependence** is the repeated use of a drug for emotional or social reasons. For example, a person might drink alcoholic beverages to feel less anxious around others or to escape from fear or sadness. Drug use becomes the center of the user's life.

▶ The FDA investigates drugs for harmful effects. For example, ephedra was once legally available as a weight loss aid and energy booster, but the FDA has banned its use.

Drug abuse can harm the mind and the body. It can weaken a person's ability to make responsible decisions. A person who abuses drugs might become violent or be pressured into sexual activity. Abusing drugs may make a person do things he or she may not usually do.

Signs of Drug Abuse

Drug dependence starts with "I might try it just once." Early warning signs of drug abuse include talking about trying a drug, lying about using drugs, hiding drugs, smelling like alcohol, suddenly getting into trouble, and spending time with peers who use drugs.

 **What is drug abuse?**

LESSON 1 REVIEW

Review Concepts

1. **List** three ways prescription and OTC drugs can benefit health.

2. **Identify** three ways in which drugs can enter the body.

3. **Explain** how each of the following factors affects the way a drug works in the body: weight, health, mood, and other drugs.

4. **Name** three guidelines to follow when taking OTC drugs and three guidelines to follow when taking prescription drugs.

Critical Thinking

5. **Compare and Contrast** What is the difference between drug misuse and drug abuse? Support your answer with examples.

6. **LIFE SKILLS** **Make Responsible Decisions** Which of the six guidelines do you follow when you say "no" to drug use and abuse? Explain your answer.

Living a Drug-Free Lifestyle

When you throw a stone into a pond, ripples spread outward in all directions. Drug abuse works in the same way. Drug abuse has a ripple effect. It disturbs the life of the person who abuses drugs and that of his or her family and friends. Remaining drug free enables you to reach your goals for a healthful future.

The Effects of Alcohol Abuse and Other Drug Abuse

Alcohol abuse and other drug abuse can lead to various problems for users and the people around them. Many of these problems have serious consequences.

Effects on the individual A person who abuses alcohol or other drugs has an increased risk of illness, damage to the body, and sleep loss. He or she may develop physical and psychological dependence. The person is more likely to be absent from school or work, depressed, anxious, and suicidal. The person might have legal problems, such as traffic violations, car crashes, and arrest for possession of illegal drugs.

Effects on the family Family members of people who abuse alcohol or other drugs may become distrustful and angry. They might experience verbal and physical abuse. A family might break up as a result. Family members may have financial problems from job loss, treatment costs, and money spent on drugs.

Effects on society All members of society are affected by those who abuse alcohol and other drugs. Abuse increases crime, such as smuggling, drug dealing, theft, homicide, and assault. It can lead to unintentional injuries, such as motor vehicle deaths and drowning. It increases health care expenses for drug treatment, medical care, and counseling. It increases the number of people who are infected with HIV from shared needles used to inject illegal drugs.

According to the Office of National Drug Control Policy, there are 50,000 drug-related deaths in the United States every year.

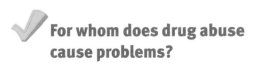
For whom does drug abuse cause problems?

▶ Being drug free helps build strong family relationships.

Why People Abuse Drugs

Do You Know?

The price of addiction is high. According to the American Cancer Society, tobacco addiction causes about 440,000 deaths in the United States each year. That is more deaths than are due to alcohol, cocaine, heroin, car crashes, fire, and AIDS combined.

Why do some people abuse alcohol or other drugs? Some people abuse drugs in order to fit in and feel accepted by their peers. They may hope to escape stress or hide their feelings of negative self-esteem. For some, abusing drugs is a way to rebel against the law or against their parents or guardians. Others abuse drugs to feel the thrill of taking a risk or because they are curious. Still others are influenced by some of the messages in the media—movies, music, TV programs, or advertisements—that encourage drug use.

People who abuse drugs can develop an addiction to them. **Addiction** is the compelling need to continue a behavior even if it is harmful. Drug addiction can begin with a single act of drug abuse.

Steps to Drug Addiction

Once a person begins abusing a drug, he or she can easily become dependent upon it. The steps that lead from drug abuse to drug addiction usually progress as follows:

Step 1: Experimental Use The person experiments with a drug such as alcohol or marijuana. He or she begins to use the substance occasionally and may try other drugs.

Step 2: Occasional Use The person takes the drug more frequently, perhaps daily. He or she develops a tolerance for the drug.

Step 3: Situational Use The person uses the drug when participating in certain activities or situations.

Step 4: Intense Use The person becomes preoccupied with the drug. He or she spends considerable time, energy, and money on the drug. Use of the drug causes problems at home and at school.

Step 5: Compulsive Use The person becomes addicted to the drug—physically, psychologically, or both. He or she needs the drug daily or even hourly.

▼ **Don't be fooled by unhealthful media messages.**

Some people start abusing drugs to make themselves feel better. Yet drug abuse eventually makes a person feel worse. When a person abuses a drug, he or she can become overwhelmed by feelings of guilt and self-loathing. To escape these feelings, the person uses the drug even more. This leads to more guilt, which leads to further drug abuse, and so on. The cycle of drug abuse and addiction continues.

Drug addiction brings serious physical consequences. People who abuse drugs may lose weight, develop organ damage, and have illnesses and premature diseases. They may have impaired memory and are at risk for committing suicide. In addition, taking toxic levels of drugs can cause heart failure, blood poisoning, and death.

✔ **What is addiction?**

▶ **There are many healthful ways to manage stress.**

ACTIVITY
LIFE SKILLS
CRITICAL THINKING

Manage Stress

Sometimes people abuse drugs as a harmful response to stress in their lives. However, there are plenty of *healthful* ways to manage stressors. Work with a group of students to make a mobile to identify ways to manage stress. The mobile has four arms made by crisscrossing two thick strips of cardboard. Label the four arms of the mobile with the names of the four steps below.

1. **Identify the signs of stress.** From this arm, hang strips of paper with labels such as "worrying," "sleeping poorly," "headaches," and "stomachaches."

2. **Identify the cause of stress.** From this arm, hang strips labeled with causes of stress, such as "tests," "bullies," and so on.

3. **Do something about the cause of stress.** From this arm, hang strips that have strategies: If the cause of stress is a test, make a plan to study and prepare for success, including help from a parent, teacher, or a tutor.

4. **Take action to lessen the harmful effects of stress.** From this arm, hang strips with healthful behaviors, such as "Get plenty of rest and sleep" and so on.

Getting Help for a Person Who Abuses Drugs

Can you recognize the signs of drug abuse? If so, you can get help for someone who might be abusing alcohol or other drugs. The behaviors listed below are some of the warning signs of drug abuse.

The person who abuses drugs

- hangs out with friends who use harmful drugs.
- stops hanging out with drug-free friends.
- may have a sloppy appearance.
- has glassy or red eyes and dilated pupils.
- has slurred speech.
- lies about activities and whereabouts.
- stops caring about school, family, and friends.
- is easily angered.
- steals or borrows money.
- stops participating in healthful activities.

Character

Show Your Support

Responsibility If someone you know has one or more of the behaviors that indicate possible signs of alcohol or other drug abuse, tell a responsible adult. By doing so, you protect the health and well-being of this person. You also protect your school by helping to keep other students in a drug-free environment. You also protect society. A person who abuses alcohol and other drugs might drop out of school activities, perform poorly in school, and participate in crime and abusive behavior. Make a "Top Ten List of Reasons Why It Is Responsible to Tell an Adult if a Person You Know Abuses Alcohol or Other Drugs."

How to Get Help for Someone Who Abuses Drugs

Follow the steps outlined below to get help for someone who abuses alcohol or other drugs.

1. **Write down the warning signs of drug abuse that you observe.** Make a list of important details, including the time and the place. For example, you might write: *Wednesday morning before school—had red eyes and couldn't remember locker combination.*

2. **Share your concerns with a responsible adult.** Tell an adult what you have noticed. Take your notes with you; the notes will help the adult decide what to do next.

3. **Listen to the advice of the adult who takes action.** The adult will decide the appropriate actions to take. Usually, the parents or guardian of a young person will be involved. There may be an **intervention,** an action by people who want someone to get treatment. With the help of a mental health professional or drug abuse treatment specialist, family members and friends can conduct an intervention. They meet with the person who abuses drugs, tell how the person's actions have hurt them, and insist that the person get help.

4. **Recognize that you were responsible when you took action to get someone help.** Some people pretend not to notice when they see drug abuse. It takes great strength to be honest and responsible enough to get someone the help he or she needs.

5. **Decide whether you need help.** If you have been affected by the behavior of a person who abuses drugs, talk to your parents or guardian. You may need counseling.

✓ **What should you do if someone you know is abusing drugs or alcohol?**

ACTIVITY

Art
L I N K
Five Steps

Make a foldout booklet containing the five steps for getting help for someone who abuses drugs. Fold and cut sheets of 8 1/2" x 11" paper to make a 16-page booklet. Include a title page, plus two, three, or four pages devoted to each step. Use scripted penmanship to design the title page. The book is your own to share with your family. Include in step 2 the names of adults you would talk to and what you might say.

Write About It!

Living Drug-free

Think about your drug-free lifestyle one year from today. What activities are you involved in? What kinds of people do you hang out with? What do you do for fun in the evenings and on weekends? Write a paragraph describing a day in your life as a drug-free teen.

Maintaining a Drug-Free Lifestyle

You can choose and maintain a drug-free lifestyle. Avoid situations where drugs are used. Choose drug-free activities that bring out the best in you and that keep you connected to your family, your friends, and the community.

There are many types of drug-free activities that give you the chance to explore interests and meet new people. You can look in the newspaper to find times and dates for concerts, plays, sports events, or other activities that interest you. Also, you can develop a new hobby, such as playing chess, making jewelry, or learning to bowl. You may choose to join a club, team, or community group. Spending time with drug-free people will help you avoid the loneliness that can lead to drug use. Doing volunteer work for others is a positive way to build your self-esteem. Helping other people stay happy and healthy will help *you* do the same.

Being drug free will improve your lifestyle, both now and in the future. In the short term, being drug free will help keep your body healthy and your mind clear. It will keep you safe. It will enable you to take leadership roles in your school and community. It will give you the time to practice—and excel at—the activities you enjoy. You will feel proud of the decision you have made, you will gain the respect of your friends and family, and you will enjoy being in control of your life.

In the long term, being drug free helps protect your health throughout your teen years and into adulthood. It helps you reach your education and career goals. You are better able to be a responsible, contributing member of society. Being drug free helps you lead a happy, fulfilled life.

▼ **Being involved in sports, hobbies, and other activities helps you maintain a drug-free lifestyle.**

Finding Help

Your school and community have resources for people who abuse alcohol and other drugs. Ask a guidance counselor or other responsible adult about these resources. Some schools offer programs that assist students with drug-related issues. Others have chapters of national groups, such as Students Against Destructive Decisions (SADD).

There are many places young people can get help for alcohol and drug abuse. These resources include hospitals, drug treatment centers, Al-Anon/Alateen, Alcoholics Anonymous, and Narcotics Anonymous.

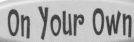

On Your Own

FOR SCHOOL OR HOME

Dialogue on Drugs

Interview an older teen or a young adult who maintains a drug-free lifestyle. What activities is the person involved in? Ask what motivates him or her to maintain a drug-free lifestyle.

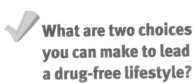 What are two choices you can make to lead a drug-free lifestyle?

▶ **Positive role models can help you live a drug-free lifestyle.**

LESSON 2 REVIEW

Review Concepts

1. **List** two ways drug abuse can affect an individual; two ways it can affect a family; and two ways it can affect society.

2. **Name** five reasons a person might begin abusing alcohol or other drugs.

3. **Outline** the steps you should take if someone you know is abusing drugs.

Critical Thinking

4. **Synthesize** Use what you have learned in this lesson to write a Drug-Free Pledge. Your pledge should include at least five "I will" statements that tell what you will do to maintain a drug-free lifestyle.

5. **LIFE SKILLS** **Manage Stress** How can managing stress help a person maintain a drug-free lifestyle? In your answer, give examples of ways to manage stress that can help a person maintain a drug-free lifestyle.

Tobacco

More young people today than ever before choose not to smoke or use smokeless tobacco products. They also try to avoid breathing the smoke from other people's cigars and cigarettes. They know that tobacco is harmful to their health. Teens who say "no" to tobacco promote their health and the health of others.

Tobacco Addiction

Tobacco is a plant whose leaves are dried and used as the main ingredient in cigarettes and cigars. Tobacco smoke contains more than 250 substances that are toxic or cause cancer. **Nicotine** is a highly addictive stimulant drug found in tobacco. It raises the heart rate and blood pressure. It may cause sweating, nausea, and diarrhea. **Tar** is a thick, sticky fluid produced when tobacco is burned. It coats the lungs and makes it difficult for oxygen to pass into the blood. Tar can cause cancer. **Carbon monoxide** is an odorless, colorless, poisonous gas in tobacco smoke. It can cause headaches, shortness of breath, nausea, and chest pain.

Tobacco use can result in physical and psychological addiction. When people are physically addicted to tobacco, their bodies crave it. Without tobacco, they sometimes feel nervous and tired and develop headaches.

People who are psychologically addicted to tobacco use it to fulfill emotional needs. Psychological addiction is as difficult to overcome as physical addiction.

Tobacco addiction can happen with a single use or over a longer period of time. It usually occurs in stages.

Stage 1: First Use A person tries a cigarette or a little snuff—to fit in, to rebel, or to experiment.

Stage 2: Occasional Use The person continues to use tobacco at certain times or with certain people.

Stage 3: Regular Use The person uses tobacco every weekend or at the same times every day. Tolerance develops.

Stage 4: Addiction The person feels a strong need for tobacco and uses it regularly. He or she may be unable to quit without help.

Tobacco use can result in addiction. People who begin using tobacco when they are young often find it difficult to stop later. Tobacco use increases the risk of other drug use. Teens who smoke are about seven times more likely than those who don't to drink alcohol and use marijuana or cocaine.

Do You Know?

Effects of a mother's smoking on an unborn child include low birth-weight, sudden infant death syndrome (SIDS), miscarriage, and prematurity (having a baby that is not fully developed). Long-term effects also include asthma, behavior problems such as hyper-activity, and lung cancer.

▼ **Warning labels tell only part of the story.**

SURGEON GENERAL'S WARNING: Smoking Causes Lung Cancer, Heart Disease, Emphysema, And May Complicate Pregnancy.

 **What is nicotine?**

The Effects of Tobacco on the Body

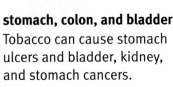
An Expensive Habit

The costs of smoking are not only physical; they are financial, too. If a person smoked one pack of cigarettes a day for the next 20 years, he or she would spend more than $20,000 on the habit. Calculate how much money a person who smoked would spend in a month if the person smoked two packs a day and each pack cost $7.

Source: Virtual Hospital

Tobacco use affects almost every part of the body. It changes the way a person looks and smells. It increases heartbeat and blood pressure, and drains a person's energy. It damages internal organs and interferes with body functions. Here is a look at the harmful effects of tobacco—from head to toe.

How Tobacco Use Affects the Body

brain
Nicotine causes the release of a chemical in the brain that makes tobacco users crave tobacco.

mouth, teeth, and throat
Tobacco causes bad breath, stains the teeth, and decreases the senses of taste and smell. It can cause gum disease and mouth, throat, and esophageal cancer.

blood vessels
Carbon monoxide reduces the amount of oxygen carried in the blood. As a result, physical activity is more difficult. Tobacco narrows the blood vessels, causing a condition called atherosclerosis.

heart
As a result of atherosclerosis, the heart must work harder to pump blood. This extra stress on the heart can lead to high blood pressure, heart attack, and stroke.

stomach, colon, and bladder
Tobacco can cause stomach ulcers and bladder, kidney, and stomach cancers.

lungs
Smoking blocks the airways, impairs the lungs, and increases the risk of lung cancer and other respiratory diseases.

skin
Smoking ages and wrinkles the skin.

fingers
Long-term tobacco use can stain the fingers yellow.

Diseases Linked to Tobacco

Tobacco use can lead to many serious diseases and disorders such as

- **cancer,** a disease in which abnormal cells grow and spread. People who smoke have an increased risk of cancers in the mouth, throat, breast, lungs, and pancreas. Smoking is the most common cause of death from cancer.

- **emphysema** (em•fuh•ZEE•muh), a condition in which the air sacs in the lungs become damaged. As a result, the body does not get all of the oxygen it needs. Emphysema is also known as chronic obstructive pulmonary disease (COPD). COPD is responsible for more than 100,000 deaths per year. Cigarette smoking causes 90 percent of all cases of emphysema.

- **asthma** (AZ•muh), a chronic condition in which the airways become narrow or blocked and breathing becomes difficult. Smoking and breathing secondhand smoke can cause asthma-related symptoms in children and teens.

- **chronic bronchitis,** a condition in which mucus blocks the airways. People with bronchitis must cough to dislodge the mucus. Smoking is the greatest risk factor for bronchitis.

▶ By avoiding tobacco, you decrease your risk for many diseases.

Science LINK

A Cilia Model

Smoking paralyzes the *cilia*, little hairlike structures in the lungs. Normally, these "brooms of the lungs" move back and forth to sweep out particles of dust and pollen. In the lungs of people who smoke, the cilia become paralyzed and cannot do their job. Dust and other materials—including the tar from cigarettes—build up. Using paper towel rolls, make two models of an air passage, one lined with healthy cilia, the other lined with paralyzed cilia, clogged with dust. Share ideas for the most effective materials to use to show the differences.

- **respiratory infections,** such as colds and pneumonia. Smoking robs the body of vitamin C, which helps keep the immune system strong.

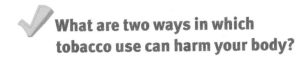
What are two ways in which tobacco use can harm your body?

D23

ACTIVITY

On Your Own

FOR SCHOOL OR HOME

Learn the Law

With a parent or guardian, visit various stores, restaurants, or office buildings in your community and ask about smoking regulations for them. Check your community's laws about smoking in public buildings.

▼ **Choose friends who do not smoke or use smokeless tobacco.**

Smokeless Tobacco and Secondhand Smoke

Tobacco can harm you even if you *don't* light up. Using smokeless tobacco is as dangerous as smoking cigarettes. Being around the smoke from other people's cigarettes and cigars can harm your body.

Forms of smokeless tobacco   Smokeless tobacco is tobacco made and sold in two forms: chewing tobacco and snuff. Chewing tobacco is chopped tobacco that is chewed. Snuff is powdered tobacco that is placed between the cheek and gums. Sucking or chewing either form of tobacco sends nicotine into the bloodstream through the tissues in your mouth. The nicotine makes smokeless tobacco addictive. Smokeless tobacco contains dangerous chemicals, including cadmium (used in car batteries), arsenic (a lethal poison), cyanide (another poison), and lead. Smokeless tobacco has 28 cancer-causing agents. Tobacco companies even add sand and fiberglass to smokeless tobacco to increase the absorption of nicotine.

Effects of smokeless tobacco Smokeless tobacco causes bad breath and stained teeth, cracked and bleeding lips, receding gums, tooth decay, stomach ulcers, heart attacks, and strokes. After seven days of using smokeless tobacco, sores and red and white patches can start to form in the mouth. The white patches have a high chance of becoming cancerous. Treatment for oral cancer includes surgery, which may disfigure the face.

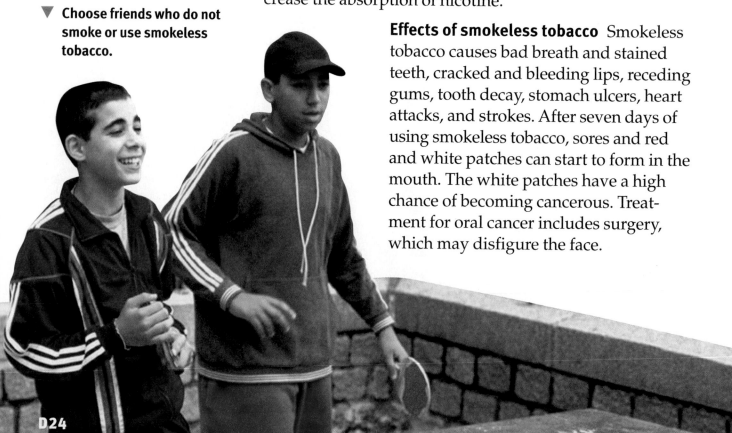

Secondhand Smoke

If someone smokes near you, you will breathe in second-hand smoke. **Secondhand smoke** is exhaled smoke and sidestream smoke. *Sidestream smoke* is smoke from a burning cigarette or cigar. Breathing secondhand smoke is harmful. Secondhand smoke contains harmful substances that can irritate the eyes, nose, throat, and lungs, and cause headaches. Secondhand smoke also causes your hair and clothes to smell. This might lead others to believe that you have been smoking, even if you have not.

Breathing secondhand smoke has been linked to serious health problems. Each year, it causes about 3,000 deaths from lung cancer. It also causes 35,000 heart disease–related deaths among nonsmokers. In children, secondhand smoke can cause asthma, pneumonia, bronchitis, and respiratory infections. About 7,500 to 15,000 children under the age of 18 months are hospitalized each year for infections caused by secondhand smoke.

Avoiding secondhand smoke Concerns about secondhand smoke have led to smoking bans in public places. Smoking is banned in many restaurants, offices, factories, and shopping malls. In some cities and towns, smoking also is banned in building entrances, in parks, and on beaches.

You can avoid the harmful effects of second-hand smoke by asking people not to smoke near you. At home, family members can adopt a non-smoking policy. When you leave the house, you can go to smoke-free places. When places are not smoke free, you can choose to sit in a smoke-free section. You can even be a health advocate by writing to a favorite restaurant to encourage the owner to make it smoke free.

✔ **What is secondhand smoke?**

This facility is smoke free.

No Smoking

▶ **Many communities ban smoking in public places.**

Resisting Pressure to Use Tobacco

Teens need to prepare themselves to say "no." Resisting the pressure to smoke tobacco, dip snuff, or chew tobacco protects your health. It will earn you the respect of other people. It may even persuade users to say "no" as well.

Most teens don't smoke or use smokeless tobacco. They know that tobacco use is harmful. They know that it is illegal for minors to purchase tobacco products. They also know that once a person starts using tobacco, it is difficult to stop.

Some teens *do* use tobacco, though. They start using it for a variety of reasons. They may experience pressure from their peers. They may falsely believe that smoking relieves stress or aids in weight loss. They may be influenced by messages in the media, such as ads for cigarettes. Some of these influences are strong ones. Nevertheless, you *can* resist the pressure to use tobacco.

ACTIVITY — LIFE SKILLS

CRITICAL THINKING

Analyze What Influences Your Health

Tobacco manufacturers pay large sums of money to write persuasive ads. Some of these ads are aimed directly at teens. They make tobacco use look fun, attractive, and harmless. One way you can resist these ads is to analyze them.

1 **Identify people and things that might influence you.** Find an ad for a tobacco product. It might show a thin, attractive person smoking on a yacht, or a rugged-looking man on horseback.

2 **Evaluate how the influence might affect your health and decisions.** Study the ad closely. What parts of the ad make smoking look fun, glamorous, or appealing? How might these images influence the viewer's decision about using tobacco?

3 **Choose positive influences on health.** Note any part of the ad that might be a *positive* influence on your health. Look carefully at all the fine print.

4 **Protect yourself from negative influences on health.** To avoid being influenced by tobacco ads, remember that they are deceptive. Remind yourself that what you *read* in ads does not match up with what you *know* about tobacco.

Taste the Great Outdoors

Resist Pressure to Use Tobacco

Use resistance skills to resist pressure to use tobacco.

- **Say "no"** with self-confidence.
- **Give reasons** for saying "no."
- **Repeat** your "no" response several times.
- **Use nonverbal behavior** to match verbal behavior.
- **Avoid situations** in which there will be pressure to make wrong decisions.
- **Avoid people** who make wrong decisions.
- **Resist pressure** to engage in illegal behavior.
- **Influence others** to make responsible decisions.

For information about resisting tobacco, contact your school nurse, your community health department, the American Cancer Society, the American Heart Association, or the American Lung Association. Some organizations also provide information about tobacco-cessation programs, which help people stop using tobacco.

 What resistance skills can you use to resist the pressure to use tobacco?

▶ **Good friends won't pressure you to use tobacco.**

LESSON 3 REVIEW

Review Concepts

1. **List** the four stages in which tobacco addiction occurs.

2. **Identify** five ways tobacco use harms the body.

3. **State** three disorders of the respiratory system caused by tobacco use.

4. **Explain** reasons why smokeless tobacco and secondhand smoke are harmful.

5. **Name** three sources of pressure to smoke and tell how you can resist each one.

Critical Thinking

6. **Synthesize** Design an ad for a campaign to encourage teens to avoid tobacco use. Draw or describe an illustration for your ad and write a slogan or a short paragraph to accompany it.

7. **LIFE SKILLS** **Analyze What Influences Your Health** Teens sometimes view celebrities as role models. As a result, a celebrity's behavior might influence a teen's decision about tobacco use. Write a paragraph that identifies people who might influence you and evaluate how the influence might affect your decision to use tobacco.

Use Resistance Skills

Dear Health Nut,

Here's the problem ... My friend has started smoking cigarettes. He thinks that smoking is cool and that it makes him look older. A couple of times he has offered me a cigarette. I don't want to smoke, but I don't want to lose my friend either. What should I do?

Distraught in Dallas

No Smoking

Dear Distraught in Dallas,

Here is how you might solve the problem . . . Use your resistance skills. You don't want to smoke—nor do you want to breathe secondhand smoke. But you aren't sure how to say so without upsetting your friend. All you have to do is say "no" with self-confidence. He'll get the message loud and clear.

Health Nut

Learn This Life Skill

Follow these four steps to use resistance skills. You can use the Foldables to help you organize your thoughts.

1 **Say "no" in a firm voice.**

Feel confident about your decision. You have made a responsible choice. You are in control of your actions.

2 **Give reasons for saying "no."**

Some reasons to give are

- it's not healthful.
- it's not safe.
- it's not legal.
- it does not show respect for myself and others. I don't want to smell like smoke.
- it does not follow the guidelines of my parents and other responsible adults.
- it does not demonstrate good character.

3 **Be certain your behavior matches your words.**

Do not hold a cigarette or pretend to inhale it. Avoid situations in which there will be pressure to make harmful decisions. Avoid being with people who make harmful decisions. Resist the pressure to do something illegal.

4 **Ask an adult for help if you need help.**

If an adult is not present and you feel uncomfortable, say that you need to be somewhere and leave immediately.

If you do this activity with a group of students, students can participate in different ways to illustrate all four steps of **using resistance skills,** such as writing, folding, or drawing. Some students may do the activity in other ways, such as by role-playing or drawing a comic strip to illustrate the four steps.

Practice This Life Skill

Activity What would you say to a classmate who pressures you to smoke? Make a list of the resistance skills you will use in this situation. Then role-play with a classmate who will pressure you while you demonstrate these resistance skills.

Alcohol

You will learn . . .

- the effects of alcohol on the body.
- the effects of drinking alcohol on decision making and relationships.
- the short- and long-term effects of drinking alcohol.
- resistance skills you can use if you are pressured to drink alcohol.

Vocabulary

- **alcohol,** D31
- **cirrhosis,** D31
- **blood alcohol concentration,** D34
- **alcoholism,** D35
- **fetal alcohol syndrome (FAS),** D35

It takes an alert mind to play a video game. It also takes physical coordination—responding quickly to what you see by pressing the right button. More than just in video games, you use mental alertness and physical coordination all the time. To protect your mind and body, choose to be alcohol free.

How Alcohol Affects the Body

Alcohol is a drug found in some beverages that slows body functions. When a person drinks alcohol, his or her body converts the alcohol into acetaldehyde. However, the body gradually converts this substance into carbon dioxide and water, which are eliminated from the body.

Excessive use of alcohol could also lead to **cirrhosis** (suh•ROH•suhs), a disease in which scar tissue replaces healthy liver cells. Cirrhosis is one of the ten leading causes of death by disease in the United States.

More than 100,000 people die from alcohol-related causes each year. Alcohol is the third leading cause of death in the United States.

Source: National Substance Abuse Index

 What is cirrhosis?

The Physical Effects of Alcohol

brain
Alcohol weakens the brain's ability to store, locate, and use information. Over time, it can *shrink* your brain!

heart
Heavy drinking can lead to high blood pressure and irregular heartbeat.

liver
Heavy drinking can poison the liver and lead to hepatitis and cirrhosis.

stomach
Too much alcohol can irritate the lining of the stomach and small intestine. Ulcers may result.

blood vessels
Alcohol causes the blood vessels to widen. With more blood passing through the veins, the person who drinks alcohol may feel warmer. In fact, more blood is flowing to the surface of the skin, which allows more body heat to escape.

Being alcohol-free allows people to develop and enjoy lasting friendships.

How Alcohol Affects Decisions and Relationships

Drinking alcohol has effects on the life skills you use when you make decisions and have relationships.

Alcohol's Effect on Decisions

Alcohol depresses, or slows down, the part of the brain used for reasoning. This means that when you drink, you lose the ability to make responsible decisions. People who drink are more likely to

- **give in to harmful peer pressure.** When people drink, even just a few sips, it is more difficult to use resistance skills.

- **communicate poorly with others.** Some people become very talkative when they drink. They say things or share feelings that they later regret. Drinking also affects the motor skills that control muscle coordination in the mouth, so it becomes difficult to speak clearly.

  - **experience depression.** Alcohol is a depressant drug. Drinking makes people depressed. At first, it might cause people to forget their problems. However, when problems remain unsolved, they become worse.

  - **become violent.** Drinking makes a person less able to resolve conflicts. It can lead to arguments, fights, and violence. In fact, alcohol is involved in about one out of two murders and one out of three sexual assaults.

  - **drive under the influence.** Every 33 minutes, someone in America dies from an alcohol-related car crash. Many people who have been drinking believe that they are capable of driving. In reality, their ability to react has slowed dramatically. People who have been drinking also might accept a ride with a driver who has been drinking.

Alcohol's Effect on Relationships

You are at an age when it is important to work on your relationships with others. Drinking alcohol can make it difficult for you to learn social skills that help you connect with others. Alcohol can affect your mood. It might make you more talkative or give you a false feeling of closeness to others. You might say and do things that you might not usually do. In this way, alcohol becomes a crutch that keeps you from developing healthful social skills.

Families Drinking alcohol affects family relationships. Your parents or guardians do not approve of you drinking alcohol. If you drink, you will have to sneak around and lie about what you are doing. This destroys the trusting relationship you want to have with them.

Friendships Drinking alcohol affects friendships. Teens who make responsible decisions don't drink and they choose to stay away from teens who do drink. You would lose the respect of teens who choose to be drug free. Their parents or guardian would not approve of them spending time with you.

Risk behaviors Drinking alcohol increases the likelihood that you will take part in risk behaviors. Alcohol affects the thinking and reasoning part of the brain. For example, you might not stick to your decision to practice abstinence from sex. In fact, one in four teens ages 13 to 18, who had been sexually active, said that they were drinking the first time they had sexual contact. The consequences might be unintended pregnancy and infection with STDs, including HIV. Drinking alcohol makes feelings intense. Many people who act violently were drinking at the time.

How might drinking alcohol affect a person's relationships?

Do You Know

There is a close link between alcohol and suicide. More than one in three eighth-grade girls who are heavy drinkers have also attempted suicide.

Source: Do It Now Foundation

Healthful family relationships are a protective factor against alcoholism.

Physical Education LINK

Make a Sports Checklist

Drinking alcohol affects fitness skills—for example, agility, balance, coordination, reaction time, and speed. Even a small amount of alcohol impairs hand-eye coordination. It makes a person run and react more slowly. Make a six-column chart. In column 1, list sports played at your school. Label the other columns with the names of the fitness skills. Demonstrate each sport with a partner and determine which fitness skills are used. Put a check mark next to each sport to indicate the skill used, as a way of showing why athletes must avoid alcohol.

Other Effects of Drinking

Drinking alcohol over many years can have long-term effects on health, such as the development of cirrhosis. However, it also has short-term effects, even after one drink. Many short-term effects depend on a person's blood alcohol concentration (BAC). **Blood alcohol concentration** is the amount of alcohol in a person's blood.

Factors That Affect BAC

Several factors contribute to a person's BAC, such as

- **amount of alcohol.** The more alcohol a person drinks, the higher his or her BAC will be.
- **rate of drinking.** Drinking faster than one's liver can process the alcohol increases a person's BAC.
- **weight.** The less a person weighs, the faster he or she feels the effects of alcohol.
- **foods eaten.** When a person's stomach is empty, alcohol enters the bloodstream more rapidly.
  - **other drugs.** If another depressant drug is in the bloodstream, the effects of alcohol will be greater.
  - **gender.** Males produce more of the enzyme that breaks down alcohol. Therefore, the BAC of females increases faster than that of males.
  - **mood.** If a person is depressed before beginning to drink, his or her depression will tend to be more severe afterward.

The higher a person's BAC, the more short-term effects the person experiences. Short-term effects include blurred vision, slurred speech, slowed reaction time, nausea, vomiting, headache, dehydration, and fatigue.

◄ Drinking alcohol damages your growing body.

Long-Term Effects

Alcoholism is a disease in which a person is dependent on alcohol. The dependence is physical and psychological. People with alcoholism might have different patterns of drinking. Some people are binge drinkers. They drink large amounts of alcohol at one time. Others drink alcohol every day.

Some people have a greater risk for developing alcoholism because of their heredity. When alcohol enters the body, it is changed into acetaldehyde, a poison. Acetaldehyde is very toxic and if it were to build up in the body, a person would become violently sick and could die. Fortunately, it is changed in the body to carbon dioxide and water and eliminated by the kidneys and lungs.

In some people, a small amount of acetaldehyde goes to the brain and becomes THIQ. THIQ is like an opiate, a drug that relieves pain. As THIQ builds up, a person becomes "hooked" or "addicted." These people have developed alcoholism. If one or more adult members of a family have alcoholism, the children are at increased risk for alcoholism. However, they can still be committed to stay alcohol free.

Alcoholism lasts a lifetime. A person who has the disease can recover, but the person cannot drink again.

Alcoholism has been called a "family disease" because there is a heredity factor—it runs in families. The family of a person with alcoholism can respond either by enabling or allowing the drinking, or they can use honest talk. Those who use honest talk confront the family member with alcoholism. They share their feelings, making it clear that the person must take steps toward recovery.

Fetal alcohol syndrome (FAS) is a condition that causes birth defects in babies born to mothers who drank alcohol during pregnancy. When a pregnant woman drinks, the baby's BAC soars. This can harm the baby in many ways. Babies born with FAS may have slow physical and mental growth. They may have poor motor skills and develop learning problems. To prevent FAS, a pregnant woman should avoid drinking alcohol.

What is alcoholism?

▶ **Family support is an important factor in continuing to live an alcohol-free life.**

Saying "No" to Alcohol

It is important that you learn to recognize and resist pressure to drink alcohol.

Someone might offer you a beer at a party or a drink of liquor at a football game. Someone might keep pressuring you to drink after you've said "no" or even make fun of you. It is easy to learn skills to avoid these pressures.

USE RESISTANCE SKILLS TO RESIST PRESSURE TO DRINK ALCOHOL	
Situation	**Response**
Someone offers you a drink at a party.	Say "no" with confidence.
The person continues to offer you a drink.	Say "no" again. Give reasons for saying "no."
You are at a sleepover. Your friend wants to sneak some of her parents' alcohol.	Use nonverbal behavior to match verbal behavior. You may need to call your family and go home.
A friend invites you to a party where there will be alcohol.	Avoid people and situations that are influences to drink alcohol.
A friend who has been drinking offers you a ride home from a party.	Resist pressure to engage in illegal behavior.
A friend says she might attend a party with older teens who drink alcohol.	Influence others to make responsible decisions.

ACTIVITY

MAKE a Difference

Maintaining a Drug-Free Lifestyle

As a high school student in Miami, Lihua Chen makes a difference. She serves as the president of her school's Drug Free Youth In Town (DFYIT) club, which offers children entertaining ways to stay alcohol and drug free. Sometimes, Lihua wonders whether her group's hard work helps other people. When she has these doubts, she reminds herself that, little by little, the work is worth the effort. Make a list of ways you can help keep your community drug free.

Other pressures are more subtle. Just being at a gathering where alcohol is present puts pressure on those who are there. The next time you are pressured to drink alcohol, use resistance skills.

 What should you do if you are pressured to drink alcohol?

Set Health Goals

1 **Write the health goal you want to set:** *I will not drink alcohol.*

2 **Tell how the goal will affect your health.** Write down five ways in which maintaining an alcohol-free lifestyle promotes health.

3 **Describe a plan you will follow. Keep track of your progress.** Develop a plan to maintain an alcohol-free lifestyle. You might spend more time pursuing a hobby or playing a musical instrument. You might help out more at home.

4 **Evaluate how your plan worked.** Evaluate your plan after a few days, then after a week. Did it work? Do you need to make changes? If the plan failed, ask a teacher or parent to help you revise it.

◀ **Resistance skills will help you say "no" to alcohol.**

LESSON 4 REVIEW

Review Concepts

1. **List** four ways in which alcohol can harm the body.

2. **Recall** how drinking alcohol can affect a person's decision making and how it can affect his or her relationships.

3. **Summarize** three short-term effects of drinking alcohol and two long-term effects of alcohol.

4. **Identify** resistance skills you can use if you are pressured to drink alcohol.

Critical Thinking

5. **Evaluate** the best way for your peers to maintain an alcohol-free lifestyle. Make a bumper sticker urging other teens to use that strategy.

6. **LIFE SKILLS** **Set Health Goals** Rewrite the following sentences. Fill in the blanks to compose your own health goal statement: *One important health goal of mine is to not drink alcohol. This protects my health by* _____ *and* _____. *My plan to do this includes* _____, _____, *and* _____.

Illegal Drug Use

You will learn ...

- the short- and long-term effects of using marijuana, inhalants, anabolic steroids, stimulants, depressants, narcotics, and hallucinogens.

Vocabulary

- **illegal drugs,** D39
- **marijuana,** D39
- **hashish,** D39
- **inhalants,** D40
- **anabolic steroids,** D41
- **stimulant,** D42
- **depressants,** D43
- **narcotics,** D44
- **hallucinogens,** D45

Illegal drugs have harmful effects on the body, the emotions, and the mind. Because of this, there are laws that forbid their manufacture, purchase, possession, sale, and use. Being drug free keeps you from breaking laws.

Marijuana

Illegal drugs are drugs for which use, possession, manufacture, and sale are against the law. The most commonly used illegal drug in this country is **marijuana,** an illegal drug that affects mood and short-term memory. Also known as pot, grass, and weed, it comes from a plant called *Cannabis sativa,* or hemp. The dried, shredded leaves of marijuana are sometimes rolled up into a cigarette (known as a joint) or a cigar (known as a blunt) and smoked. Marijuana can also be smoked in pipes or brewed as tea. **Hashish** is an illegal drug made from marijuana that has stronger effects.

Both marijuana and hashish contain over 400 chemicals. The most dangerous of these is THC. In the short term, THC causes problems with memory, learning, and concentration. It affects a person's vision, hearing, sense of touch, and sense of time. It can cause a loss of coordination, an increase in heart rate, and nervousness.

The smoke from marijuana and hashish affects people the same way tobacco smoke does, but to a greater degree. In fact, smoking one joint puts about four times as much tar into the lungs as smoking one tobacco cigarette. Over long periods, using marijuana and hashish can lead to addiction. It can cause cancer, brain damage, lung disease, and heart attack. It can also impair judgment and weaken the immune system, making a person more likely to catch colds. Using these drugs often leads to the use of other illegal drugs, such as heroin and cocaine. For this reason, marijuana has been nicknamed "the gateway drug."

✔ **What is an illegal drug?**

BUILD ACTIVITY

Character

Inform Others

Honesty When discussing illegal drugs, it is important to be honest with others. Sharing true information about the dangers of illegal drugs may persuade others to avoid drug use. You might even save someone's life. Improvise and perform a scene about how you can help a person by educating him or her with the facts about drug use.

▼ **By avoiding illegal drugs, you reduce your risk for many diseases.**

MY CHOICE...
DRUG-FREE.

Red H___ ___P NATIONAL CAMP___

Inhalants

Inhalants (in·HAY·luhnts) are chemicals that are breathed in or inhaled. These substances give off strong gases, or fumes, that can be inhaled to produce a high. Many inhalants are common household products, such as nail polish remover, glue, cleaning fluids, and paint. When used as inhalants, these products often are sniffed directly from the container. They also can be "huffed" from a rag soaked in the substance or inhaled out of a bag. Inhaling these products to produce a high is illegal and harmful. Inhalant abuse causes more than 1,000 deaths a year in the United States.

When the gases in inhalants are breathed in, they replace the oxygen that the body needs. The gases travel to the brain and cause a light-headed feeling known as a "rush" or a "buzz." After a few minutes, the rush wears off. The body labors to replace lost oxygen. The user may experience fatigue, headaches, nausea, vomiting, slurred speech, loss of coordination, and wheezing.

People who abuse inhalants are at risk for sudden sniffing death syndrome (SSDS). SSDS can happen the very first time someone breathes in fumes. Using inhalants to become high can produce irregular heart rhythms, heart failure, and death. Using inhalants often can cause sores around the mouth and the eyes and a red, runny nose. It can result in brain damage. Regular use leads to tolerance and dependence.

ACTIVITY

Science LINK

Diagram the Effects of Inhalants

Some of the chemicals in inhalants get absorbed by the fatty tissues in the brain and spinal cord. One of these tissues, myelin, coats and protects the spinal cord. The spinal cord carries messages from the brain to the rest of the body. Over time, the chemicals in inhalants break down myelin. The result is that the brain can no longer tell the body what to do. Draw a diagram to show the effect inhalants have on myelin and the nervous system.

Anabolic Steroids

Anabolic steroids (a•nuh•BAH•lik STIR•oydz) are drugs used to increase muscle size and strength. These drugs have medical uses and can be prescribed by a physician. Nonanabolic steroids, such as cortisone, are used to treat medical problems such as asthma and arthritis. Anabolic steroids are sometimes used illegally without a prescription. Most people who abuse anabolic steroids are athletes who want to boost their performance. In recent years, the abuse of anabolic steroids by teen males has risen.

Anabolic steroids are taken as pills or injected directly into the muscles. Anabolic steroids can produce a range of harmful side effects, including breast enlargement and damage to reproductive organs in males, breast reduction in females, stunted growth, and severe acne.

Anabolic steroids can also cause hardening of the arteries, high blood pressure, liver damage, mood swings, and aggressive or violent behavior. Withdrawal from anabolic steroids can lead to depression.

The health effects of anabolic steroids in teens are disturbing. If teens take anabolic steroids before their growth spurt, their growth may stop. As a result, they may remain short for the rest of their lives.

 Why is it harmful and unsafe to use inhalants and anabolic steroids?

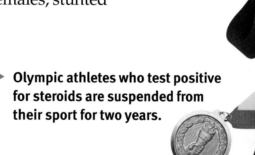

▶ **Olympic athletes who test positive for steroids are suspended from their sport for two years.**

ACTIVITY LIFE SKILLS

CRITICAL THINKING

Set Health Goals

Use a health behavior contract to set a health goal.

1 **Write the health goal you want to set:** *I will not misuse or abuse drugs.*

2 **Tell how the goal will affect your health.** A healthful way to increase muscle strength is to exercise and remain drug free, including free from anabolic steroids.

3 **Describe a plan you will follow. Keep track of your progress.** Make a daily exercise plan to increase muscle strength. Check with your family and with a coach for their approval.

4 **Evaluate how your plan worked.** Review your plan after you have used it for a week. Did you stick to your exercise plan? If not, how can you improve the plan for the coming week?

Stimulants

A **stimulant** is one of a group of drugs that speed up the body's functions. Stimulants increase heart rate and blood pressure. They make people feel more alert and awake. They also can make people feel restless and irritable. Tolerance and addiction to stimulants can develop quickly.

Caffeine *Caffeine* is a stimulant found in chocolate, coffee, tea, some soft drinks, and some prescription and OTC drugs. It stimulates the circulatory, respiratory, and nervous systems. Caffeine is a legal stimulant.

Illegal stimulants *Cocaine* is an illegal, addictive stimulant made from the leaves of the coca plant. Cocaine is usually snorted or sniffed. Its use can result in anxiety, loss of appetite, sleeplessness, paranoia, and depression. Even a single use of cocaine can result in a heart attack. Its many side effects include burns and sores in the nose, loss of interest in daily activities, hallucinations, stroke, seizures, and brain infections.

Crack is an illegal drug that is a stronger form of cocaine. Highly addictive, it has the same short- and long-term effects as cocaine.

Amphetamines are stimulants that suppress the appetite and keep a person awake. A physician may prescribe them for certain medical conditions, including some sleep disorders. However, amphetamines are highly addictive. All uses of amphetamines other than those prescribed by a physician are illegal. Amphetamines are often made and sold illegally. People who abuse amphetamines can become violent and paranoid. They can experience fever, sweating, headaches, blurred vision, and dizziness. Amphetamines can cause irregular heartbeat, loss of coordination, and heart failure. All people who abuse amphetamines are at increased risk for becoming addicted, being infected by HIV or hepatitis (if injected), and of death by overdose.

NEW-GENERATION STIMULANTS

Stimulants speed up the body's functions by changing the way the brain works. Stimulants change the way nerve cells communicate. New-generation stimulants include:

Crystal meth	a powder form of amphetamine that can be injected, inhaled, or swallowed
Ice and Glass	amphetamines that are smoked to produce a fast, strong effect
Crank	amphetamines that come in tablets or capsules; a nickname for all forms of street stimulants, or "speed"

Depressants

Depressants are a group of drugs that slow down the body's functions. They relax the muscles, calm the nerves, and make people sleepy. They also decrease the heart rate and blood pressure. Depressants interfere with brain activity. They slow down brain cells and affect reasoning and judgment.

Alcohol is a depressant drug. Other depressants include barbiturates and tranquilizers.

Barbiturates A *barbiturate* (bar•BI•chuh•ruht) is a drug that causes sleepiness. A tranquilizer is a drug that relieves anxiety. Both can be prescribed for medical conditions. Barbiturates and tranquilizers also can be abused and used illegally.

Barbiturates are odorless powders that come in tablet or capsule form. They are the most dangerous of all depressants. People who use barbiturates experience slowed heart rates, confusion, and a feeling of dullness. They can also become emotional, violent, depressed, and anxious. Like alcohol, barbiturates can cause slurred speech, hostility, and clumsiness. In large doses, they can cause unconsciousness and death. Tolerance of barbiturates occurs rapidly. Withdrawal symptoms include an increased risk of suicide.

Tranquilizers *Tranquilizers* are drugs that relieve anxiety and can be taken orally or by injection. They can produce sleepiness, confusion, depression, and blurred vision. In large doses, a tranquilizer can magnify a person's behavior. For example, it might make a person who is loud become louder or a person who is sad become sadder. Tranquilizers also can cause slurred speech, sleeplessness, and rage. When barbiturates or tranquilizers are used together or with alcohol, the person using them may fall into a coma and die.

 How are stimulants different from depressants?

On Your Own
FOR SCHOOL OR HOME

Make a Harmful/ Healthful Card

Fold a piece of drawing paper in half. Make a chart that looks like this, with *Harmful* on one half and *Healthful* on the other. Add more items to each side of the chart.

Harmful	Healthful
Friends who smoke	Friends who are drug free
Drinking beer	Drinking juice

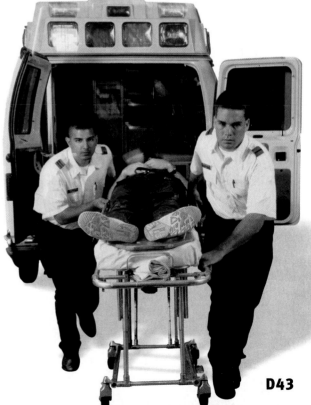

▼ **Illegal drug use can have harmful consequences.**

Narcotics

Narcotics are a group of drugs that slow down the nervous system and relieve pain. They are made from opium, a substance found in the poppy plant. Narcotics also can put a person into a deep sleep. Physicians prescribe some narcotics for medicinal purposes. Using narcotics without a prescription is against the law.

Narcotics include morphine, codeine, and heroin. *Morphine* (MAWR•feen) is a narcotic used to control pain. It may be swallowed or injected. A person who uses morphine may be unable to concentrate and may experience mild anxiety. Morphine constricts the pupils, so vision can become blurred. An overdose of morphine can cause coma or death. Long-term use can change brain function. Stopping morphine use can cause severe withdrawal symptoms.

Codeine (KOH•deen) is a narcotic painkiller made from morphine. It has a calming effect and can produce sleep. It also slows reaction time, increasing the chance of unintentional injuries. Codeine is addictive. In large doses, it can cause coma and death.

Heroin (HER•uh•wuhn) is an illegal narcotic made from the same substance as morphine. It is used illegally to produce a "FALSE" warm, happy feeling. Using heroin can be fatal. It may be injected, sniffed, or smoked. Heroin use can cause dry mouth, slurred speech, vomiting, and constipation. Long-term use can cause pneumonia; brain damage; and lung, liver, and kidney infections. In addition to the effects of the drug itself, street heroin may have additives that do not dissolve. These substances might clog the blood vessels that lead to the heart, lungs, liver, and brain. This can cause the death of small patches of cells in vital organs. Sharing a needle to inject heroin increases the risk of transmitting HIV. Withdrawal symptoms include sleeplessness, joint pain, cold flashes, and sometimes death.

CAREERS IN HEALTH

DEA Agent

DEA agents work for the U.S. Drug Enforcement Administration (DEA). DEA agents enforce drug laws by investigating cases of possible drug abuse. They sometimes go undercover to investigate criminals suspected of breaking drug laws. DEA agents must be honest and have good judgment. They also must be familiar with the law. To become a DEA agent, you must have a college degree and special training with the FBI.

 LOG ON Visit **www.mmhhealth.com** to find out more about this and other health careers.

Hallucinogens

Hallucinogens (huh•LOO•sin•uh•jins) are a group of illegal drugs that cause a person to feel different sensations. They affect the way a person perceives his or her surroundings. These drugs cause people to see and hear things that are not real. Hallucinogens impair a person's judgment and increase the risk of accidents and injuries. All are addictive.

Hallucinogens include LSD, PCP, and mescaline. *LSD* is an illegal hallucinogen sold in tablets, capsules, or liquid form. It can cause blurred vision, lowered body temperature, nausea, and rapid heart rate. Long-term effects of LSD use include depression and flashbacks.

PCP is an illegal hallucinogen that speeds up or slows down body functions. It is also known as angel dust and Supergrass. PCP can exist in a pure, white crystal powder or in capsules or tablets. It may cause people who abuse it to feel detached from their surroundings.

▲ **Hallucinogens distort reality, even for spiders.**

It may cause numbness, slurred speech, and clumsiness. People who use PCP become violent and engage in risk behaviors.

Mescaline (MES•kuh•luhn) is an illegal hallucinogen made from the peyote cactus plant. Button-shaped parts of the plant are chewed or soaked to produce a liquid. Mescaline can cause people to see and hear things that aren't there. They may develop a blank stare or rapid eye movements. Mescaline can cause flashbacks long after it is used.

 **What are hallucinogens?**

LESSON 5 REVIEW

Review Concepts

1. **List** three short-term and three long-term effects of smoking marijuana or hashish.

2. **Explain** how an inhalant affects the brain.

3. **Identify** three harmful side effects of anabolic steroids.

4. **Name** one stimulant, one depressant, one narcotic, and one hallucinogen, and describe the effects of each.

Critical Thinking

5. **Synthesize** Suppose you were pressured to try one of the drugs described in this lesson. Write a paragraph that describes resistance skills you might use.

6. **LIFE SKILLS** **Set Health Goals** A friend is setting a goal of not misusing or abusing drugs. What are some healthful actions that your friend can carry out daily to be sure to reach or maintain that goal? For example, your friend may avoid gangs and spend more family time at home.

CHAPTER **7** REVIEW

Chapter Summary

Lesson 1 • Over-the-counter and prescription drugs help maintain and improve health when used as directed. Following guidelines for their safe use protects health and prevents drug abuse.

Lesson 2 • Abusing alcohol and other drugs harms the individual involved in the abuse, his or her family, and society. Choosing a drug-free lifestyle protects individuals, families, and society.

Lesson 3 • Using tobacco products can lead to addiction and can harm many of the body's organs and systems. Resisting tobacco protects health.

Lesson 4 • Using alcohol can harm health. Using resistance skills when offered alcohol products protects health.

Lesson 5 • The misuse, abuse, or illegal use of the following drugs harms health: marijuana, inhalants, anabolic steroids, stimulants, depressants, narcotics, and hallucinogens. Obeying drug laws and following family guidelines for drug use protect the health and safety of you and others.

Use Vocabulary

drug, D5

medicine, D5

tolerance, D7

drug abuse, D10

addiction, D14

nicotine, D21

alcoholism, D35

illegal drug, D39

depressant, D43

Choose the correct term from the list to complete each sentence.

1. Any substance that can change the way your body or your mind works is a(n) _____?_____.

2. A drug used to prevent or cure illness or disease, or to relieve pain is called a(n) _____?_____.

3. Someone who needs larger and larger doses of a substance to get the same effect has developed a(n) _____?_____ to that drug.

4. A person whose body or mind depends on a substance has developed a(n) _____?_____.

5. A drug that slows down the body's functions is a(n) _____?_____.

6. Heroin is never prescribed by a physician. It is a(n) _____?_____.

7. The intentional use of a substance for nonmedical purposes is called _____?_____.

8. The addictive substance found in all tobacco products is _____?_____.

9. The disease that causes a person to lose control over how much alcohol he or she consumes is called _____?_____.

Answer each question in complete sentences.

10. What is the difference between an over-the-counter drug and a prescription drug?

11. In addition to the individual who uses, who else is affected by drug abuse?

12. Why are smokeless tobacco and second-hand smoke harmful to health?

13. How does drinking alcohol affect a person's ability to make decisions?

14. Name three side effects caused by the use of anabolic steroids.

Reading Comprehension

Answer each question in complete sentences.

Drug misuse is the harmful use of a legal drug that is not done on purpose. Lack of knowledge might lead to drug misuse. If you do not follow the instructions for the proper use of a drug, you are misusing it. You might misread a medicine label in the middle of the night and take too big a dose. These are examples of drug misuse.

15. Does drug misuse always happen on purpose?

16. What can you do to avoid misusing a drug?

Critical Thinking/Problem Solving

Answer each question in complete sentences.

Analyze Concepts

17. Why are drug misuse and drug abuse harmful and unsafe?

18. What warning signs suggest that someone may be using drugs?

19. Describe how tobacco use can lead to addiction.

20. How might drinking alcohol affect a person's relationships?

21. Why is marijuana known as the "gateway drug"? Why is it harmful?

Practice Life Skills

22. Use Resistance Skills Your friend says, "Let's go outside for a few minutes. I'll give you one of my cigarettes." With a classmate, role-play resistance skills.

23. Make Responsible Decisions At a friend's family gathering, a guest offers Meg a glass of wine. Meg knows she should not take the wine but is worried that she might offend her hosts. What is the responsible decision she should make. How would she use the Guidelines for Making Responsible Decisions™?

Read Graphics

Use the text in the visual below to answer the questions.

24. By what percent did inhalant abuse among eighth graders decrease from 1993 to 1999?

25. In what year did the most eighth graders abuse inhalants?

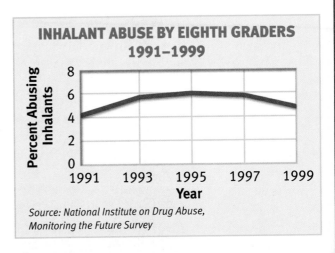

INHALANT ABUSE BY EIGHTH GRADERS 1991–1999

Source: National Institute on Drug Abuse, Monitoring the Future Survey

 LOG ON Visit **www.mmhhealth.com** to find out how much you know about alcohol, tobacco, and other drugs.

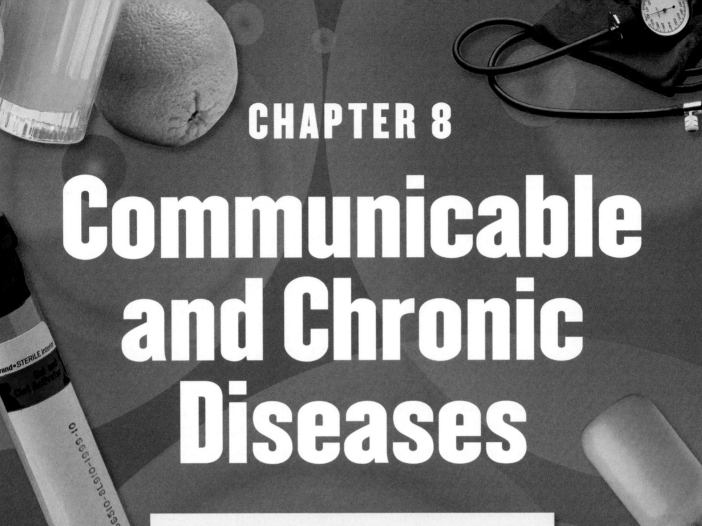

CHAPTER 8
Communicable and Chronic Diseases

Lesson 1 • Communicable Diseases, D50

Lesson 2 • Sexually Transmitted Diseases, HIV Infection, and AIDS, D56

Lesson 3 • Noncommunicable Diseases, D62

Lesson 4 • Managing Chronic Illnesses, D70

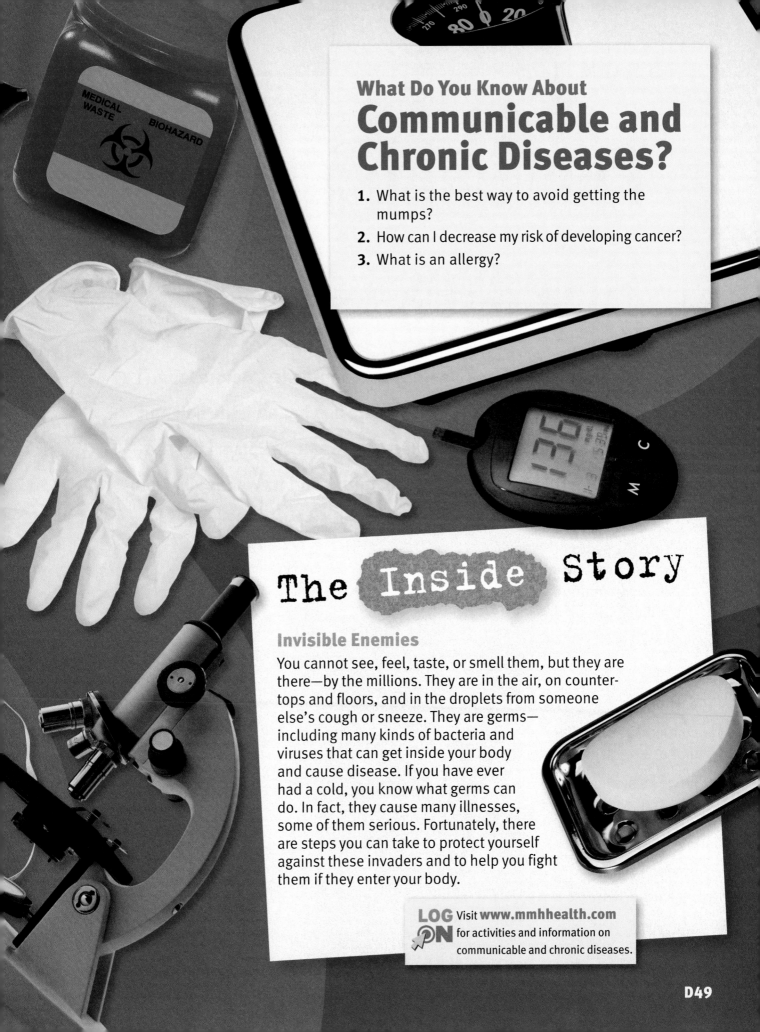

What Do You Know About
Communicable and Chronic Diseases?

1. What is the best way to avoid getting the mumps?
2. How can I decrease my risk of developing cancer?
3. What is an allergy?

The Inside Story

Invisible Enemies

You cannot see, feel, taste, or smell them, but they are there—by the millions. They are in the air, on counter-tops and floors, and in the droplets from someone else's cough or sneeze. They are germs—including many kinds of bacteria and viruses that can get inside your body and cause disease. If you have ever had a cold, you know what germs can do. In fact, they cause many illnesses, some of them serious. Fortunately, there are steps you can take to protect yourself against these invaders and to help you fight them if they enter your body.

LOG ON Visit **www.mmhhealth.com** for activities and information on communicable and chronic diseases.

Communicable Diseases

You will learn ...

- types of pathogens and how they enter the body.
- how body defenses protect against pathogens.
- the causes, symptoms, and prevention of common communicable diseases.

Vocabulary

- **pathogens,** D51
- **communicable disease,** D51
- **immune system,** D52
- **white blood cells,** D52
- **antibodies,** D52
- **immunity,** D53
- **vaccines,** D53

You are at soccer practice. Before long, each teammate has handled the ball and has passed it to someone else. Like the soccer ball, germs can travel rapidly from person to person and spread diseases.

What Are Communicable Diseases?

Pathogens (PA•thuh•juhns) are living organisms or particles that can cause disease. A **communicable** (kuh•MYOO•ni•kuh•buhl) **disease** is a disease caused by pathogens that can be spread from person to person. Chances are good that you have had one such illness, like the common cold. Communicable diseases can spread in a short time throughout schools and families.

Types of Pathogens

Just as there are different ways for pathogens to spread, there are many types of pathogens, such as

viruses—microscopic particles that can reproduce inside living cells, leading to such illnesses as colds, flu, and hepatitis (types A, B, and C).

bacteria—one-celled organisms that live almost everywhere on Earth. Most are harmless or even helpful. However, many kinds of bacteria cause diseases such as strep throat, gonorrhea, tuberculosis, Lyme disease, and anthrax.

fungi—living organisms that have some characteristics of plant cells but cannot make their own food. Fungi feed off living or nonliving organisms. Some forms cause diseases such as athlete's foot, ringworm, and jock itch. However, not all fungi cause disease.

protozoa—one-celled organisms that are larger and more complex than bacteria. Not all protozoa cause disease. However, some forms do, causing malaria and toxoplasmosis.

How They Enter the Body

Pathogens can cause diseases when they enter a person's body. They can enter the body in a number of ways, including

direct contact—touching, kissing, or other close contact with a person who carries a pathogen. For example, a mother may pass a pathogen to her unborn child or pathogens may spread when people shake hands.

indirect contact—contact with objects used by a person who has a pathogen, such as handrails, doorknobs, the water in a swimming pool, eating utensils, or contact with droplets from that person's cough or sneeze. This is a common way of spreading the common cold.

using a needle that has infected blood on it, through tattooing, piercing body parts, or injecting a drug.

inhaling air, eating food, or drinking liquid that carries pathogens.

being bitten by an animal or insect that carries pathogens.

What causes communicable diseases?

ACTIVITY

Science
LINK
Glittering Handshakes

Want to see how quickly a communicable disease can spread? Rub a small amount of glitter on your hand and then shake hands with a classmate. This student should then shake hands with another, and so forth until five students have shaken hands. The fifth student will have some glitter on his or her hand. You see, a person who is ill can spread the disease to someone with whom he or she has never had contact.

Your Body's Defense Against Communicable Diseases

If pathogens are everywhere, how do people stay healthy most of the time? Our bodies have a special system that helps protect us from the invaders around us. The **immune** (i•MYOON) **system** is a system of body organs, tissues, and cells that destroy pathogens. The immune system provides three lines of defenses that can stop many pathogens before they have a chance to get deep inside the body.

Our First Line of Body Defenses

Healthy, unbroken skin blocks many pathogens. Inside of body openings, such as the nose and mouth, we have mucous membranes. These make mucus, a thick, sticky substance that traps some pathogens. The air passages through which you breathe are lined with tiny hairs called cilia. Cilia trap some pathogens, which you then exhale or sneeze out.

Our Second Line of Body Defenses

Other parts of the immune system provide a second line of defenses that can kill invading pathogens. These systems include

- acids in the stomach that can kill pathogens.
- fever—a higher-than-normal body temperature that can kill some pathogens.
- **white blood cells** fight pathogens that cause infection and illness. Some kinds of white blood cells form **antibodies,** protein substances in blood that can find, weaken, or destroy certain pathogens. Other types of white blood cells attack pathogens by surrounding and digesting them.

◄ Clean hands help prevent many illnesses.

Immunity—Third Line of Defense

The body makes antibodies after it is exposed to a pathogen. Often, a person becomes ill before he or she has enough antibodies to fight off the pathogen. Yet the antibodies remain to protect the person from future attacks by the pathogen. This means that he or she has **immunity** (i•MYOO•nuh•tee), or resistance to a particular disease. Some diseases have potentially deadly effects, so it is better to have a vaccine, if one is available, than to expose a person to the pathogen.

Vaccines are dead or weakened pathogens given for immunity. You might be given a vaccine in a shot or by mouth. The vaccine causes your body to make antibodies to fight the pathogen for a specific disease. The antibodies kill or weaken live pathogens if they enter your body. Common childhood vaccines include

- hepatitis B.
- polio.
- diphtheria, pertussis, and tetanus (DPT).
- pneumococcal disease.
- measles, mumps, and rubella.
- varicella (chicken pox).
- *Haemophilius influenzae* type b (Hib).

 **What are two ways to develop immunity?**

CAREERS IN HEALTH
Microbiologist

Microbiology is the study of microscopic organisms, including most pathogens. Microbiologists study communicable diseases, but they may also work in other fields, such as helping farmers deal with pests that destroy crops. To be a microbiologist, you need to study math and science in school. Most microbiologists go to college, and many earn advanced degrees, such as a doctorate.

LOG ON Visit **www.mmhhealth.com** to find out more about this and other health careers.

The Immune System at Work

1. Pathogen invades body.

2. Certain white blood cells make antibodies to the pathogen.

3. Antibodies attach to invading pathogens. This signals other cells to attack the pathogen.

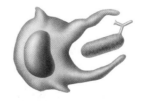

4. Other white blood cells destroy the pathogen.

Colds spread when droplets that contain a cold virus are inhaled or transferred by touch.

Common Communicable Diseases

Some common communicable diseases are discussed in the table below. The table includes symptoms of each disease. The most common is the common cold, which is caused by viruses and is spread when infected people cough and sneeze.

COMMUNICABLE DISEASES

Illness	Cause	Symptoms	Prevention	Treatment
Common cold	One of many different viruses	Sore throat, runny nose, sneezing, cough, headache, fever	Avoid people who have colds; wash hands	Rest, medicine
Influenza ("the flu")	One of many different viruses	Fever, headache, muscle aches, runny nose, sore throat, upset stomach, fatigue	Avoid contact with people who have the flu; wash hands; get a flu vaccine	Rest, medicine
Lyme disease	Bacteria passed through the bite of an infected tick	Round "bull's-eye" rash, fever, aches and headache, joint pain	Avoid tick bites by wearing protective clothing and applying insect repellent; remove ticks immediately	Antibiotics
West Nile virus	Virus passed by bite of an infected mosquito	Fever, headache, muscle aches, rash, swollen glands, brain swelling in severe cases	Avoid mosquito bites by wearing protective clothing and using insect repellent; get rid of standing water, where mosquitoes breed	Rest, medicines; severe cases may require hospitalization
Mononucleosis ("mono")	A virus	Fatigue, fever, sore throat, sore muscles, swollen glands in neck, armpits, and groin	Avoid contact with people who have mononucleosis	Rest, medicines, medical treatment in severe cases
Hepatitis (types A, B, C)	Infection of liver, each type caused by a different virus	Fatigue, muscle aches, fever, upset stomach, diarrhea, yellowing of skin and whites of eyes	Wash hands after using bathroom; for type A, avoid contaminated food and water; get vaccines for types A and B; practice abstinence from sex and drug use for types B and C	Rest, medicines, medical treatment
Tuberculosis	Bacteria, often infecting lungs	Long-lasting fever and coughing, night sweats, coughing up blood	Avoid contact with people who have tuberculosis	Long-term antibiotics
Strep throat	Bacterial infection in throat	Fever, sore throat, nausea, a bright red skin rash; the bacteria that causes strep can cause other diseases, such as scarlet fever	Avoid contact with people who have strep	Antibiotics

A symptom is a change in the way a person behaves or the body functions. This change is a sign that the person might have the disease.

Avoiding Communicable Diseases

Follow these guidelines to avoid catching or spreading a disease to others.

- Wash your hands for at least 20 seconds with soap and warm water before and after preparing food, before eating, and after using the bathroom.

- Keep your fingers away from your eyes, nose, and mouth. Touching objects and then touching the eyes and nose is a common way of spreading cold viruses.

- Cover your mouth and nose with a tissue when you cough or sneeze.

- Don't share personal items, such as toothbrushes, drinking glasses, or bottles.

 What kinds of illnesses can be treated with antibiotics?

 LIFE SKILLS

CRITICAL THINKING

Practice Healthful Behaviors

Perhaps there have been many mosquitoes around your home, especially in the evening. Mosquitoes can transmit West Nile virus to humans. How can you protect yourself from West Nile virus?

1. **Learn about a healthful behavior.** Go to the library or use the Internet to research ways that you can prevent mosquito bites. By protecting yourself, you are practicing a healthful behavior, rather than a risk behavior.

2. **Practice the healthful behavior in the correct way.** Make a list of the ways you can prevent mosquito bites. Practice them.

3. **Ask for help if you need it.** Make a list of people you can ask for help.

4. **Make the healthful behavior a habit.** Keep a log and list how many ways to prevent mosquito bites you think of each day for a week.

LESSON 1 REVIEW

Review Concepts

1. **Discuss** four types of pathogens.

2. **Explain** the lines of defense that your body has against disease.

3. **Discuss** symptoms that are common to many communicable diseases.

Critical Thinking

4. **Categorize** Classify the ways in which pathogens can enter the body and cause disease.

5. **LIFE SKILLS** **Practice Healthful Behaviors** Identify at least four common communicable diseases and what you can do to help prevent them.

Sexually Transmitted Diseases, HIV Infection, and AIDS

You will learn . . .

- the signs, symptoms, diagnosis, and treatment for sexually transmitted diseases.

- the causes of and treatment for HIV infection and AIDS.

- how HIV is and is not spread.

- how to reduce the risk of HIV infection and STDs.

Vocabulary

- **helper T cells,** D58
- **AIDS,** D58

Abstinence means choosing not to engage in risk behaviors, such as sexual activity. Practicing abstinence is the only sure way to prevent the possible unintended outcomes of sexual activity. Abstinence is the responsible decision to make to protect yourself.

What Are Sexually Transmitted Diseases?

A sexually transmitted disease (STD) is a disease spread through sexual contact. STDs are also called sexually transmitted infections (STIs). Some STDs can also be spread through casual contact. STDs are spread when pathogens from an infected person enter a partner. The partner is then infected with the pathogen and has an STD. The best way to prevent STDs is by practicing abstinence. The chart below describes some common STDs.

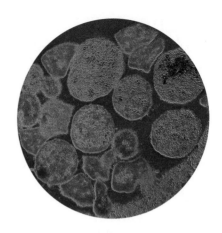

▲ **Bacteria cause some types of STDs.**

 **What is an STD?**

COMMON STDs

Disease	Cause	Symptoms	Treatment	Long-term effects (if untreated)
Chlamydia (kluh•MI•dee•uh)	Bacteria	Often, few or no symptoms; pain when urinating; discharge from penis or vagina; itching or burning of penis; swelling of scrotum	Antibiotics	Sterility (inability to have children) in women; harm to babies born to infected mothers
Gonorrhea (gah•nuh•REE•uh)	Bacteria	May cause few early symptoms, especially in women; pain when urinating; discharge from penis or vagina	Antibiotics	Sterility; heart and joint damage; harm to babies born to infected mothers
Syphilis (SI•fuh•luhs)	A type of bacteria, called a spirochete	Painless sores on mouth, penis, or vagina; flu-like symptoms; skin rash; symptoms may be hard to notice	Antibiotics	Can spread to brain, heart, and other organs; harm to babies born to infected mothers; death
Genital herpes (HER•peez)	Virus	Painful blisters on or around penis or vagina; genital tenderness	No cure; medicines can manage discomfort	Can spread to eyes; harm to babies born to infected mothers
Hepatitis B	Virus (spread by contact with infected blood and body fluids)	Some people have no symptoms, but others have nausea, vomiting, and abdominal pain	Injection of antibodies, bed rest; vaccination is available for hepatitis B	Cirrhosis or cancer of the liver
Pubic lice	Insects that attach to pubic hair and feed on blood	Small black spots on the skin near the pubic hair; itching and swelling in the pubic area	Special shampoo containing a drug to kill lice	Blisters, itching, infection
Genital warts	Virus	For males, warts on the penis; for females, warts in the vaginal area	No treatment can completely eliminate the virus; once infected, a person will always carry the virus	Recurring warts, increased risk of cancers of the cervix and penis

What Are HIV and AIDS?

One type of cell that plays an active part in the immune system is the helper T cell. **Helper T cells** are white blood cells that trigger the production of antibodies, protecting the body against disease. HIV, or the *human immunodeficiency* (I•myuh•noh•di•FI•shuhn•see) *virus*, is a virus that destroys helper T cells. As helper T cells are destroyed, there are fewer and fewer antibodies to fight pathogens. Infections become more common and severe. The immune system weakens.

Over time, HIV leads to **AIDS**, or *acquired immune deficiency syndrome*, which is a breakdown in the body's ability to fight infection. When a person has AIDS, infections take over the body.

HIV Infection and Treatment

When people are first infected with HIV, they may have no symptoms, or they may become ill with flu-like symptoms. Many people infected with HIV seem healthy for 12 years or more. This means that people can have HIV and not even know it. This also means that they can infect others. Still, during that time the virus is at work, attacking the immune system.

This is one of the reasons that testing for HIV is very important. If people learn that they have the infection, they can take medicines to help protect their health. HIV cannot be cured. However, some drugs are used to slow down HIV so it does not multiply as quickly. Another drug decreases the amount of HIV in the blood. A newer treatment for HIV helps restore functioning of the immune system.

How HIV Attacks the Immune System

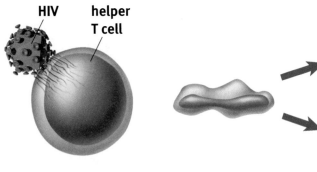

HIV   **helper T cell**

1. HIV attacks a helper T cell. Helper T cells play a vital role in the immune system. For example, they help in making antibodies, in destroying pathogens, and in destroying cancer cells.

2. HIV uses the helper T cell to make new copies of itself and destroys the helper T cell.

How HIV Is Spread

HIV is in the body fluids of infected people. These fluids include blood, semen, vaginal fluids, and breast milk. When fluids from an infected person come in contact with and enter another person's body, the virus can also enter the other person. This is most likely to happen

- during close sexual contact.
- when sharing a needle, such as for using drugs or piercing body parts.
- when infected blood is used for a transfusion (unlikely in the United States because of strict blood testing).
- from infected mother to child—during pregnancy or childbirth, or sometimes through breast-feeding.

HIV has also been found in saliva and tears. However, HIV has not been known to be spread by contact with these fluids.

How HIV Is NOT Spread

According to the Centers for Disease Control and Prevention (CDC), HIV is not passed by

- hugging or shaking hands.
- touching pencils, books, and other objects.
- using public or shared bathroom facilities.
- kissing someone with your mouth closed (kissing is a risk if blood could be in or on a person's mouth).
- donating blood.
- breathing the same air as an HIV-infected person.
- mosquito or other insect bites.

 Why is it important to get tested for HIV infection?

ACTIVITY
LIFE SKILLS
CRITICAL THINKING

Analyze What Influences Your Health

How can the media, such as newspapers, books, and magazines, affect a person's attitudes and behavior?

1 **Identify people and things that might influence you.** List the kinds of media that you read. Do they portray realistic and responsible behaviors?

2 **Evaluate how the influence might affect your health and decisions.** Keep a log of newspapers, books, and magazines that you read over the course of a week. Do these media discuss sensitive issues such as STDs or AIDS?

3 **Choose positive influences on health.** Review your notes. Which stories gave accurate and appropriate messages about the risks of STDs? Which did not?

4 **Protect yourself from negative influences on health.** List the newspapers, books, and magazines that you will not read and explain why. Make a decision to avoid these media that give inaccurate or unhealthful information.

The Fine Points of Needle Safety

Tattooing and ear piercing can only be done safely by qualified professionals who follow strict standards. However, rules and regulations vary by state. In some states, there are few legal requirements for providers of these services. With an adult's help, find the number of a local ear piercing studio. Call and ask which measures they take to ensure customer safety.

How Can I Protect Myself from HIV and STDs?

The only sure way to prevent the transmission of STDs is to practice abstinence. Vaccines will not protect you from STDs. You can't tell if a person has an STD just by looking at him or her. You must choose behaviors to reduce the risk of infection of HIV and STDs. Here are some precautions to take.

- **Discuss ear piercing with a parent or guardian.** Receive permission and have them accompany you if you have your ears pierced. Avoid having other body parts pierced. Follow health precautions. Never share a needle for ear piercing.

- **Do not get a tattoo.** Discuss tattooing with a parent or guardian. Know the laws about getting tattoos. Know that many people regret having gotten a tattoo and that sharing a needle to get a tattoo can cause HIV infection or hepatitis B or C.

- **Recognize that blood used for transfusion in the United States is screened for HIV.** Check the safety level of the blood supply in other countries if you travel.

- **Do not drink alcohol.** Drinking alcohol or using other drugs can make it difficult to say "no" to risk behaviors.

Universal Precautions

There are some steps you can take to keep from having contact with pathogens in body fluids. These steps can help protect you from HIV and other pathogens found in blood and body fluids. Follow these steps whenever you might have contact with blood and other body fluids.

◀ **Always obtain approval from your parent or guardian before having your ears pierced.**

1. Wear disposable gloves.
2. Do not wear the gloves more than once.
3. Wash your hands with soap and water after you take the gloves off.
4. Wear a face mask or shield if you give first aid for breathing.
5. Do not use the face mask or shield more than once without sterilizing it.
6. Cover cuts, scrapes, or rashes on your body with plastic wrap or a sterile dressing.
7. Do not eat or drink anything while giving first aid.
8. Do not touch your mouth, eyes, or nose while caring for a person on whom you are performing first aid.

 What are two ways besides sexual contact that STDs can spread?

ACTIVITY LIFE SKILLS

CRITICAL THINKING

Be a Health Advocate

Plan a campaign to bring the message of HIV awareness to your class. Be sure to check with your teacher first.

1 **Select a health-related concern to communicate.** Identify the key HIV messages you want to communicate—for example, that people can have and pass HIV without knowing it.

2 **Gather reliable information.** Use library and Internet resources to research facts and figures about HIV, such as rates of infection among young adults.

3 **Identify your purpose and target audience.** Your purpose is to make others more aware of HIV. Your target audience is the students in your class.

4 **Develop a convincing and appropriate message.** Choose the best way to reach your audience—for example, posters, handouts, newsletters, or displays. Distribute or display the results of your research for the benefit of your classmates.

LESSON 2 REVIEW

Review Concepts

1. **Discuss** the symptoms and long-term effects of STDs.

2. **Recall** the causes and treatments for HIV infection and AIDS.

3. **Describe** how HIV is spread.

Critical Thinking

4. **Generalize** Why is abstinence the best approach to the prevention of HIV and STDs?

5. **LIFE SKILLS Analyze What Influences Your Health** How can you protect yourself from negative influences that increase your risk of contracting AIDS or other STDs?

6. **LIFE SKILLS Be a Health Advocate** Why is it important for students to promote HIV awareness and protection?

Noncommunicable Diseases

You will learn . . .

- why you should keep a family health history.
- the causes, symptoms, and risk-reducers for cancer.
- the causes, symptoms, and risk-reducers for heart disease.
- ways to care for someone with a noncommunicable disease.

Vocabulary

- **cancer,** D63
- **carcinogen,** D63
- **cardiovascular diseases,** D66
- **heart attack,** D66
- **stroke,** D67
- **high blood pressure,** D67

Communicable diseases are caused by pathogens that can be spread from person to person. Many other types of diseases are not spread by pathogens. They include serious diseases such as heart disease and cancer. You can take steps to help lower your risk for these diseases.

Noncommunicable Diseases

Diseases that are not spread from person to person are called noncommunicable diseases. They can be caused by several possible factors.

- A person may inherit a disease or the likelihood of developing one from a biological parent. Diabetes is an example of an inherited disease.
- A person's lifestyle can lead to good health—or to disease. For example, using tobacco is known to cause **cancer,** a disease in which abnormal cells multiply and spread. The lack of regular physical activity can increase the risk of heart disease.
- Substances in the environment can cause serious health problems or make existing health problems worse. For example, pollution in the air can trigger an asthma attack. Exposure to certain chemicals can contribute to cancer and other health problems. A **carcinogen** is a substance that causes cancer.

Your Family Health History

Scientists do not fully understand why some people get certain noncommunicable diseases and others do not. One place to find clues of risks you may face is in your family health history. This includes information about the health of your biological relatives. Ask your parents or guardian about your family health history.

▶ **Pollution may contribute to some health problems.**

Keep a Personal Health Record

A personal health record is a record of a person's health, health care, and health care providers. It keeps all of your health information in one place. Your physician can use it to help make treatment decisions. A personal health record should include

- a copy of your birth certificate.
- a copy of your family health history.
- a list of the immunizations you have had.
- information about your health and habits.
- a record of your visits to health care providers.
- a copy of your family's health insurance policy.

 **What are some possible causes of noncommunicable diseases?**

▼ **Using sunscreen can help reduce your risk of skin cancer.**

Cancer

The spread of abnormal cells caused by cancer can interfere with normal body functions. *Metastasis* (muh•TAS•tuh•suhs) is the spreading of cancer cells to different body parts. Sometimes, the abnormal cells form growths that become lumps called *tumors* (TOO•muhrs). As tumors grow, they may spread and damage other tissues and organs. Not all tumors are cancerous.

A normal cell can change to a cancer cell for different reasons. Viruses, certain chemicals, radiation, and heredity can cause cells to change. Carcinogens from the environment can cause changes in normal cells. For example, cigarette smoke and tar contain carcinogens that cause cancer in cells of the lungs and other organs.

Cancer can affect many body organs and parts. It can also affect the blood and the fluid of the lymphatic system. This system aids in fighting off illness. Some factors that may increase the risk of cancer are

- unprotected exposure to the sun.
- overexposure to carcinogens, such as insect or pest sprays and X rays.
- use of tobacco products.
- an unhealthful diet, especially one high in fat.
- drinking alcoholic beverages.
- the use of certain medicines.
- lack of daily, regular physical activity.

Reducing the Risk of Cancer

There are steps you can take to prevent cancer. Do not use tobacco in any form, and avoid secondhand tobacco smoke. Avoid sun overexposure by wearing long sleeves, hats, and sunglasses. Avoid tanning booths and sun lamps. When you cannot avoid the sun, use a sunscreen. Check the label to make sure that it says it has a sun protection factor (SPF) of at least 15. Follow a balanced diet that is low in fat and high in fruits, vegetables, and whole-grain products. Do not drink alcohol. Avoid unnecessary exposure to chemicals, such as insect sprays and solvents.

Treating Cancer

Early detection of cancer is important. The treatment of cancer and its chances of success depend on the type of cancer, where it is, how far it has progressed, and the patient's overall health and attitude.

Treatments for cancer include surgery to remove the cancerous body parts. Chemotherapy is the use of special medicines to kill cancer cells. Radiation, a powerful kind of energy, kills cancer cells and shrinks the size of tumors. Other treatments, such as biological therapy, aim to boost the body's own cancer-fighting system. Some people receive treatments that prevent certain types of cancers from getting the hormones they need to grow.

 What is cancer, and how does it affect the body?

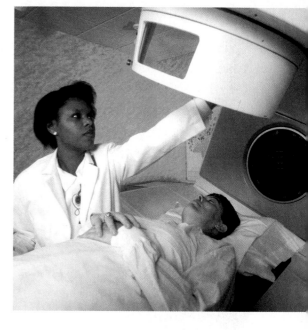

▲ **Physicians use advanced technologies to treat cancer.**

Use Communication Skills

Your brother likes to get a deep tan. You are concerned that his sun exposure places him at risk for cancer. Role-play a conversation with another student in which you tell your brother about your concern.

1 **Choose the best way to communicate.** Plan your conversation before you start. Write out the main ideas you want to get across. Decide if you will have your conversation privately or with others present. (You may need others in your role play.)

2 **Send a clear message. Be polite.** Review your notes before you start. Check that your main ideas are clear. Be respectful of your brother's feelings. Use I-messages.

3 **Listen to the other person.** Encourage your brother (the other person in your role play) to express his opinions.

4 **Make sure you understand each other.** Restate what you think you heard and ask the other person to confirm that it is correct.

Cardiovascular Diseases

Diseases of the heart and the blood vessels are called **cardiovascular** (kar•dee•oh•VAS•kyuh•luhr) **diseases**. They cause more deaths than any other type or category of illness. Here are some common cardiovascular diseases and their causes.

- **Heart attack** is a condition that results when the blood supply to the heart muscle is blocked off or interrupted, leading to damage to the heart muscle. When this happens, the heart muscle tissue does not get the oxygen and nutrients it needs and tissue dies as a result. A heart attack requires emergency treatment in order to save a life. A person who survives a heart attack may return to health by following an established routine of healthful behaviors, including healthful nutrition and physical activity, under care from a physician.

◀ Choosing healthful foods can reduce the risk of cardiovascular disease.

ACTIVITY — LIFE SKILLS

CRITICAL THINKING

Set Health Goals

Use a health behavior contract to set a health goal. To reduce your risk of cardiovascular disease, it is important to follow a diet high in magnesium, potassium, calcium, whole-grain products, and vitamins C and E.

1. **Write the health goal you want to set:** *I will choose behaviors to reduce my risk of cardiovascular diseases.*

2. **Tell how the goal will affect your health.** List the positive effects on your cardiovascular system of setting this goal.

3. **Describe a plan you will follow. Keep track of your progress.** Make a list of foods you should choose to reduce your risk of cardiovascular disease. You should consult the Dietary Guidelines and the Food Guide Pyramid to make your list. Decide how you can add these foods to your diet. Prepare a menu for the week to help you carry out your plan.

4. **Evaluate how your plan worked.** Did you follow your plan successfully? Do you have to make any changes as you continue your plan in the weeks ahead?

- **Stroke** is a blockage or break in a blood vessel that brings blood flow to the brain. As a result, blood flow to a part of the brain is limited. Nerve cells in that part of the brain do not get the oxygen and nutrients they need. Depending on the part of the brain affected, a person who has had a stroke may have trouble speaking or moving. A person who is having a stroke requires emergency medical treatment in order to reduce the extent of damage from the stroke.

- **High blood pressure** means the blood is pressing very hard on the walls of the arteries when the heart beats. This harms the arteries and can lead to stroke, heart attack, and other health problems.

The buildup of fatty deposits, or plaque, inside artery walls is called atherosclerosis (A•thuh•ROH•skluh•ROH•sus). Plaque can lead to blockages in arteries that cause heart attack and stroke.

Reducing the Risk of Cardiovascular Disease

Follow these steps to reduce the risk of cardiovascular disease.

- Avoid tobacco and secondhand smoke.
- Learn to manage stress.
- Choose foods that are low in salt.
- Avoid foods that have cholesterol and fat, especially saturated and trans fats.
- Eat a variety of foods from each of the food groups. Be sure to eat plenty of fruits, vegetables, whole grains, and low-fat dairy products. Include fish and nuts.

- Maintain a healthful weight.
- Get regular physical activity.
- Get regular health care.

Treating Cardiovascular Disease

There are several ways to treat cardiovascular disease. Physicians choose the treatment method based on the patient and the nature of the illness. Drugs may be prescribed to lower blood pressure, dissolve blood clots, and keep the heartbeat regular. In addition, surgery can unblock or bypass clogged arteries. Pacemakers, devices that help control heartbeat, can be placed in the body. In some cases, physicians can replace a diseased heart with a transplant.

 How does diet help prevent cardiovascular disease?

If Someone Has a Noncommunicable Disease

Having a health condition such as cancer or cardiovascular disease can be very difficult. People in this situation need support and understanding. If you know someone who has one of these health problems, you may be able to help.

Cardiovascular disease sometimes can lead to emergency situations. Knowing how to provide life-saving first aid is one way you can support people with serious health problems.

It is a good idea to learn cardiopulmonary resuscitation (CPR). If you are trained in CPR, you can help a person whose heart and breathing have stopped.

FIRST AID

First Aid for Stroke

1. **Recognize the symptoms of stroke.** According to the American Stroke Association, the warning signs of stroke include
   - sudden numbness or weakness of the face, arm, or leg, often affecting just one side of the body.
   - confusion or trouble speaking or understanding.
   - difficulty seeing.
   - trouble walking, including dizziness and loss of balance.
   - severe headache.
2. **Understand that stroke is a medical emergency.** Do not let the person talk you out of acting. Act right away!
3. **Call for emergency medical help**—9-1-1 in many places.

First Aid for a Heart Attack

1. **Recognize the symptoms of heart attack.** These symptoms may develop slowly. They include
   - chest discomfort that feels like pressure or squeezing—may come and go.
   - discomfort in other areas, which can include the arms, jaw, stomach, back, or neck.
   - shortness of breath.
   - nausea, sweating, or lightheadedness.
2. **Understand that heart attack is a medical emergency.** Do not let the person talk you out of acting. Act right away!
3. **Call for emergency medical help**—9-1-1 in many places.

Terminal Illness

A terminal illness is one that is certain to end in death. Sometimes, noncommunicable illnesses are terminal illnesses. People who have a terminal illness and their families need a great deal of support.

One way to help is to spend time with the people who are affected. Do not allow yourself to avoid them. If you are not sure whether it is a good time to visit, ask. Be a good listener. Let others share their feelings. Remember, you cannot solve the crisis. Just be there for support.

Another basic guideline is to act as normally as possible. Try not to treat people differently just because they are dealing with a serious illness.

Talk to an adult you trust about your own feelings. Helping people deal with death is very difficult. Do not ignore your own needs.

Sometimes people who are dying receive care from a hospice. A hospice provides many services that help the ill person and his or her loved ones prepare for death. These services are meant to meet both the physical and the emotional needs of the person facing death.

BUILD Character
ACTIVITY

Plan for Emergencies

Responsibility Knowing whom to call when a medical emergency occurs might save a life. Rehearse and act out what you would do to call for emergency help if someone was having a heart attack or stroke. State out loud which symptoms the person might be experiencing and how you would react. Know what to tell the person who answers the call: the name, address, and condition of the person.

 What should you do if you suspect that someone is having a stroke or a heart attack?

LESSON 3 REVIEW

Review Concepts

1. **Recall** why you should keep a family health history.

2. **Discuss** the major causes, symptoms, and risk-reducers for cancer.

3. **Describe** the major causes, symptoms, and risk-reducers for cardiovascular disease.

Critical Thinking

4. **Contrast** How do cancer and cardiovascular disease differ from each other?

5. **LIFE SKILLS Use Communication Skills** Write a letter that expresses support for a friend whose family has to deal with a terminal illness.

Managing Chronic Illnesses

You will learn . . .

- some of the most common chronic health conditions.
- ways to manage asthma and allergies.
- ways to manage chronic health conditions.

Vocabulary

- chronic health condition, D71
- insulin, D71
- epilepsy, D71
- allergy, D73

Almost everyone becomes ill at one time or another. However, you may know someone who has to manage a health condition all the time. For such a person, managing the condition is an important part of his or her daily life—and the key to enjoying the best possible health.

Chronic Health Conditions

A **chronic health condition** is one that lasts for a long time or keeps coming back. Often, a chronic health condition can be successfully managed. Choosing healthful behaviors may control the effects of the condition.

Diabetes

Diabetes (dy•uh•BEE•teez) is a disease in which the body does not produce enough or cannot use enough **insulin** (IN•suh•luhn), a hormone that helps the body use sugar from foods for energy. In diabetes, sugar builds up in the blood. There are two main types of diabetes.

1. In **type 1 diabetes,** the body makes no insulin. Type 1 may begin in people early in life. People with type 1 diabetes take insulin injections or use an insulin pump for the rest of their lives. Type 1 symptoms include extreme hunger or thirst, tiredness, weight loss, mood changes, and frequent urination. People with type 1 diabetes have high levels of sugar in their blood and urine. A young person with diabetes might have very high or low blood sugar.

2. In **type 2 diabetes,** the body makes insulin. However, the body cannot use it properly, or there is not enough of it. Type 2 usually begins in adulthood. However, a growing number of children and adolescents are being diagnosed with type 2 diabetes. People with type 2 diabetes control it with a special diet and physical activity, prescribed by a physician.

Epilepsy

Epilepsy (E•puh•lep•see) is a condition in which nerve messages in the brain are disturbed for brief periods of time. Epilepsy is a general term that includes different types of seizures. A seizure is a brief period in which there is loss of mental and physical control. A seizure can last for a few seconds up to a few minutes. People with epilepsy have had more than one seizure, and they may have had more than one kind of seizure. There are two types of seizures. Partial seizures occur in just one part of the brain and may involve a change in or loss of consciousness. Generalized seizures may cause a loss of consciousness, falls, or muscle spasms. You can take actions to protect a person who has a seizure.

- Do not try to stop the person from moving.
- Move objects that could cause injury away from the person.
- Stay calm.
- Help the person rest and feel comfortable after the seizure.

 **What is insulin?**

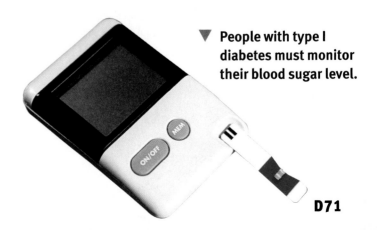

▼ **People with type I diabetes must monitor their blood sugar level.**

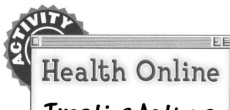

Health Online

Treating Asthma

e-Journal

Many people your age have asthma. Research and report on asthma using the e-Journal writing tool. Visit **www.mmhhealth.com** and click on **e-Journal**.

On Your Own
FOR SCHOOL OR HOME

At home with a parent or guardian, make a checklist of possible allergens that may exist at your home.

Managing Asthma and Allergies

Asthma (AZ•muh) is a chronic condition in which breathing becomes difficult. Asthma is the leading reason that children miss school due to chronic illness. In people with asthma, the airways become narrow or blocked. Young people with asthma feel like they are breathing through a narrow straw. Other symptoms include wheezing, tightness in the chest, and a dry cough. Symptoms occur when their lungs react to certain triggers in the environment, such as

- animal dander or feathers.
- colds and other infections.
- smoke and other air pollutants.
- exercise or physical activity.
- pollen, dust, or mold.
- cold air.
- certain foods.

Asthma cannot be cured, but it can be controlled. Young people with asthma must work with a physician to make a plan. They might use an inhaler, which is a small handheld device that contains medication. The medication relaxes and widens the air passages.

The Bronchial Tubes

normal airway

narrowed airway caused by asthma

Allergies

An **allergy** (A•ler•jee) is a condition in which the body reacts to foods or other substances. An allergen (A•ler•jen) is a substance that causes an allergic reaction.

Common allergens include dog and cat dander, grass, pollen, dust, and mold. Some foods, such as milk, eggs, and tomatoes, also contain allergens.

The body reacts to an allergen as if it was a harmful invader. Cells in the body act as if they are under attack and release chemical substances to fight the invader. These chemical substances cause allergy symptoms to appear.

Allergy symptoms vary among people. Symptoms may include a runny nose, tearing eyes, coughing, and congested lungs. A person may have a stuffed-up feeling in the nose, ears, and chest. He or she may have a headache, hives, or a feeling of itchiness.

An allergist is a physician who treats people with allergies. The allergist might test a person for different allergens. He or she would place the allergens in the person's body through small scratches in the skin. The allergist then checks the person's reaction to the different allergens and prescribes treatments. The treatments reduce a person's reaction to an allergen. Some treatments cause the reaction to disappear.

People who are at risk for severe allergic reactions should carry special medicine called epinephrine. It can provide life-saving help in an emergency.

What do allergies and asthma have in common?

▲ Allergens such as pollen produce symptoms in many people.

Write About It!

Managing Illness

Many books feature characters who have dealt with illnesses. Some that you might like to read include

- *Weaver's Daughter,* by Kimberly Brubaker Bradley
- *Sugar Was My Best Food: Diabetes and Me,* by Carol Antoinette Peacock, Adair Gregory, and Kyle Carney Gregory
- *Bluish,* by Virginia Hamilton

Take a trip to the library to find other books that you would like to read. Ask a librarian for suggestions. Then write a brief summary of how a character in a story managed his or her illness.

Managing Chronic Health Conditions

Many young people have a chronic health condition. They can manage these conditions in four ways.

1. **Follow a plan for optimal health.** Optimal health is the highest level of health that can be achieved. To achieve optimal health, a person must put together a health care team. The team might include the person, the parents or guardian, the physician, and the school nurse. In some cases, a dietitian, respiratory therapist, or physical therapist might be part of the team. The team's plan for optimal health might include medicine and a special diet or a program of exercise. The plan might include frequent checkups and lab tests.

2. **Cooperate with adults, such as a parent, guardian, or school nurse.** Some adults help with the plan. For example, a young person might need injections of insulin. A parent or guardian might give the injections at home. The school nurse might give the injections during school. In the case of an emergency, responsible adults will know what to do.

Science LINK

Genes, Culture, and Disease

Members of racial and ethnic groups are likely to share similar genetic makeup. Thus, a flawed gene may be to blame for why certain health conditions are more common among certain cultures. For example, sickle cell anemia tends to occur in people whose ancestors came from Africa. Tay-Sachs disease, which affects the nervous system, occurs much more often in the descendants of Jewish people from Eastern Europe. Cystic fibrosis, a chronic lung disease, is more common in the United States among whites than among other racial groups. Choose one of these three diseases and research what is thought to be its genetic cause. Write a newspaper article reporting the results of your investigation.

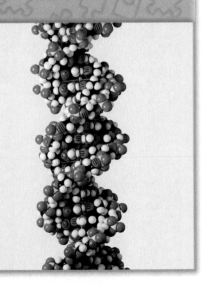

3. **Wear medical alert jewelry.** Medical alert jewelry contains the medical information of the person who wears it. Young people wear the jewelry to alert others to their conditions. In the case of an emergency, a person can read the jewelry. When calling for help, the person can tell the dispatcher what is on the jewelry.

4. **Attend support meetings.** Support groups exist for young people with chronic health conditions and their families. Group members discuss ways to cope. They provide each other with support and encouragement.

 **What is medical alert jewelry?**

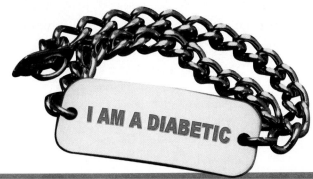

Be a Health Advocate

Suppose your class was about to get a new student who had a chronic illness, such as type 1 diabetes. Write a plan for what your class and school should do to support the new student.

1 **Select a health-related concern to communicate.** You want to help prepare the class to understand this student's special needs.

2 **Gather reliable information.** Use library and Internet resources to find out what kinds of challenges and special needs this person may face, such as diet, emergency plans, and medication.

3 **Identify your purpose and target audience.** Your purpose is to understand the needs of someone with a chronic illness. Your target audience is your classmates.

4 **Develop a convincing and appropriate message.** Write your plan and share it with your class. Why is it important to prepare emergency plans for people with chronic illnesses?

◀ **Jewelry such as this alert others to a person's medical condition.**

LESSON 4 REVIEW

Review Concepts

1. **Define** *chronic health condition.*

2. **Describe** the difference between the two main types of diabetes.

3. **Recall** the main symptom of epilepsy.

4. **Describe** what happens during an asthma attack.

Critical Thinking

5. **Integrate** What health conditions described in other lessons of this chapter might be considered chronic health conditions? Explain.

6. **(LIFE SKILLS)** **Be a Health Advocate** Use the Internet and library resources to research the causes of diabetes. You can also review Chapter 4 of your textbook. Using this information, make a flyer that encourages fellow students to take specific steps to prevent diabetes.

Access Valid Health Information, Products, and Services

Dear Health Nut,

Here is my problem . . .

I must settle an argument. We were talking in class today about HIV infection. Some kids in class said they would worry about getting HIV just from being in the same room with an infected person. I say that is not possible. Who is right?

Jed in Tennessee

Straight Talk About AIDS

How to Avoid HIV and AIDS

HIV/AIDS Get the Facts

AIDS and HIV Infection

Dear Jed in Tennessee,

Here is how you might solve the problem . . . Your classmates need to learn the facts about HIV and other health risks. There is a lot of incorrect information out there. You need to find out how to access valid health information. In this case, follow the steps on the next page to help access valid health information, products, and services.

Health Nut

Learn This Life Skill

Follow these four steps to access valid health information, products, and services. You can use the Foldables to help you organize your thoughts.

1 Identify when you need health information, products, and services.

When it comes to HIV, you need valid health information all the time. This information can keep you from taking dangerous health risks. It can also help you help others know what is and is not dangerous.

2 Identify where you can find health information, products, and services.

What are reliable sources of health information? It may come from health care providers, the Internet, books, or other sources.

3 Locate health information, products, and services.

Ask the school nurse or another health care provider if he or she has any information about HIV. In addition, use your library or the Internet to find information. (Make sure a responsible adult helps you.)

4 Evaluate what you found.

Consider where the information came from. Also consider how old the information is. For many topics such as HIV, information that is more than a couple of years old may not be valid anymore.

Practice This Life Skill

Activity How can you find out about flu vaccines available for "flu season"?

> 1. Identify when you need health information, products, and services.
>
> 2. Identify where you can find health information, products, and services.
>
> 3. Locate health information, products, and services.
>
> 4. Evaluate what you found.

If you do this activity with a group of students, students can participate in different ways to illustrate all four steps of **accessing valid health information, products, and services,** such as writing, folding, or drawing. Some students may do the activity in other ways, such as by role-playing or drawing a comic strip to illustrate the four steps.

Chapter Summary

By learning about the different forms of diseases, you can better protect yourself from communicable diseases and successfully manage noncommunicable diseases.

Lesson 1 • Communicable diseases are spread from person to person. Your body has a powerful system for resisting these diseases, and you can take steps to protect yourself from them.

Lesson 2 • One type of communicable disease is sexually transmitted diseases, or STDs. Abstinence is the only sure way to prevent the sexual transmission of these diseases.

Lesson 3 • Some diseases are not passed from person to person. These noncommunicable diseases often result from heredity, lifestyle, or environmental factors.

Lesson 4 • People must often live with chronic health conditions. In many cases, they can be managed successfully.

Use Vocabulary

immune system, D52

antibodies, D52

vaccine, D53

AIDS, D58

carcinogens, D63

cardiovascular disease, D66

stroke, D67

chronic health condition, D71

epilepsy, D71

allergy, D73

Choose the correct term from the list to complete each sentence.

1. When you get a(n) _____?_____, your body is exposed to a dead or harmless form of a pathogen.

2. Diabetes is a(n) _____?_____ that can be managed with diet, exercise, and medication.

3. Infection with HIV causes _____?_____.

4. One possible result of untreated _____?_____ is a heart attack.

5. You can reduce your cancer risk by cutting exposure to _____?_____.

6. The _____?_____ is made up of body organs, tissues, and cells that destroy pathogens.

7. _____?_____ is a condition in which nerve messages in the brain are disturbed for brief periods of time.

8. Protein substances in blood that can find, weaken, or destroy certain pathogens are _____?_____.

9. _____?_____ occurs when a blockage or break in a blood vessel limits blood flow to the brain.

10. A(n) _____?_____ is a condition in which the body reacts to food or other substances.

Review Concepts

Answer each question in complete sentences.

11. What are some ways to manage asthma and allergies?

12. What are some of the causes of cancer?

13. How can a person decrease his or her risk of becoming infected with HIV?

14. How does the body protect itself against pathogens?

15. Why should you keep a family health history?

Reading Comprehension

Answer each question in complete sentences.

When people are first infected with HIV, they may have no symptoms, or they may become ill with flu-like symptoms. Many people infected with HIV seem healthy for 12 years or more. This means that people can have HIV and not even know it. This also means that they can infect others. Still, the virus is at work, attacking the immune system.

16. What are the symptoms when someone first gets infected with HIV?

17. Why is it important to understand that people with HIV may seem healthy?

Critical Thinking/Problem Solving

Answer each question in complete sentences.

Analyze Concepts

18. Defend why it is worth the small risk of infection in order to receive a vaccine.

19. Compare and contrast type 1 and type 2 diabetes.

20. Specify practices that can help decrease a person's risk of cancer.

21. Evaluate the possible causes of noncommunicable diseases.

Practice Life Skills

22. **Access Valid Health Information, Products, and Services** You propose visiting a friend whose father has cancer. Another friend says she does not want to go because she does not want to get sick, too. How can you show her that someone cannot "catch" cancer?

23. **Make Responsible Decisions** One of your friends gives a misleading report about how STDs are passed and how a person can stay safe from them. Use the Guidelines for Making Responsible Decisions™ to evaluate your choices of actions to take and make a responsible decision.

Read Graphics

Use the text in the visual below to answer the questions.

24. According to the graph, how many fewer teens gave birth in 2001 than in 1997?

25. Why do you think that the number of teens who had babies fell each year from 1997 to 2001?

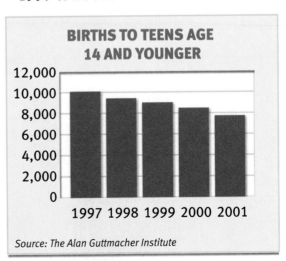

BIRTHS TO TEENS AGE 14 AND YOUNGER

Source: The Alan Guttmacher Institute

LOG ON Visit **www.mmhhealth.com** to find out how much you know about communicable and chronic diseases.

D79

Effective Communication

Organize an Advertising Campaign

Use library and Internet sources as well as this textbook to gather information about the dangers of drug abuse. Then organize an advertising campaign that encourages young people to resist pressures to use illegal drugs. Share your campaign with the class.

Say NO to Drugs

Self-Directed Learning

Plan a Celebration

What if you were in charge of planning the end-of-season celebration for your soccer team? What healthful foods and drinks would you put on the menu? What activities would you suggest for the party? Design an invitation to the celebration.

Critical Thinking and Problem Solving

Compare Conditions

Gather information about two chronic health conditions. Write a report in which you explain how people manage these conditions. Include information about how others can show support for a person with a chronic health condition.

Responsible Citizenship

Make a Speech

What health issues that have been in the news recently concern you? Pick one health-related news story and present the issue to your class in a short speech. Be sure to include an outline listing the important points of your speech to hand out to the audience.

Flu Outbreak Seen As Worst In Years

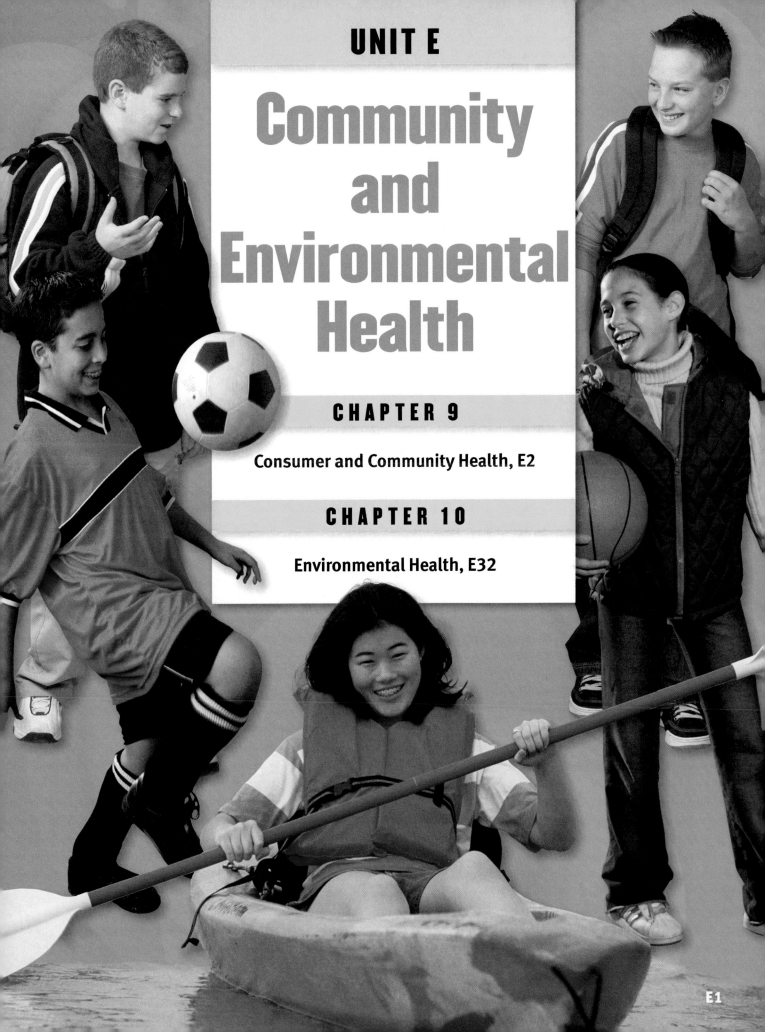

UNIT E

Community and Environmental Health

CHAPTER 9

Consumer and Community Health, E2

CHAPTER 10

Environmental Health, E32

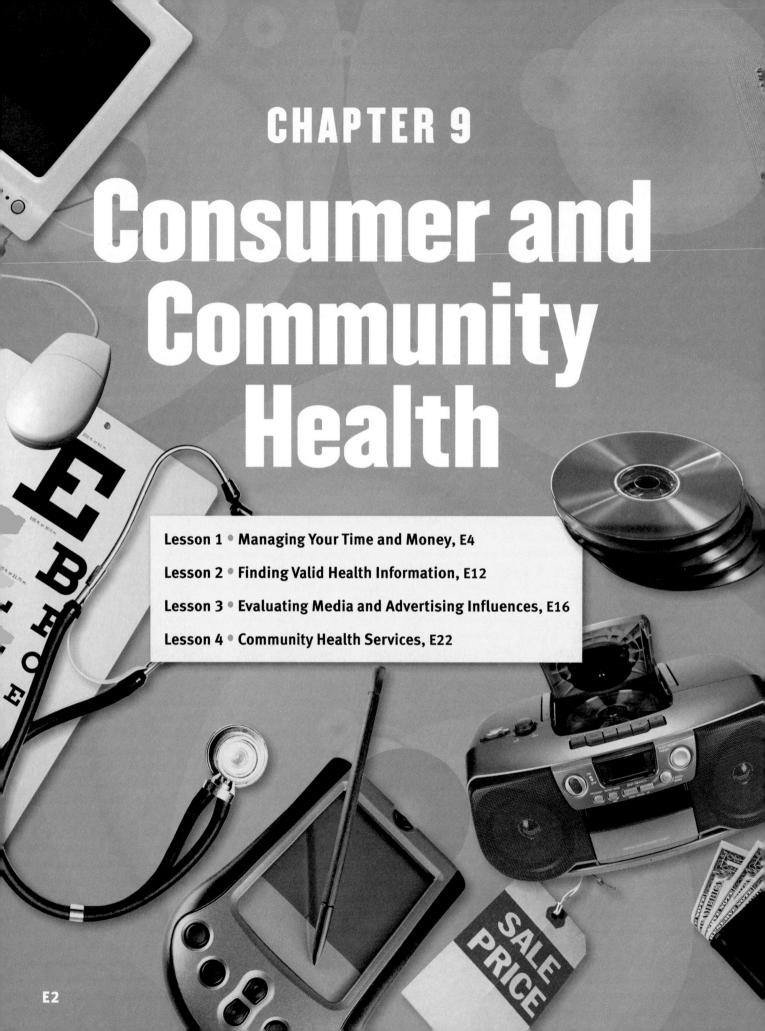

CHAPTER 9

Consumer and Community Health

Lesson 1 • Managing Your Time and Money, E4

Lesson 2 • Finding Valid Health Information, E12

Lesson 3 • Evaluating Media and Advertising Influences, E16

Lesson 4 • Community Health Services, E22

What Do You Know About
Consumer and Community Health?

1. What is a time management plan?
2. Where can you find reliable health care information?
3. What tactics do advertisers use to influence your consumer choices?

My Weekly Budget

Income		
	Allowance	$10.00
	Childsitting	6.00
Expenses		
	Movies	$16.00
	Snacks	$5.00
Savings	Music Downloads	4.00
		3.00

CREDIT CARD

Garage SALE

The Inside Story

Spending by Young People

Do you know how much money you spend on clothes and entertainment in a year? Last year, young Americans spent about $170 billion on such items. Companies have taken notice of the awesome spending power of young people. You are part of an age group that advertisers seek to influence. From movies and snacks to music and fashions, ads can influence you in ways you may not expect.

LOG ON Visit **www.mmhhealth.com** for activities and information on consumer and community health.

Managing Your Time and Money

You will learn . . .

- how to manage your time.
- how to practice money management.
- how to recognize shopping and entertainment addictions.

Vocabulary

- **time management plan,** E5
- **schedule,** E5
- **currency,** E6
- **money management,** E6
- **budget,** E6
- **financial goal,** E7
- **shopping addiction,** E8
- **entertainment addiction,** E9

Your favorite band is holding a concert in your area in a couple of days, but you do not have enough money to buy a ticket. To make matters even more difficult, a class project is due the day after the concert and you have not started it yet. Time and money are limited resources. To succeed in life, you must learn to manage both your time and your money.

How to Manage Time

A  is a plan that shows how a person will spend time. Learning to manage time ensures that a person can accomplish his or her top priorities.

Think of all the people and tasks in your life that require your time. Family members, chores, school activities, friends, and hobbies all fill up your day. When you add quiet time for yourself and rest and sleep, fitting everything in may seem overwhelming. Managing time helps you avoid making too many commitments, which may cause you to be stressed. It enables you to set and reach important goals. See the chart on page E6 for the benefits of managing your time wisely.

Many people use a schedule as part of their time management plan. A **schedule** is a list of times, events, or things to do. List daily activities on your schedule and rank them in order of importance. Accomplish the most important or time-sensitive activities first.

On Your Own
FOR SCHOOL OR HOME

Track Your Time

Coordinating a family schedule into your time management plan requires careful planning. Design a chart to help organize your time. Start by planning just one day. Remember to include time for family activities and household chores. Your chart should also allow time for homework, relaxation, and friends. Evaluate how your plan worked and adjust if necessary.

✔ **What is a schedule?**

▲ **A time management plan can help reduce stress.**

How to Manage Money

Currency is the money used in a country. All around the world, people are earning, spending, and trying to save money. If you are like most people, the amount of money you have is limited. You must learn to manage money so that you do not waste it. Learning to manage your money will help you plan ahead so you don't run out unexpectedly.

Money management is a skill used in spending and saving money. There are two main ways to practice money management. One way is to help your family save money by making wise choices. Another way is to make a **budget**, a plan for spending and saving money.

To organize a weekly budget:

- Start by adding up all the money you earn or receive in a week. You might earn money by receiving an allowance or doing chores.

- Decide how much money to save and how much to spend. Always try to save some money.

Even if you do not have money of your own right now, you should know how to make a budget. This skill will be handy when you do earn money.

▲ Making a budget will help you decide how much money you can spend on entertainment.

THE ADVANTAGES OF SAVING TIME AND MONEY	
Advantages of Saving Time	**Advantages of Saving Money**
You can build stronger relationships with family members.	You help your family maintain its budget.
You do not feel overwhelmed by your workload.	You will not be overwhelmed by debt.
You are not late for appointments.	You do not accumulate items that you don't need.
You can pursue activities that challenge your body and mind.	You will feel better about yourself for being responsible.
You have more time to spend with friends.	You do not need to ask your friends for money.

How to Save Money

A careful consumer makes wise choices with money. To make wise choices, you must plan ahead. You must consider different choices and pick the best one. Here are some guidelines to help you save money.

1. **Develop the habit of saving.** Even if you have only a small amount of money, you can save some. For example, you could make it a habit to save the coins you receive as change from purchases. Put the coins in a jar. When the jar is full, open a savings account.

2. **Trade your services.** Suppose you want to learn to play the guitar but can't afford the cost of the lessons. You might offer to trade services with the person giving guitar lessons. You might offer to mow the lawn, run errands, or clean a room in return for guitar lessons. Perhaps you would like to attend a play or a sports event. Ask how you might help at the event in exchange for paying to see it.

3. **Select low-cost entertainment.** Choose entertainment that is a good value. Go to a bargain movie or a matinee rather than the evening show. Look for family bargain events at the zoo, ballpark, and circus. The library is a good source of low-cost entertainment. You can watch movies, check out videos, and borrow books for free from your public library.

▶ **Saving money can help you reach your financial goals.**

4. **Select low-cost physical activities.** Many physical activities are enjoyable and low in cost. For example, you could play basketball at the local gym or playground. You could take a walk or jog through the park. Use equipment that you already have. Ride your bicycle. Swim at a public beach or lake.

Financial Goals

A **financial goal** is a goal to save or accumulate a certain amount of money needed for a specific reason. Financial goals vary from person to person. Setting a financial goal helps you succeed at your long-term plans, such as college or a trip you may want to take when you get older. You can also set a short-term financial goal, a goal for right now or the near future. What is a short-term financial goal you might have?

 **What is a budget?**

ACTIVITY **BUILD**

Character

Choose Entertainment Responsibly

Responsibility Develop a plan to spend your time and money on healthful entertainment. Make a list of 10 to 20 healthful activities that you enjoy. List qualities of these activities that show they are healthful. Make it a practice to consistently choose the items on your list.

ACTIVITY

LIFE SKILLS

CRITICAL THINKING

Shopping and Entertainment Addiction

Do you know someone who cannot stop buying things? A **shopping addiction** is an uncontrollable urge to shop and spend. Young people who buy on impulse or who always want to shop may have a shopping addiction. They usually do not need what they buy. Many young people with this addiction do not know how to cope with feelings of boredom, loneliness, or depression. They may not have any hobbies or more meaningful ways of spending their time. Some may shop to reduce anxiety. Shopping addiction can result in debt and can continue as a person grows older. Young people who have shopping addiction need help to learn healthful coping skills.

Set Health Goals

Your class trip is in ten weeks. The trip will cost each student $75. You currently have $5. You need to raise money to be able to afford to go on the trip. Use a health behavior contract to set a health goal.

1 **Write the health goal you want to set:** *I will make a plan to manage time and money.*

2 **Tell how the goal will affect your health.** List reasons to explain why learning to manage your money is beneficial to your well-being.

3 **Describe a plan you will follow. Keep track of your progress.** Design a plan to save money by changing your spending habits. Perhaps you will eat meals at home rather than buying meals at the food court, or rent a video instead of going to the movies. Set up a budget to help you meet your financial goal.

4 **Evaluate how your plan worked.** After a week, review your spending habits. How much money did you save? Will you earn enough money for the trip? If not, how can you alter your plan to meet your financial goal?

Another common addiction is **entertainment addiction**, the uncontrollable urge to be entertained. Young people with this addiction spend most of their time doing activities such as watching television or playing computer games. They don't put aside time for physical activity, homework, or their families. This addiction harms their physical, mental and emotional, and family and social health. A young person may develop entertainment addiction as a way of coping with problems and should find healthful ways to cope.

Healthful Entertainment

What you see, hear, and read can influence the way you act. Healthful entertainment promotes your physical, mental and emotional, and family and social health. To healthfully entertain yourself, follow family guidelines. Entertainment should be appropriate for your age group. Entertainment should not talk about or include violent or sexual language, drug use, or teen sex.

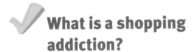
What is a shopping addiction?

Do You Know

A recent survey suggests that many people believe they watch too much television. Two out of five adults and seven out of ten young people think that they spend too much time in front of the TV.

Source: A.C. Nielsen Company, New York Times

▼ **Family guidelines will help you choose healthful entertainment.**

LESSON **1** REVIEW

Review Concepts

1. **List** two ways you can practice money management.

2. **Summarize** how to recognize shopping addiction and entertainment addiction.

3. **Explain** the benefits of managing your time.

Critical Thinking

4. **Solve** Pam never seems to have enough time to spend with her best friend. She receives an allowance, but she never seems to have money left to buy school supplies. How might you help Pam solve these problems?

5. **LIFE SKILLS** **Set Health Goals** Write an outline that other students could use to make a time management plan. List daily activities with suggestions for ranking and allocating time for them.

Make Responsible Decisions

Dear Health Nut,

Here's the problem ... My friend received a video game system for his birthday. He invites me to his house every day after school. We play for hours and usually don't have enough time for homework. Now our grades are dropping. When I try to go home to study, my friend always says, "just one more game," and we end up playing for another hour or two. How can I change this behavior?

Hooked in Houston

Dear Hooked in Houston,

Here is how you might solve the problem . . . You recognize that playing video games has caused your grades to drop. You can choose to go straight home after school so you're not tempted to play games. You might really want to go to your friend's house, though. In this case, use the steps on the next page to help you make the responsible decision.

Health Nut

Learn This Life Skill

Follow these four steps for making responsible decisions. You can use the Foldables to help you organize your thoughts.

1 **Identify your choices. Check them out with your parent or another trusted adult.**

List the possible choices.

2 **Evaluate each choice. Use the Guidelines for Making Responsible Decisions™.**

Not all the questions listed in the Guidelines will apply to every situation. Which questions apply to the situation described here? Use them to evaluate each choice.

3 **Tell what the responsible decision is. Check this out with your parent or another trusted adult.**

Use your answers to the questions above to make a responsible decision.

4 **Evaluate your decision.**

What are the consequences of acting on the decision you made?

Practice This Life Skill

Activity You will have a test in three days. You need to study. However, you had promised friends to spend time on a class project with them this week. Write a skit that illustrates how you can use the Guidelines for Making Responsible Decisions™ in the decision-making process.

Guidelines for Making Responsible Decisions™

- Is it healthful?
- Is it safe?
- Is it legal?
- Do I show respect for myself and others?
- Do I follow the guidelines of responsible adults, such as my parents or guardian?
- Do I demonstrate good character?

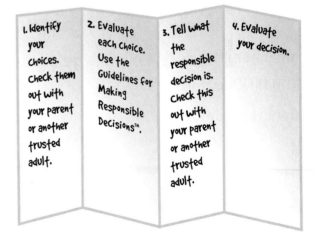

If you do this activity with a group of students, students can participate in different ways to illustrate all four steps of **making responsible decisions,** such as writing, folding, or drawing. Some students may do the activity in other ways, such as by role-playing or drawing a comic strip to illustrate the four steps.

Finding Valid Health Information

You will learn . . .

- sources of valid health information.
- how you can be safe when learning about health online.

Vocabulary

- **consumer**, E13
- **valid information**, E13
- **support groups**, E14, E15

If you developed a rash, would you know what to do? What if you felt sick after eating a spicy meal? It is important for you to learn where to find health information that you can trust to be accurate.

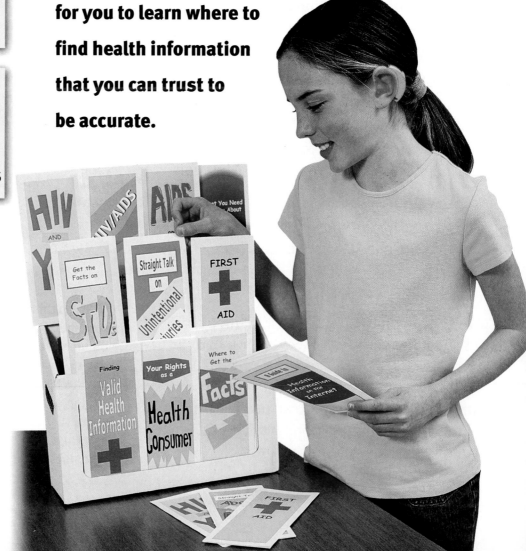

Valid Health Information

You are a consumer. A **consumer** is a person who evaluates information and buys products and services. You might buy health products such as soap and bandages. When buying products or dealing with health issues, try to find **valid information,** information that is accurate.

When researching health information, use reliable sources. Reliable sources are individuals or organizations that provide information you can depend on to be accurate. A parent, guardian, physician, a school nurse, professional organizations, and government agencies are reliable sources. You can find information by interviewing a person, researching health books and magazines, and searching the Internet.

On Your Own
FOR SCHOOL OR HOME

Valid Sources

Conduct an interview with someone who may help you find valid information. For example, you might interview a school nurse or nutritionist. You could also interview a school librarian or visit your local public library and interview a librarian there.

 **What is a consumer?**

SOURCES OF HEALTH INFORMATION

Sources	Examples	Tips
Licensed Health Care Providers	physicians, dentists, nurses, counselors, physician assistants, nurse practitioners	Consult licensed professionals who are trusted through word of mouth or credentials.
Professional Associations	American Medical Association; American Public Health Association	Contact the best-known association for your specific issue.
Private Organizations	Better Business Bureau; Consumers Union	Contact these organizations when you have questions about companies, health products, and services.
Community Organizations	American Cancer Society; American Red Cross; American Lung Association	These organizations often have a local office in your area.
Federal Government Agencies	Food and Drug Administration; Centers for Disease Control and Prevention	Government agencies often have large staffs and offer lots of information about health issues.
State and Local Agencies	child health programs, drug abuse programs	These agencies provide useful health services in your area.
Media	TV news programs, radio talk shows, videos	Readily accessible, these sources often deal with current topics.
Printed Materials	books, medical dictionaries, encyclopedias, textbooks, medical journals, magazines, newspapers	Use sources published by reputable associations or agencies.
Computer-Based Sources	Internet, CD-ROM, e-mail newsgroups	Evaluate the sources of information you find online.

Online Information

Health Online

find Valid Health Information

e-Journal

How can you find valid health information on the Internet? Research and report on the validity of online information using the e-Journal writing tool. Visit **www.mmhhealth.com** and click on **e-Journal**.

Most schools and libraries have computers that enable you to connect to the Internet. Most professional groups, government agencies, and private organizations have Web sites. With permission from your parents or guardian, you can use these sites to get valid health information.

Support groups can provide information. **Support groups** are groups of people who meet to comfort and help one another. Often they can share information and sources of information. Some support groups are available online.

Safety Tips When Using the Computer

When you use the computer, you need to act safely. Always get permission from a parent or guardian before going online. Also, never give out personal data such as your first and last name, address, password, or phone number. Always evaluate online health information carefully.

Do not buy a product online without permission from a parent or guardian. Be aware of the time you spend online and the cost.

LIFE SKILLS

CRITICAL THINKING

Use Resistance Skills

How can you best say "no" in this situation? You have participated in an online support group for several months. You have learned useful health information. The last time you logged on, however, someone asked you to e-mail your name and address. The person claimed to want to mail you more information.

1 Say "no" in a firm voice. Write a statement that you would use to best say "no" and mean it. Practice saying it out loud so that you can tell that the statement will be effective.

2 Give reasons for saying "no." Tell the person that the information requested from you is personal and private. Some people use this information for illegal purposes.

3 Be certain your behavior matches your words. Do not share information with anyone else you talk to online. If the person keeps asking you for information, stop participating in the support group. Report the person to the administrator of the Web site.

4 Ask an adult for help if you need help. Ask for help from a parent, guardian, or another responsible adult.

How to Check Sources

To find valid health information, you must check the source. Professional associations, government agencies, and community organizations are reliable sources. Search for information based on research rather than opinion. The material should contain researched facts. Find out if other health care professionals trust the information. You can ask your health care provider or another professional if he or she believes what you have found. Double-check the information. Trustworthy Web sites provide notes so you can check their research.

 What types of Web sites can you visit to learn about health?

▲ **Ask a responsible adult to help you find health information online.**

LESSON 2 REVIEW

Review Concepts

1. **Describe** how to determine if health information is valid.

2. **List** three sources of valid health information, providing an example of each source.

3. **Summarize** ways you can be safe when using online support groups to gather health information.

Critical Thinking

4. **Evaluate** You have a friend who has been getting health information from a company's Web site. You suspect the information is not valid. What is the responsible thing for you to do?

5. **LIFE SKILLS** **Use Resistance Skills** Certain members of your online support group announce that they are doing a survey. They ask for the name of your school. Others in the group have sent in their schools' names. What should you do? Why?

E15

Evaluating Media and Advertising Influences

You will learn . . .

- ways to recognize influences on consumer choices.
- how advertisers can influence you.
- ways to evaluate health care products.
- your rights as a consumer.

Vocabulary

- **advertisement,** E17
- **commercial,** E17
- **fad,** E17
- **media influence,** E18
- **brand,** E18
- **generic,** E18
- **media literacy,** E18
- **quackery,** E20

Messages urging you to buy particular products or services are everywhere. You hear them on your radio. You see them on TV. They even pop up on your computer screen when you are online. How can you tell if the claims they make are true?

LIMITED TIME ONLY!

BUY NOW!!

FREE TRIAL OFFER

Operators Standing By

WAIT, THERE'S MORE . . .

Influences on Consumer Choices

A consumer judges information and buys products and services. When you shop, you choose between products. You evaluate the messages sent out by the people and companies that want you to buy products and services.

Advertisements An **advertisement,** or ad, is an announcement designed to persuade or influence choice. A **commercial** is an ad on television or radio. Advertising is a way to sell products and services. They attempt to persuade you that you need a certain product or service. They contain convincing appeals. Sometimes ads use repetition to drive a message home. You may see the same ad many times in a single day.

Family and friends The people in your life also may influence your consumer choices. For example, your parents or guardian may spend freely, or they may clip coupons and hunt for bargains. You might develop the same habits as family members. Your friends may buy certain brands of clothing. You may feel pressured to buy the same things they do. Emotions can influence shopping styles as well. Sometimes people shop to relieve boredom or depression. Buying items fills up their time with something to do.

Culture Culture also may influence your spending habits. You may be influenced by your family's ethnic background. You may follow their traditions by using the same products they do. You may also be influenced by the culture of your surroundings. Many people follow the crowd. They want what everyone else has.

Fads Some influences can change quickly, however. A **fad** is something that is very popular for a short time. For example, a style of shoe that everyone bought last year may seem silly now that the fad is over. Avoiding the purchase of a fad product can help save you money.

 **What is a fad?**

▼ **Ads and commercials can influence your consumer choices.**

Advertising Techniques

Are you aware of how advertisers influence you? **Media influence** is the way in which forms of communication, including magazines, radio, television, newspapers, and the Internet, affect a person.

Some companies spend millions of dollars on advertising. They want you to buy their product or service. With so much money at stake, advertisers work hard to design the most persuasive ads they can. They use several methods to target young people.

Some ads show well-known actors or athletes using a product. These ads imply that you can be like the celebrity if you buy that item. In reality, the celebrity earns money to endorse, or support, the product. The celebrity may not use the product at all. Ads target a young person's desire to be part of the crowd. They promise that people will like you if you buy a certain product. Advertisers may try to convince you that their product is "in." They claim that their product is new and stylish.

A **brand** is a product made by a certain company or a well-known manufacturer. Some people believe that buying certain brands gives them status. However, a **generic** is a product that meets certain standards but does not have fancy packaging or brand name recognition. A generic item is often of the same quality as a brand-name product.

Becoming a Smart Shopper

Although some ads may try to mislead you, you can learn how to tell fact from fiction. **Media literacy** is the ability to recognize and evaluate messages in the media. Being informed helps you spot false advertising. When you read an advertisement, identify the advertising techniques that are being used. Determine if the ad has a factual basis. Just because a popular star promotes a product does not mean that the claims are true.

▼ **Responsible shopping involves comparing products carefully.**

Most young people want to be liked. Ads appeal to this desire. They often suggest that buying a product will make you popular. For example, do you want to wear the latest fashions? Many young people are concerned about clothes. They want to look sharp. Ads for some brand-name clothes try to convince you that their clothes will make you more popular or more stylish. Their message is "everybody who is anybody wears this brand."

Owning a product or buying a certain brand of clothing may make you liked for a while. However, your character, your personality, and your personal strengths are the lasting qualities that can make you respected by others.

Smart shoppers also think about *when* to buy something—that is, when they *need* a product—and they avoid buying on impulse. They also consider *where* to buy products. They look for stores that offer discounted prices or have special sales.

▼ **Ads attempt to appeal to a young person's desire to be fashionable.**

 **What is a brand?**

Access Valid Health Information, Products, and Services

How can you find out what causes acne and how to treat it?

1 **Identify when you need health information, products, and services.** Why might you be concerned about acne?

2 **Identify where you can find health information, products, and services.** You might talk to a physician, the school nurse, or a pharmacist about how to treat acne. You might ask your parent or guardian for help. You also might use valid Web sites to gather information.

3 **Locate health information, products, and services.** Review your sources. With a parent or guardian, go online to look for information from the valid sources you identified.

4 **Evaluate what you found.** Compare the information you obtained from different sources. Are there major differences in the information you found? Which information will you use?

Evaluating Health Care Products

Quackery is a method of selling worthless products and services. Ads promote products and services by making convincing appeals. Quackery sells by making false or exaggerated claims.

For example, a young person may see an ad for a special cream to treat acne. The ad claims that the product is so new that physicians don't know about it. The ad states that the cream clears up acne overnight. Before-and-after pictures of a young person show how well the cream works. Someone who has acne may be tempted to buy this product without researching it.

In reality, acne will not go away overnight. Physicians know about new products. The before-and-after pictures probably have changes other than the appearance of the skin to make the young person more attractive. This ad makes false claims. Don't be tempted by quackery.

You need to choose health care products carefully and responsibly. Doing so will keep you safe and save you money. Read the ad or label carefully. Quackery often uses words such as *breakthrough* or *miracle* to describe the product. The ad may promise instant results. In addition, beware of ads for a single product that claim to fix many problems at once. A good rule to follow is that if something sounds too good to be true, it probably is. If you still can't figure out if a product will work or is safe, talk to a physician. Find out if a legitimate consumer protection group has tested the item. Research possible side effects. Check government health agencies for possible warnings about the product.

NEW KLEERO

Clears skin instantly!

CALL NOW: 555-1234

◀ **Don't be fooled by products that make exaggerated claims.**

How Agencies Protect Your Rights

The Food and Drug Administration (FDA) is a federal agency that checks food, drugs, medical devices, and cosmetics to make sure they are safe to use. Another agency that protects you from quackery is the Federal Trade Commission, or the FTC. The FTC makes sure that the ads in newspapers, in magazines, and on TV are true.

 How can you avoid quackery when shopping for health care products?

PRODUCT GUIDE

Product	What to Look For
Vitamins	FDA approval; percentage of the recommended daily allowance
Sunscreen	SPF protection of at least 15; water resistance
Soap and shampoo	lowest prices—comparing prices can save hundreds of dollars
Acne cream	dermatologist approval; safe ingredients
Prescription medicines	check with a physician if a generic medicine will work as well as a brand-name medicine

On Your Own

FOR SCHOOL OR HOME

Compare Shampoos

With a parent, guardian, or another respected adult, visit the shampoo aisle of a drug or grocery store. Note the range of prices. Do a side-by-side comparison of the ingredients in one of the most expensive brands and one of the least expensive brands of shampoo. Do you notice a difference? Draw a poster that illustrates your findings.

LESSON 3 REVIEW

Review Concepts

1. **Identify** what influences consumer choices.

2. **List** resources for evaluating health care products.

3. **Describe** how advertisers influence people to buy their products.

Critical Thinking

4. **Summarize** What guidelines would you offer other students for evaluating health care products, such as shampoo, toothpaste, or bandages?

5. **LIFE SKILLS** **Access Valid Health Information, Products, and Services** How would you be able to identify a newspaper or magazine ad as an example of quackery? What guidelines could you offer other students your age?

Community Health Services

You will learn . . .

- how you can get health care and how the costs of health care are paid.
- how the government plays a role in health care.
- how the community meets special needs.
- how you can volunteer.
- about health careers.

Vocabulary

- **health care,** E23
- **providers,** E23
- **facilities,** E23
- **consumer costs,** E23
- **volunteer,** E26
- **service learning,** E27

Your younger sister falls and injures her ankle. Would you know whom to call? It is important for you to know where to go for health care. Learn which resources are available in your community.

Health Care Providers and Facilities

Health care is the management of physical and mental well-being by professionals, such as physicians, nurses, and hospital workers. A community's health care system includes many different people, places, and companies.

Providers are suppliers of what is needed or wanted, as in health care. Health care providers include physicians, dentists, school nurses, physical therapists, nurse practitioners, physician assistants, and counselors. Specialists, such as allergists, are also health care providers.

Facilities are places that serve a specific purpose. A health care facility is a place where people receive health care. Health care facilities include hospitals, physicians' offices, school-based health centers, and dental offices. Places like walk-in clinics, drug treatment centers, and nursing homes are also health care facilities.

Right now, your parents or guardian might choose where you go for health care. When a person needs to find a physician, family members, friends, and neighbors may recommend a provider. Hospitals often have physician referral services. The American Medical Association (AMA) can provide a list of physicians in your area. Contact the AMA, the American Board of Medical Specialties, or your local hospital to check on a health care provider's training. Find out what your costs will be to see the provider.

Consumer costs are the items given up in order to buy and use up resources. Once you decide on a physician, he or she can recommend health care facilities.

 **What is health care?**

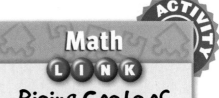

Math LINK

Rising Costs of Health Care

Health insurance is a plan that helps pay the cost of health care. In recent years, the price of health insurance has skyrocketed. In 2001, about 41.2 million Americans did not have health insurance. Experts estimate that by 2006, up to 53.7 million people will be without insurance. Draw a bar graph that shows this information. What is the change in the number of Americans who do not have health insurance between 2001 and 2006?

▼ **Health care is available at several types of facilities.**

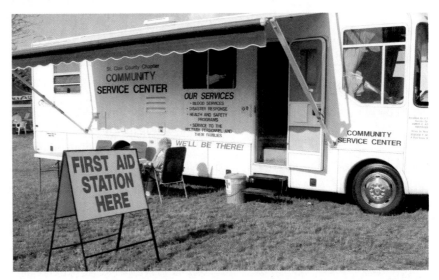

E23

The Government's Role

Federal and state governments help many people who can't afford health care.

Federal government The federal government offers two main programs: Medicare and Medicaid. Through Medicare, the government pays part of the health care costs for people over the age of 65. People with certain disabilities also receive benefits from this program. Medicaid provides insurance for those with a low income and needy people of any age.

State government State governments provide health care services through health departments. These health departments set health standards for restaurants, schools, and other public facilities. Other branches run vaccination programs to protect citizens from disease. State health departments also publish booklets to inform the public about health issues.

Local government Local government agencies work with the state on many health programs. Local officers enforce health policy, such as anti-litter laws. Local groups run recycling campaigns and maintain water quality. Local governments also provide services for people with special needs. For example, communities install ramps and elevators for people who use wheelchairs. Some towns have crosswalk lights that beep to warn people with visual impairments. Communities also install public restrooms and water fountains that are wheelchair accessible.

Write About It!

The History of Health Care

Medicare and Medicaid are important federal health care programs. Research the history of one of these programs. Write a news article explaining how the program came about. Note which groups and individuals were the major supporters of the program.

GOVERNMENT HEALTH SERVICES

Level of Government	Services
Federal	funds Medicare and Medicaid; distributes health information; protects the rights of citizens with disabilities; funds medical research; regulates food and drugs; regulates medical devices; fights false advertising
State	sets health standards; passes health legislation; runs immunization programs; prints health literature; answers questions from the public; regulates public facilities; inspects food and water; eliminates disease-spreading insects and rodents; maintains vital records
Local	helps enforce health laws; provides facilities for people with special needs; establishes health education programs; removes trash

Special Needs

Some people in the community have special needs. They might have a disability or a handicap. A disability is something that changes a person's ability to perform certain activities. Some people with disabilities have handicaps. A handicap is anything that makes it difficult for a person to perform a task. Follow these guidelines to protect the rights of people with special needs.

1. Do not park a bicycle in a handicap space.
2. Do not use a restroom for the handicapped.
3. Do not use a wheelchair ramp for skateboarding or play.
4. Allow someone with special needs to get on an elevator first.
5. Protect the safety of people with special needs when you are using trails to in-line skate or bicycle.
6. Show respect and courtesy at all times.

Some people receive health insurance from a health maintenance organization (HMO). Members of an HMO choose a provider from a list of participating physicians. This provider arranges for all of the member's health care. Members pay the same amount each month, and often a small fee for each office visit.

What health services do local governments provide?

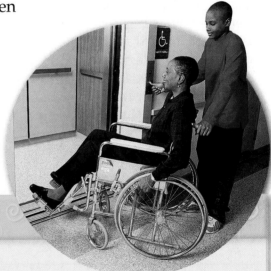

CRITICAL THINKING

Analyze What Influences Your Health

What are some health services local government agencies in your area provide? See page E24 for possible examples.

1. **Identify people and things that might influence you.** Make a poster of the health services provided by local government agencies in your area. In the poster, explain what each service does.

2. **Evaluate how the influence might affect your health and decisions.** As you present your poster to the class, describe how a person's health would be affected without the services identified.

3. **Choose positive influences on health.** State ways that you can support local government health services. What can you do to make them more effective?

4. **Protect yourself from negative influences on health.** In your presentation, explain how the health of the community would be affected without any of these services.

MAKE a Difference

Help Others

Young people can make a difference. Teen sisters Jessica and Elizabeth Annis of Bainbridge Island, Washington, have been volunteers since they were in fifth and sixth grade. In one project, they collected stuffed animals for children in shelters. Within two months, the sisters had gathered more than 700 stuffed toys. The teens also spent their spring break repairing a church and serving meals to the homeless. Conduct a survey with your classmates to learn about ways they would like to help the community.

Voluntary Health Organizations

Groups that are not part of the federal or state government also promote health. Many of these health agencies rely on volunteers and donations. To **volunteer** is to provide a service without getting paid. Voluntary health groups provide many services. They support medical research. They promote efforts to prevent diseases. Voluntary health organizations educate the public about a variety of health issues.

You may have heard of some voluntary health organizations. The American Red Cross provides blood and assists people in emergencies. Other well-known voluntary health organizations include the American Heart Association, the March of Dimes, and the American Cancer Society. Follow these guidelines when you are looking for ways to help others.

- **Consider a way to volunteer.** Ask yourself: What are my interests? What issues concern me? How much time do I have? Do I have friends who will join me?

  - **Get permission.** Ask a parent or guardian for permission. You might also need permission from a teacher, principal, community organization, or community official.

  - **Make a plan.** Identify who you will need to contact. Set a date or schedule. Identify the supplies, equipment, or transportation you might need.

  - **Evaluate your project when it is complete.** Did the project help the community? What did you learn? How could the service be improved? Would you do it again?

◄ Consider becoming a volunteer for a cause that interests you.

The Personal Benefits of Volunteering

When you choose to volunteer, you help others. The decision can make you feel good about yourself. Volunteering is a meaningful way of coping with feelings of boredom or low self-esteem. Doing work for others is a healthful alternative to substance use. Volunteering is a great way to use your talents, form friendships, and learn new skills. Volunteer work may even be part of your school program. **Service learning** is volunteer work done by students in the community that is connected to the classroom. You may learn skills and services that you may eventually use in your career—and learn about career opportunities at the same time.

Local Opportunities

You can promote health in your area by volunteering. There are many chances for you to volunteer. For example, you may work at a summer camp for youth with special needs. You may help at an assisted living center. You could help deliver food to people who are ill or physically challenged. There are many ways for you to promote health as a volunteer. You can

- make cards to take to a children's hospital.
- take part in a walk-a-thon.
- collect used clothing for people in need.
- wash cars to raise money for a community organization.
- plant a tree.
- write letters to local officials about a health cause.
- stock shelves at the library.
- help out at local after-school youth clubs.
- participate in local cleanup efforts.

What services do voluntary health organizations provide?

Social Studies

ACTIVITY

L I N K
Community Volunteers

Work with a group of students to make a directory of possible opportunities to volunteer in your neighborhood. For example, list names and addresses of senior centers, schools that have after-school tutoring programs for younger children, school fund-raising activities that you may have at your own school, and so on.

▼ **When you volunteer, you help others and yourself.**

Art LINK
Career Mural

Design a mural on butcher paper or a large poster board to represent health careers. You can find information from a library and draw pictures or cut out pictures from magazines to represent what people in these careers do. Your mural also can include requirements for these careers, such as a four-year college degree, a two-year college degree, special training in a medical technology school, and so on.

Technology and Health Careers

Advances in medical technology have improved health care. In the past 100 years, the human life span has increased from about 49 years to 75 years. This increase is due in large part to advances in medical technology. For example, in 1896 Emil H. Grube became the first physician in the United States to use X rays to treat breast cancer. Scientists perfected a polio vaccine in the 1950s. This vaccine virtually wiped out one of the worst diseases in history. These are just two of many historical examples that have changed health care in the United States.

Modern medicine continues to evolve. In the past, patients with artificial hearts had to have wires hooked up to machinery outside the body. Today, an artificial heart may be battery powered. Surgeons can replace joints with human-made materials.

Communities, however, do not benefit equally from medical advances. People without health plans cannot afford high-cost procedures. How to bring the benefits of modern medicine to all people has become a challenge for our nation's leaders.

▲ Advances in health care have benefited many people.

CAREER OPPORTUNITIES IN THE TECHNOLOGY AND HEALTH CARE FIELDS

Job	Function
anesthesiologist	provides patient with relief from pain during and after an operation
cardiologist	studies and treats diseases of the heart
neurologist	diagnoses and treats disorders of the nervous system
radiologist	diagnoses disorders by using radiation, such as an X ray
oncologist	diagnoses and treats cancers
medical technician	performs laboratory tests

Technological Developments and Career Opportunities

As technology changes, health experts need to learn new skills. Some advances have opened up new careers because of the level of training involved and the use of high-tech tools. For example, trained technicians perform magnetic resonance imaging (MRI) scans, which use magnets and radio waves to view the inside of the body. Specialists perform other scanning methods as well, such as X rays and computer-assisted tomography (CAT) scans. Recently, advances in laser technology have led to new careers in corrective laser eye surgery.

 **What does an oncologist do?**

◀ **Physicians, researchers, and other health care workers must keep up with new technologies.**

CAREERS IN HEALTH
Health Inspector

Health inspectors are an important part of a community health system. They work for governmental agencies and private businesses. Inspectors check conditions at places such as schools, restaurants, swimming pools, and beaches. They make sure public places follow written health standards. In cases of serious violations, a health inspector's report may shut down a business. They also educate businesses on how to follow health standards. Health inspectors need good observational and investigative skills. They should have a strong background in science. Many colleges offer programs of study that specialize in public health. Next time you are dining at your favorite restaurant, look to see if a health inspection certificate is on display.

 LOG ON Visit **www.mmhhealth.com** to find out more about this and other health careers.

LESSON 4 REVIEW

Review Concepts

1. **Explain** how communities assist people who have special needs.

2. **List** six different places in your community where a person could receive health care.

3. **Recall** the ways a person can volunteer.

4. **Describe** how technology has changed health careers.

Critical Thinking

5. **Contrast** Think of a health care procedure you have received over the past year, such as a dental checkup or a physical. How might that procedure have been performed 50 to 100 years ago? Explain possible differences.

6. **LIFE SKILLS** **Analyze What Influences Your Health** How can federal, state, and local governments influence people's health?

Chapter Summary

Lesson 1 • Time and money management skills will help you achieve your goals.

Lesson 2 • Health information is available from many types of sources. You can learn to find valid sources of health information.

Lesson 3 • Advertising and the media influence your choices as a consumer. You can learn to make wise choices when shopping for health care products.

Lesson 4 • A system of health care providers and health care facilities supplies a community's health services. It is important to know about the resources in your community.

Use Vocabulary

schedule, E5
budget, E6
valid information, E13
media influence, E18
generic, E18
media literacy, E18
providers, E23
facilities, E23
service learning, E27

Choose the correct term from the list to complete each sentence.

1. The ability to recognize and evaluate messages in the media is _____?_____.

2. Suppliers of what is needed or wanted, as in health care, are called _____?_____.

3. Making a plan for spending and saving money is called a _____?_____.

4. Places that serve a specific purpose are _____?_____.

5. The way in which forms of communication, including magazines, radio, television, newspapers, and the Internet, affect a person is called _____?_____.

6. A list of times, events, or things to do is called a _____?_____.

7. Knowledge or facts that are true make up what is called _____?_____.

8. A product that meets certain standards but does not have a brand name is _____?_____.

9. When students participate in volunteer work that is connected to the classroom, it is called _____?_____.

Review Concepts

Answer each question in complete sentences.

10. What is a shopping addiction?

11. How can you protect your personal safety online?

12. Why might an advertiser use a celebrity to promote a product?

13. Why should you question ads that promise immediate results?

14. How does the government help people over 65 afford health insurance?

Reading Comprehension

Answer each question in complete sentences.

A time management plan is a schedule that details how a person will organize his or her time. Managing time well ensures that a person has time for his or her top priorities. Managing time helps you avoid making too many commitments so you will not feel overwhelmed and stressed. It helps you to set and reach important goals.

15. How does managing your time keep you from feeling stressed?

16. In what ways do you manage your time?

Critical Thinking/Problem Solving

Answer each question in complete sentences.

Analyze Concepts

17. Compare wisely managing your time with wisely managing your money.

18. Define the goal of a support group.

19. Summarize the ways that you can check the validity of online information.

20. Contrast an advertisement with a commercial.

21. How has technology provided new jobs in the health care field?

Practice Life Skills

22. **Make Responsible Decisions** You are trying to save money for a new sweater. Your friend encourages you to go to the arcade every weekend and spend money there. What is the responsible decision to make in this situation?

23. **Make Responsible Decisions** A commercial for a "miracle" weight loss pill guarantees that you will lose 10 pounds in one week without diet or exercise. You are tempted to try it. What is the responsible decision to make in this situation?

Read Graphics

Use the text in the visual below to answer the questions.

24. About what portion of the students earn money by working? What percentage receive an allowance?

25. Based on the chart, why is it important for you to learn money management skills now?

SOURCES OF TEEN INCOME

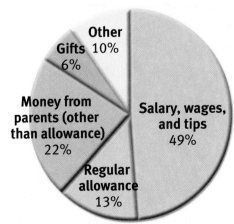

Source: Parents Make a Difference

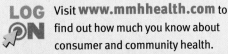

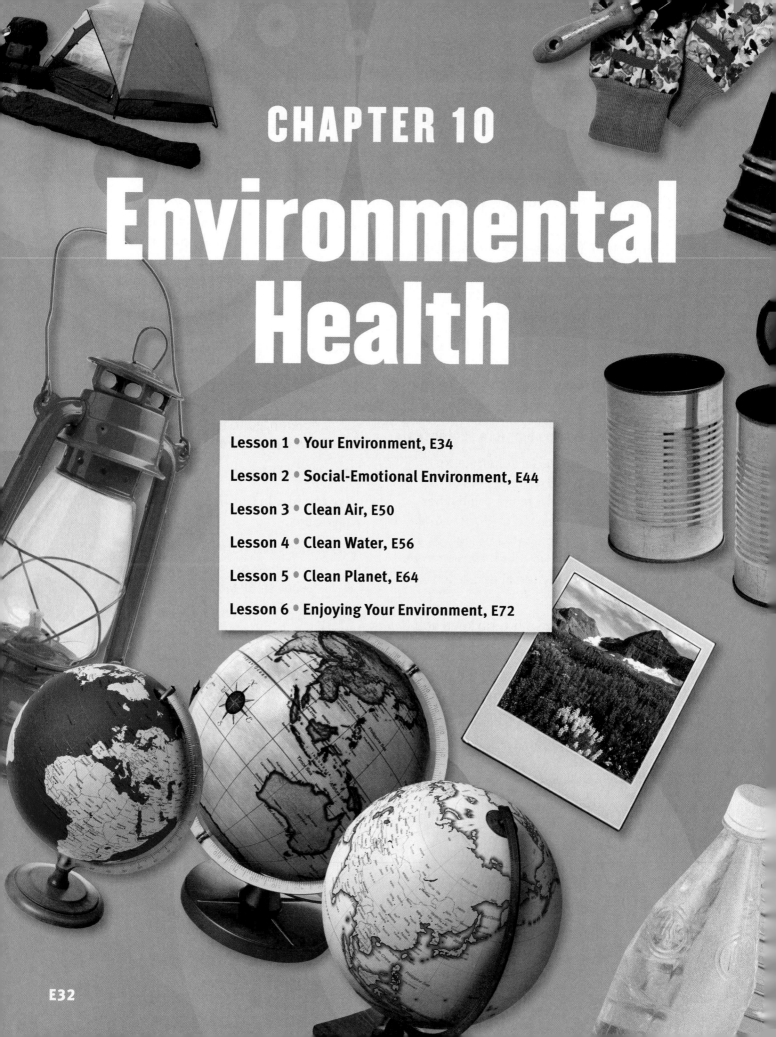

CHAPTER 10
Environmental Health

Lesson 1 • Your Environment, E34

Lesson 2 • Social-Emotional Environment, E44

Lesson 3 • Clean Air, E50

Lesson 4 • Clean Water, E56

Lesson 5 • Clean Planet, E64

Lesson 6 • Enjoying Your Environment, E72

What Do You Know About
Environmental Health?

1. What is acid rain?
2. Name a common household substance that can pollute the water supply.
3. What are renewable resources?

CARPOOLS ONLY 2 OR MORE PERSONS PER VEHICLE

The Inside Story

Danger in the Air

You have to breathe to stay alive. When you swim underwater, you try to hold your breath as long as you can. Eventually, you have to come to the surface and your body forces you to take in air. Sometimes, though, breathing could actually make a person ill. This could happen when the air contains harmful substances. Being aware of these threats and learning how to prevent them can help you breathe much easier. How clean is the air in your community?

LOG ON Visit **www.mmhhealth.com** for activities and information on environmental health.

E33

Your Environment

You will learn . . .

- what makes up your environment.
- how to improve your social-emotional environment.
- what makes up your physical environment.
- how to keep noise at a safe level.

Vocabulary

- physical environment, E35
- emotional environment, E35
- social environment, E35

Your surroundings are one of many factors that influence your health. Some things that you may take for granted have a huge impact on your life. Being aware of these factors can help you make healthful decisions.

The Parts of Your Environment

What makes up the world around you? Depending upon where you live, your "world" may include tall buildings, farms, or ocean beaches. No matter where you live, your world includes air, water, and land. It includes your daily weather and overall climate. It also includes the people around you and how you react to them. All these things influence your life. The environment is everything that is around you.

You already know that your overall health has physical, mental and emotional, and family and social aspects. Each individual's environment also contains different parts. The **physical environment** is the living conditions around a person. The **emotional environment** is the feeling of trust and caring around a person. Lastly, **social environment** is the contact a person has with people around him or her.

Everything in your environment affects your health. That is why many people are health advocates for the environment. A health advocate for the environment is a person who promotes health for self and others for the purpose of protecting the environment. He or she does not take actions that might harm the environment. For example, he or she would not throw trash on the ground. Instead, a health advocate for the environment might organize a trash cleanup day at a local park.

 **What are the three parts of a person's environment?**

Science LINK
Water Source

Most people get their water from a community water supply system. Most of these supply systems rely on surface water, such as lakes, rivers, and reservoirs, while others use groundwater from wells. Before water enters your home, it has to be filtered and purified. Experiment by trying to remove different contaminants from water. Fill four small plastic cups with tap water. Add oil to one cup, tea leaves from an open tea bag to another cup, soil or sand to the third cup, and broken crackers to the last cup. Once water has been polluted, is it easy to return it to purity? Decide for yourself.

▶ **A class volunteer day at a local park can help keep the environment clean.**

Sports and Self-Esteem

Write a short story about a student who moves to a new town and joins a sports team as a way of meeting new friends. Your story should show some of the ways that team sports improve social-emotional health. For example, you might show how team sports help build friendships and make people feel more valuable.

Your Social-Emotional Environment

Your environment is more than just what you can see around you. The feelings you have and your relationships with others are also important parts of your environment.

Emotional environment Your emotional environment includes all the emotions that you feel and that others feel about you. The care you receive from your parents or guardian is part of your emotional environment. So is the feedback you receive from parents, teachers, and friends. Feedback is a response to what you say or do. Feedback may be positive or negative. The care, trust, and feedback you get from and give to others affects how you feel about yourself.

Social environment Your social environment includes the contact you have with all the people around you from day to day. Your family, your teachers, and your friends are all part of your social environment. So are the people you see only casually, such as your bus driver or the clerk at the local store. Like the emotional environment, a person's social environment may be positive or negative. Having a positive social environment helps make your life more satisfying.

Social-emotional environment The social environment and the emotional environment involve the people in your life and the way you interact with them. The two parts of your environment put together are known as your social-emotional environment. Together, your social-emotional environment can have an effect on your self-esteem—that is, how you feel about yourself. A positive social-emotional environment can increase a person's self-esteem.

◀ **Your family is an important part of your emotional environment.**

Parts of Your Social-Emotional Environment

Your social-emotional environment includes all the places where you meet and interact with the important people in your life. These places include

- **Your home** This is where you spend time with your parents and guardians, the people who care for you. You may also interact with siblings or other relatives who live with you.

- **Your school** Here you meet and spend time with many of your close friends. You also form relationships with other people who affect your health, such as teachers and coaches.

- **Your community** You may have meaningful relationships with neighbors and other people in your community. In addition, your community helps care for you by providing police and fire protection.

You also may meet people in a variety of other places, such as a summer camp or an after-school program. Hobbies, such as music or sports, may give you a chance to make new friends. Volunteering in your community is another good way to connect with other people.

How does your social-emotional environment affect your self-esteem?

▶ **Trash on the beach spoils the natural beauty and can injure wildlife.**

Your Physical Environment

How big is your physical environment? There is no single answer. Right now, your physical environment includes your classroom and the desk where you are sitting. However, these things are part of a larger environment. Your physical environment includes your home, your school, the town where you live, and planet Earth itself, with all its land, air, and water.

Parts of Your Physical Environment

You know you need air and water to survive. The air that you breathe and the water that you drink are important parts of your physical environment. Substances in the air and water, such as pathogens, carcinogens, and other poisons, can enter your body and harm your health.

Your physical environment also includes some things you may not think about most of the time. For example, noise is a part of your physical environment that affects your health. You also are affected by the weather and by the amount of space you have in your home and community.

Your physical environment may pose threats to your safety. For example, busy streets increase the risk of car crashes. You must be aware of your physical environment so you can protect yourself from unintentional injuries. Unintentional injuries are the leading cause of death for young people.

A healthful and safe physical environment promotes health. Clean air keeps lungs healthy. A safe noise level protects hearing.

▶ The physical environment plays an important role in your health.

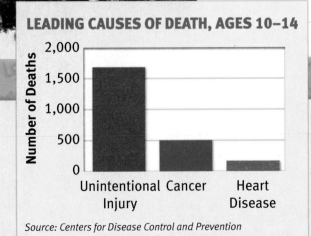

Math LINK

The Biggest Risk

This graph shows three of the top causes of death for people between the ages of 10 and 14. How common were deaths from unintentional injury as compared to deaths from cancer and heart disease?

LEADING CAUSES OF DEATH, AGES 10–14

Number of Deaths (2,000 / 1,500 / 1,000 / 500 / 0)

Unintentional Injury · Cancer · Heart Disease

Source: Centers for Disease Control and Prevention

Improving Your Physical Environment

Because your physical environment affects your health, it makes sense to take good care of it. Here are steps you can take to improve your physical environment.

- **Keep it clean.** Dispose of trash properly. Do not litter. You can also try to persuade others not to pollute the environment.

- **Protect your hearing.** Stay away from loud noises. If you have to go someplace noisy, wear ear plugs or other forms of hearing protection.

- **Stay away from weapons.** If you ever come across a gun—in someone's hands, on the ground, or at a friend's house—do not touch it. Leave immediately and tell a responsible adult. Stay away from people who buy, sell, or use weapons.

- **Set goals.** If you are not happy where you are, you can work to build a better life for yourself. Work hard in school, make plans for a successful future, and learn job skills by volunteering.

✔ **What is the leading cause of death for young people?**

▶ **Taking care of the physical environment can improve your health.**

ACTIVITY — **LIFE SKILLS**

CRITICAL THINKING

Be a Health Advocate

A group of friends meet in a park after school each day for a snack. They always leave litter behind them. Plan an education campaign to convince them to change their behavior.

1 **Select a health-related concern to communicate.** You want to educate your classmates about the benefits of a positive physical environment.

2 **Gather reliable information.** Give examples of other towns or places that offer positive physical environments. List the benefits of such environments. List steps your classmates can take to promote this kind of environment.

3 **Identify your purpose and target audience.** Clarify your message before you begin your campaign. Think of ways you need to get your message across to your classmates.

4 **Develop a convincing and appropriate message.** Choose at least two methods of communication for your campaign, such as posters, songs, and e-mail.

Noise Pollution

Loud noises are more than an annoyance. They can harm your hearing and cause a range of other health problems. Noise pollution is loud or constant noise that causes hearing loss and stress.

A single very loud noise can harm hearing. So can exposure to noise over a long period of time. Even common sounds such as road traffic and lawn mowers can cause harm in some cases. Hearing damage may include loss of hearing or tinnitus, a ringing or buzzing in the ears.

Being exposed to loud noise harms health. High levels of noise trigger the stress response. Noise pollution can cause blood pressure and heartbeat rates to increase. Loud noise might cause headaches, tension, and anxiety. It often is difficult to sleep or relax near loud noise.

Wear ear protection when you are exposed to high levels of noise.

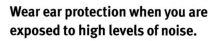

The important first step in reducing the harmful effects of noise is to become aware of the noise. The next step is to take action to lower the noise. In some cases, the noise can't be reduced. A person may live on a busy street or have planes flying overhead throughout the day. You can take other healthful actions. You should sit at a safe distance from music speakers. Wear earplugs when you are around loud noise, such as a lawn mower or weed cutter. When you listen to music through headphones, keep the sound low enough to hear someone talking.

You can rate the sounds you hear in your environment by comparing them to the sounds listed in this chart. You can classify sounds as barely audible, quiet, moderate, noisy, and unbearable. Sounds below 30 decibels are barely audible. Sounds from 30 decibels to 50 decibels are quiet. Moderate sounds start at 50 decibels. Sounds at 70 to 110 decibels are noisy. Sounds above 110 decibels are unbearable.

✔ **How is noise harmful to health?**

NOISE LEVELS AND HEARING

Sound	Loudness in Decibels
Softest sound heard with normal hearing	0
Rustling leaves	10
Whisper	20
Nighttime noises in a house	30
Soft radio	40
Classroom	50
Ordinary conversation	60
Inside a car on highway	70
Busy city street	80
Subway	90
Siren (30 meters away)	100
Thunder	110
Pain threshold	120
Indoor rock concert	120
Jet engine at takeoff	140

▲ The term *decibel* is used to measure sound. Repeated exposure to sounds above 85 decibels can damage hearing over time.

LESSON 1 REVIEW

Review Concepts

1. **List** the three parts of your environment.

2. **Describe** some of the things that make up your physical environment.

3. **Explain** how to avoid the harmful effects of noise.

Critical Thinking

4. **Compare** Explain how social environment and emotional environment are related.

5. **LIFE SKILLS** **Be a Health Advocate** A video arcade where Ben likes to play pinball is so noisy that he can't even think. How could he convince the management to keep the noise down?

Practice Healthful Behaviors

Dear Health Nut,

Here's my problem . . . I love music, and I really like it loud. I like to listen to CDs by putting on my headphones and really cranking up the volume on my favorite songs. My friend says that doing this could harm my hearing. How can I enjoy using my headphones and protect my hearing at the same time?

Music Lover in Minnesota

Dear Music Lover in Minnesota,

Here is how you might solve the problem . . . If you really love music, you need to take care of your hearing. Otherwise, you won't be able to enjoy music anymore. You need to adjust the volume control on your CD player so that you can hear people talking. A friend sitting 2 feet away from you should not be able to hear sounds coming from your headphones.

Health Nut

Learn This Life Skill

There are four steps to practicing healthful behaviors. Use a portable music player to figure out what volume level is safe for listening to music. Use the Foldable to help you organize this information.

1 **Learn about a healthful behavior.**
Identify the risk behavior and the healthful behavior.

2 **Practice the healthful behavior in the correct way.**
Describe how you could work with a partner to adjust the sound on your headphones. How could your partner help you determine if your volume control is set too high?

3 **Ask for help if you need it.**
When you actually wear headphones, how can others help you determine if the volume control is too high?

4 **Make the healthful behavior a habit.**
Use what you learn in Steps 2 and 3 to carry out a plan to wear headphones each day. Check to see if others around you can hear music from your headphones. If they can hear you, lower the volume control. Record your results each day.

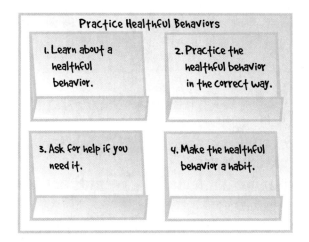

If you do this activity with a group of students, students can participate in different ways to illustrate all four steps of **practicing healthful behaviors,** such as writing, folding, or drawing. Some students may do the activity in other ways, such as by role-playing or drawing a comic strip to illustrate the four steps.

Practice This Life Skill

Activity Spread the word. Work with a partner to demonstrate to others how to determine a safe volume level for listening to music with headphones. Organize your demonstration with a scripted text and include posters. Be careful not to let the volume ever get loud enough to hurt your ears.

Social-Emotional Environment

You will learn . . .

- how your social-emotional environment affects your health.
- how to improve your social-emotional environment.
- ways to manage anxiety.

Vocabulary

- **resilient,** E48

You have some control over how people feel and act toward you. Your behavior toward others affects how they interact with you. The thing you may not know yet is how to improve a negative social-emotional environment.

How Social-Emotional Environment Affects Health

Your social-emotional environment can affect your health in many ways. This part of the environment includes the quality and amount of contact you have with people and the feeling of trust and caring around you. This environment is positive when people treat you with trust and caring. People encourage you and praise your good work and strengths. As a result, you feel better about yourself.

A positive social-emotional environment promotes and protects health. You have the feelings of trust and caring you need to succeed. You have the support you need to take risks to grow and learn.

However, think about what it might be like to live in a negative social-emotional environment. For example, you might feel put down. Your strengths and talents might not be noticed. Young people who are abused have a negative social-emotional environment.

A negative social-emotional environment can be harmful to health. People who feel put down and discouraged may become ill more often than those in a positive social-emotional environment. Because they may not value themselves, they may not take care of their health. Instead, they may choose risk behaviors. They might not make responsible decisions about their health.

Your relationships with others affect your health as well. When you have close, caring relationships, you always have someone to share in your good times and support you in hard times. Friends and family members can support you through tough decisions and help you make healthful choices. Having no close relationships, by contrast, can lead to trouble. Loneliness can sometimes lead people to give in to peer pressure. Their need to fit in may tempt them to engage in risk behaviors such as drug use or sexual activity.

✓ **What is the risk of having few or poor relationships?**

▶ **Trust and support promote a positive social-emotional environment.**

Improving Your Social-Emotional Environment

You can take action to improve your social-emotional environment. Much of what you say and do has a direct effect on the interactions of others with you. To understand what you can do, think about the social environment and emotional environment separately.

Improving Your Social Environment

Building a better social environment means developing positive relationships. Here are some ideas.

- **Get involved in healthful activities.** You could join a club or a sports team, or get involved at a local community center or hospital. Fill times of loneliness with positive actions. Learn a new hobby or skill.

- **Meet peers at a camp.** There are many kinds of camps from which you can choose. You might attend a Girl Scout or a Boy Scout camp. You might enjoy soccer, basketball, or lacrosse camps. You might enjoy a drama camp or an art camp. Some camps offer scholarships to young people who cannot afford to pay. Ask a parent, guardian, or teacher about attending these camps. Young people from other communities will be at camp. You will have a chance to make new friendships.

- **Find a pen pal.** Ask a parent, guardian, or teacher how to find a pen pal. You can write or e-mail a pen pal. Develop a long-distance relationship.

- **Develop a skill or hobby.** Fill times of loneliness with positive actions. Learn new hobbies and skills. Share them later when you meet other young people.

◀ **You can share fun times with and learn from an older person.**

- **Become friends with an older person.** Older people may often feel lonely. They may have friendship needs. They might share your interests. Many nursing homes, assisted living facilities, and senior centers have programs to match older people with young people.

- **Ask a responsible adult for advice.** Share feelings of loneliness. Discuss ways to meet other young people. Share concerns if you live in a neighborhood where peers are involved in sex, drugs, or crime. Parents, teachers, coaches, and other responsible adults may have more ideas about how you can meet new people.

Improving Your Emotional Environment

Take action to improve your emotional environment. Follow these steps.

- **Think positively about yourself.** Remember to praise yourself for your accomplishments. At the same time, always be honest with yourself about things you need to work on. Make sure these self-criticisms are constructive. Use self-statements, words you say to yourself to stay in control. Don't let put-downs or criticism you do not deserve influence you.

- **Don't use alcohol, tobacco, or other drugs.** These substances will not solve any of your problems. They will damage your physical and emotional health.

- **Do not cope or try to get even by choosing risk behaviors.** Risk behaviors will harm you. Your goal is to protect yourself.

ACTIVITY

Music LINK
Friends in Tune

With a group, select a tune that you have learned in music class. Each person listens to or sings the tune alone. Then group members sing the tune together, sway to the rhythm, and clap to keep the beat. Discuss how this activity can help people interact in healthful ways, as well as help them relax.

- **Take care of your health.** Get plenty of rest and sleep, eat healthful foods, and exercise. Practice ways to reduce stress.

- **Ask a parent, guardian, or other responsible adult about counseling.** Talking with a counselor can help you discover new insights and possibilities to explore.

- **Develop a relationship with a mentor.** A mentor is a responsible person who helps a younger person. A mentor whom you like and trust can give you honest feedback about your strengths and weaknesses. He or she can guide you to other sources of help.

How can adults help you improve your social and emotional environments?

Managing Anxiety

Do You Know?

Researchers have studied young people who have gone through war, terrorist attacks, and other trauma. Studies indicate that resilient children can learn to overcome terrible events and build positive lives.

A negative social-emotional environment may cause a person to feel anxiety. *Anxiety* is a feeling of worry or uneasiness about something harmful or disappointing that may happen. For example, being bullied or having friends who engage in risk behaviors may cause a person to have anxiety.

Many people feel some anxiety about day-to-day challenges. Anxiety may sometimes help a person work harder to reach a positive goal. However, when anxiety begins to interfere with a person's daily life, the anxiety may require professional help.

Becoming more resilient (ri•ZIL•yuhnt) can help a person manage anxiety. Being **resilient** means being able to bounce back and learn from misfortune or change. Here are some strategies for managing anxiety by becoming more resilient.

- **Learn to manage stress.** Help yourself relax by playing games, talking to friends, breathing deeply, or thinking of soothing mental images. Make a schedule.

- **Remember your values.** Base your decisions on the beliefs and ideas that are most important to you. Having a set of values to guide your decisions helps you feel connected to other people and to society as a whole.

- **Think positively.** Try to convince yourself that you can bring positive change to your life. When bad things happen, try to see them as temporary setbacks and not as permanent problems. Remind yourself of all the things you can do to take control of your life and your future.

- **Find and talk to an adult you can trust.** You will be able to deal with your problems more easily if you have an adult to help you through them. A trusted adult—a parent, guardian, or other responsible adult—will listen to you and offer guidance, care, and support.

▼ **A coach can help you develop fitness and good sportsmanship.**

Overcoming Anxiety

An important part of managing anxiety is being willing and able to take control of your life. One way to do this is by taking the lead in activities. For example, you could start a new club and invite others to join. If you are afraid of failing, begin with something small that will enable you to gain skills. Try reaching out to just one person you would like to know better. If you succeed, you will gain the self-esteem to try again, perhaps on a larger scale.

You also can manage anxiety by dealing with problems. Use the Guidelines for Making Responsible Decisions™ to decide what to do. If your first solution does not work, try another approach. Learning how to resolve conflicts is a key to having a positive social-emotional environment.

 **What does it mean to be resilient?**

Resolve Conflicts

Role-play a situation with a partner. One partner is a bully trying to get the other to cut class and go to a movie. Before you start, each partner thinks of what to say. Use these steps to resolve the conflict.

1. **Stay calm.** List three guidelines for staying calm. For example, keep from shouting. A third partner can help by warning you when you seem to be getting angry.

2. **Talk about the conflict.** Be sure you and the other person agree on the problem you are trying to solve. Think of the problem, not the other person, as the source of the conflict.

3. **Discuss possible ways to settle the conflict.** Work together to brainstorm possible solutions. Remember to use the Guidelines for Making Responsible Decisions™.

4. **Agree on a way to settle the conflict. You may need to ask a trusted adult for help.** Evaluate the possible solutions until you decide on one that will succeed.

LESSON 2 REVIEW

Review Concepts

1. **Identify** the health risks of a negative social-emotional environment.

2. **List** three ways to improve your social-emotional environment.

3. **Describe** strategies for managing anxiety.

Critical Thinking

4. **Draw Conclusions** How can being resilient help you cope with a disappointment or sad event?

5. **LIFE SKILLS Resolve Conflict** After playing a baseball game, two friends on opposing teams begin to argue over which is the better team. The argument becomes angry and they are about to fight. How might you help them resolve this conflict?

E49

Clean Air

You will learn . . .

- why clean air is important.
- how air pollution changes air quality.
- ways to keep the air clean.

Vocabulary

- **pollution,** E51
- **fossil fuels,** E51
- **radon,** E52
- **sick building syndrome (SBS),** E52
- **acid rain,** E53
- **ozone layer,** E53
- **greenhouse effect,** E53
- **global warming,** E53

Nothing is more basic to life than breathing. The body must inhale air several times a minute to get the oxygen it needs. However, the air you breathe also contains many other substances, some of which may be harmful. This is why it is important to keep the air clean.

The Need for Clean Air

All plants and animals take in oxygen from the air and use it to produce energy for their life activities. As a result of this process, they release carbon dioxide. Plants have a special ability to use carbon dioxide and produce oxygen. Plants and the plantlike algae that live close to water surfaces replenish our planet's oxygen supply.

If the air is not clean, it can harm the health of all living organisms. It can reduce Earth's ability to support life. **Pollution** is a harmful change in the physical environment. Pollution can affect Earth's land, water, and air. Air pollution occurs when the air is contaminated with harmful substances. Common pollutants include

- natural pollutants, including once living matter that is decaying, and matter from volcanoes.

- tobacco smoke.

- exhaust from motor vehicles.

- particulates—particles of soot, ash, and dirt.

- gases produced from the burning of trash and **fossil fuels,** which are coal, oil, and natural gas burned to produce energy.

These pollutants affect air outdoors as well as indoors. They threaten human health in several ways. For example, polluted air may contain harmful substances that can cause illness, pain, or even death to humans. It also can harm the plants and animals that humans rely on to survive.

Smog Among the pollutants in car exhaust are gases that can react with other gases in the air and produce smog. *Smog* is a combination of smoke and fog. Smog hangs like a thick, smelly brown cloud over many American cities. Smog affects people with asthma and allergies. It can result in lung diseases, including cancer.

 **What is pollution?**

Science LINK
Trees Map

Trees greatly improve the quality of the air, especially in cities. Make a map of your neighborhood to show the locations of trees. You may have tree-lined streets, parks, clusters of trees on street corners, or you may have just a few scattered trees if you live in a busy city. Indicate locations where trees are missing.

▶ Pollution damages your health.

E51

On Your Own
FOR SCHOOL OR HOME

Home Safety

With your family, set up a checklist for keeping your home safe from carbon monoxide and radon. Your checklist should include testing your home for these gases.

- Keep gas appliances properly adjusted.
- Use the correct fuel in kerosene space heaters.
- Have a trained professional inspect, clean, and tune-up the central heating system once a year.

▼ A carbon monoxide detector can help protect your family.

Pollution at Home and Around the World

Some forms of air pollution are easy to recognize, such as the smoke that pours out of factory smokestacks. Other forms are less obvious.

Indoor Air Pollution

The air inside schools, homes, and other buildings may contain pollutants. Poorly working furnaces, stoves, and water heaters can produce carbon monoxide. Carbon monoxide is an odorless, colorless, and poisonous gas. Breathing in too much of it can cause sickness and death. Other indoor pollutants include

- **Secondhand tobacco smoke** Secondhand smoke is tobacco smoke that enters the air nonsmokers breathe. It can cause lung cancer.
- **Radon** Radon is an odorless, colorless, and radioactive gas. Radon enters buildings through cracks in floors and basement walls. Breathing it over a long time adds to the risk of lung cancer. It is possible to test houses for radon and have it removed if necessary.
- **Asbestos and lead** These pollutants are mainly found in the paint and building materials of older homes. Asbestos is known to cause lung cancer, and lead is known to cause brain damage. A qualified professional must remove lead or asbestos from a building.

Other indoor air pollutants include mold and allergens, substances that can trigger an allergic response. Fumes from common household chemicals, such as paints, cleansers, and glues can also pollute the air indoors.

Sick building syndrome (SBS) is an illness caused by indoor air pollution. Its symptoms include headaches, eye irritation, and nausea. SBS increases the risk of respiratory infections and asthma attacks. Getting fresh air can relieve the symptoms.

Worldwide Concerns About Air Pollution

Smog is only one of many worldwide problems related to air pollution.

Acid rain is precipitation that is high in acid content as a result of pollution. It harms plants, animals, bodies of water, and even buildings.

The **ozone layer** is a layer of the upper atmosphere that traps ultraviolet (UV) rays from the sun, protecting life on Earth from these rays. Some air pollutants rise into the atmosphere and damage the ozone layer. This damage means that more UV rays reach Earth's surface. Increased exposure to UV rays can cause skin cancer.

The **greenhouse effect** is the trapping of heat from the sun by gases in Earth's atmosphere. This effect might cause global warming. **Global warming** means an increase in Earth's temperature. Some scientists think Earth will get warmer. Others think that we cannot predict how Earth will change.

 What is radon?

Analyze What Influences Your Health

Role-play this situation with a group. A group of older students meets after school to play ball. They have asked you to join them. After your first game, some of them offer you a cigarette. What should you do?

1. **Identify people and things that might influence you.** Identify the influences, including people and things, on your health if you spend your after-school time with this group.

2. **Evaluate how the influence might affect your health and decisions.** For each influence you listed in Step 1, list a possible effect on your health.

3. **Choose positive influences on health.** Make a list of activities to show how you might spend your after-school time in more healthful ways.

4. **Protect yourself from negative influences on health.** How do you show refusal to any of the members of this group who offer you a cigarette?

◀ The glass of a greenhouse traps radiation from the sun inside the greenhouse in the form of heat. This effect occurs in Earth's atmosphere as well.
blue arrows = incoming sunlight that passes through the glass into the greenhouse
red arrows = heat from inside the greenhouse that does not readily escape through the glass

E53

Science LINK

Diffusion Model

With a responsible adult, walk through your home looking for any containers of household chemicals, such as cleaners and paints. Make sure that the containers are tightly sealed. If they are not tightly sealed, fumes from the chemicals can diffuse, or spread out, from the containers. You can make a model to understand how the fumes spread. Fill a clear glass with water. Put one drop of food coloring into the water. Do not stir. Observe the food coloring over an hour. The water represents the air in a room. The food coloring represents fumes from a loosely covered container. Explain what happens.

▼ **Recharging batteries is one way to conserve energy.**

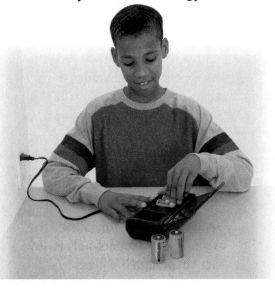

Doing Your Part

You can help reduce air pollution. Here are some ideas.

- **Do not smoke cigarettes.** In addition to protecting your health, not smoking means you will not produce secondhand smoke, a major indoor pollutant.

- **Limit car rides.** Automobiles are a leading source of air pollution in this country. Talk to a parent or guardian about cutting down on car trips. Take advantage of public transportation. Walk or ride your bicycle when it is safe to do so.

- **Limit electricity use.** Many electrical power plants contribute to air pollution. You can help by turning off lights and appliances when you are not using them.

- **Reduce.** Cutting down on your purchases can reduce pollution. Look for products and brands that reduce the amount of packaging for their products.

- **Reuse.** Rather than throwing products out, think of ways to reuse them.

- **Plant trees.** Green plants can remove carbon dioxide from the air and produce oxygen. They also provide shade on hot days.

Ways to Keep Indoor Air Clean and Safe

You and your family can take steps to reduce air pollution inside and around your home.

- Limit the use of household cleaners in aerosol cans.
- Use household cleaners, paints, and other chemicals only in well-ventilated rooms. Carefully read labels on these cleaners and follow instructions.
- Have the home checked for asbestos and have any asbestos removed or sealed in place.
- Install a carbon monoxide detector in your home.
- Check to see that space heaters, furnaces, and water heaters are working properly.
- Check the home for radon levels.
- Have a no-smoking policy.

Addressing Worldwide Concerns

Measures are being taken on a world-wide level to reduce air pollution. For example, the United States Congress passed the Clean Air Act of 1963 to protect air. Additional measures were added in 1967, 1970, 1977, and 1990. Since the 1970s, various air pollutants have decreased significantly.

As a result of these laws, car manufacturers have reduced the amount of harmful wastes released. "Clean coal" methods were introduced to lower the amount of harmful wastes that result in acid rain. Power plants that burn coal can wash coal before burning it to remove sulfur. Sulfur can result in acid rain when the coal burns.

However, Earth's rain forests are being depleted. The plants in these vast forest areas help remove carbon dioxide from the air and replace it with oxygen. These forests are being cleared to make room for homes and farms. Efforts to address this issue are being discussed worldwide.

How can you reduce air pollution?

CAREERS IN HEALTH
Climatologist

A climatologist studies weather patterns to find the effects of climate on our surroundings. Will there be a flood? Are we in a drought? These are questions that climatologists try to answer. Climatologists work for state and federal governments and private companies. Some teach at colleges. To become a climatologist, a person needs a strong background in math and science. Some climatologists work in a laboratory, while others travel to different areas to do research.

LOG ON Visit **www.mmhhealth.com** to find out more about this and other health careers.

LESSON 3 REVIEW

Review Concepts

1. **Explain** how poor air quality can both directly and indirectly harm human health.

2. **Name** one form of indoor air pollution and one form of outdoor air pollution.

Critical Thinking

3. **Analyze** Explain how reusing products can help reduce air pollution.

4. **Summarize** Write a letter to a friend stating the importance of clean indoor air and summarizing important steps that can be taken to make sure indoor air is clean and safe.

5. **LIFE SKILLS Analyze What Influences Your Health** Suppose that you live in a house that was built in the 1930s, and your family is planning a renovation project. How might this project affect the air quality in your home?

Clean Water

You will learn . . .

- why clean water is important.
- how water pollution changes water quality.
- ways to keep the water clean.
- ways to conserve water.

Vocabulary

- **runoff,** E58
- **sewage,** E58
- **conservation,** E62

Water is as important to our survival as air. In fact, our bodies are made up mostly of water. We can live without it for only a short time. Unfortunately, there are many threats to the quality of our water supply. You can learn to help protect our sources of water.

The Need for Clean Water

All organisms depend on water. We need water for drinking, for washing, and to raise the crops and animals we depend on for food. Without a supply of clean water, we would not be able to survive.

Our planet has a great deal of water. However, people can use and drink only a very small part of this water—less than 1 percent. We cannot drink salt water from the ocean without spending money to remove the salt in it. Much of Earth's freshwater is frozen in the planet's ice caps and glaciers.

Water cycle Although we use water at a very rapid rate, water is returned to Earth's surface through the ongoing water cycle. Water, including used water, evaporates from Earth's surface, rises into the atmosphere, and eventually returns as rain, snow, sleet, or hail. However, water is not evenly distributed across Earth's surface. Many areas go without rain for many months of the year. Places that may get large amounts of rain in one season may have a drought because of weather changes. It is important for people to take good care of the water we have.

Water pollution Like the air, water can become polluted. For example, poisons and carcinogens of many types can get into the water. Some forms of water pollution occur naturally, such as contamination with certain pathogens and dissolved radon gas. However, a great deal of pollution comes from human activities. Both our use of chemicals and the natural wastes we produce can harm water. In some cases, we can clean up polluted water supplies. Other pollutants, however, are very difficult to remove.

Almost every county in the United States contains wetlands—marshes, bogs, swamps, and similar areas. About half of the nation's original wetlands have been destroyed. These areas help clean our water, reduce flood and storm damage, and provide a place for many kinds of fish and animals to live.

▼ Clean water is important for your health and for recreation.

✔ What percentage of Earth's water is safe for drinking?

How Pollution Gets into Our Water

Pollution can be managed to reduce threats to public health, safety, and the environment. Pollution can enter water through industrial waste, human waste (or sewage), or runoff from rainwater. This polluted water is called wastewater. All the wastewater produced by a city eventually ends up in a river, lake, or ocean.

Sources of Pollution

Water pollution is water contaminated with harmful substances. It results from several main sources.

Runoff **Runoff** is water from rain or melted snow that flows across the land and into surface water. Runoff also carries chemicals from cars off the roadways into water supplies. Pollution can get into the water supply when runoff picks up pesticides used on crops.

Sewage Pathogens are another common pollutant in water. A major source of water pollution is sewage. **Sewage** is waste liquid and matter carried off by sewers. If sewage is not treated properly, pathogens from human wastes can enter the water and infect people who drink it.

Air pollution A third form of water contamination comes from air pollution. When air pollution mixes with water in clouds, it can fall back to Earth as acid rain. This can harm plants, animals, and humans.

Illegal dumping Some water pollution occurs when people or industries pour pollutants directly into the water or onto the ground. Laws help to prevent this type of pollution.

Household pollutants Finally, water pollution can come from people's homes.

sunlight

pollution from smoke

acid rain

◀ Air pollutants, mostly from industrial smoke, combine with sunlight and water vapor to form acid rain. Some of the pollutants in acid rain result from lightning activity.

How Water Pollution Affects the Food Chain

Organisms need food to survive. All food comes from organisms called producers. Producers use energy from sunlight to make their own food from water and carbon dioxide. Green plants and some one-celled organisms, such as algae, are producers. Animals are consumers. Consumers are organisms that eat producers or other organisms. Together producers and consumers make up a food chain. A food chain is a path of the sun's energy from producer to consumers.

Water pollution can disrupt the food chain. For example, acid rain in a stream may destroy the insects living there. Then the fish in the stream will die out since they have nothing to eat. In turn, the food supply is removed. In this way, damage to just one part of the food chain can harm many kinds of animals.

Pollution can also cause health risks for animals near the top of the food chain. Poison that enters the bottom of the food chain can become more concentrated as it moves up. For example, mercury exists in low levels in small fish species. However, because sharks and swordfish eat so many of the smaller fish, they may have high mercury levels in their bodies. That can present a health risk for people who eat those fish.

ACTIVITY

Science
LINK
Food Chains

Make flowcharts to trace all the foods you eat in a day back to producers. For example, fish might have eaten other fish and smaller marine consumers, which in turn may have eaten algae. How would you show a food chain for each ingredient in a chicken sandwich, which may have meat, bread, lettuce, and tomatoes? Make a food chain flowchart for all the foods in your breakfast, lunch, and dinner.

✓ **What is runoff?**

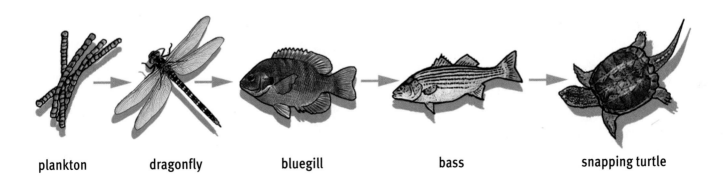

| plankton | dragonfly | bluegill | bass | snapping turtle |

▲ The red arrows show the path of the sun's energy from organism to organism. What happens if part of the food chain is broken?

E59

Stopping Water Pollution

Each person in the United States uses about 80 to 100 gallons of water per day. Most of that water is used to flush toilets. Many local governments now require faucets, toilets, and showers to allow only a limited amount of water flow per minute.

As a result of the responsible efforts of people in the United States since the 1970s, fresh-water pollution has fallen significantly.

Like air pollution, water pollution is a large problem with many causes. However, individuals can take action to reduce water pollution and protect the water supply.

One way that people in a community can fight water pollution is by cleaning up surface water—in streams, rivers, ponds, and lakes. Local cleanup programs aim to remove garbage from riverbanks and lakeshores. If no such programs exist in your community, talk to an adult about how one can get started.

Cleaning up surface water is just one way people can be health advocates for the environment. Health advocates for the environment take steps to improve the quality of all parts of the environment. Cleanup programs help improve water quality and build a healthier environment for the plants and animals that live in the water.

Learn About Water Treatment

Most public water supplies are treated to ensure that they are safe for people to drink. Water treatment usually involves several steps for removing the dirt, plant material, and pollutants that normally get into water. It may also involve adding chemicals to the water to kill pathogens.

Talk to an adult about visiting a local water treatment plant. There you will learn about the quality of water in your area and about what you can do to help keep water clean.

▲ Everyone can help keep the water supply clean.

Cut Down on Water Pollutants

Many household chemicals, such as gasoline, motor oil, and paint thinner, can pollute water. Spilling even small amounts of these products down the drain can harm water supplies. Chemicals spilled on the ground can seep down through the ground and pollute groundwater. Groundwater is underground water that may be pumped to the surface for use.

Talk to a parent or guardian about chemicals in your home. Make sure that the chemicals are stored and used properly. Many household products have labels that explain how to dispose of them safely. Follow these guidelines. Make sure to keep products in their original containers so you will have the labels on hand. You also can cut down on your use of harmful chemicals by using safer alternatives, such as vinegar or baking soda for cleaning.

Other sources of water pollution are lawn and garden fertilizers and pesticides. Runoff may carry these chemicals into water sources far from your home. Learn about ways to cut down on the use of these products, such as fertilizing lawns with mulch or compost. Many hardware stores offer less harmful chemicals for the lawn and garden.

Why is it important to handle chemicals safely even if you live far from rivers and lakes?

ACTIVITY
LIFE SKILLS
CRITICAL THINKING

Be a Health Advocate

Design a poster fact sheet describing how to properly get rid of household wastes.

1 **Select a health-related concern to communicate.** Learning how to dispose of household wastes properly helps to avoid polluting the water supply.

2 **Gather reliable information.** Contact your local sanitation or public health department. Ask if your community has a household chemical waste collection site or event. If the answer is no, ask how people should dispose of these products.

3 **Identify your purpose and target audience.** Choose a group of people you think could make use of the information you have gathered. For instance, you might target young people, home owners, or business owners.

4 **Develop a convincing and appropriate message.** Produce your fact sheet using what you have learned. Make your language and design suitable for your target audience.

NO DUMPING Ⓢ
Flows To Waterways

◀ Many products found in your home can pollute the water supply. What are some nonpolluting alternatives to the products shown here?

E61

Conserving Water

Conserve at School

Citizenship Public buildings, including schools, use a lot of water. Brainstorm a list of ways you could encourage water conservation in your school. For instance, you might encourage students to drink at the fountain for 10 seconds or wash their hands for only 20 seconds. Post your suggestions on a bulletin board in the school hallway.

The amount of fresh water on our planet is limited, and in some areas, water supplies are shrinking quickly. You can help protect water supplies by conserving water. **Conservation** means saving resources, such as water, energy, or land. You can conserve water by not polluting water and by using less water.

Conserving Water Indoors

People use water at home in many ways. Showering, washing dishes, washing laundry, drinking water—it all adds up. Fortunately, there are many ways to save water on all these activities. Here's a room-by-room look at how you and your family can save water at home. Many of these tips can also help you save energy and reduce air pollution that could lead to acid rain.

Saving Water at Home

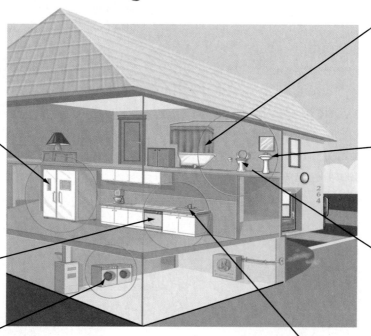

Refrigerator Keep a pitcher of water in the refrigerator so you do not have to run the water to wait for it to get cold.

Dishwasher Run the dishwasher only when it is full.

Washing machine Run the washing machine only when it is full. Consider replacing an old machine with a newer one that uses less water.

Shower Take short showers rather than baths. Turn the water off while you soap up and shampoo. Install a low-flow shower head.

Bathroom sink Fix leaky faucets. Do not leave the water running while you brush your teeth.

Toilet Make sure the toilet does not leak. Newer toilets use as little as 1.6 gallons of water per flush.

Kitchen sink Fix leaky faucets. Even a small leak can add up to gallons of water going down the drain each day. Install a low-flow faucet head.

▲ Use this picture to make a checklist of ways to save water that you can follow at home.

Conserving Water Outdoors

People also use a lot of water outdoors for activities like washing cars and watering plants. Here are some ways you and your family can conserve water outdoors.

- Do not open hydrants.
- For your yard or window box, choose plants that will do well in your climate. Do not choose plants that require lots of water.
- Water your plants during the coolest part of the day to keep the water from evaporating. Try to choose a time when it is not windy.
- Put mulch around plants and shrubs to cut down on evaporation.
- Check for and repair leaks outside your home.
- When you wash the car, do not leave the hose running.

 What is conservation?

ACTIVITY LIFE SKILLS

CRITICAL THINKING

Set Health Goals

Use a health behavior contract to set a health goal.

1 **Write the health goal you want to set:** *I will protect the natural environment.*

2 **Tell how the goal will affect your health.** List the ways conserving water can affect you, your family, and the environment.

3 **Describe a plan you will follow. Keep track of your progress.** Set a specific goal for how much you want to reduce your water use. Follow the strategies on these pages. Keep track of how much water you save for one week.

4 **Evaluate how your plan worked.** At the end of a week, figure out how much water you saved. If you did not meet your goal, try adding some more strategies for conserving water.

◀ **Follow directions for the care of your plants to avoid overwatering.**

LESSON **4** REVIEW

Review Concepts

1. **List** three ways that humans use water.

2. **Identify** two sources of water pollution.

3. **Summarize** how the burning of fossil fuels contributes to water pollution.

Critical Thinking

4. **LIFE SKILLS** **Be a Health Advocate** You want to convince your local government to conserve water. Write a paragraph explaining why conservation is important and listing steps your town could take to reduce water use.

5. **LIFE SKILLS** **Set Health Goals** You want to reduce the use of harmful chemicals in your home. Describe a plan your family could follow to meet this goal.

Clean Planet

You will learn . . .

- how we rely on Earth's resources.
- how Earth gets polluted.
- ways to keep Earth clean.
- ways to conserve energy and land.

Vocabulary

- **renewable resource,** E65
- **landfill,** E66
- **hazardous waste,** E66
- **biodegradable,** E67
- **recycling,** E68
- **composting,** E69
- **humus,** E69

Our physical environment extends to the entire planet. We depend on Earth and on its resources for our health and our way of life. Anything that damages these natural resources also harms our health.

Earth and Its Resources

A resource is something that people can use. All organisms on Earth depend on natural resources. For human beings, natural resources also provide the energy that we rely on for heat, light, and other necessities that help us enjoy life.

Renewable Resources

A renewable resource is a resource that can be replaced. Water, for example, is a renewable resource. Some resources are renewable only up to a point. For example, if people cut down trees and use the wood, new trees will grow to replace them. However, if people cut too many trees without planting new ones, then the forests will not grow back fast enough to keep up with wood use.

Nonrenewable Resources

Nonrenewable resources cannot be replaced after they are used. If people keep using them, in time these resources will become less available and their prices will rise. Earth's supply of minerals, such as the metals aluminum, gold, iron, and silver, are nonrenewable.

Energy Resources

Energy is the ability to do work. People use energy to power cars, run computers, and heat buildings. The main source of Earth's energy is the sun. This energy, called solar energy, also can be turned into electricity and used for powering household appliances.

Other sources of energy include the wind, running water, and heat deep within Earth, geothermal energy. As long as wind blows, its energy can be captured by windmills to produce electricity.

However, we also depend on many nonrenewable resources for our energy supplies. These include fossil fuels, such as oil, natural gas, and coal. If supplies of fossil fuels fall, their prices will rise. This change will encourage finding more supplies and substitutes. It will also encourage people to conserve these fossil fuels voluntarily. Conserving these fuels can make supplies last longer. It also will reduce air pollution.

✓ **What is a renewable resource?**

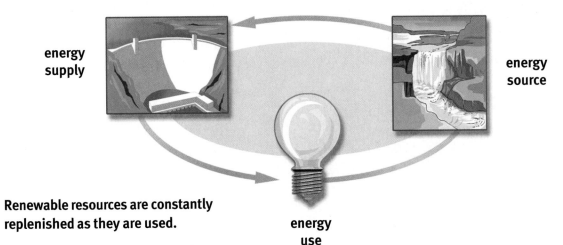

energy supply

energy source

energy use

▶ Renewable resources are constantly replenished as they are used.

How Land Gets Polluted

Social Studies LINK

ACTIVITY

Where Does Your Trash Go?

What happens to the trash in your community? Check your phone book to find out what local government agency collects and disposes of solid waste. Ask how trash is collected from homes and businesses and where it goes afterward.

Think about how many times a day you throw something in the garbage can. Every time you open a package, you produce waste. In addition, many businesses produce large amounts of waste. All of this waste has to go somewhere. Unfortunately, much of it ends up polluting a precious resource, land.

Solid Waste and Landfills

Solid waste is trash or garbage. In this country, most solid waste goes into a **landfill,** a specially designed place for collecting and burying waste. One potential problem with landfills is that water from rain and snow seeps down through them and picks up pollutants. To keep this polluted water from getting into water supplies, modern landfills have liners and other systems for collecting the water.

Landfills require a lot of land. In many communities, it is difficult or even impossible to find space for a landfill. These communities must ship their waste to distant locations.

Some solid waste is burned in specially designed incinerators. However, not all wastes will burn. The ash that is left behind must be buried in a landfill. Burning trash also produces gases that can pollute the air.

▼ There is a good chance that the garbage from your home winds up in a landfill.

A Sanitary Landfill

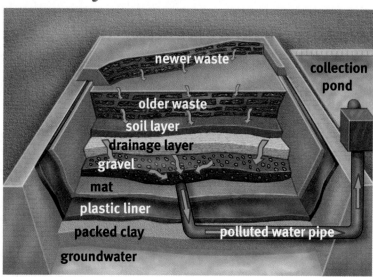

newer waste

collection pond

older waste

soil layer

drainage layer

gravel

mat

plastic liner

packed clay

polluted water pipe

groundwater

Hazardous Waste

Some wastes require special handling. **Hazardous waste** is waste that is poisonous, flammable, or otherwise dangerous. These wastes must be disposed of carefully to avoid polluting the land and harming our health. Hazardous waste includes poisonous industrial or household chemicals; medical wastes that can carry dangerous pathogens; and radioactive wastes from nuclear power plants, which give off potentially harmful radiation.

Littering

A surprising amount of solid waste is not disposed of properly. Some people throw trash in the street and not in the garbage can. No matter how littering occurs, it is a serious problem for everyone.

Some litter is **biodegradable,** or capable of breaking down into harmless substances by natural means. Some dishwashing detergents and laundry detergents are made of biodegradable products. These products are dumped into water and eventually become part of lakes, streams, and rivers.

Many common types of litter, however, may take hundreds of years to break down. As a result, these types of litter simply build up every day on Earth. Some forms of litter, such as broken glass, can cause injury. Others carry pathogens that may threaten people's health. Litter can clog storm drains, leading to flooding. It can also harm waterways and organisms that live in them. Cities and towns spend huge amounts of money to get rid of trash dumped along roads and on vacant lots.

▲ **Disposing of waste properly is everyone's responsibility.**

 What is a landfill?

CRITICAL THINKING

Be a Health Advocate

You notice that people toss litter from cars. Develop a campaign to encourage people to stop this form of littering.

1 **Select a health-related concern to communicate.** You can help prevent littering by encouraging people not to throw trash from their cars.

2 **Gather reliable information.** Use this book and library and Internet resources to take notes about the costs and problems related to littering.

3 **Identify your purpose and target audience.** Your purpose is to cut down on litter. Your audience could include drivers and anyone else who rides in a car on a regular basis.

4 **Develop a convincing and appropriate message.** Brainstorm a list of slogans that will motivate people not to litter. Put your best slogan on a button, a sticker, or a poster.

Doing Your Part

Even when we throw trash in the proper place, it takes its toll on Earth. You can reduce this impact by cutting down on the amount of waste you produce.

Recycling

Recycling means turning waste into new, usable products. Recycling has many benefits. It saves resources by using a single resource many times. It also uses less energy than making products from new resources. By saving energy, it also reduces pollution. Because it uses products that would otherwise be thrown away, recycling saves landfill space.

Many items can be recycled, including

- plastic bottles and jugs.
- aluminum cans and foil.
- newspapers and magazines.
- cardboard.
- juice boxes.
- metal cans.
- paper at school.

However, not every community can recycle all these items. In addition, each community has its own rules about recycling. For example, metal cans may need to be rinsed and crushed. Check with your sanitation department to find out what items you can recycle and how.

Do You Know?

What if your school held a paper recycling drive? For every ton of paper recycled, the students would save 17 trees from being cut down to make new paper. A ton is equal to 2,000 pounds.

▶ Products marked with the symbol below are recyclable. Check to see which items can be recycled in your community.

Precycling

Precycling means taking steps to reduce the amount of waste you produce. The simplest way to do this is to consume less. If you avoid buying items you don't need, these products will not enter the waste stream. If you choose goods with less packaging, you will have less material to throw out or recycle.

Another way to precycle is to extend the life of the things you use. Try to repair broken items instead of throwing them away and buying new ones. You can also reuse items, such as empty bottles and jars. This may help you save money as well as conserve resources.

Composting

A lot of the space in our landfills is taken up by yard waste and food scraps. We can save landfill space by putting this waste to use. **Composting** is a method for turning certain types of waste into humus. **Humus** (HYOO•muhs) is a natural, soil-like material produced by the breaking down of plant and animal remains.

Follow these steps to compost at home.

1. Get a large box—at least 3 feet wide and deep. Place it outside, away from your home.
2. Line the bottom and sides of the box with garbage bags.
3. Put down a layer of grass, leaves, and food scraps. (Do not put meats, dairy products, or fats in the pile.) Mix in some straw and soil.
4. Pour water on the pile—just enough to moisten it.
5. Keep adding layers until the box is two thirds full.
6. Mix the pile every three to four days. In one to two months, you will have humus.

Your community may have rules and guidelines for composting. Call your sanitation or health department before you build your compost.

Name three benefits of recycling.

How much could composting help reduce our solid waste? According to the United States Environmental Protection Agency, about one fourth of household solid waste could be composted.

▼ **When you compost you reduce, reuse, and recycle.**

Conserving Resources

Here are some ideas you can use to conserve resources. How many more can you name?

- **Practice precycling and recycling.** You also can "complete the cycle" by buying products made from recycled materials. Check product labels to see whether they contain any recycled materials. Recycling will work in the long term only if people are willing to buy recycled goods.

- **Conserve energy.** By conserving energy, you will reduce air pollution and conserve our precious resources of fossil fuels. By practicing the tips on page E71, you can have a direct, positive impact on the environment. This will reduce air pollution and conserve fossil fuels.

- **Conserve water.** The strategies that you learned in Lesson 4 to help you conserve water are likely to save energy as well. For example, taking shorter showers saves both water and the energy used to heat the water. Running the washing machine less often saves water and electricity. In addition, every time you conserve water you help reduce the energy required for pumping and treating water supplies.

On Your Own
FOR SCHOOL OR HOME

Saving Energy at Home

Talk to a parent or guardian about home improvements that can be made to conserve resources at home. Check the tips on page E71. For example, you might ask about switching to energy-saving lightbulbs or installing a low-flow showerhead.

LIFE SKILLS

CRITICAL THINKING

Set Health Goals

Use a health behavior contract to set a health goal.

1 **Write the health goal you want to set:** *I will help conserve energy and natural resources.*

2 **Tell how the goal will affect your health.** Explain how conserving resources can affect your health.

3 **Describe a plan you will follow. Keep track of your progress.** Make a list of specific steps you will take, such as recycling or turning down the heat. For one week, check off each action that you take.

4 **Evaluate how your plan worked.** At the end of the week, look at the conservation actions that you did not take. Identify ways you can take those actions in the next week.

Tips for Conserving Energy at Home and in School

- Ride a bicycle or walk to reduce using fuels in cars.
- Carpool with friends to school and community activities.
- Turn off lights and all electronic appliances when not in use.
- Wear warm clothes instead of turning up the heat.
- Seal air leaks around doors and windows.
- Keep windows and doors closed in air-conditioned places. Keep air conditioning at about 78°F.
- Wash clothes in warm, rather than hot, water. Wait for a full load before running a dish-washer or laundry machine.
- Use energy-saving light bulbs.
- Use fuel-efficient appliances.
- Use a microwave or toaster oven to heat up a small amount of food.
- Preheat the oven for as short a time as possible.

 Identify three ways you can cut down on energy use.

Consumer Wise
ACTIVITY

Going Organic

Organic foods and products are made without the use of harmful pesticides and fertil-izers. Buying these products can help prevent pollution. However, they are often more expensive than other products. Visit your local supermarket and compare the prices of organic and nonorganic foods. Calculate how much more organic foods cost on average. Make an ad-vertisement comparing the prices and possible advan-tages of organic foods with other foods.

USDA CERTIFIED ORGANIC

◀ **Recycled materials have many uses.**

LESSON 5 REVIEW

Review Concepts

1. **Compare** renewable and nonrenewable resources.
2. **List** at least two methods of precycling.
3. **Identify** two benefits of conserving energy.

Critical Thinking

4. **Evaluate** Which do you think is a better method for disposing of trash: landfills or incin-erators? Explain why.

5. **LIFE SKILLS** **Be a Health Advocate** You want to convince people in your community to start a recycling program, or to use the program that you already have. Explain what strategy you would use to send this message and why.

6. **LIFE SKILLS** **Set Health Goals** You want to reduce the amount of trash your household pro-duces by half. List five specific steps you could take to reach this goal.

Enjoying Your Environment

You will learn . . .

- what kinds of activities you can enjoy outdoors.
- where you can go to enjoy the outdoors.
- how a pleasant visual environment can help you improve your health.

Vocabulary

- **ecosports,** E73
- **ecology,** E75
- **visual environment,** E76

Enjoying the outdoors can be one of life's great pleasures. Everyone can find some ways to spend time outside and experience their natural environment.

Enjoyable Outdoor Activities

The best way to enjoy the outdoors is by taking part in activities that do not harm the environment. Try physical activities that are friendly to the environment. **Ecosports** are outdoor sports activities that do not harm the environment. Here are some examples of activities to do with your family.

- **Kayaking and canoeing** These activities enable you to get out on the water without polluting it. Be sure to follow all safety rules, including wearing the required personal flotation device and riding with an adult.

- **Hiking or running** Exploring trails is a great way to get close to the natural environment. However, you should not go out alone, and you should make sure you have some way to call for help if you are injured.

- **Rock climbing** This exciting activity takes special training and equipment. You will need to take a course to learn special skills before you try it.

- **Camping** Be sure you camp only in places where it is allowed and always camp in a group with an adult.

- **Mountain biking** Make sure that biking is allowed on a trail before you use it.

- **Swimming** Swim only in designated areas, and never swim alone.

Another excellent way to enjoy the outdoors is to plant a garden. Many cities have community garden plots you may be able to use.

The motors on off-road, all-terrain vehicles can emit lots of pollutants. These vehicles account for about 90 percent of certain types of air pollution at Yellowstone National Park, even though cars and other types of vehicles outnumber them by 16 to 1.

What is an ecosport?

▲ **What are some other ways to enjoy the outdoors?**

ACTIVITY
Social Studies
L I N K
Parks Map

The National Park System began in the 1870s, when the United States Congress set aside the Yellowstone area in the Wyoming and Montana territories. This was the first national park in the world. On a map of the United States, plot the locations of major national parks. You may plot them with pencil on an outline map or use stick-on notes on a wall map. Which national park is closest to you?

Where to Enjoy the Outdoors

The United States contains countless places where people can enjoy the outdoors. Even city areas have parks and green spaces people can use.

Parks

One of the nation's great resources is its system of national parks. There are more than 84 million acres of land devoted to parks, memorials, seashores, lakeshores, and more. These lands offer a wide range of recreation options. For example, there are miles of hiking paths, hundreds of campgrounds, and thousands of acres of waterways to explore.

Each state also has its own system of parks, preserves, beaches, and forests. You can find out about these resources through your state government.

Local governments—cities and towns—also have outdoor recreation facilities. Check with local officials about options in your area. You may discover local parks with playgrounds, sports fields, or swimming areas.

Other Settings

You can enjoy nature in a variety of settings other than parks. For example, you can hike beside lakes, rivers, and streams, as well as use them for boating and swimming (in designated areas). You also can go walking through fields and woods. Campgrounds provide a place to sleep outdoors in a natural environment.

Nature preserves and wildlife refuges are a special kind of place to enjoy the outdoors. These places are set aside to help protect habitats for plants and animals. Refuges are good places to observe wildlife and appreciate the beauty of nature.

◀ **Have you ever visited a national park?**

Respecting the Outdoors

When you enjoy the outdoors, remember to protect and conserve our natural resources. **Ecology** is the relationship of plants and animals to their physical and biological environment. Disturbing any part of the environment can disrupt all the plants and animals that live there.

"Leave no trace." When you visit a park, preserve, or other outdoor place, a good rule to follow is "leave no trace." Do not take resources from the land, such as plants and animals. Do not feed wild animals or eat wild plants. Do not carve your name into trees or break off branches to build campfires. You also should avoid littering. Be prepared to take out any waste you make or bring in.

Follow rules. Many outdoor places may have their own rules, as well. For example, signs in parks may request that you stay only on marked paths. Straying from paths can damage fragile environments, such as sand dunes or thin mountain soils. There may also be rules about bringing pets into natural places or about camping and eating only in certain areas. Be sure to follow any posted rules.

Be extra careful with fires. Never build a fire without adult supervision, and use only spots set aside for fires or barbecues. Be sure to put out all fires completely before you leave the area. Drown a fire with water or bury it with soil or sand that is free of debris.

✓ How many acres of land does the National Park System include?

Do You Know

In the year 2002, there were nearly 280 million visits to sites in the National Park System. That is nearly one visit for every person living in the United States.

▼ Take only photos; leave only footprints.

Your Visual Environment

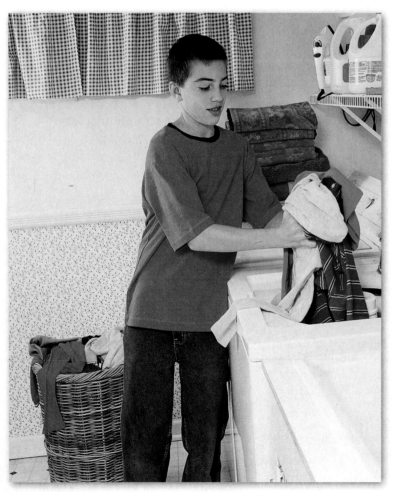

ACTIVITY

Art
LINK
Brighten Your Space

Design a piece of art to enhance your living space. You may draw or paint a picture or make a collage. Include scenes, colors, or images you find pleasing. Consider framing your work or mounting it on cardboard to keep it neat.

Having a pleasing living space can you help relax. You probably share some spaces, such as the living room, with other members of your family. Maybe you have your own bedroom or you share it with another family member. No matter how you share your living space, you will enjoy it more if you promote a pleasing environment.

The **visual environment** is everything a person sees regularly. Making your room and your home more pleasant to look at can help reduce stress. Also, feeling good about your environment is likely to improve your self-esteem and encourage responsible behavior. When you care for your living space, you maintain self-respect.

Keep it clean. You will enjoy your living space more if you keep it clean and tidy. Keeping your space clean can also help you avoid conflict with others in your home. Keep your bed made and your things picked up. Organize your study area. Run the vacuum and dust from time to time. These tips apply to other parts of your home, too. Try not to leave your belongings lying scattered around.

Fix it up. If you are not happy with your living space, talk to a parent or guardian about improving it. New paint, wallpaper, or curtains may help. Adding plants can brighten up a room. Ask for more lighting in the room if you need it. You also can improve the outdoor environment by planting flowers or shrubs.

◀ How can cleaning your living space show that you respect yourself and those around you?

Sharing Space

If you share living space with someone else, such as a sibling, work together to set up rules for keeping the place in order. You may wish to establish a cleaning schedule. Also, agree on times when you will need quiet for studying and times when it is okay to talk on the phone or watch television.

You and the person you share the space with may not agree about how the area should look. In this situation, you may have to compromise. Decide which things are most important to each of you and try to include both of them.

 **What is the visual environment?**

Practice Healthful Behaviors

You probably spend several hours a day at your television and computer. Practice using these appliances safely.

1 **Learn about a healthful behavior.** Following some simple guidelines can help reduce eye-strain and stress on the body.

- Sit at least 36 inches away from a 19- to 21-inch TV screen. Sit farther from larger ones.
- Look off in the distance for 20 seconds every 20 minutes when using a computer.
- Sit at least 13 inches from a computer monitor. It should be at the right height for your eyes.
- Be sure your chair is comfortable. Use good posture while watching TV or using a computer.

2 **Practice the healthful behavior in the correct way.** Decide which of these guidelines you need to improve. Make a plan to improve it.

3 **Ask for help if you need it.** You may need to talk to a parent or guardian about replacing some furniture.

4 **Make the healthful behavior a habit.** Follow your plan every day for a week. How well did you do? What might you need to adjust to continue your plan?

◀ **If you share living space, ask those around you if they mind listening to music.**

LESSON **6** REVIEW

Review Concepts

1. **List** three activities you can enjoy outdoors.

2. **Name** two guidelines you should follow in outdoor settings.

3. **Describe** one way to improve the quality of your visual environment.

Critical Thinking

4. **Conclude** Why do you think the United States government decided that it was important to set aside land for national parks?

5. **LIFE SKILLS** **Practice Healthful Behaviors** Name an outdoor sport and explain what steps you should take to protect your safety while doing it.

Chapter Summary

Lesson 1 • Your environment includes three parts: physical, emotional, and social. All three parts can affect your health.

Lesson 2 • You can protect your health by improving your social-emotional environment.

Lesson 3 • Air pollution can threaten the health of plants, animals, and humans. You can take steps to protect the environment.

Lesson 4 • Water pollution poses a health risk. You can take steps to prevent pollution and to conserve water.

Lesson 5 • Conserving resources and reducing waste are two important ways to help keep Earth clean and healthy.

Lesson 6 • Outdoor activities offer a chance to enjoy the natural environment. You can also improve your visual environment indoors.

Use Vocabulary

physical environment, E35

resilient, E48

pollution, E51

runoff, E58

renewable resource, E65

recycling, E68

ecology, E75

Choose the correct term from the list to complete each sentence.

1. The process of turning waste into new, usable products is called _____?_____.

2. _____?_____ is a harmful change in the physical environment.

3. _____?_____ from farms and streets can contribute to water pollution.

4. To be _____?_____ is to bounce back and learn from misfortune or change.

5. _____?_____ is the living conditions around a person.

6. Solar energy is an example of a(n) _____?_____.

7. The science of _____?_____ deals with the way living things interact in their environment.

Review Concepts

Answer each question in complete sentences.

8. What makes up your social-emotional environment?

9. What causes acid rain?

10. How does sewage contribute to water pollution?

11. Name three common ways of disposing of solid waste.

12. Compare and contrast recycling and precycling.

13. List three places you can go to enjoy the outdoors.

14. What is your visual environment?

Reading Comprehension

Answer each question in complete sentences.

Air pollution can threaten human health in several ways. For example, polluted air may contain harmful substances that can cause illness, pain, or even death to humans. It can also harm the plants and animals that humans rely on to survive.

15. What are two ways that air pollution can threaten the health of humans?

16. What are two other things that pollution can damage?

Critical Thinking/Problem Solving

Answer each question in complete sentences.

Analyze Concepts

17. How are risk behaviors and poor emotional environment connected?

18. How does the burning of fossil fuels contribute to global warming?

19. Describe two ways that water pollution can affect the food chain.

20. Describe the benefits of composting.

21. Explain why it is important to "leave no trace" in parks, preserves, and other natural habitats.

Practice Life Skills

22. **Practice Healthful Behaviors** How can you conserve natural resources?

23. **Make Responsible Decisions** You are cleaning out the basement and you find an old container of cleaning fluid. You do not know whether this substance is hazardous. Explain your options and which one you think is the responsible decision.

Read Graphics

Use the text in the visual below to answer the questions.

24. What percentage of the world's energy supply comes from fossil fuels?

25. What percentage comes from renewable resources (hydroelectric, burning of waste and renewable fuels)? Predict how this percentage may change in the future.

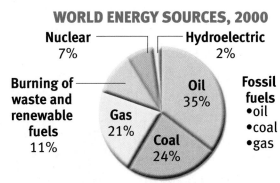

WORLD ENERGY SOURCES, 2000

Nuclear 7%
Hydroelectric 2%
Burning of waste and renewable fuels 11%
Gas 21%
Coal 24%
Oil 35%
Fossil fuels
• oil
• coal
• gas

Source: International Energy Administration

LOG ON Visit **www.mmhhealth.com** to find out how much you know about caring for your physical, emotional, and social environment.

Effective Communication

Make a Poster

Think of a cause that you would like to help as a volunteer. Then, make a poster that describes the efforts of the cause and encourages others to get involved. Display the poster in school.

Self-Directed Learning

Manage Your Time

Organize a schedule for yourself for the next week. Be sure to block off the time you spend in school, studying, and sleeping. Make it a point to schedule time for physical activity, rest, and sleep.

Critical Thinking and Problem Solving

Write an Editorial

Work with a small group. Each of you chooses an environmental issue, such as noise, air, land, or water pollution. Use library and Internet resources and this textbook to gather facts and opinions about the issue. Then, write an editorial that explains what you believe should be done about the issue. Present your editorials in a roundtable discussion in front of the whole class.

Responsible Citizenship

Recycle Products

With a responsible adult, check items at stores for brands that use recycled products. Look for a recycle logo on packages. Summarize your findings into a list of products that use recycled materials and products that people can recycle.

Remove All Paper

Plastic Bag Recycling Center

Clean, Dry Bags ONLY
Remove All Paper

Glossary

LOG ON Visit **www.mmhhealth.com** for an audio Glossary in English and in Spanish.

A

abdominal thrust A thrust to the abdomen that helps dislodge an object. *(p. C79)*

abstinence The act of avoiding risk behaviors. *(p. A7)*

abstinence from sex Voluntarily choosing not to be sexually active. *(p. A62)*

abuse The harmful treatment of another person. *(p. A52)*

acid rain Precipitation that is high in acid content as a result of pollution. *(p. E53)*

acne A skin disorder that results in pimples, whiteheads, and blackheads. *(p. C7)*

active listening A way of responding that shows you hear and understand. *(p. A45)*

addiction The compelling need to continue a behavior even if it is harmful. *(p. D14)*

adolescence The period between childhood and adulthood. *(p. B17)*

adrenaline (uh•DRE•nuhl•uhn) A hormone that prepares the body for quick action. *(p. A24)*

advertisement An announcement designed to persuade or influence choice. *(p. E17)*

aerobic exercise Exercise that requires oxygen use for a period of time. *(p. C29)*

affection A warm feeling. *(p. A66)*

AIDS Acquired Immune Deficiency Syndrome, which is a breakdown in the body's ability to fight infection. *(p. D58)*

airway A passage in the body that takes in air. *(p. C77)*

alcohol A drug found in some beverages that slows body functions. *(p. D31)*

alcoholism A disease in which a person is dependent on alcohol. *(p. D35)*

allergy (A•ler•jee) A condition in which the body reacts to foods or other substances. *(p. D73)*

anabolic steroids (a•nuh•BAH•lik STIR•oydz) Drugs used to increase muscle size and strength. *(p. D41)*

anaerobic exercise Exercise in which the body's demand for oxygen is greater than the supply. *(p. C29)*

anemia A condition in which the blood does not have enough red blood cells. *(p. B48)*

anorexia nervosa (a•nuh•REK•see•uh nehr•VOH•suh) An eating disorder in which a person starves himself or herself and has a low body weight. *(p. B67)*

antibodies Protein substances in blood that can find, weaken, or destroy certain pathogens. *(p. D52)*

artery (AR•tuh•ree) A blood vessel that carries blood away from the heart. *(p. B12)*

asthma (AZ•muh) A chronic condition in which the airways become narrow or blocked and breathing becomes difficult . *(p. D23)*

astigmatism (uh•STIG•muh•ti•zuhm) A vision problem in which the cornea or the lens of the eye is curved unevenly, causing blurred vision. *(p. C16)*

B

balanced diet Meals and snacks that provide the proper number of servings of foods from each group daily. *(p. B39)*

binge eating disorder An eating disorder in which a person frequently stuffs himself or herself with food but does not purge to get rid of the food. *(p. B67)*

biodegradable Capable of being broken down into harmless substances by natural means. *(p. E67)*

blizzard A heavy snowstorm with strong winds. *(p. C69)*

blood alcohol concentration The amount of alcohol in a person's blood. *(p. D34)*

body composition The proportion of fat tissue to lean tissue in the body. *(p. B62)*

body image The feeling a person has about the way his or her body looks. *(p. B65)*

Body Mass Index A measure of mass compared to height. *(p. B62)*

brand A product made by a certain company or a well-known manufacturer. *(p. E18)*

budget A plan for spending and saving money. *(p. E6)*

bulimia nervosa (buh•LEE•mee•uh nehr•VOH•suh) An eating disorder in which a person stuffs himself or herself and then tries to rid the body of food. *(p. B67)*

Glossary

bullying Hurting or threatening someone younger, weaker, or smaller. *(p. C56)*

burglary A crime in which a person breaks into a shop, house, or other location to steal something. *(p. C66)*

calorie A unit of energy available from food for use by the body. *(p. B44)*

cancer A disease in which abnormal cells multiply and spread. *(p. D63)*

carbohydrates (KAHR•boh•HY•drayts) The body's main source of energy. *(p. B37)*

carbon monoxide An odorless, colorless, poisonous gas in tobacco smoke. *(p. D21)*

carcinogen A substance that causes cancer. *(p. D63)*

cardiopulmonary resuscitation (CPR) A way to restore heartbeat and breathing. *(p. C80)*

cardiovascular (kar•dee•oh•VAS•kyuh•luhr) **diseases** Diseases of the heart and the blood vessels. *(p. D66)*

cartilage Soft material on the end of bones. *(p. B6)*

cavity A hole in the enamel of a tooth. *(p. C24)*

character The effort a person uses to act on responsible values. *(p. A11)*

chewing tobacco Chopped tobacco that is chewed. *(p. D24)*

chromosomes (KROH•muh•sohmz) Strands of matter found in the nucleus of a cell through which a person inherits traits. *(p. B27)*

chronic health condition A condition that lasts for a long time or keeps coming back. *(p. D71)*

circulatory system The body system that transports oxygen, food, and waste through the body. *(p. B12)*

cirrhosis (suh•ROH•suhs) A disease in which scar tissue replaces healthy liver cells. *(p. D31)*

commercial An ad on television or radio. *(p. E17)*

communicable (kuh•MYOO•ni•kuh•buhl) **disease** A disease caused by pathogens that can be spread from person to person. *(p. D51)*

communication The sharing of feelings, thoughts, and information with another person. *(p. A41)*

composting A method for turning certain types of waste into a humus. *(p. E69)*

conflict A disagreement. *(p. A38)*

conflict resolution skills Steps that you take to settle a disagreement in a healthful way. *(p. A38)*

conjunctivitis A very contagious infection in which the tissue around the eye and inside the eyelid swells. *(p. C17)*

conservation To save resources. *(p. E62)*

consumer A person who evaluates information and buys products and services. *(p. E13)*

consumer costs The items given up in order to buy and use up resources. *(p. E23)*

cool-down A period of three to five minutes of reduced physical activity. *(p. C37)*

currency The money used in a country. *(p. E6)*

cut An opening caused by something sharp. *(p. C42)*

Daily Value The amount of a nutrient that a person needs each day. *(p. B51)*

dental plaque A sticky substance containing bacteria that forms on teeth. *(p. C22)*

depressants A group of drugs that slow down the body's functions. *(p. D43)*

depression A lasting feeling of being sad, unhappy, or discouraged. *(p. A28)*

dermatologist A physician who screens for and treats skin disorders. *(p. C7)*

dermis The thick inner layer of the skin. *(p. C6)*

diabetes (dy•uh•BEE•teez) A disease in which the body cannot use or does not produce enough of a necessary chemical called insulin. *(p. B46)*

Dietary Guidelines for Americans A set of guidelines for healthful eating and living for healthy Americans ages two years and older. *(p. B40)*

digestive system The body system that breaks food down so that it can be used by the body. *(p. B14)*

dislocation The movement of a bone away from its joint. *(p. C42)*

distress Negative stress that prompts a harmful response. *(p. A24)*

divorce A legal end to a marriage. *(p. A50)*

domestic shelter A place where family members can stay safe. *(p. A53)*

dose The amount of a drug taken at one time. *(p. D7)*

drug A substance that changes the way the body or mind works. *(p. D5)*

drug abuse The harmful use of any drug on purpose. *(p. D10)*

drug misuse The harmful use of a legal drug that is not done on purpose. *(p. D10)*

eating disorder An emotional problem that leads to harmful changes in eating habits. *(p. B66)*

ecology The relationship of plants and animals to their physical and biological environment. *(p. E75)*

ecosports Outdoor sports activities that do not harm the environment. *(p. E73)*

electrical storm A storm with bolts of lightning. *(p. C69)*

embryo (EM•bree•oh) The name of the developing baby from fertilization until the eighth week. *(p. B28)*

emergency A serious situation that calls for quick action. *(p. C75)*

emotional abuse Harmful verbal or non-verbal treatment that lowers a person's self-esteem. *(p. C50)*

emotional environment The feelings of trust and caring around a person. *(p. E35)*

emphysema (em•fuh•ZEE•muh) A condition in which the air sacs in the lungs become damaged. *(p. D23)*

empty calories Foods that are high in fat or sugar and calories but low in other nutrients. *(p. B47)*

endocrine system The body system made up of glands that produce hormones. *(p. B18)*

endurance The ability to perform an extended activity without becoming overly tired. *(p. C28)*

entertainment addiction The uncontrollable urge to be entertained. *(p. E9)*

environment Everything that surrounds you. *(p. A11)*

epidermis The thin outer layer of the skin. *(p. C6)*

epilepsy (E•puh•lep•see) A condition in which nerve messages in the brain are disturbed for brief periods of time. *(p. D71)*

esophagus (i•SAH•fuh•guhs) A tube through which food passes to the stomach. *(p. B14)*

eustress (YOO•stres) Positive stress that prompts a healthful response. *(p. A24)*

facilities Places that serve a specific purpose. *(p. E23)*

fad Something that is very popular for a short time. *(p. E17)*

fad diet A weight-loss program based on popular trends rather than scientific evidence. *(p. B61)*

family and social health The condition of a person's relationships with others. *(p. A5)*

family guideline A rule a family makes to help members live in a responsible way. *(p. A51)*

farsightedness A vision problem in which close objects appear blurred while distant objects are seen clearly. *(p. C16)*

fats Nutrients that provide energy and help the body store vitamins. *(p. B37)*

fertilization (fuhr•tuh•luh•ZAY•shun) The joining of a sperm cell and an egg to make a single cell called a fertilized egg. *(p. B27)*

fetal alcohol syndrome (FAS) A condition that causes birth defects in babies born to mothers who drank alcohol during pregnancy. *(p. D35)*

fetus (FEE•tuhs) During pregnancy, the name of the developing baby from the end of the eighth week until birth. *(p. B28)*

fiber The part of grains and plant foods that cannot be digested. *(p. B40)*

financial goal A goal to save or accumulate a certain amount of money needed for a specific reason. *(p. E7)*

first aid The temporary and immediate care given to a person who has a sudden illness or injury. *(p. C75)*

flammable Able to catch fire easily. *(p. C64)*

flexibility The ability to bend and move the joints through a full range of motion. *(p. C28)*

flood The overflowing of a body of water onto dry land. *(p. C73)*

fluoride (FLAW•ryd) A mineral that helps prevent tooth decay. *(p. C23)*

food group Foods that provide similar nutrients. *(p. B38)*

Food Guide Pyramid A guide prepared by the United States Department of Agriculture that shows how many servings you need to eat from each food group every day. *(p. B38)*

Glossary

food labels Panels of nutritional information that appear on food packages. *(p. B51)*

fossil fuels Coal, oil, and natural gas burned to produce energy. *(p. E51)*

frostbite A condition in which a person's body tissues freeze. *(p. C71)*

gang A group of people who usually are involved in dangerous or illegal activities. *(p. C57)*

gene (JEEN) A tiny piece of information found in a chromosome that controls heredity. *(p. B27)*

generic A product that meets certain standards but does not have fancy packaging or brand name recognition. *(p. E18)*

gesture A movement of the body that communicates what a person is thinking. *(p. A44)*

gingivitis (jin•juh•VY•tuhs) The first stage of periodontal disease; it is a condition in which the gums are sore and bleed easily. *(p. C25)*

global warming An increase in Earth's temperature. *(p. E53)*

gonads Reproductive glands. *(p. B21)*

greenhouse effect The trapping of heat from the sun by gases in Earth's atmosphere. *(p. E53)*

grief Intense sadness caused by loss or death. *(p. A29)*

grooming Everything people do to stay clean and have a healthful appearance. *(p. C5)*

hallucinogens (huh•LOO•sin•uh•jins) A group of illegal drugs that cause a person to feel different sensations. *(p. D45)*

hashish An illegal drug made from marijuana that has stronger effects. *(p. D39)*

hazardous waste Waste that is poisonous, flammable, or otherwise dangerous. *(p. E66)*

hazards Possible sources of harm or danger in and around the home. *(p. C63)*

health The state of a person's body, mind, and feelings, and how he or she gets along with others. *(p. A5)*

health behavior contract A written plan to practice a life skill, in order to reach a health goal. *(p. A17)*

health care The management of physical and mental well-being by professionals, such as physicians, nurses, and hospital workers. *(p. E23)*

healthful weight A weight that is desirable for a person. Healthful weight varies from person to person. *(p. B59)*

health goals A healthful aim or purpose that a person can take steps to achieve over a lifetime. *(p. A7)*

health-related fitness The ability of the heart, lungs, muscles, and joints to perform well. *(p. C28)*

heart attack A condition that results when the blood supply to the heart muscle is blocked off or interrupted, leading to damage to the heart muscle. *(p. D66)*

heat exhaustion Extreme tiredness from being in hot temperatures. *(p. C70)*

heatstroke An overheating of the body that is life threatening. *(p. C70)*

helper T cells White blood cells that trigger the production of antibodies. *(p. D58)*

heredity The sum of the traits transmitted to a person by his or her biological parents, or inherited. *(p. A5)*

high blood pressure A condition that results when the blood presses very hard on the walls of the arteries when the heart beats. *(p. D67)*

hormone A chemical messenger that regulates body activities. *(p. B18)*

human immunodeficiency (I•myuh•noh•di•FI•shuhn•see) **virus (HIV)** A virus that destroys helper T cells. *(p. A64)*

humus (HYOO muhs) A soil-like material produced by the breaking down of plant and animal remains. *(p. E69)*

hypothermia A condition in which a person's body temperature drops from exposure to cold. *(p. C71)*

illegal drugs Drugs for which use, possession, manufacture, and sale are against the law. *(p. D39)*

I-message A statement that refers to a specific behavior or event, describes the effect of the event on a person, and identifies the feelings that result. *(p. A42)*

immune (i•MYOON) **system** System of body organs, tissues, and cells that destroy pathogens. (p. D52)

immunity (i•MYOO•nuh•tee) Resistance to a particular disease. (p. D53)

inhalants (in•HAY•luhnts) Chemicals that are breathed in or inhaled. (p. D40)

insulin (IN•suh•luhn) A hormone that helps the body use sugar from foods for energy. (p. D71)

intervention An action by people who want someone to get treatment. (p. D17)

intestine A tube that digests food and moves remaining waste through the body. (p. B14)

joint A point at which two bones meet. (p. B6)

kidney An organ through which blood circulates as wastes are filtered. (p. B15)

labor A series of stages that result in the birth of a baby. (p. B29)

landfill A specially designed place for collecting and burying waste. (p. E66)

life cycle The different stages of growing, developing, aging, and dying. (p. B17)

life skill An ability that helps maintain and improve health. (p. A6)

lifestyle The way in which a person lives. (p. A5)

limit A boundary. (p. A66)

loyalty A strong and lasting affection and support. (p. A58)

lungs The main organs of the respiratory system. (p. B11)

malnutrition A harmful condition caused by not eating enough food or not eating the right kinds of food. (p. B46)

malocclusion (ma•luh•KLOO•zhuhn) The abnormal fitting together of teeth in the jaw. (p. C25)

marijuana An illegal drug that affects mood and short-term memory. (p. D39)

media influence The way in which forms of communication, including magazines, radio, television, newspapers, and the Internet, affect a person. (p. E18)

media literacy The ability to recognize and evaluate messages in the media. (p. E18)

mediation A process in which a responsible adult helps settle a conflict. (p. A39)

mediator A trusted adult who helps settle a conflict. (p. C53)

medicine A drug used to prevent or cure illness or disease, or to relieve pain. (p. D5)

menstrual (MEN•struhl) **cycle** A monthly series of changes that occur in a female's body. (p. B21)

mental and emotional health The condition of a person's mind and how he or she expresses feelings. (p. A5)

minerals Nutrients that are involved in many body processes. (B37)

money management A skill used in spending and saving money. (p. E6)

muscle A bundle of tissues that moves certain parts of the body. (p. B6)

muscular system The body system that helps a person move and maintain posture. (p. B6)

narcotics A group of drugs that slow down the nervous system and relieve pain. (p. D44)

natural disaster An event caused by nature that results in heavy damage. (p. C69)

nearsightedness A vision problem in which distant objects appear blurred while close objects are seen clearly. (p. C16)

neglect The failure to provide proper care and guidance. (p. A52)

negotiate To discuss a conflict in order to reach an agreement. (p. A38)

nerves Bundles of fibers that carry messages from the brain to the spinal cord and other parts of the body. (p. B8)

nervous system The body system for communication and control. (p. B8)

Glossary

nicotine A highly addictive stimulant drug found in tobacco. *(p. D21)*

noise pollution Loud or constant noise that causes hearing loss. *(p. C17)*

nonverbal communication The use of actions rather than words to express oneself. *(p. A44)*

nutrients The substances in foods that the body needs for growth and repair of cells, for body processes, and for energy. *(p. B37)*

Nutrition Facts The title of the food label. Food labels list serving size, calories per serving, and calories from fat. *(p. B51)*

obesity Having too much body fat. *(p. B62)*

ophthalmologist A physician who treats diseases and injuries to the eye. *(p. C12)*

optometrist A health care professional who is trained and licensed to examine people's eyes and prescribe eyeglasses or contact lenses. *(p. C12)*

orthodontist A dentist who treats malocclusion. *(p. C25)*

osteoporosis A disease in which bones are thin and break easily. *(p. B46)*

over-the-counter (OTC) drug A medicine that can be purchased without a prescription. *(p. D5)*

overweight Above a healthful weight. *(p. B61)*

ozone layer A layer of the upper atmosphere that traps ultraviolet (UV) rays from the sun, protecting life on Earth from these rays. *(p. E53)*

pathogens (PA•thuh•juhns) Living organisms or particles that can cause disease. *(p. D51)*

peer pressure Influence or pressure that people of a similar age place on a person to behave in a certain way. *(p. A20)*

Percent Daily Value The percentage of the recommended daily amount of a nutrient that is found in a serving of food. *(p. B51)*

periodontal (pehr•ee•oh•DAHN•tuhl) **disease** A disease of the gums and other tissues that support the teeth. *(p. C25)*

personality A person's unique blend of physical, mental, social, and emotional traits. *(p. A11)*

perspiration A mixture of water, salt, and waste products produced by sweat glands in the skin. *(p. C7)*

pharmacist A licensed professional who distributes drugs that are prescribed. *(p. D8)*

physical abuse Harmful treatment of a person that results in physical injury. *(p. C50)*

physical dependence Repeated drug use that causes tolerance. *(p. D11)*

physical environment The living conditions around a person. *(p. E35)*

physical fitness plan A written schedule of physical activities to do to develop health-related fitness and skill-related fitness. *(p. C33)*

physical health The condition of a person's body. *(p. A5)*

pituitary gland The body's master gland, which secretes hormones that control the other glands. *(p. B18)*

pollution A harmful change in the physical environment. *(p. E51)*

pregnancy The time during which an offspring develops within the female parent. *(p. A65)*

prejudice An opinion formed before all the facts are known. *(p. C49)*

prescription drug A medicine that can be obtained only with a written order from a physician. *(p. D5)*

President's Challenge A physical fitness test that measures student fitness in five areas. *(p. C34)*

PRICE A treatment for muscle soreness, muscle spasms, strains, sprains, and bruises that involves protection, rest, ice, compression, and elevation. *(p. C43)*

priority Something that deserves first attention. *(p. A19)*

protective factors The ways a person behaves or characteristics of a person's surroundings that promote health and safety. *(p. C55)*

proteins Nutrients needed for growth and repair of body cells. *(p. B37)*

providers Suppliers of what is needed or wanted, as in health care. *(p. E23)*

psychological (sy•kuh•LAH•juh•kuhl) **dependence** The repeated use of a drug for emotional or social reasons. *(p. D11)*

puberty (PYOO•ber•tee) The period in which gonads first begin to make hormones. *(p. B21)*

quackery A method of selling worthless products and services. *(p. E20)*

radon An odorless, colorless, and radioactive gas. *(p. E52)*

random events Events over which a person has little or no control. *(p. A5)*

recycling Turning waste into new, usable products. *(p. E68)*

relationship The connection a person has with other people. *(p. A35)*

reliable A characteristic of a person who can be trusted and depended on. *(p. A58)*

renewable resource A resource that can be replaced. *(p. E65)*

reproductive system The body system that enables living beings to produce offspring. *(p. B27)*

reputation The quality of a person's character as judged by others. *(p. A64)*

rescue breathing Breathing air into an unconscious person who has a pulse. *(p. C80)*

resilient (ri•ZIL•yuhnt) Able to bounce back and learn from misfortune or change. *(p. E48)*

resistance skills Skills that help a person say "no" to an action or leave a situation. *(p. A21)*

respect Treating others with dignity and consideration. *(p. A14)*

respiratory system The body system that helps the body use air that is inhaled. *(p. B11)*

resting heart rate The number of times your heart beats each minute when you are standing still. *(p. C36)*

risk behavior An action that can harm people. *(p. A7)*

runoff Water from rain or melted snow that flows across the land and into surface water. *(p. E58)*

schedule A list of times, events, or things to do. *(p. E5)*

scrape The wearing away of the skin caused by rubbing against a rough surface. *(p. C42)*

secondhand smoke Exhaled smoke and sidestream smoke. *(p. D25)*

self-esteem What a person thinks about himself or herself. *(p. A12)*

self-protection Taking steps to protect oneself. *(p. C55)*

self-respect Having high regard for oneself because one behaves in responsible ways. *(p. A64)*

separation A situation in which a husband and wife remain married but live apart. *(p. A50)*

service learning Volunteer work done by students in the community that is connected to the classroom. *(p. E27)*

sewage Waste liquid and matter carried off by sewers. *(p. E58)*

sexual abuse Sexual behavior that is forced on a person. *(p. C50)*

sexually transmitted disease (STD) A disease spread through sexual contact. *(p. A64)*

shock A dangerous drop in blood flow. *(p. C83)*

shopping addiction An uncontrollable urge to shop and spend. *(p. E8)*

sick building syndrome (SBS) An illness caused by indoor air pollutants. *(p. E52)*

side effect An unwanted reaction to a drug. *(p. D7)*

skeletal system The body system that serves as a support framework. *(p. B6)*

skill-related fitness the ability to perform well in sports and physical activities. *(p. C33)*

smoke alarm A device that alerts individuals to dangerous levels of smoke. *(p. C64)*

smokeless tobacco Tobacco made and sold as chewing tobacco or snuff. *(p. D24)*

snuff Powdered tobacco that is placed between the cheek and gums. *(p. D24)*

social environment The contact a person has with the people around him or her. *(p. E35)*

spinal cord A thick band of nerves through which messages enter and leave the brain. *(p. B8)*

sprain An injury to the tissue that connects bones to a joint. *(p. C42)*

stimulant One of a group of drugs that speed up the body's functions. *(p. D42)*

street smart Being aware of possible danger and knowing what to do. *(p. C55)*

Glossary

stress The body's reaction to the demands of daily living. *(p. A23)*

stressor A cause of stress. *(p. A24)*

stroke A blockage or break in a blood vessel that brings blood flow to the brain. *(p. D67)*

suicide The taking of one's own life on purpose. *(p. C49)*

support groups Groups of people that meet to comfort and help one another. *(p. E14)*

sympathetic Feeling or showing sympathy toward your friends. *(p. A58)*

tar A thick, sticky fluid produced when tobacco is burned. *(p. D21)*

target heart rate A heart rate of 60 to 75 percent of maximum heart rate. *(p. C36)*

tendon (TEN•duhn) Tough bands of tissue that connect muscle to bone. *(p. B7)*

time management plan A plan that shows how a person will spend time. *(p. E5)*

tolerance A condition in which increasing amounts of a drug are needed to produce the desired effects. *(p. D7)*

underweight Below a healthful weight. *(p. B60)*

unit price The price of food by weight, serving, or some other unit. *(p. B52)*

universal precautions Steps taken to keep people from having contact with pathogens in body fluids. *(p. C76)*

urinary system The body system that removes liquid wastes from the body. *(p. B15)*

uterus (YOO•tuh•rus) A muscular organ in a woman's body that supports the development of the fertilized egg during pregnancy. *(p. B27)*

vaccines Dead or weakened pathogens given for immunity. *(p. D53)*

valid information Information that is accurate. *(p. E13)*

values The principles and standards that guide the way a person acts. *(p. A11)*

vein (VAYN) A blood vessel that returns blood to the heart. *(p. B12)*

violence The use of force to harm someone or destroy property. *(p. A52)*

visual environment Everything a person sees regularly. *(p. E76)*

vitamins Nutrients that help the body use carbohydrates, proteins, and fats. *(p. B37)*

volunteer To provide a service without getting paid. *(p. E26)*

warm-up A period of three to five minutes of easy physical activity. *(p. C37)*

weapon Any device used to inflict violence. *(p. C49)*

wellness A state of balanced health or well-being. *(p. A5)*

white blood cells Blood cells that fight pathogens that cause infection and illness. *(p. D52)*

whiteout A severe blizzard in which a person cannot see the horizon and can only make out dark shapes. *(p. C69)*

wound An injury to the body's soft tissues. *(p. C82)*

you-message A statement that blames or shames someone. *(p. A42)*

Glosario

LOG ON Visita **www.mmhhealth.com** para escuchar el glosario en inglés y en español.

A

abdominal thrust/presión en el abdomen Presión que se ejerce en el abdomen para forzar la salida de un objeto. *(pág. C79)*

abstinence/abstinencia Acción de evitar comportamientos arriesgados. *(pág. A7)*

abstinence from sex/abstinencia sexual Elección voluntaria de no llevar una sexualidad activa. *(pág. A62)*

abuse/abuso Trato que lastima a otra persona. *(pág. A52)*

acid rain/lluvia ácida Precipitación con elevado contenido ácido como resultado de la contaminación. *(pág. E53)*

acne/acné Afección de la piel como granos, puntos blancos y puntos negros. *(pág. C7)*

active listening/escucha activa Manera en que una persona responde para demostrar que escucha y comprende. *(pág. A45)*

addiction/adicción Fuerte deseo de hacer algo aunque sea perjudicial. *(pág. D14)*

adolescence/adolescencia Periodo entre la niñez y la edad adulta. *(pág. B17)*

adrenaline/adrenalina Hormona que prepara al cuerpo para emprender una acción rápida. *(pág. A24)*

advertisement/anuncio Aviso diseñado para persuadir e influir una selección. *(pág. E17)*

aerobic exercise/ejercicio aeróbico Ejercicio que requiere uso de oxígeno durante un cierto periodo. *(pág. C29)*

affection/afecto Sentimiento de cariño por otra persona. *(pág. A66)*

AIDS/SIDA El síndrome de inmunodeficiencia adquirida (SIDA) debilita la capacidad del cuerpo para combatir las infecciones. *(pág. D58)*

airway/vías respiratorias Conductos en el cuerpo por donde ingresa el aire. *(pág. C77)*

alcohol/alcohol Droga que se encuentra en algunas bebidas que disminuye las funciones del cuerpo. *(pág. D31)*

alcoholism/alcoholismo Enfermedad en que una persona se vuelve dependiente del alcohol. *(pág. D35)*

allergy/alergia Condición en la cual el cuerpo reacciona ante algunos alimentos u otras sustancias. *(pág. D73)*

anabolic steroids/esteroides anabólicos Droga usada para aumentar el tamaño y la fortaleza de los músculos. *(pág. D41)*

anaerobic exercise/ejercicio anaeróbico Tipo de ejercicio en que el cuerpo necesita más oxígeno del que le es suministrado. *(pág. C29)*

anemia/anemia Afección en que la sangre no tiene suficientes glóbulos rojos. *(pág. B48)*

anorexia nervosa/anorexia nerviosa Trastorno alimentario en que una persona se priva de alimentos por su propia cuenta y tiene un peso bajo. *(pág. B67)*

antibodies/anticuerpo Sustancia en la sangre que ayuda a encontrar y combatir algunos agentes patógenos. *(pág. D52)*

artery/arteria Vaso sanguíneo que lleva sangre desde el corazón al resto del cuerpo. *(pág. B12)*

asthma/asma Enfermedad en que las vías respiratorias se estrechan u obstruyen, dificultando la respiración. *(pág. D23)*

astigmatism/astigmatismo Problema de la visión en que la córnea o lente del ojo no tiene una curvatura uniforme, por lo cual se produce visión borrosa. *(pág. C16)*

B

balanced diet/dieta balanceada Comidas y alimentos que proveen el número apropiado de porciones diarias de cada grupo de alimentos. *(pág. B39)*

binge eating disorder/trastorno alimentario por glotonería Trastorno alimentario en que una persona de manera incontrolable pero no se purga. *(pág. B67)*

biodegradable/biodegradable Que puede ser degradado en sustancias inofensivas mediante mecanismos naturales. *(pág. E67)*

blizzard/ventisca Tormenta de nieve con vientos fuertes. *(pág. C69)*

blood alcohol concentration/concentración de alcohol en la sangre Cantidad de alcohol presente en la sangre de una persona. *(pág. D34)*

body composition/composición corporal Proporción de tejido graso y tejido magro en el cuerpo. *(pág. B62)*

body image/imagen corporal Manera de sentirse una persona debido al aspecto de su cuerpo. *(pág. B65)*

Body Mass Index/índice de masa corporal Medida del peso en comparación con la estatura. *(pág. B62)*

brand/marca Nombre de producto hecho por una determinada compañía o fabricante. *(pág. E18)*

budget/presupuesto Plan para gastar y ahorrar el dinero. *(pág. E6)*

bulimia nervosa/bulimia nerviosa Trastorno alimentario en que una persona ingiere gran cantidad de comida y en seguida trata de eliminarla de su cuerpo. *(pág. B67)*

bullying/intimidar Lastimar o atemorizar a otra persona más joven, débil o pequeña. *(pág. C56)*

burglary/robo con allanamiento de morada Delito en que una persona entra en un almacén, casa u otro sitio para robar algo. *(pág. C66)*

C

calorie /caloría Unidad de energía disponible en los alimentos para uso del cuerpo. *(pág. B44)*

Glosario

cancer/cáncer Enfermedad en que células se multiplican y proliferan de manera anormal. *(pág. D63)*

carbohydrates/carbohidratos Principal fuente de energía para el cuerpo. *(pág. B37)*

carbon monoxide/monóxido de carbono Gas venenoso, incoloro e inodoro que proviene de la quema de combustibles. *(pág. D21)*

carcinogen/carcinógeno Sustancia que produce cáncer. *(pág. D63)*

cardiopulmonary resuscitation (CPR)/reanimación cardiopulmonar (RCP) Técnica de primeros auxilios para restablecer el ritmo cardiaco y la respiración a una persona. *(pág. C80)*

cardiovascular disease/enfermedad cardiovascular Enfermedad del corazón y los vasos sanguíneos. *(pág. D66)*

cartilage/cartílago Tejido blando en el extremo de los huesos. *(pág. B6)*

cavity/caries Cavidad en el esmalte de un diente. *(pág. C24)*

character/carácter Esfuerzo de una persona para actuar de acuerdo a valores responsables. *(pág. A11)*

chewing tobacco/tabaco de mascar Tabaco picado que se mastica. *(pág. D24)*

chromosomes/cromosomas Estructuras que se encuentran en el núcleo de las células que trasmiten la información genética. *(pág. B27)*

chronic health condition/afección crónica Enfermedad o trastorno que dura un tiempo prolongado o que se repite. *(pág. D71)*

circulatory system/sistema circulatorio Sistema corporal que transporta por todo el cuerpo el oxígeno, los alimentos y las sustancias de desecho. *(pág. B12)*

cirrhosis/cirrosis Enfermedad en que el tejido cicatricial reemplaza células sanas del hígado. *(pág. D31)*

commercial/anuncio comercial Anuncio en la televisión o en el radio. *(pág. E17)*

communicable disease/enfermedad contagiosa Enfermedad causada por agentes patógenos que se puede transmitir de una persona a otra. *(pág. D51)*

communication/comunicación Acto de compartir sentimientos, pensamientos e información con otra persona. *(pág. A41)*

composting/compostaje Método para descomponer ciertos desechos en abono. *(pág. E69)*

conflict/conflicto Desacuerdo. *(pág. A38)*

conflict resolution skills/destrezas para la resolución de conflictos Pasos que se usan para resolver un desacuerdo de manera saludable. *(pág. A38)*

conjunctivitis/conjuntivitis Infección muy contagiosa que se caracteriza por la inflamación del tejido alrededor del ojo y la parte interior del párpado. *(pág. C17)*

conservation/conservación Protección de los recursos naturales. *(pág. E62)*

consumer/consumidor Persona que juzga la información para comprar y usar productos y servicios. *(pág. E13)*

consumer costs/costos para el consumidor Aquello que se entrega para comprar y consumir recursos. *(pág. E23)*

cool-down/enfriamiento Periodo de tres a cinco minutos para disminuir la actividad física. *(pág. C37)*

currency/moneda Dinero que se usa en un país. *(pág. E6)*

cut/corte Rotura ocasionada sobre la piel por un elemento cortante. *(pág. C42)*

D

Daily Value/valor diario La cantidad de nutrientes que una persona necesita cada día.

dental plaque/sarro Una sustancia pegajosa que se forma sobre los dientes y que contiene bacteria.

depressants/sedantes Un grupo de drogas que reduce las funciones del cuerpo.

depression/depresión Un sentimiento duradero de estar triste, infeliz o desanimado.

dermatologist/dermatólogo El médico que detecta y trata problemas de piel.

dermis/dermis La capa gruesa inferior de la piel.

diabetes/diabetes Una enfermedad donde el cuerpo no puede usar o no puede producir suficiente insulina, un químico necesario.

Dietary Guidelines for Americans/Guía Alimenticia para Estadounidenses Las recomendaciones de dieta y estilo de vida para Estadounidenses saludables de dos años de edad y mayores.

digestive system/sistema digestivo El sistema del cuerpo que descompone el alimento para poder ser usado por el cuerpo.

dislocation/dislocación El mover el hueso de su articulación.

distress/estrés negativa Una respuesta dañina a algo estresante.

divorce/divorcio Terminación legal de una matrimonio.

domestic shelter/casa de refugio El lugar donde los miembros de una familia pueden estar sin peligro.

dose/dosis La cantidad de una droga tomada en una sóla vez.

drug/droga Una sustancia que cambia la manera en que funciona el cuerpo o la mente.

drug abuse/abuso de drogas El usar a propósito una droga nociva.

drug misuse/uso incorrecto de drogas El mal uso de drogas sin intención.

eating disorder/trastorno alimentario Problema emocional que conduce a cambios en los hábitos alimentarios de manera perjudicial. *(pág. B66)*

ecology/ecología La relación de plantas y animales a su ambiente físico y biológico. *(pág. E75)*

ecosports/ecodeportes Actividades deportivas al aire libre que no causan daño al ambiente. *(pág. E73)*

electrical storm/tormenta eléctrica Tempestad caracterizada por truenos y rayos. *(pág. C69)*

embryo/embrión Bebé en desarrollo desde la fecundación hasta la octava semana que se adhiere a las paredes del útero durante el embarazo. *(pág. B28)*

emergency/emergencia Situación grave que requiere de acción inmediata. *(pág. C75)*

emotional abuse/abuso emocional Trato verbal dañino o acción que afecta la autoestima de una persona. *(pág. C50)*

emotional environment/ambiente emocional Sentimientos que rodean a una persona, como la confianza y el afecto. *(pág. E35)*

emphysema/enfisema Enfermedad en la que los alvéolos de los pulmones se dañan. *(pág. D23)*

empty calories/calorías vacías Se dice de los alimentos que son altos en grasa o azúcar y en calorías pero bajos en otros nutrientes. *(pág. B47)*

endocrine system/sistema endocrino Sistema corporal conformado por glándulas que producen hormonas. *(pág. B18)*

endurance/resistencia Capacidad para realizar una actividad prolongada sin sentirse demasiado cansado. *(pág. C28)*

entertainment addiction/adicción al entretenimiento Necesidad incontrolable de estar divirtiéndose. *(pág. E9)*

environment/ambiente Todo lo que rodea a una persona. *(pág. A11)*

epidermis/epidermis Capa externa y delgada de la piel. *(pág. C6)*

epilepsy/epilepsia Afección en que los mensajes nerviosos que van hacia el cerebro son interrumpidos por breves periodos. *(pág. D71)*

esophagus/esófago Conducto a través del cual el alimento llega al estómago. *(pág. B14)*

eustress/eustrés Estrés positivo que conduce a una respuesta saludable. *(pág. A24)*

facilities/instalaciones Lugares que sirven para un propósito específico. *(pág. E23)*

fad/moda Algo que es muy popular durante un periodo corto. *(pág. E17)*

fad diet/dieta de moda Programa para perder peso basado en tendencias populares y no en evidencia científica. *(pág. B61)*

family and social health/salud familiar y social Condición de las relaciones de una persona con los demás. *(pág. A5)*

family guideline/norma familiar Regla que una familia establece para ayudar a sus miembros a vivir de manera responsable. *(pág. A51)*

farsightedness/hipermetropía Problema de la visión en que los objetos cercanos se ven borrosos mientras que los que se encuentran distantes se ven con claridad. *(pág. C16)*

fats/grasas Nutrientes que suministran energía y que ayudan a almacenar vitaminas. *(pág. B37)*

fertilization/fecundación Unión de un espermatozoide y un óvulo para constituir una sola célula denominada óvulo fecundado. *(pág. B27)*

fetal alcohol syndrome (FAS)/síndrome de alcohol fetal (FAS, por su sigla en inglés) Presencia de defectos de nacimiento s en bebés nacidos de madres que bebían alcohol durante el embarazo. *(pág. D35)*

fetus/feto Nombre del bebé en desarrollo durante el embarazo, desde el final de la octava semana hasta el nacimiento. *(pág. B28)*

fiber/fibra Parte de los cereales y alimentos vegetales que el cuerpo no puede digerir. *(pág. B40)*

financial goal/meta financiera Meta para ahorrar o acumular una determinada cantidad de dinero, necesaria por una razón específica. *(pág. E7)*

first aid/primeros auxilios Atención inmediata y temporal que se presta a una persona que se ha enfermado de repente o ha sido herida. *(pág. C75)*

flammable/inflamable Que puede encenderse con facilidad. *(pág. C64)*

flexibility/flexibilidad Capacidad para doblar y mover las articulaciones en una completa variedad de movimientos. *(pág. C28)*

flood/inundación Desbordamiento de una masa de agua sobre terrenos secos. *(pág. C73)*

fluoride/fluoruro Mineral que ayuda a evitar la caries dental. *(pág. C23)*

food group/grupo alimenticio Alimentos que contienen nutrientes similares. *(pág. B38)*

Food Guide Pyramid/ Pirámide Alimenticia Guía preparada por el Departamento de Agricultura de Estados Unidos que muestra cuántas porciones diarias se deben consumir de cada grupo de alimentos. *(pág. B38)*

Glosario

food labels/rótulo nutricional Información nutricional que aparece en los empaques de los alimentos. *(pág. B51)*

fossil fuels/combustible fósil Carbón, petróleo y gas natural que se queman para producir energía. *(pág. E51)*

frostbite/congelación Cuando se congelan tejidos del cuerpo. *(pág. C71)*

gang/ganga Grupo de personas involucradas en actividades violentas o criminales. *(pág. C57)*

gene/gen Unidad mínima de información en los cromosomas que controla la herencia. *(pág. B27)*

generic/genérico Producto que satisface ciertos estándares pero que no tiene un empaque de lujo o reconocimiento de marca. *(pág. E18)*

gesture/gesto Movimiento del cuerpo que muestra lo que una persona está pensando. *(pág. A44)*

gingivitis/gingivitis Etapa inicial de la enfermedad periodontal, en la que las encías se inflaman y sangran con facilidad. *(pág. C25)*

global warming/calentamiento global Aumento de la temperatura de la Tierra. *(pág. E53)*

gonad/gónada Glándula de la reproducción. *(pág. B21)*

greenhouse effect/efecto invernadero Dificultad de disipación del calor del Sol por gases en la atmósfera. *(pág. E53)*

grief/duelo Profunda tristeza causada por una pérdida o muerte. *(pág. A29)*

grooming/aseo Acciones para mantener el cuerpo limpio y lucir saludable. *(pág. C5)*

hallucinogen/alucinógeno Droga ilegal que ocasiona que las personas tengan diferentes sensaciones. *(pág. D45)*

hashish/hachís Droga ilegal elaborada a partir de la marihuana y que tiene efectos más fuertes. *(pág. D39)*

hazardous waste/desecho peligroso Basura que puede ser venenosa, inflamable o representar otros riesgos. *(pág. E66)*

hazard/riesgo Algo que puede causar daño o lesión dentro y fuera del hogar. *(pág. C63)*

health/salud Estado del cuerpo, la mente y los sentimientos de una persona, y cómo se relaciona con los demás. *(pág. A5)*

health behavior contract/compromiso de comportamiento saludable Plan escrito para practicar destrezas para la vida para alcanzar una meta relacionada con la salud. *(pág. A17)*

health care/cuidado de la salud Atención del bienestar físico y mental de una persona, por parte de profesionales, como médicos, enfermeras y trabajadores hospitalarios. *(pág. E23)*

health goals/metas de salud Objetivos o propósitos de salud que una persona busca alcanzar a lo largo de su vida. *(pág. A7)*

healthful weight/peso saludable Peso recomendado para una persona y que varía de persona a persona. *(pág. B59)*

health-related fitness/buen estado de salud Capacidad del corazón, pulmones, músculos y articulaciones para funcionar en óptimas condiciones. *(pág. C28)*

heart attack/ataque cardiaco Afección que se presenta cuando el suministro de sangre hacia el músculo cardiaco se bloquea o interrumpe, produciendo un daño en dicho músculo. *(pág. D66)*

heat exhaustion/agotamiento por calor Cansancio extremo producido por altas temperaturas. *(pág. C70)*

heatstroke/insolación Exposición excesiva a los rayos solares que puede ser peligrosa. *(pág. C70)*

helper T cells/linfocitos T auxiliares Glóbulos blancos que activan la producción de anticuerpos. *(pág. D58)*

heredity/herencia Conjunto de los rasgos transmitidos a una persona por sus padres biológicos o heredados. *(pág. A5)*

high blood pressure/ presión sanguínea alta Condición en que la sangre presiona sobre las paredes de las arterias cuando late el corazón. *(pág. D67)*

hormone/hormona Mensajeros químicos que regulan actividades corporales. *(pág. B18)*

human immunodeficiency virus (HIV) /virus de inmunodeficiencia humana (VIH) Virus que destruye los linfocitos T auxiliares. *(pág. A64)*

humus/humus Material parecido a la tierra que resulta del compostaje de residuos vegetales y animales. *(pág. E69)*

hypothermia/hipotermia Afección en la que la temperatura del cuerpo desciende por exposición al frío. *(pág. C71)*

illegal drugs/drogas ilegales Drogas cuyo uso, posesión, fabricación y venta están contra la ley. *(pág. D39)*

I-message/mensaje inteligente Enunciado que se refiere a un comportamiento o evento específico; describe el efecto del evento sobre una persona e identifica los sentimientos que produce. *(pág. A42)*

immune system/sistema inmunológico Sistema de órganos, tejidos y células que destruyen los agentes patógenos. *(pág. D52)*

immunity/inmunidad Resistencia a una enfermedad en particular. *(pág. D53)*

inhalants/inhalantes Sustancias químicas que se aspiran o inhalan. *(pág. D40)*

insulin/insulina Hormona que regula el nivel de azúcar en la sangre tomado de los alimentos como energía. *(pág. D71)*

intervention/intervención Acción de personas que quieren que alguien siga un tratamiento. *(pág. D17)*

intestine/intestino Conducto del aparato digestivo que digiere el alimento consumido y expulsa las sustancias de desecho. *(pág. B14)*

joint/articulación Punto del cuerpo donde se unen dos o más huesos *(pág. B6)*

kidney/riñón Órgano que filtra los desechos de la sangre. *(pág. B15)*

labor/parto Proceso durante el nacimiento de un bebé. *(pág. B29)*

landfill/vertedero Sitio designado para acumular y enterrar la basura. *(pág. E66)*

life cycle/ciclo de vida las diferentes etapas de crecimiento, desarrollo, envejecimiento y muerte. *(pág. B17)*

life skills/destrezas para la vida Habilidad para mantener y mejorar la salud. *(pág. A6)*

lifestyle/estilo de vida Manera vivir de una persona. *(pág. A5)*

limit/límite Frontera. *(pág. A66)*

loyalty/lealtad Afecto y apoyo fuertes y duraderos. *(pág. A58)*

lung/pulmón Órgano principal del sistema respiratorio. *(pág. B11)*

malnutrition/malnutrición Afección causada por no comer suficiente alimento o no ingerir las clases correctas de alimentos. *(pág. B46)*

malocclusion/maloclusión Ajuste anormal de los dientes cuando las mandíbulas se cierran. *(pág. C25)*

marijuana/marihuana Droga ilegal que afecta la memoria de corto plazo. *(pág. D39)*

media influence/influencia de los medios de comunicación Manera en que las formas de comunicación, incluidos revistas, radio, televisión, periódicos e Internet, afectan a una persona. *(pág. E18)*

media literacy/conocimiento de los medios de comunicación Capacidad para reconocer y evaluar mensajes en los medios de comunicación masiva. *(pág. E18)*

mediation/mediación Proceso mediante el cual un adulto responsable ayuda a resolver un conflicto. *(pág. A39)*

mediator/mediador Adulto neutral y confiable que ayuda a resolver un conflicto. *(pág. C53)*

medicine/medicamento Droga legal que se usa para prevenir o curar una enfermedad, o para aliviar el dolor. *(pág. D5)*

menstrual cycle/ciclo menstrual Serie de cambios que ocurren cada mes en el cuerpo de una mujer. *(pág. B21)*

mental and emotional health/salud mental y emocional Condición de la mente de una persona y la manera de expresar sus sentimientos. *(pág. A5)*

minerals/minerales Nutrientes que intervienen en diferentes procesos del cuerpo. *(pág. B37)*

money management/administración del dinero Habilidad para gastar y ahorrar dinero. *(pág. E6)*

muscle/músculo Conjunto de tejidos que mueve determinadas partes del cuerpo. *(pág. B6)*

muscular system/sistema muscular Sistema corporal que ayudan a una persona a moverse y conservar la postura. *(pág. B6)*

narcotics/narcóticos Grupo de drogas que reduce la actividad del sistema nervioso y alivia el dolor. *(pág. D44)*

natural disaster/desastre natural Evento causado por la naturaleza y que produce serios daños. *(pág. C69)*

nearsightedness/miopía Problema de la visión en que los objetos distantes se ven borrosos mientras que los que se encuentran cerca se ven claramente. *(pág. C16)*

neglect/negligencia Falla al proporcionar cuidados y orientación apropiados. *(pág. A52)*

negotiate/negociar Dialogar para llegar a un acuerdo en un conflicto. *(pág. A38)*

nerves/nervios Conjunto de fibras nerviosas que llevan mensajes del cerebro a la médula espinal y otras partes del cuerpo. *(pág. B8)*

nervous system/sistema nervioso Sistema corporal que controla la comunicación entre las distintas partes del cuerpo. *(pág. B8)*

nicotine/nicotina Droga estimulante altamente adictiva que se encuentra en el tabaco. *(pág. D21)*

noise pollution/contaminación sonora Ruido alto o constante que causa pérdida de la audición. *(pág. C17)*

nonverbal communication/comunicación no verbal Uso de acciones en lugar de palabras para expresarse. *(pág. A44)*

Glosario

nutrients/nutrientes Sustancias en los alimentos que el cuerpo necesita para el crecimiento y reparación de las células, y que suministran energía. *(pág. B37)*

Nutrition Facts/información nutricional Título del rótulo nutricional que presenta una lista con el tamaño de la porción, las calorías por porción y las calorías a partir de las grasas. *(pág. B51)*

obesity/obesidad Acumulación excesiva de grasa corporal. *(pág. B62)*

ophtalmologist/oftalmólogo(a) Médico especialista en el tratamiento de enfermedades y lesiones de los ojos. *(pág. C12)*

optometrist/optómetra Profesional de la salud capacitado y con licencia para examinar los ojos de las personas y prescribir anteojos o lentes de contacto. *(pág. C12)*

orthodontist/ortodontista Dentista especializado en corregir la posición de los dientes. *(pág. C25)*

osteoporosis/osteoporosis Enfermedad en que los huesos se debilitan y fracturan con facilidad. *(pág. B46)*

over-the-counter (OTC) drug/medicamento de venta libre Medicamento que se puede comprar sin receta médica. *(pág. D5)*

overweight/sobrepeso Peso superior al que es saludable. *(pág. B61)*

ozone layer/capa de ozono Capa superior de la atmósfera que protege a todos los seres vivos en la Tierra de la radiación ultravioleta. *(pág. E53)*

pathogen/agente patógeno Organismo vivo o partícula que puede causar una enfermedad. *(pág. D51)*

peer pressure/presión de los compañeros Influencia que compañeros de la misma edad ejercen sobre uno o más de ellos para que se comporten de determinada manera. *(pág. A20)*

Percent Daily Value/Porcentaje del valor diario Porcentaje de la cantidad diaria recomendada de un nutriente presente en la porción de un alimento o bebida. *(pág. B51)*

Periodontal disease/enfermedad periodontal Enfermedad de las encías y demás tejidos que sostienen los dientes. *(pág. C25)*

personality/personalidad Mezcla particular de características físicas, mentales, sociales y emocionales de una persona *(pág. A11)*

perspiration/transpiración Mezcla de agua, sal y productos de desechos producida por glándulas sudoríparas en la piel. *(pág. C7)*

pharmacist/farmacéutico Profesional que tiene licencia para distribuir medicamentos con receta. *(pág. D8)*

physical abuse/abuso físico Uso excesivo de la fuerza que ocasiona una lesión física. *(pág. C50)*

physical dependence/dependencia física Uso repetido de una droga que llega a causar tolerancia. *(pág. D11)*

physical environment/ambiente físico Los lugares y las cosas que constituyen las condiciones de vida de una persona. *(pág. E35)*

physical fitness plan/plan para ponerse en forma Plan escrito de actividades físicas para ponerse en forma. *(pág. C33)*

physical health/salud física Estado del cuerpo de una persona. *(pág. A5)*

pituitary gland/glándula pituitaria Principal glándula del cuerpo que segrega hormonas que controlan otras glándulas. *(pág. B18)*

pollution/contaminación Cambio que produce daño en el ambiente físico. *(pág. E51)*

pregnancy/embarazo Periodo durante el cual se desarrolla un vástago en la madre. *(pág. A65)*

prejudice/prejuicio Formarse una opinión antes de conocer todos los datos. *(pág. C49)*

prescription drug/medicamento con receta Medicamento que se puede conseguir solamente con receta escrita por un médico. *(pág. D5)*

President's Challenge/prueba de presidente Prueba en cinco áreas con respaldo del gobierno para medir el estado físico de las personas. *(pág. C34)*

PRICE/PRICE Tratamiento para la fatiga muscular, espasmos musculares, calambres, esguinces y contusiones que requiere protección, reposo, hielo, compresión y elevación. *(pág. C43)*

priority/prioridad Algo que merece atención en primer lugar. *(pág. A19)*

protective factors/factores de protección Formas de comportamiento de la persona o de las características del medio ambiente para mantener la salud y la seguridad. *(pág. C55)*

protein/proteína Nutriente necesario para el crecimiento y la reparación de las células del cuerpo. *(pág. B37)*

provider/proveedor Persona o entidad que suministra lo que se necesita o desea, como la asistencia médica. *(pág. E23)*

psychological dependence/dependencia psicológica Necesidad emocional o social para usar repetidamente una droga. *(pág. D11)*

puberty/pubertad Etapa del crecimiento en el que las gónadas empiezan a segregar hormonas. *(pág. B21)*

quackery/charlatanería Fraude o engaño para vender productos o servicios inútiles. *(pág. E20)*

radon/radón Gas inodoro, incoloro y radiactivo. *(pág. E52)*

random event/hecho aleatorio Evento que está fuera del control de una persona. *(pág. A5)*

recycling/reciclaje Convertir productos de desecho en productos nuevos utilizables. *(pág. E68)*

relationship/relación Interacción de dos o más personas. *(pág. A35)*

reliable/confiable Característica que distingue a una persona en la que se puede confiar. *(pág. A58)*

renewable resource/recurso renovable Recurso que se puede remplazar. *(pág. E65)*

reproductive system/sistema reproductivo Sistema corporal que permite que los seres vivos se reproduzcan. *(pág. B27)*

reputation/reputación Calidad del carácter de una persona según como la juzgan los demás. *(pág. A64)*

rescue breathing/respiración artificial Dar respiración a una persona inconsciente que no respira pero que tiene pulso. *(pág. C80)*

resilient/resiliente Se dice de la persona que puede recuperarse y aprender del infortunio o los cambios. *(pág. E48)*

resistance skills/destrezas de resistencia Habilidad de una persona para decir "no" ante una acción o para alejarse de una situación. *(pág. A21)*

respect/respetar Tratar a otros con dignidad y consideración. *(pág. A14)*

respiratory system/sistema respiratorio Sistema corporal que ayuda al cuerpo a utilizar el aire aspirado. *(pág. B11)*

resting heart rate/ritmo cardiaco en reposo Número de veces que el corazón late cada minuto cuando una persona se encuentra en posición de descanso. *(pág. C36)*

risk behavior/comportamiento arriesgado Acción que puede ser perjudicial para una persona. *(pág. A7)*

runoff/escurrimiento Agua lluvia o nieve derretida que no es absorbida en el suelo y pasa a las corrientes. *(pág. E58)*

schedule/agenda Lista de horarios y eventos o actividades por realizar. *(pág. E5)*

scrape/raspadura Lesión producida en la piel al raspar una parte del cuerpo contra una superficie dura o áspera. *(pág. C42)*

secondhand smoke/humo de segunda mano Humo exhalado por un fumador y que aspira otra persona. *(pág. D25)*

self-esteem/autoestima Concepto que una persona tiene de sí misma. *(pág. A12)*

self-protection/autoprotección Tomar medidas para protegerse. *(pág. C55)*

self-respect/autorrespeto Alta estima que tiene una persona de sí misma porque se comporta con responsabilidad. *(pág. A64)*

separation/separación Acuerdo entre marido y esposa para vivir separados sin disolver el matrimonio. *(pág. A50)*

service learning/aprendizaje al servicio de la comunidad Trabajo voluntario realizado por estudiantes en comunidades y que se relaciona con el aprendizaje en el salón de clases. *(pág. E27)*

sewage/aguas residuales Desechos líquidos y sólidos que se descargan en las alcantarillas. *(pág. E58)*

sexual abuse/abuso sexual Contacto sexual al que se obliga a una persona. *(pág. C50)*

sexually transmitted disease (STD)/enfermedad de transmisión sexual (ETS) Enfermedad causada por contacto sexual. *(pág. A64)*

shock/shock Disminución peligrosa del flujo sanguíneo en el cuerpo. *(pág. C83)*

shopping addiction/compra compulsiva Impulso incontrolable de ir de compras y gastar dinero. *(pág. E8)*

sick building síndrome (SBS)/síndrome del edificio enfermo Enfermedad causada por la contaminación del aire dentro de una edificación. *(pág. E52)*

side effect/efecto secundario Cambio indeseado en el cuerpo después de ingerir un medicamento. *(pág. D7)*

skeletal system/sistema esquelético Sistema que sirve de armazón de apoyo del cuerpo. *(pág. B6)*

skill-related fitness/estado físico competitivo Capacidad para desempeñarse bien en los deportes y las actividades físicas. *(pág. C33)*

smoke alarm/alarma de humo Mecanismo que alerta a las personas sobre niveles peligrosos de humo. *(pág. C64)*

smokeless tobacco/tabaco que no se fuma Tabaco que se prepara y vende para ser masticado o como rapé. *(pág. D24)*

snuff/rapé Hojas de tabaco molidas finamente que se ponen el carrillo y las encías. *(pág. D24)*

social environment/ambiente social Contacto que una persona tiene con las personas que la rodean. *(pág. E35)*

spinal cord/médula espinal Banda gruesa de nervios que transporta mensajes hacia el cerebro y desde el cerebro. *(pág. B8)*

sprain/esguince Lesión en el tejido que une los huesos a la articulación. *(pág. C42)*

stimulant/estimulante Un grupo de drogas que acelera las funciones del cuerpo. *(pág. D42)*

street smart/precavido en las calles Se dice de la persona que está consciente de un posible peligro y sabe qué hacer. *(pág. C55)*

stress/estrés Reacción del cuerpo ante las exigencias de la vida diaria. *(pág. A23)*

stressor/factor estresante Causa de estrés. *(pág. A24)*

stroke/apoplejía Bloqueo o rompimiento de un vaso sanguíneo que transporta sangre al cerebro. *(pág. D67)*

suicide/suicidio Quitarse intencionalmente la vida. *(pág. C49)*

support groups/grupos de apoyo Grupos de personas que se reúnen para animarse y ayudarse mutuamente. *(pág. E14)*

sympathetic/comprensivo(a) Sentimiento o manifestación de agrado hacia los amigos. *(pág. A58)*

tar/alquitrán Fluido espeso y pegajoso que se produce al quemar el tabaco. *(pág. D21)*

target heart rate/ritmo cardiaco ideal Frecuencia cardiaca entre 60% y 75% del ritmo cardiaco máximo. *(pág. C36)*

tendon/tendón Fibra de tejido resistente que une los músculos a los huesos o a otras partes del cuerpo. *(pág. B7)*

time management plan/plan de administración del tiempo Plan que muestra cómo una persona distribuye su tiempo. *(pág. E5)*

tolerance/tolerancia Estado en el cual se necesitan cantidades cada vez mayores de un medicamento para producir los efectos deseados. *(pág. D7)*

underweight/bajo peso Peso menor que el saludable. *(pág. B60)*

unit price/precio unitario Valor del alimento por peso, porción o alguna otra unidad de medida. *(pág. B52)*

universal precautions/precauciones universales Procedimientos que ayudan a las personas evitar contacto con agentes patógenos en fluidos corporales. *(pág. C76)*

urinary system/sistema urinario Sistema que elimina los desechos líquidos del cuerpo. *(pág. B15)*

uterus/útero Órgano muscular del cuerpo de la mujer que alberga el óvulo fecundado durante el embarazo. *(pág. B27)*

vaccine/vacuna Agentes patógenos inactivos o debilitados que se suministran para inmunizar. *(pág. D53)*

valid information/información válida Datos que son verdaderos. *(pág. E13)*

values/valores Principios y normas que guían el comportamiento de una persona. *(pág. A11)*

vein/vena Vaso sanguíneo que transporta sangre hacia el corazón. *(pág. B12)*

violence/violencia Uso de la fuerza para lastimar a alguien o para destruir bienes. *(pág. A52)*

visual environment/ambiente visual Todo lo que una persona ve regularmente. *(pág. E76)*

vitamin/vitamina Nutriente que ayuda al cuerpo a usar carbohidratos, proteínas y grasas. *(pág. B37)*

volunteer/voluntario Persona que provee un servicio sin esperar recibir pago. *(pág. E26)*

warm-up/calentamiento Periodo de tres a cinco minutos de actividad física suave. *(pág. C37)*

weapon/arma Objeto usado para cometer actos violentos. *(pág. C49)*

wellness/bienestar Estado de equilibrio de la salud. *(pág. A5)*

white blood cells/glóbulos blancos Células de la sangre que atacan los agentes patógenos que causan infecciones y enfermedades. *(pág. D52)*

whiteout/cortina de nieve Ventisca severa en la cual una persona no puede ver el horizonte y sólo puede divisar formas oscuras. *(pág. C69)*

wound/herida Lesión en los tejidos blandos del cuerpo. *(pág. C82)*

you-message/mensaje no inteligente Enunciado que acusa o hace avergonzar a otra persona. *(pág. A42)*

Index

Note: Page numbers in *italics* refer to photos and illustrations. See *Table of Contents* for all feature types.

A

AAHPERD. *See* American Alliance for Health, Physical Education, Recreation, and Dance (AAHPERD)
Abdominal thrust, C79
Abstinence, A7, A62–A69, B31
  living up to adult expectations and, A63, A64, *A65*
  reasons to practice, A64–A65
  resistance skills and, A68–A69, *A68*, B30
  setting limits, A66–A67
Abstinence from sex, A62
Abuse, A52, C50–C51, *C50*
  drug. *See* Drug abuse
  in family, A52–A53
  forms of, C50
  recognizing, C51
  reporting, C51, C58
  social-emotional environment and, E45
Accidents, C63. *See also* Unintentional injuries
Acetaldehyde, D31, D35
Acid rain
  food chain destroyed by, E59
  reducing, E55
  water pollution from, E58, *E58*
  worldwide concerns about, E52
Acne, B20, C5, C7
  finding valid information on, E19, E20
Acne cream product, evaluating, E21
Acquired immune deficiency syndrome (AIDS), A65, D58. *See also* Human immunodeficiency virus (HIV)
Active listening, A45, A47
Activities, taking the lead in, E49
Addiction
  entertainment, E9
  shopping, E8
Addiction, drug, D14–D15
  marijuana, D39
  stimulants, D42
  tobacco, D21
Adolescence, B17
  emotional and intellectual changes in, B22

physical changes of, B20–B21
social changes in, B23
special dietary needs in, B48–B49
Adrenal glands, *A24*, *B18*, B19
Adrenaline, A24, *A24*, B19
Adults
  abdominal thrust on conscious/unconscious, C79
  CPR for, C80–C81
Adults, responsible
  asking for advice from, E47
  drug abuse help from, D16, D17, *D17*
  help in coping from, E48
  influence on personality, A11
  living up to expectations of, A63, *A65*
  managing chronic illness with help of, D74
Advertisements, E17, *E17*
Advertising, E17, E18–E21
  jingles, E20
  quackery and, E20, *E20*
  spending by young people and, E3
  techniques, E17, E18–E19
  tobacco ads, D26
Advocate, health. *See* Health advocate, being
Aerobic exercise, C29
Affection, A66, A67
After-school activities, avoiding gangs and, C56, *C56*
Age, drug effects and, D7
Agility, C33
Aging, life cycle and, B17
AIDS, A65, D58. *See also* Human immunodeficiency virus (HIV)
Air, E50–E55
  harmful substances in, E33, E38
  need for clean, E51
  pathogens spread by, D51
  quantity inhaled and exhaled, B3
Air pollutants, B11, E51, E52
Air pollution, E51–E55, *E51*, E73
  body defenses against, B11
  health effects of, E51, *E51*
  indoor, E52, E54
  reducing, E54–E55
  water pollution from, E58
  worldwide concerns about, E53, E55
Airways
  asthma and narrowing of, D72

checking injured person for open, C77
Al-Anon/Alateen, D19
Alcoholics Anonymous, A52, D19
Alcoholism, D35
Alcohol use and abuse, D10, D30–D37, D43
  avoiding, B29, B30, B41, C52, D60, D64, E47
  blood alcohol concentration (BAC), D34
  cost of abuse of, A66
  effect on decisions, A66, D32
  effect on relationships, D13, *D13*, D33, D33
  long-term effects of, D35
  physical effect of, D13; D31, *D31*, D36
  during pregnancy, B29, B30, D35
  resistance skills to avoid, D36–D37, *D37*
  sex and, A66, D33
  short-term effects of, D35
  society and, D13
  among teens, D16
  tobacco use and, D21
  violence and, C49, D32, D33
Allergens, D73, *D73*
  indoor air pollution from, E52
Allergies, D73
  anaphylactic shock and, C83
  food, B54–B55, *B54*
Allergist, D73
All-terrain vehicles, pollution from emissions, E73
Alveoli, B11, *B11*
American Alliance for Health, Physical Education, Recreation, and Dance (AAHPERD), C35
American Board of Medical Specialties, E23
American Cancer Society, D27, E26
American Dental Association (ADA)
  brushing and flossing, C22
  fluoride recommendations, C23
  Seal of Acceptance, C21
American Heart Association, D27, E26
American Lung Association, D27
American Medical Association (AMA), E23

American Red Cross, E26
American Speech-Language-Hearing Association, E40
American Stroke Association, D68
Ammonia, D21
Amphetamines, D42
Anabolic steroids, D41, *D41*
Anaerobic exercise, C29
Anaphylactic shock, C83
Anemia, B48
  sickle cell, D74
Anesthesiologist, E28
Anger, A23
  managing, C53
Animal bite, pathogens spread by, D51
Animals, respecting outdoors and, E75
Ankle sprain, C84
Annis, Jessica and Elizabeth, E26
Anorexia nervosa, B67
Antibiotic ointment, C42, C82
Antibiotics, D5
Antibodies
  as defense against pathogens, D52
  immunity and, D53, *D53*
Antiperspirants, C7
Anvil (ear), *C14*
Anxiety
  and puberty, B22
  shopping addiction and, E8
  ways to manage, A25, E48–E49
Appeals, advertising, E17, E19, *E19*
Appearance. *See also* Body image; Personal health care
  major changes in, suicidal thoughts and, C52
  physical activity and, C27
Appetite, physical activity and, C27
Armstrong, Lance, D68
Arsenic, D24
Artery(ies), B12
  plaque buildup in, D67
Artificial heart, E28
Artificial tears, C13
Art Link, A44, A55, C42, C58, D17, D64, E28, E76
Asbestos, E52, E54
Asia, HIV/AIDS in, D58
Asthma, D23, D72
  tobacco use and, D23
Astigmatism, C16
Atherosclerosis, D22
Athletes, anabolic steroid abuse by, D41. *See also* Sports

Index

Athletic shoes, C41, *C41*
Auditory nerve, *C14*

B

Baby
  birth of, B29
  development of fetus, *B28*
  low birth weight, A65
  prenatal care and health of, B29
Bacteria, D49, D51
  common communicable diseases caused by, D54
  sexually transmitted diseases caused by, D57, *D57*
  tooth decay and, C24
Balance, C33
  healthful weight and better, B59, *B59*
Balanced diet, B39, B46, *B46*
Ball-and-socket joint, B6, *B6*
Bandages. *See also* First aid
  for injuries, C42, C43
  for wounds, C82
Barbiturates, D43
Bargain events, going to, E7
Bathing
  skin care and, C6
  washing hair, C8
  washing hands, C63, D55, D61
Behavior(s)
  family guidelines for, A51
  healthful, A6, B68
  matching nonverbal and verbal, A21, A68–A69
  personality and, A11
  risk, A7, A59, A60–A61, *A60*, B23, D33, E47
Benzene, D21
Beta-endorphins, A27
  physical activity and, C27
Bicuspids. *See* Premolars
Biking, E73
  safety, C40, C65
Binge drinkers, D35
Binge eating disorder, B67
Bingeing, B67
Biodegradable products, E67
Biological therapy, D65
Birth, premature, B29
Birth defects, fetal alcohol syndrome and, D35
Birthrate among teens, A65. *See also* Pregnancy
Birth weight, low, A65
Bladder, urinary, B15, *B15*, D22
Bleeding from wound
  care for, C82–C83
  heavy, C83
  shock from, C83

Blended family, A50
Blizzard, C69, *C69*
Blood, B12
Blood alcohol concentration (BAC), D34
Blood pressure, C11
  high, B41, D67
Blood pressure gauge, *C11*
Blood sample, C11
Blood transfusion, HIV and, D59, D60
Blood vessels, B12
  alcohol use and, *D31*
  cardiovascular diseases of, D66–D67
  tobacco use and, *D22*
Body composition, B62
  exercise to improve, C29
  healthful, C28
Body fat, B62, C28
Body fluids
  HIV spread by, D59
  universal precautions to prevent contact with, D60–D61
Body image, B64–B69
  defined, B65
  developing positive, B65, *B65*, B68–B69
  eating disorders and, B66–B67
  factors influencing, B65, *B67*, B68
  negative, B66
Body language, A44
Body Mass Index, B62, *B62*
Body odor, C5, C7
Body systems, B4
  circulatory system, B12–B13, *B12*
  digestive system, B14–B15, *B15*
  endocrine system, B18–B19, *B18*
  integumentary system, B5
  interaction of, B7, B9, B13
  nervous system, B8–B9, *B9*
  reproductive system, B27
  respiratory system, B11, *B11*
  skeletal system, B6–B7, *B6*
  urinary system, B15, *B15*
Body temperature
  fever, C11, D52
  taking, C11
  weather extremes and, C70, C71
Body type, healthful weight and, B63, *B63*
Body weight. *See* Weight

Bones, B6–B7
  broken, C84
  physical activity and, C27
Boredom, A25, E8
Botulism, B51
Bowel movement, B15, *B15*
Braces for teeth, C25
Brain, B8, *B9*, B13
  alcohol use and, *D31*
  depressants and, D43
  depression and, A29
  physical activity and blood flow to, C27
  stress and, *A24*
  stroke and damage to, D67
  tobacco use and, *D22*
Brain stem, B8, *B9*
Brainstorming, A42
Brand, E18
Breakfast, healthful, B44, *B44*
Breast-feeding, HIV and, D59
Breathing
  asthma and, D72
  checking injured person for, C76
  rescue, C80, C83
  secondhand smoke, D23, D25, E52
  stress and, *A24*
Broken bones, first aid for, C84
Bronchial tubes, B11, *B11*
  asthma and, *D72*
Bronchitis, chronic, D23
Brushing teeth, C22, *C22*
Budget, E6, *E6*
Build Character
  caring, A42, A65, B54, C5, E46
  choosing friends, A63
  citizenship, C76, E18, E62
  honesty, D39
  honesty/respect/ responsibility/fairness/ caring/citizenship, B17
  respect, B62, E37
  responsibility, A15, A53, A60, B69, C43, C50, D16, D25, D69, E8
Bulimia nervosa, B67
Bullying, C56
Burglary, C66
Burns, C85
  first aid for, C85
  in kitchen, avoiding, C63
Bushan, Amit, B12

C

Cadmium, D24
Caffeine, D42
  in hot weather, avoiding, C70

during pregnancy, avoiding, B29
Calcium, B8, B37, B48
  for strong teeth, C23
Calculus, C25
Calming down to manage anger, C53
Calories
  burning, B59, B60
  defined, *B44*
  empty, B47
  maintaining healthful weight and, B60–B61
Calories from fat, B52
Camp, meeting peers at, E46
Campgrounds, E74
Camping, E73
  safety, C65
Cancer, D63–D65
  causes of, D23, D63
  colon, B40
  deaths from, age 10–14, E38
  factors increasing risk of, D64
  lung, D25, E51, E52
  oral, D25
  reducing risk of, D64, *D64*
  skin, E53
  surviving, D68
  treating, D65, *D65*
  warning signs of, D64
Canines, C21, *C21*
Cannabis sativa, D45
Canned goods, danger of bulging or damaged, B51
Canoeing, E73
Capillary, B12
Carbohydrates, B37
  simple, B41
Carbon dioxide, plants' use of, E51
Carbon monoxide, D21, E54
  in tobacco smoke, D21, D22
Carbon monoxide detectors, E54
Carcinogens, D63, D64
Cardiac muscles, B7
Cardiologist, E28
Cardiopulmonary resuscitation (CPR), C80–C81
  for shock, C83
  training in, D68
Cardiorespiratory endurance, C28
  physical activities for, C29, C36, *C36*
  test of, C35
Cardiovascular diseases, D66–D67

life-saving first aid for, D68
reducing risk of, D66, *D66,*
D67
Careers in Health, E28–E29
aerobics instructor, C29,
C29
camp counselor, A12
climatologist, E55
DEA agent, D44
disaster relief worker, C80
endocrinologist, B19
farmer, B39
grief counselor, A51
health inspector, E29
microbiologist, D53
in technology and health
care field, E28
Caring, A14
for grieving people, A29,
A29
paying a compliment, E46
as friendship quality, A58
social-emotional environ-
ment and, E45
Cars. *See* Motor vehicles
Cartilage, B6
Cavities, C24, *C24*
Celebrity, advertising using,
E18
Cell membrane, *B5*
Cell phones, A41
Cells, B5, *B5*
in blood, B12
egg, B21, B27
growth, D64
red blood cells, B12, B13
sperm, *B9,* B27
white blood cells, B12, D52,
D53, D58, *D58*
Cementum, *C21*
Centers for Disease Control
and Prevention (CDC),
A65
on HIV, D59
Cerebellum, B8, *B9*
Cerebrum, B8, *B9*
alcohol's effect on, A67
Character, A11
abstinence and, A64
self-esteem and, A12–A13
traits of good, A14–A15
Checkups, C10–C19
being health advocate for,
C18–C19
dental, C23
for ears, C14–C15
eye and ear problems,
C16–C17
for eyes, C12–C13, *C13*
physical examinations, C11,
C11

Chemicals
avoiding unnecessary expo-
sure to, D64
household, E52, E54, E61,
E61, E66
inhalants, D40
Chemotherapy, D652
Chen, Lihua, D36
Chewing tobacco, D24
Child abuse, C50
Childbirth, B29, *B29*
Child Help USA, A52
Childhood, stages of, B17
Children
abdominal thrust on con-
scious/unconscious, C79
CPR for, C81
Childsitter, safety at home
with, C67
Chlamydia, D57
Choking, C79
Cholesterol, B41, B47
avoiding, D67
in common foods, B47
Chromosomes, B27
Chronic bronchitis, D23
Chronic health conditions,
D70–D75
allergies, D73
asthma, D72
among certain racial and
ethnic groups, D74
defined, D71
diabetes, B46, D71, *D71*
epilepsy, D71
managing, D74–D75
medicines for, D5
Chronic obstructive pul-
monary disease (COPD),
D23
Cigarettes, chemicals in, D21.
See also Smoking; Tobacco
Cilia, B11
as defense against
pathogens, D52
in lungs, smoking and, D23
Circulatory system, B12–B13,
B12
Cirrhosis, D31, D34
Citizenship, responsible, A9
being prepared for emer-
gency, C76
character trait, A14
exercising consumer rights,
E18
water conservation in
school and, E62
Clean air, need for, E51
Clean Air Act (1967), E55
"Clean coal" methods in
power plants, E55

Cleaning your living space,
E76, E77
Clean water, need for, E57,
E57
cleanup programs and,
E60
Clostridium botulinum, B51
Clothing
for biking, C65
for cold weather, C71, *C71*
for hot weather, C70
outdoor physical activity
and, C40
Coach, developing good
sportsmanship from,
E48
Cocaine, D21, D42
Cochlea, *C14*
Codeine, D44
Cola drink, B44
Cold weather, safety precau-
tions in, C40, C71, *C71*
Colon, tobacco use and, D22
Colon cancer, B40
Commercials, E17, *E17*
Common cold, D54
Communicable diseases,
D50–D61
avoiding, D55
body defenses against,
D52–D53, *D53*
common, D54
defined, D51
sexually transmitted dis-
eases, D56–D61
spread of, D51
Communication, A40–A47
effective, A9
in family, A49
healthful, A42–A43, *A43,*
A45, A49
nonverbal, A44–A45, *A44*
verbal, A41, *A41,* A43, *A43*
Communication skills. *See
also* Life Skills Activity
alcohol's effect on, D32
using, A46–A47, B23
Community
safety in, C55, C59
social-emotional environ-
ment in, E37
Community health services,
E22–E29
government's role in,
E24–E25
health care providers and
facilities, E23
technology and health
careers in, E28–E29
voluntary health organizations, E26–E27

Community organizations
as sources of valid health
information, E13
for victims of violence,
C52
Compliment, paying a, E46
Compost, E61
Composting, E69, *E69*
Compress, in PRICE treat-
ment, C43
Compulsive use of drug, D14
Computer, guidelines for us-
ing, E77
Computer-assisted tomogra-
phy (CAT) scans, E29
Computer-based sources of
valid information, E13
Conflict, A38
managing anger in, C53
resolving, A45, C53, *C53,*
C60–C61, E49
Conflict resolution skills,
A38–A39, *A38. See also*
Life Skills Activity
SAVE and, A42
Conjunctivitis (pinkeye), C17
Conservation, E62
energy, *E54,* E70, E71
of resources, E70–E71
water, E62–E63, *E62,* E70
Consumer, E13
advertising and, E17,
E18–E21
evaluating health care products, E20–E21
finding reliable health information, E12–E15
influences on choices, E17
money management by,
E6–E7, E8
spending by young people,
E3
Consumer costs, E23
Consumer rights, E18, E21
Consumers (food chain), E59
Consumer Wise Activity
costs of smoking, D22
evaluating advertisement,
E17
finding help for families,
A52
food safety tips, B41
hair care products, C8
microwave safety demon-
stration, C63
needle safety in tattooing
and ear piercing, D60
organic foods and products,
E71
responsible buying deci-
sions, A20, B22

school lunches, choosing foods at, B43
taking medicines, D5
tooth-whitening products, C21
Contact lenses, C13, C16
Control, taking, E49
Cooking foods, B53
Cool-down, C37, C39, C42
Coordination, C33
COPD. *See* Chronic obstructive pulmonary disease (COPD)
Coping with negative social-emotional environment, E48–E49
Cornea, *C12*
scratched, C17
Corn sugar, B47
Corn syrup, B47
Counseling, E47
Couple family, A50
CPR. *See* Cardiopulmonary resuscitation (CPR)
Crack, D42
Crank (amphetamine), D42
Creams (drug), D6
Cresol, D21
Crime. *See also* Violence
burglary, C66
drug abuse and, D13
hate, C49
Critical thinking, A9
Crown of tooth, C21, *C21*
Crystal meth, D42
Culture
disease and, D74
influence on consumer choices, E17
Curl-ups, C34, *C34*
Currency, E6
Cuspids. *See* Canines
Cut, C42
Cuticles, C9
Cyanide, D24
Cystic fibrosis, D74
Cytoplasm, *B5*

D

Daily Value, B51
Dairy products, B41
Dandruff shampoo, C8
Dating, family guidelines for, A63, *A63*
DEA. *See* U.S. Drug Enforcement Administration (DEA)
Deafness, C17
Death(s), B17
alcohol-related, D31
changes in family due to, A50

drug-related, D13, D14, D42
grief over, *A28*, A29, A50
leading causes of, age 10–14, E38
terminal illness and, D69
tobacco use as cause of, D26
Decibels, C14, *C15*, E41, *E41*
Decision making, alcohol's effect on, A66, D32. *See also* Responsible decisions, making
Defenses against communicable disease, D52–D53, *D53*
Delivery of baby, B29
Dental checkups, C23
Dental health plan, C22–C23
Dental plaque, C22, C23
gingivitis and, C25
tooth decay and, C24, *C24*
Dentin, C21, *C21*
Deodorants, C7
Dependence, drug, A52
of alcoholism, D35
physical dependence, D11, D35
psychological dependence, D11, D35
Depressants, D43. *See also* Alcohol use and abuse
Depression, A28
abuse and, C51
alcohol and, D32
shopping addiction and, E8
signs of, A28
suicide and, C52
Dermatologist, C7
Dermis, C6, *C6*
Dextrose, B47
Diabetes, B46, D71, *D71*
Diet, B37
balanced, B39, B46, *B46*
fad, B61
to reduce risk of cancer, D64
special dietary needs in adolescence, B48–B49
for teeth and gums, C23
Dietary guidelines, B36–B41
eating out and, B43
Food Guide Pyramid, B38–B39, *B38*, B40, B44, B46, *B47*, B55
nutrients, B14, B37, *B37*
Dietary Guidelines for Americans, B40–B41, B46
ethnic foods and, B56–B57
Digestive system, B14–B15, *B15*
Direct contact, pathogens spread by, D51
Disability, E25

Disease(s). *See also* Chronic health conditions; Communicable diseases; Noncommunicable diseases
healthful weight and reducing risk of, B59
marijuana and, D45
medicines to fight, D5
physical activity and prevention of, C27
tobacco use and, D23, *D23*
Dishwasher, water conservation and, E62, E70, E71
Dislocation, C42
Distress, A24, A35
Divorce, A50, A52
among teens, B31
DNA, B27
Domestic shelter, A53
Domestic violence, C49
Dominant gene, B27
Dose, drug, D5, D7, *D7*, D9
Drinking alcohol. *See* Alcohol use and abuse
Driving under the influence, D32
Drops (drug), D6
Drought, E57
Drug(s). *See also* Alcohol use and abuse; Drug abuse; Tobacco
avoiding, C52, E47
blood alcohol concentration and other, D34
for cardiovascular diseases, D67
defined, D5
dose of, D5, D7, *D7*, D9
effect on body, D7
entry into body, D6, *D6*
illegal, D10, D38–D45
living drug-free lifestyle, D18–D19, *D18, D19*
medicines, D3, D4–D11
misuse and abuse of, D10–D11
over-the-counter (OTC), D5, D8, *D8*
prescription, D5, *D5*, D9, *D9*, E21
safe use of, D8–D9
violence and, C49
Drug abuse, D10–D11, D12–D17
defined, D10
effects of, D11, D13
getting help for, D16–D17
reasons for, D14–D15
among teens, D16
warning signs of, D16, D17

Drug addiction, D14–D15
marijuana, D39
stimulants, D42
tobacco, D21
Drug dependence, A52
alcoholism, D35
physical dependence, D11, D35
psychological dependence, D11, D35
Drug-free lifestyle, D18–D19
maintaining, D36
Drug labels, D8, *D8*, D9, *D9*
Drug misuse, D10–D11
Drug use, D10
Dumping, illegal, E58
Duration of exercise, C34

E

Ear(s), *C14*
caring for, C14–C15
problems with, C17
Early childhood, B17
Ear piercing, D60, *D60*
Earplugs, using, C15, E39, E41
Earthquakes, C73
Eating. *See also* Nutrition
during pregnancy, B29
stress management with healthy, A26
teeth used for, C21
Eating disorders, B66–B67
Eating habits, B42–B49
breakfasts, B44, *B44*
eating out and, B43
health and, B46–B47
snacking, B44–B45, *B45*, B49
special dietary needs of teens, B48–B49
Eating out, Dietary Guidelines and, B43
Ecology, E75
Ecosports, E73
Ectomorph, B63
Education, income and level of, B31
Effective communication. *See* Communication
Egg cells, B21, B27
Electrical storm, C69
Electricity use, limiting, E54
Electric shock, preventing, C64
Elevation of injured part, in PRICE treatment, C43
Embryo, B28
Emergency, C75. *See also* First aid
cardiovascular diseases and, D68
knowing whom to call, D69
preparation for, C75, C82

Index

Emergency kit for natural disasters, C72, C73
Emergency phone numbers, C75
  and childsitting, C67
Emotional abuse, C50
Emotional environment, E35, E36, *E36. See also* Social-emotional environment
  improving, E47
Emotions, A22–A29
  in adolescence, B22
  depression, A28
  expressing, A23, E47
  grief, *A28*, A29, A50
  influence on consumer choices, E17
  stress and, A23, *A23*, A24–A27
  violence and, C49
Empathy, A29, A65
Emphysema, D23
Empty calories, B47
Enamel, tooth, C21, *C21*
Endocrine system, B18–B19, *B18*
  emotional and intellectual changes and, B22
  physical changes of adolescence and, B20–B21
Endomorph, B63
Endurance, C28
  cardiorespiratory, C28, C29, C35, C36, *C36*
  muscular, C28, C29, C34, C35
Endurance run/walk, C35
Energy, E65
  healthful weight and, B59
Energy conservation, *E54*, E70, E71
Energy resources, E65
Entertainment
  choosing responsibly, A67, *A67*, E8
  healthful, A67, *A67*, E9, *E9*
  influence on decisions about sex, A66
  low-cost, E7
Entertainment addiction, E9
Environment, A11, E34–E41
  air and air pollution, E50–E55
  asthma and, D72
  being health advocate for, E35, *E35*, E60
  defined, A11
  disease caused by, D63
  Earth's resources, E64–E71
  enjoying, E72–E77
  influence on physical activities, C31

noise pollution and, C17, E40–E41
  parts of, E35
  personality and, A11
  physical, E33, E35, E38–E39, *E38*
  social-emotional, E36–E37, E44–E49
  visual, E76–E77
  water and water pollution, E56–E63
Environmental Protection Agency, E69
Ephedra, D11
Epidermis, C6, *C6*
Epilepsy, D71
Epinephrine, C83, D73
Equipment
  for physical activities, C33
  safety, *A21*, C39, C40
  sports, C41
Esophagus, B14, *B15*
Estrogen, B20
Ethnic foods, B56–B57
Eustachian tube, *C14*
Eustress, A24, A35
Evans, Nickole, A42
Exercise. *See also* Physical activity
  aerobic, C29
  anaerobic, C29
  for circulatory health, B13
  components of, C34
  correct techniques, C34–C35, *C34, C35*
  for health-related fitness, C29
  during pregnancy, B29
  for respiratory health, B11
  at target heart rate, C36, *C36*
  warm-up and cool-down, C37, *C37*, C39, C42
Expectations, living up to adult, A63, A64, *A65*
Experimental use of drug, D14
Extended family, A50
Eye(s), *C12*
  caring for, C12–C13, *C13*
  laser eye surgery, E29
  problems with, C16–C17
  similarity to camera, C12
Eyeglasses, C12, C13, C16

F

Face mask, universal precaution of wearing, D61
Facial expressions, A44, A45
Facilities, E23
  health care, E23
  physical activity, C33
Fad diet, B61

Fads, E17
Fairness, A14, C27
Falls, preventing, C64
False advertising, recognizing, E18, E20
Family(ies), A48–A53
  abuse and violence in, A52–A53, C49
  adjusting to changes in, A50–A51, *A50*
  alcohol-free life and, *D35*
  alcoholism in, D35
  alcohol use and relationship with, D33
  drug abuse effects on, D13, *D13*
  emotional environment and, E36, *E36*
  finding help for, *A52*, A53
  healthful communication in, A49
  healthy relationship with, B23
  influence on consumer choices, E17
  physical activity with, C27, C30–C31
  social environment and, E36
  types of, A50
Family and social health, A5, *A5*
  abstinence, practicing, A62–A69
  communication, A40–A47
  family life, A48–A53
  friends, A54–A61
  physical activity and, C27
  relationships, A34–A39
Family counselor, A52, A53
Family guidelines, A51
  for dating, A63, *A63*
  following, A58
  for healthful entertainment, E9, *E9*
Family health history, D63
Family violence, C49
Farsightedness, C16
Fast food, B52
  fit in Food Guide Pyramid, B55
Fathers, teen, B31. *See also* Marriage; Pregnancy
Fats, B37
  reducing intake of, B47
  saturated, B41, B47, D67
  trans, B47, B52, D67
Fat tissue, B62, C28
FDA. *See* Food and Drug Administration (FDA)
Federal government role in health care, E24

Federal Trade Commission (FTC), E21
Feedback, E36
Feelings, expressing, A41. *See also* Emotions
Females, body changes during puberty, B20
Fertilization, B27, B28
Fertilizers
  organic foods without, E71
  reducing use of, E61
Fetal alcohol syndrome (FAS), D35
Fetus, B28
Fever, C11
  as defense against pathogens, D52
Fiber, B40
Fighting, C49
Fillings, C24
Financial goal, E7, *E7*
Fires
  outdoors, E75
  preventing, C64
First aid, C74–C85
  abdominal thrusts, C79
  bleeding, controlling, C82–C83
  broken bones, C84
  burns, C85
  checking injured person, C76, C77
  CPR, C80–C81
  first steps in, C76–C77
  for heart attack, D68
  items in first aid kit, C75
  permission from injured person for, C75
  rescue breathing, C80, C83
  for shock, C83
  sprains, C84
  for stroke, D68
  universal precautions in, C76–C77, D61
First-degree burn, C85
Fitness, B40
  health-related, C28–C29
  for life, C30–C31
  physical fitness plan, C32–C37
  skill-related, C33
  tests to measure, C34–C35, *C34, C35*
Fitness skills, C33
  alcohol and, D34
Fixed joint, B6
Flammable, C64
Flash flood, C73
Flexibility, C28
  exercise for, C29

Index

Floating in water, demonstrating, C65
Floods, C73
Flossing, C22
Flu (influenza), D54
Fluoride, C23, C24
Foldables™, A17, A47, B25, B57, C19, C61, D29, D77, E11, E43
Food(s)
  blood alcohol concentration and, D34
  digestion of, B14–B15
  organic, E71
  pathogens spread by, D51
  reducing risk of cardiovascular disease, D66, *D66*, D67
  servings of, B39
Food allergies, B54–B55, *B54*
Food and Drug Administration (FDA), D5, E21
  ephedra investigation, D11
Foodborne illness, preventing, B53, C63
Food chain, water pollution and, E59, *E59*
Food choices, B50–B57
  ethnic foods, B56–B57
  food allergies and, B54–B55, *B54*
  food labels and, B51–B53, *B51, B52*
Food group, B38
Food Guide Pyramid, B38–B39, *B38*, B40, B44, B46
  fitting fast food in, B55
  limiting servings from top of, *B47*
Food intolerance, B54
Food labels, B51–B53
  comparing foods by reading, *B51*, B52–B53, *B52*
  fats on, B47
  food allergies and checking, B54, B55
  ingredients on, B55
  sugars on, B47
Food safety, B40, B41, B53
  on vacation, B35
Food storage and preparation, B53
Footwear, athletic, C41, *C41*
Forests, rain, E55
Formaldehyde, D21
Fossil fuels, E51, E65
Foster family, A50
Fractures, C84
Frequency of exercise, C34

Friends, A54–A61
  alcohol use and relationship with, D33
  choosing, A55, A63
  emotional environment and, E36
  ending harmful relationships, A37, A59
  importance of, A55
  influence on body image, B65, *B67*, B68
  influence on consumer choices, E17
  keeping, A58–A59
  making new, A56–A57, *A56*
  older people, becoming friends with, E46, E47
  opposite sex, A63
  physical activity with, C27, C30–C31
  qualities of good, A58, *A58*
  resisting negative peer pressure, A60–A61
  social environment and, E36
Frostbite, C71
Fruits and vegetables, B40, *B40*
  for snacks, B44
  washing, C63
FTC. *See* Federal Trade Commission (FTC)
Fumes
  from household chemicals, diffusion of, E54
  unintentional inhaling of, D40
Fungi, D51

G

Gang Resistance Education and Training (G.R.E.A.T.) Program, C56
Gangs, avoiding, C52, C56, C57
Garden, planting, E73
Gender, blood alcohol concentration and, D34
Generalized seizures, D71
Generic, E18
Genes, B27. *See also* Heredity
  disease and, D74
Genital herpes, A65, D57
Genital warts, A65, D57
Geothermal energy, E65
Germs, D49. *See also* Bacteria; Viruses
  food safety and, B53
Gestures, A44, A45
Gingivitis, C25
Glands
  endocrine, B18–B19, *B18*
  oil, *C6*

reproductive, *B18*, B19, B21
  sweat, *C6*, C7
Glass (amphetamine), D42
Gliding joint, B6
Global warming, E53
Goals
  financial, E7, *E7*
  health, A7, *A7*
  to improve physical environment, E39
  realistic, A13
Gonads, B21
Gonorrhea, D57
Government agencies
  consumer rights protection and, E21
  role in health care, E24–E25
  as sources of valid health information, E13
Grains, eating, B40, B44
Grass. *See* Marijuana
Greenhouse effect, E53, *E53*
Grief, *A28*, A29, A50
  comforting grieving person, A50
Grooming, C5–C9, *C5*
  benefits of, C5
  hair care, C8, *C8*
  nail care, C9, *C9*
  skin care, C6–C7, *C7*
Groundwater, reducing pollution of, E61
Group dates, A63
Growth and development. *See also* Adolescence
  life cycle, changes in, B16–B23
  pregnancy and childbirth, B26–B31
  support and control systems, B4–B9
  transport systems, B10–B15
Growth hormone, B18, B20
Growth spurt, B20
Grube, Emil H., E28
Guidelines, family, A51
Guidelines for Making Responsible Decisions™, A19. *See also* Responsible decisions, making
  taking control of problems using, E49
Guilt
  abstinence and, A64
  drug abuse and, D15
Gums
  caring for, C22–C23, *C22*
  problems, preventing and treating, C24–C25, *C24*
  structure of, C21, *C21*
  tobacco use and, D22

Guns, C55
  avoiding, E39
  in home, avoiding danger with, C66
  school shootings, C56

H

Habits
  breaking harmful, A15
  eating, B42–B49
  saving money, E7
Hair, B5
  caring for, C8, *C8*
  pubic, B20
Hallucinogens, D45, *D45*
Hammer (ear), *C14*
Handicap, E25
Handshakes, disease spread by, D52
Hand signals for biking, C65
Hand washing, C63, D55, D61
Harmful habits, breaking, A15
Harmful relationships, A35
  ending, A37, A59
Harmony Sidewalk Murals project, C58
Hashish, D39
Hate crime, C49
Hazardous waste, E66
Hazards, C63
  at home, C64
  outdoors, C65
Headphones, using, C15, E41, E42–E43
Health
  defined, A5
  effect of drug and, D7
  factors affecting, A5
  influences on, analyzing, A13, *A13*
  optimal, D74
  taking care of, E47
  taking responsibility for, A6–A7, *A6*
  three parts of, A5
Health advocate, being, A14. *See also* Learning Life Skills; Life Skills Activity
  for checkups, C18–C19
  for environment, E35, *E35*, E60
  HIV awareness and, D61
  litter prevention campaign, E67
  for smoke-free public places, D25
Health behavior contract, *A16*, A17
  to set health goal, A27, A51, B13, B45, C9, C58, C71, D41, D66, E8, E63, E70

Index

Health care, A5, E23. *See also*
    Personal health care
    costs of, D13, E23
    facilities, E23
    government's role in,
        E24–E25
    prenatal, B29, B30
    providers, C16, E23, E25
    technology and health ca-
        reers in, E28–E29
Health care facilities, E23
Health care products, evaluat-
    ing, E20–E21
Health care providers, E23
    getting information on, C16
    HMO, E25
Health care team, D74
Health departments, state, E24
Healthful activities, getting in-
    volved in, E46
Healthful behaviors, A6
    positive body image and,
        B68
    practicing. *See* Life Skills
        Activity
Healthful diet, B37
Healthful entertainment, A67,
    A67, E9, *E9*
Healthful relationships, A35,
    A36–A37, *A37*
Healthful weight, B58–B63
Health goals, setting, A7, *A7*.
    See also Life Skills Activity
    for self-esteem, A16–A17
Health insurance, E23, E25
Health literacy, A9
Health maintenance organiza-
    tions (HMOs), E25
Health Online, A26, A68, B18,
    B52, C40, C72, D7, D72,
    E58
Health record, C11
    personal, D63
Health-related fitness,
    C28–C29
    tests to measure, C34–C35
Hearing
    caring for ears and,
        C14–C15
    problems, C17
    protecting your, E39, *E40*,
        E41
Hearing aid, C17, *C17*
Hearing loss, C16, C17
    noise pollution and, E40
    in students, E40
Heart, *B5*, B12, *B12*
    alcohol use and, *D31*
    artificial, E28
    cardiovascular diseases of,
        D66–D67, D68

stress and, *A24*
tobacco use and, *D22*
Heart attack, D66
    first aid for, D68
    symptoms of, D68
Heart disease, D63
    cardiovascular diseases,
        D66–D67, D68
    deaths from, age 10–14,
        E38
Heart rate
    resting, C36
    target, C36
Heat exhaustion, C70
Heatstroke, C70
Height, measuring, C11
Helmets, wearing, C39
Help, asking for
    for alcohol and drug abuse,
        D19
    to break harmful habit, A15
    in emergency, C75
    for person abusing drugs,
        D16–D17
    to resist pressure, A69
    violence or abuse and, C58,
        C59
Helper T cells, D58, *D58*
Helping others
    with noncommunicable dis-
        ease, D68–D69
    volunteering and, E26–E27
Hemp, D45
Hepatitis, D54, D60
Hepatitis B, D57
Heredity, A5, B27, *B27*
    alcoholism and, D35
    body type and, B63
    defined, A5
    personality and, A11
Heroin, D44
Herpes, genital, A65, D57
High blood pressure, D67
    salt intake and, B41
Hiking, E73
    planning for hiking trip,
        C41
    safety, C65, *C65*
Hinge joint, B6, *B6*
HIV. *See* Human immunodefi-
    ciency virus (HIV)
HMOs. *See* Health mainte-
    nance organizations
    (HMOs)
Hobbies
    developing, E46
    drug-free lifestyle and, D18,
        D18
Home
    energy conservation at, E70,
        E71

reducing air pollution in,
    E54
safety in, C64, C66–C67
social-emotional environ-
    ment at, E37
water conservation at, E62
Homicide, C49
Honesty, A14
    constructive self-criticisms,
        E47
    in information about illegal
        drugs, D39
Hormones, B18
    emotional and intellectual
        changes and, B22
    insulin, D71
    physical changes of adoles-
        cence and, B20–B21
    stress and, A24
    synthetic, B20
Hospice, D69
Hospitals, E23
Hot weather, safety precau-
    tions in, C40, C70, *C70*
Household chemicals, E66
    diffusion of fumes from,
        E54
    indoor air pollution from,
        E52
    inhalants among, D40
    proper storage and disposal
        of, E61
    reducing use of, *E61*
Household pollutants, E58
Human immunodeficiency
    virus (HIV), A64, D58,
    D58
    abstinence to avoid, A65
    accessing valid information
        about, D76–D77
    drug abuse and, D13
    infection and treatment,
        D58
    protecting self from,
        D60–D61
    spread of, D44, D59
Humus, E69
Hurricanes, C72
Hydrogenated, B47
Hypothermia, C71

I

Ice, in PRICE treatment, C43
Ice (amphetamine), D42
Ideas, sharing, A41, *A41*
Illegal drugs, D10, D38–D45
    anabolic steroids, D41, *D41*
    defined, D39
    depressants, D43
    hallucinogens, D45, *D45*
    inhalants, D40

marijuana, D21, D39
narcotics, D44
stimulants, D42
Illegal dumping, water pollu-
    tion from, E58
Illness, changes in family due
    to, A50. *See also* Disease(s)
I-messages, A42, A45, A47,
    A49
    to resolve conflict, C53, *C53*,
        C61
Immune system, D52
    defenses against pathogens,
        D52–D53, *D53*
    HIV and, D58, *D58*
    marijuana and, D45
Immunity, D53
Incinerators, E66
Incisors, C21, *C21*
Income, education level and,
    B31
Indirect contact, pathogens
    spread by, D51
Indoor air pollution, E52
    ways to reduce, E54
Industrial wastes, E66
Infancy, B17
Infant
    chest thrust on choking,
        C79
    CPR for, C81
Infections
    ear and eye, C17
    respiratory, D23
    secondhand smoke and,
        D25
Infertility, sexually transmit-
    ted diseases and, A65
Influences. *See also* Life Skills
    Activity
    on consumer choices, E17
    on health, analyzing, A13,
        A13
Influenza (flu), D54
Information
    accessing valid health,
        A8–A9
    finding reliable, E12–E15
    misleading, taking action
        over, A8
Ingredients on food label, B55
Inhalants, D40
Inhaled medicines, D6
Inhaler, D72
Inherited disease, D63
Injection of drugs, D6
Injuries. *See also* First aid
    from abuse, C51
    accidents, C63
    checking injured person,
        C76, C77

Index

eye, C17
healthful weight and reducing risk of, B59
medicines for, D5
outdoors, C40–C41
during physical activity, preventing, C39–C41, *C40*
preventing, C47
to teeth, preventing, C23
treating, C42–C43
unintentional, C63, *C63*, C64, C65, D13, E38
Inner ear, *C14*
Insect bite, pathogens spread by, D51
Insect repellant, wearing, C40
Inside Story, A3, A33, B3, B35, C3, C47, D3, D49, E3, E33
Insulin, D71
Insurance, health, E23, E25
Integumentary system, B5
Intellectual changes in adolescence, B22
Intense use of drug, D14
Intensity of exercise, C34
Interests
drug-free lifestyle and exploring, D18
friends with similar, A56, *A59*
influence on physical activities, C30
Internet
health information on, E14–E15
search on, A8
Intervention, D17
Intestines, B14–B15, *B15*
stress and, *A24*
Involuntary muscles, B7
Iris, *C12*
Iron, B48

J

Jingles, advertising, E20
Joint, B6
dislocation of bone at, C42
sprain at, C42, C84
Joint-custody family, A50

K

Kayaking, E73
Kidney, B15, *B15*
Kitchen, safety in, C63
Knives, using, C63

L

Labels
drug, D8, *D8*, D9, *D9*
food, B47, B51–B53, *B51*, *B52*, B54, B55

household products, disposal guidelines on, E61
tobacco, *D21*
Labor and delivery, B29
Landfill, E66, *E66*
saving space in, E68, E69
Land pollution, E66–E67
Large intestine, B15, *B15*
Laser technology, E29
Lashley, Tyrell, C73
Late childhood, B17
Laws
for clean air, E55
drug, D44
illegal drug use, D38–D45
Lead
indoor air pollution from, E52
in smokeless tobacco, D24
Lean tissue, C28
Learning
self-directed, A9
service, E27
Learning Life Skills
access valid health information, products, and services, D76–D77
analyze what influences your health, B56–B57
be a health advocate, C18–C19
make responsible decisions, E10–E11
manage stress, B24–B25
practice healthful behaviors, E42–E43
resolve conflicts, C60–C61
set health goals, A16–A17
use communication skills, A46–A47
use resistance skills, D28–D29
Left turn hand signal, C65
Lens, *C12*
Lice, C8
pubic, D57
Lie detector test, A23
Life cycle, B16–B23
stages in, B17, *B17*
Life skills, A6
Life Skills Activity
access valid health information, products, and services, A49, B53, C13, C16, E19
analyze what influences your health, A13, C31, C51, D26, D59, E25, E53
be a health advocate, A39, B19, B66, C81, D61, D75, E39, E61, E67

make responsible decisions, A20, A59, B14, B48, C23, C41, C67, D10
manage stress, C77, D15
practice healthful behaviors, B8, B39, B61, C7, D55, E77
resolve conflicts, A45, E49
set health goals, A7, A27, A51, B13, B45, C9, C37, C58, C71, D37, D41, D66, E8, E63, E70
use communication skills, B23, D65
use resistance skills, A61, A69, B30, E14
Lifestyle, A5
dietary needs and, B49
disease caused by, D63
drug-free, D18–D19
healthful weight and lifestyle choices, B63
physically active, C30
Lightning, C69
Limit, A66–A67
Liquid, drugs dissolved in, D6
Listening, active, A45, A47
Literacy, health, A9
Littering, E39, E67
Liver, alcohol use and, *D31*
Living space, pleasing, E76–E77
Local government, role in health care, E24, E25
Local opportunities for volunteering, E27
Local parks, E74
Locks, safety at home with, C66, *C66*
Loneliness, E45
shopping addiction and, E8
ways to reduce, E46–E47
Loud noises, C17, E40–E41
Love, A49, A50, A71
Low birth weight, A65
Loyalty, as quality of good friend, A58
LSD, D45
Lung cancer, D25, E51, E52
Lungs, B11, *B11*
cilia in, D23
tobacco use and, *D22*, *D23*
Lyme disease, D54
Lymphatic system, D64

M

Magnetic resonance imaging (MRI) scans, E29
Make a Difference Activity
banning smoking in public places, B12

brainstorming for the greater good, A42
dealing with violence, C58–C59
helping in disaster, C73
helping others, E26
maintaining drug-free lifestyle, D36
Males, body changes during puberty, B20
Malnutrition, B46
Malocclusion, C25
March of Dimes, E26
Marijuana, D21, D39
Marriage
abstinence before, A64
teen parenting and, B31
Mask, wearing protective, B11
Math Link, A65, B8, B55, B60, C16, C30, C36, C82, D9, E6, E23, E38
Meats, B41
Media
drug abuse and, D14, *D14*
as valid health information source, E13
Media influence, E18
on body image, B65, *B67*, B68
on health behaviors, D59
Media literacy, E18–E19
Mediation, A38, A39
Mediator, C53
Medicaid, E24
Medical checkups, regular
for endocrine health, B19
physical examination, C11, *C11*, C34, C39
Medical alert jewelry, D75
Medical technician, E28
Medical technology, advances in, E28–E29
Medical wastes, E66
Medicare, E24
Medicines, D3, D4–D11. *See also* Drug(s); Drug abuse
effect on body, D7
entry into body, D6, *D6*
misuse and abuse of, D10–D11
safe use of, D8–D9
ways drugs are used as, D5
Melanin, B5, *C6*
Menstrual cycle, B20, B21, *B21*
Menstrual period, B21
Mental and emotional health, A5, *A5*. *See also* Emotions
character and personality, A10–A15
grooming and, C5

Index

physical activity and, C27
responsible decision-making, A18–A21
Mentor, developing relationship with, E47
Mentoring programs, C59
Menu, choosing foods from, B43
Mercury poisoning, E59
Mescaline, D45
Mesomorph, B63
Metastasis, D64
Microbiology, D53
Microwave safety demonstration, C63
Middle childhood, B17
Middle ear, *C14*
Middle ear infection, C17
Milk and milk products, food intolerance to, B54
Minerals (nonrenewable resource), E65
Minerals (nutrient), B37
Minor wounds, C82
Mode of exercise, C34
Molars, C21, *C21*
Mold, indoor air pollution from, E52
Money management, E6–E7, E8
  for physical activities, C33
  saving, E6, E7, *E7*
Mononucleosis, D54
Mood
  alcohol and, D33, D34
  effect of drug and, D7
Mood swings in adolescence, B22, *B22*
Morphine, D44
Mothers, teen, B31. *See also* Marriage; Pregnancy
Motor neurons, B9
Motor skills, alcohol's effect on, D32
Motor vehicles
  driving under the influence, D32
  limiting car rides, E54
  safety in, C65
Mountain biking, E73
Mouth
  drugs taken by, D6
  tobacco use and, *D22*
Mouth guard, using, C23
Movies
  choosing healthful, A67, *A67*
  influence on decisions about sex, A66
  relationships in, influence of, C51

Moving natural disasters, C72–C73
MRI. *See* Magnetic resonance imaging (MRI) scans
Mucous membranes
  as defense against pathogens, D52
  drugs absorbed through, D6
Murals, C58
  career, E28
Muscle(s), B6
  physical activity and, C27
  stress and, *A24*
  types of, B7
Muscle soreness, C42
Muscular endurance, C28
  exercise for, C29
  tests of, C34, C35
Muscular strength, C28
  anabolic steroids and, D41
  exercise for, C29
  tests of, C34, C35
Muscular system, B6, B7, *B7*
  circulatory system interaction with, B13
  nervous system interaction with, B9
Music
  headphones to listen to, C15, E41, E42–E43
  volume of, C14, C15
Music Link, A36, C14, E20, E47
Myelin, inhalants' effect on, D40
Myopia, C16

N

Nails, B5, C8
  caring for, C9, *C9*
Narcotics, D44
Narcotics Anonymous, D19
National Academy of Sciences, B8
National Center for Victims of Crime, C58
National Park System, E74, E75
National Safety Council, E52
Natural disasters, C69
  moving, C72–C73
  safety in, C71, C72–C73
Natural resources. *See* Resources
Nature preserves, E74
Nearness, friends due to, A56
Nearsightedness, C16
Needles, pathogens spread by, D51
  HIV, D59

Negative peer pressure, A35
  resisting, A20–A21, A43, A60–A61
  violence and, C49
Negative self-esteem, A12
Negative social-emotional environment, E45
  coping with, E48–E49
Neglect, A52, C50
Negotiate, A38, *A39*
Nerves, B8, *B9*
Nervous system, B8–B9, *B9*
  circulatory system interaction with, B13
  inhalants' effect on, D40
Neurologist, E28
Neurons, B8, B9
Neurotransmitters, A29
New-generation stimulants, D42
Nicotine, D21, D22
  in smokeless tobacco, D24
9-1-1, calling, C52, C55, C64, C75
Noise, E38
  protection from loud, C15, E39, E41
Noise levels, C14
  common, in decibels, *C15*
Noise pollution, C17, E40–E41
Noncommunicable diseases, D62–D69. *See also* Cancer, Diabetes
  cardiovascular diseases, D66–D67, D68
  factors causing, D63
  helping person with, D68–D69
  terminal illness, D69
Nonrenewable resources, E65
Nonverbal communication, A44–A45, *A44*
Nosebleeds, first aid for, C82
Nucleus, *B5*
Nutrients, B14, B37, *B37*
  on food labels, B51
Nutrition
  body image and, B64–B69
  choosing foods, B50–B57
  dietary guidelines, B36–B41
  eating habits, healthful, B42–B49
  healthful weight and, B58–B63
Nutrition Facts, B51, *B52*

O

Obesity, B62
Occasional use of drug, D14
  tobacco, D21
Oil glands, *C6*

Ointments, D6
Older people, becoming friends with, *E46*, E47
Oncologist, E28
Online health information, E14–E15, *E15*
On Your Own Activity
  alcohol model, D32
  chart your chores, A19
  community laws about smoking, D24
  comparing shampoos, E21
  energy conservation at home, E70
  eye and ear protection, C15
  finding valid information, A8
  gathering first aid supplies, C85
  harmful/healthful card, making, D43
  interview about drug-free lifestyle, D19
  interview with source of valid information, E13
  listing your qualities, B68
  mediating conflict, A38
  over-the-counter drugs, D8
  promoting positive body image, B65
  radon testing, E52
  safety tour of home, C66
  time line of birth weights and heights, B29
  time management plan, E5
Ophthalmologist, C12
Opiates, D35
Opinions, sharing, A41
Opium, D44
Opposite sex friendships, A63
Optic nerve, *C12*
Optimal health, D74
Optometrist, C12
Organic foods and products, E71
Organism, B5
Organs, B5, *B5*
Organ systems, B5. *See also* Body systems
Orthodontist, C25
Osteoporosis, B46
OTC drugs. *See* Over-the-counter (OTC) drug
Other-centered, being, A65
Outdoor environment, E72–E75
  activities in, E73, *E73*
  places to enjoy, E74–E75, *E74*
  respecting, E75, *E75*
  water conservation in, E63, *E63*

INDEX

Index

Outdoor safety, C40–C41, C65, *C65*
Outer ear, *C14*
Ovaries, B20, B21, *B21*
Over-the-counter (OTC) drug, D5, D8, *D8*
Overweight, B61
Oxygen
　breathing, B3
　plants and production of, E51
Ozone layer, E53

Ⓟ

Packaging, buying products with less, E54
Pain
　muscle soreness, C42
　narcotics to relieve, D44
　stopping physical activity and, C39
Pancreas, *B18*, B19
Parenthood
　being other-centered in, A65
　teen parenting, A68, B31
　teen pregnancy and, A33
Parents and guardians. *See also* Family(ies)
　abuse, C50
　alcohol use and relationship with, D33
　choosing friends and, A57, A58
　choosing healthful entertainment, A67, *A67*
　drug abuse and rebellion against, D14
　emotional environment and, E36
　expectations of, living up to, A63, A64, *A65*
　gun safety at home and, C66
　influence on body image, B65
　influence on physical activities, C30–C31
　letting them know where you are, C55, *C55*
　managing chronic illness with help of, D74
　permission for ear piercing, D60, *D60*
　permission to buy products online, E15
　permission to go online, E14
　permission to volunteer, E26
　relationship with, A35
　setting limits with, A66, *A66*
　social environment and, E36

Parks, E74
　rules in, E75
Partially hydrogenated, B47
Partial seizures, D71
Partners for physical activities, C33
Pathogens, D51. *See also* Communicable diseases
　entry into body, D51
　foodborne illness and, C63
　in sewage, E58
　sexually transmitted, D57
　types of, D51
　universal precautions to avoid contact with, C76–C77
PCP, D45
Peanuts, food allergy to, B54, *B54*, B55
Peer pressure, A20
　in adolescence, B23
　alcohol and giving in to harmful, D32
　loneliness and, E45
　negative, A20–A21, A35, A43, A60–A61, C49
　positive, A39
　resisting, A20–A21, A43, A60–A61, D26–D29
　to use tobacco, D26–D29
Peers
　at camp, E46
　drug abuse and, D14
Pen pals, E46
Pentagon, September 11, 2001, attack on, C73
Percent Daily Value, B51
Periodontal disease, C25
Personal health care
　checkups, C10–C19
　for ears, C14–C15
　eye and ear problems, C16–C17
　for eyes, C12–C13, *C12, C13*
　grooming, C5–C9, *C5*
　hair care, C8, *C8*
　nail care, C9, *C9*
　physical examinations, C11, *C11*
　skin care, C6–C7, *C7*
　for teeth, C20–C25
Personal health record, D63
Personality, A11. *See also* Character
Perspiration, C5, C7
　stress and, *A24*
Pesticides
　organic foods without, E71
　reducing use of, E61
　washing foods to remove, C63

Pets
　effect on health, A14
　stress management with, A26
Pharmacist, D8, D9
Physical abuse, C50
Physical activity, C26–C43
　benefits of, C27, *C30*
　dietary needs and, B49, *B49*
　factors affecting choice of, C30–C31, *C31*
　fitness and, B40
　health-related fitness from, C28–C29
　low-cost, E7
　maintaining healthful weight and, B61
　outdoor, E73, *E73*
　physical fitness plan and, C32–C37
　preventing injuries during, C39–C41, *C42*
　resources, C33
　safety in, C38–C43
　stress management with, A26, A27
　treating injuries, C42–C43, *C43*
　trends in, C3
Physical addiction to tobacco, D21
Physical changes of adolescence, B20–B21
Physical dependence, D11, D35
Physical Education Link, C33, C41, C65, D34
Physical environment, E33, E35, E38–E39, *E38. See also* Air; Land pollution; Noise; Water; Weather
　improving, E39, *E39*
　parts of, E38
Physical examination, C11, *C11*
　to assess fitness, C34
　before starting exercise program, C39
Physical fitness plan, C32–C37
　developing, C36–C37
　physical activity resources and, C33
　tests to measure level of fitness, C34–C35, *C34, C35*
Physical growth, life cycle and, B17
Physical health, A5, *A5*
　drug addiction and, D15
　physical activity and, C27

Physicians, E28
　allergist, D73
　dermatologist, C7
　ophthalmologist, C12
　referral services to find, E23
　as sources of valid health information, E13
Pinkeye, C17
Pituitary gland, B18, *B18*
　during adolescence, B21
Pivot joint, B6, *B6*
Plan, to break harmful habit, A15
Plants
　oxygen produced by, E51
　respecting outdoors and, E75
　watering, E63, *E63*
Plaque
　inside artery walls, buildup of, D67
　dental, C22, C23, C24, *C24,* C25
Plasma, B12
Platelets, B12
Poisoning
　in food chain, water pollution and, E59
　preventing, C64
Police
　calling, C52
　safety in communities and, C59
Polio vaccine, E28
Pollen, as allergen, *D73*
Pollutants
　air, B11, E51, E52
　household, E58
　water, E57, E61
Pollution, E51
　air, E51–E55, *E51*, E58, E73
　land, E66–E67
　noise, C17, E40–E41
　water, E57, E58–E61
Polonium-210, D24
Positive attitude, E48
Positive body image, developing, B68–B69, *B68, B69*
Positive peer pressure, A39
Positive self-esteem, A12, *A12*
Positive social-emotional environment, E45, *E45*
Posture, A44, B11
Pot. *See* Marijuana
Power, C33
Power plants, "clean coal" methods in, E55
Precycling, E69, E70
Pregnancy, B28–B31
　abstinence to avoid, A65
　alcohol during, avoiding, B29, B30, D35

Index

defined, *A65*
developing baby, *B28*
fetal alcohol syndrome and, D35
HIV spread during, D59
labor and delivery, B29
prenatal care in, B29
teen, A33, A65, B30–B31
Prejudice, C49
violence and, C49
Premature birth, B29
Premolars, C21, *C21*
Prenatal care, B29, B30
Prescription drug, D5, *D5*, D9, *D9*
evaluating product, E21
President's Challenge, C34–C35, C36
Pressure, resisting, A68–A69. *See also* Peer pressure
Pressure points, C83
PRICE treatment, C42, C43, *C43*
for sprains, C84
Printed materials, valid health information from, E13
Priority, A19
Private organizations, valid health information from, E13
Problems, taking control of, E49
Producers, E59
Products
accessing valid health, A8–A9
advertising to sell, E18–E19
biodegradable, E67
dissatisfaction with, A8
evaluating health care, E20–E21
with less packaging, buying, E54
reusing, E54, E69
Professional organizations, valid health information from, E13
Protective eyewear, C13
Protective factors, C55, C56
Proteins, B37
at breakfast, B44
Protozoa, D51
Providers, health care, E23
getting information on, C16
HMO, E25
Psychological addiction to tobacco, D21
Psychological dependence, D11, D35
Puberty, B21
body changes and need for grooming in, C5

changes in eyes during, C16
emotional and intellectual changes in, B22
physical changes in, B20
stress from changes in, B24–B25
Pubic hair, B20
Pubic lice, D57
Public health, E29
Public water supplies, E60
Pull-ups, C35
Pulmonary artery, *B12*
Pulmonary veins, *B12*
Pulp of tooth, C21, *C21*
Puncture wounds, first aid for, C82
Pupil (eye), *C12*
Purging, B67
Pus, C42

Q

Quackery, E20–E21, *E20*

R

Racial and ethnic groups, chronic health conditions in certain, D74
Radiation treatment, D65
Radioactive wastes, E66
Radiologist, E28
Radon, E52, E54
Rain, acid. *See* Acid rain
Rain forests, depletion of, E55
Random events, A5
Rape, C49, C50
Raw foods, preparing and storing, B53
Reaction time, C33
Recessive gene, B27
Recycling, E68, *E68*, E70
use of recycled materials, *E71*
Red blood cells, B12, B13
Red bone marrow, B13
Reflex action, B8
Reflex checker, *C11*
Relationships, A34–A39. *See also* Family(ies); Friends
alcohol's effect on, D13, *D13*, D33, *D33*
dating, A63
defined, A35
ending, A37, A59
harmful, A35, A37, A59
health and, E45
healthful, A35, A36–A37, *A37*
improving social environment by developing, E46–E47

in movies and TV, influence of, C51
steps to improve, A37
Relationship Scale, The, A36, A37
Relaxing, reducing stress and, A25
Reliable, A58
Reliable health information, finding, E12–E15
online, E14–E15
sources, E13
Remarriage, A52
Renewable resources, E65, *E65*
Reporting
abuse, C51, C58
facts, A41
sexual harassment, C56
Reproductive glands, *B18*, B19, B21
Reproductive system, B27
Reputation, A64
Rescue breathing, C80
for shock, C83
Research, to evaluate health care products, E20
Resilient, E48–E49
Resistance skills, A21. *See also* Life Skills Activity
abstinence and using, A68–A69, B30
online, E14
to resist pressure to drink alcohol, D36–D37, *D37*
to resist pressure to use tobacco, A61, D27, D28–D29
using, A61
Resources, E64–E71
conserving, E70–E71
energy, E65
help for drug-related issues, D19
land, E66–E67
nonrenewable, E65
renewable, E65
waste disposal and, E66–E69
Respect, A14, A37
abstinence and, A64
accepting differences and, B62
character trait, A14
drug-free lifestyle and, D18
keeping friends that others respect, A59
for new student in school, E37
for outdoors, E75, *E75*
relationships and, A37
self-respect, A64

Respiratory infections, tobacco use and, D23
Respiratory system, B11, *B11*
circulatory system interaction with, B13
Responsibility
character trait, A14, *A15*
shared, in family, *A49*
Responsibility, taking
getting help for person abusing drugs, D16, D17
for health, A6–A7, *A6*
role playing, A15
Responsible citizenship, A9, A14, C76, E18, E62
Responsible decisions, making, A18–A21, E10–E11. *See also* Life Skills Activity
about abstinence, A67
alcohol use and ability to make, D32, *D32*
choosing responsible friends, A57, *A57*, A59
about drugs, D10
method of, A19
resisting negative peer pressure, A20–A21
selecting restaurant, B48
Rest, benefits of, A26, C5
Resting heart rate, C36
Retina, *C12*
Reusing products, E54, E69
Right turn hand signal, C65
Risk, C63
Risk behaviors, A7
in adolescence, B23
alcohol and, D33
avoiding, E47
friends engaging in, A59
resisting negative peer pressure for, A60–A61, *A60*
Rock climbing, E73
Role-play
taking responsibility, A15
using resistance skills, A69
Running, E73
Runoff, water pollution from, E58, E61

S

Sadness, grief and, *A28*, A29, A50
Safety, C54–C59
biking, C40, C65
in community, C55, C59
finding help, C58, *C59*
food, B35, B40, B41, B53
in home, C64, C66–C67
in kitchen, C63
in natural disasters, C71, C72–C73

outdoor, C40–C41, C65, *C65*
during physical activity, C38–C43
physical environment and, E38
promoting, C59
in school, C56–C57, *C56*, C59
in severe weather, C68–C72
water, C65
from weapons, C55
when using computer, E14–E15
Safety equipment, C40
wearing, *A21*, C39
Salary, education level and, B31
Saliva, B14
Salivary glands, B14, *B15*
Salt, B41, B49
reducing intake, B47
Saturated fats, B41, B47, D67
SAVE. *See* Students Against Violence Everywhere (SAVE)
Saving money, E6, E7, *E7*
Savings account, E7
Schedule, E5
School
abuse and performance in, C51
energy conservation at, E71
safety in, C56–C57, *C56*, C59
social-emotional environment at, E37
water conservation at, E62
School nurse, managing chronic illness with help of, D74
School shootings, C56
Science Link, A23, A28, A41, B5, B27, B40, B51, C6, C12, C70, D23, D40, D52, D67, D74, E35, E54, E59
Sclera, *C12*
Scrape, C42, C43
Sealants, C24
Seat belts, using, C23
Secondary sex characteristics, B20, B21
Second-degree burn, C85
Secondhand smoke, D25
asthma and, D23
indoor air pollution from, E52
Seizures, epilepsy and, D71
Self, abdominal thrust on, C79
Self-assessment, A11
Self-concept, A11
Self-directed learning, A9

Self-esteem, A12–A13
drug abuse and negative, D14
emotional abuse and, C50
grooming and, C5, *C5*
healthful weight and positive, B59
physical activity and, C27
setting health goals for, A16–A17
social-emotional environment and, E36
sports and, E36
violence and negative, C49
visual environment and, E76
Self-protection, C55
Self-respect, A64
abstinence and, A64
grooming and, C5
Self-statements, E47
body image and, B68
Semicircular canals, *C14*
Separation, A50
September 11, 2001, disaster services on, C73
Service learning, E27
Services
accessing valid health, A8–A9
dissatisfaction with, A8
trading, E7
Servings of food, B39
Sewage, water pollution, E58
Sexual abuse, C50
Sexual activity, A33
abstinence from, A7, A62–A69, B31
alcohol and, A66, D33
and the law, A64
risks of early, B31
Sexual harassment, C49, C50
in school, C56
Sexually transmitted diseases (STDs), A64, D56–D61
abstinence to avoid, A65
common, D57
defined, D57
HIV and AIDS, A64, D58–D61
preventing, D60–D61
Shampoos, C8, E21
Sharing ideas, opinions, and decisions, A41, *A41*
Sharing living space, E77, *E77*
Shellfish, food allergy to, B54, *B54*
SHINE, C58
Shock, C83
burns and, C85
first aid for, C83, *C83*

Shoes, athletic, C41, *C41*
Shopper, becoming smart, E18–E19, *E18*
Shopping addiction, E8
Shower head, low-flow, E62
Shuttle run, C34, *C34*
Sick building syndrome (SBS), E52
Sickle cell anemia, D74
Side effects, drug, D7
of anabolic steroids, D41
of cocaine, D42
Sidestream smoke, D25
Single-custody family, A50
Single-parent family, A50
Sit and reach exercise, C35
Situational use of drug, D14
Skating, safety while, C65
Skeletal system, B6–B7, *B6*
circulatory system interaction with, B13
nervous system interaction with, B9
Skill-related fitness, C33
Skin, B5, C6, *C6*
care for, C6–C7, *C7*
as defense against pathogens, D52
drugs absorbed through, D6
scrape on, C42, C43
tobacco use and, *D22*
Skin cancer, E53
Skin conditions, C7
Skin graft, C6
Sleep, benefits of, A26, C5
Small intestine, B14, *B15*
Small talk, using, A41
Smog, E51
worldwide concerns about, E52
Smoke alarm, C64
Smokeless tobacco, D24
Smoking. *See also* Tobacco
avoiding, B11, B13, B19, B29, B30, E54
banned in public places, B12, D25, *D25*
costs of, D22
by friends, influence on health of, E53
marijuana and hashish, D45
during pregnancy, effects of on unborn child, B29, B30, D21
resistance skills to avoid, A61, D27, D28–D29
secondhand smoke from, D23, D25, E52
Smooth muscles, B7
Snacking habits, B44–B45, *B45*, B49

Snowstorm, C69
Snuff, D24
Soap product, evaluating, E21
Social changes in adolescence, B23
Social-emotional environment, E36–E37, E44–E49
health and, E45
improving, E46–E47
negative, E45, E48–E49
parts of, E37
positive, E45, *E45*
Social environment, E35, E36
Social health, grooming and, C5
Social skills
alcohol and, D33
dating and, A63
Social Studies Link, B31, B49, C52, D58, E27, E66, E74
Society, drug abuse effects on, D13
Sodium, B41. *See also* Salt
Solar energy, E65
Solid waste, E66
composting, E69, *E69*
littering, E39, E67
precycling, E69, E70
recycling, E68, *E68*, E70
Sound(s)
decibel level, C14, E41, *E41*
noise pollution, C17, E40–E41
Specialists, E23
Special needs, people with
protecting rights of, E25
services for, E24
Speed, C33
Sperm cells, B21, B27
Spinal cord, B8, *B9*
Spinal cord injury, C83
Spine, B8
Sports
dietary needs for, B49
drug-free lifestyle and, D18, *D18*
ecosports, E73
self-esteem and, E36
Sports equipment, C41
Spouse abuse, C50
Sprains, C42, C84
Sprays (drug), D6
SSDS. *See* Sudden sniffing death syndrome (SSDS)
Starches, B37
State government, role in health care, E24
State parks, E74
STDs. *See* Sexually transmitted diseases (STDs)

Index

Stealing, C49

Sterility, sexually transmitted diseases causing, D57

Steroids, anabolic, D41, *D41*

Stethoscope, C11, *C11*

Stimulants, D42

Stirrup (ear), *C14*

Stitches for deep cut, C42

Stomach, B14, *B15*
  alcohol use and, *D31*
  stress and, *A24*
  tobacco use and, *D22*

Stomach acid, as defense against pathogens, D52

Stop hand signal, C65

Stop Tobacco in Restaurants (STIR) campaign, B12

Storms, safety in, C69

Strangers, dealing with, C52
  avoiding danger at home, C66

Street smart, C55

Strep throat, D54

Stress, A3, A23, *A23*, A24–A27
  causes and signs of, A24–A25, *A24*
  from changes in puberty, B24–B25
  drug abuse and, D15
  in emergency, dealing with, C77
  keeping low, B13
  managing, A24, A26–A27, D15, *D15*, E48
  negative, A24, A35
  noise pollution and, E40
  physical activity and, C27
  positive, A24, A35
  reducing, A25, C27, E5, *E5*
  time management plan and, E5, *E5*
  violence and, C49
  visual environment and, E76

Stress management skills, A26–A27

Stressor, A24, A25

Striated (striped) muscles, B7

Stroke, D67
  first aid for, D68
  warning signs of, D68

Students Against Destructive Decisions (SADD), D19

Students Against Violence Everywhere (SAVE), A42

Sub-Saharan Africa, HIV/AIDS in, D58

Sucrose, B47

Sudden sniffing death syndrome (SSDS), D40

Suffocation, preventing, C64

Sugar, B37, B41
  reducing intake of, B47
  tooth decay and, C23, C24

Suicide, C49
  alcohol and, D33
  barbiturates and risk of, D43
  drug addiction and, D15
  warning signs of, C52

Sun exposure, protection from, D64

Sunglasses, wearing, C13, *C13*, C40

Sun protection factor (SPF), C6, C40, D64

Sunscreen
  evaluating product, E21
  wearing, C6, *C7*, C40, D64, *D64*

Support and control systems, B4–B9
  cells, tissues, organs, B5, *B5*
  integumentary system, B5
  muscular system, B6, B7, *B7*
  nervous system, B8–B9, *B9*
  skeletal system, B6–B7, *B6*

Support for people with non-communicable disease, D68–D69. *See also* Caring; Social-emotional environment

Support groups, E14
  for chronic health conditions, D75
  online, E14

Surface water, cleanup programs aimed at, E60, *E60*

Surgery for cancer treatment, D65

Sweat glands, *C6*, C7

Swimming, E73
  care of ears after, C15
  floating, C65
  water safety, C65

Sympathetic, A58

Symptoms, C11, D55
  medicines to treat, D5

Synthetic hormones, B20

Syphilis, D57

T

Talking
  to manage anger, C53
  stress management with, A25, A26

Tanning booths, avoiding, C6, D64

Tar (in marijuana smoke), D45

Tar (in tobacco smoke), D21

Target heart rate, C36

Tattooing, D60

Tay-Sachs disease, D74

T cells, helper, D58, *D58*

Teachers
  emotional environment and, E36
  social environment and, E36

Teamwork, C27

Technology
  cell phones, A41
  medical, advances in, E28–E29, *E28*

Teen parenthood, A68, B31

Teen pregnancy, A33, A65, B30–B31, D33

Teeth, C20–C25
  caring for, C22–C23, *C22*
  problems, preventing and treating, C24–C25, *C24*
  structure of, C21, *C21*
  tobacco use and, *D22*

Telephone communication, A57

Television
  choosing healthful, A67, *A67*
  guidelines for using, E77
  influence on decisions about sex, A66
  relationships on, influence of, C51
  time spent watching, A6, E9

Temperature
  changes during day, C70
  in refrigerator, C63

Temperature, body
  fever, C11, D52
  taking, C11
  weather extremes and, C70, C71

Tendon, B7

Terminal illness, D69

Testes, B20, B21

Testosterone, B20

Tetanus, C82

THC, D45

Thermometer, *C11*

Third-degree burn, C85

Throat, tobacco use and, *D22*

Thyroid, *B18*, B19

Time for physical activity, C33

Time management plan, E5, *E5*, E8
  advantages of saving time, E6
  reducing stress and, A25
  stress management with, A26, *A26*

Tinnitus, E40

Tissues, B5, *B5*

Tobacco, D10, D20–D29
  addiction to, D14, D21
  avoiding, B11, B13, B19, B29, B30, D64, E47, E54
  diseases linked to, D23, D63
  effects on body, D22–D23, *D22*
  resisting pressure to use, A61, D26–D29, *D27*
  secondhand smoke from, D23, D25, E52
  smokeless, D24

Tolerance, drug, D7, D11
  barbiturates, D43
  stimulants, D42
  tobacco, D21

Tooth decay, C24, *C24*
  preventing, C23

Tooth-whitening products, C21

Tornadoes, C72, *C72*

Trachea, B11, *B11*

Traditional family, A50

Traffic
  biking safety in, C65
  outdoor safety and, C40

Traits
  of good character, A14–A15
  inheritance of, B27
  personality, A11

Tranquilizers, D43

Trans-fatty acids (trans fats), B47, B52, D67

Transport systems, B10–B15
  circulatory system, B12–B13, *B12*
  digestive system, B14–B15, *B15*
  respiratory system, B11, *B11*
  urinary system, B15, *B15*

Trash. *See* Wastes

Trauma, resiliency and overcoming, E48

Trees
  planting, E54
  as renewable resource, E65

Trust, social-emotional environment and, E45

Tuberculosis, D54

Tumors, D64

Type 1 diabetes, D71, *D71*

Type 2 diabetes, D71

U

Ultraviolet (UV) radiation
  ozone layer and, E53
  protection from, C13

Umbilical cord, B28

Underweight, B60

Index

Unintentional injuries
  deaths from, age 10-14, E38
  drug abuse and, D13
  in home, C64
  in kitchen, C63, *C63*
  outdoors, C65
United States, HIV/AIDS in, D58
United States Department of Agriculture, B40
U.S. Drug Enforcement Administration (DEA), D44
United States Food and Drug Administration (FDA), D5, D11, E21
Unit price, B52
Universal precautions, C76–C77, D60–D61
Urethra, B15, *B15*
Urinary bladder, B15, *B15, D22*
Urinary system, B15, *B15*
Urine, B15
Uterus, B21, B27
  fetus in, B28

 V

Vacation, food safety on, B35
Vaccination programs, E24
Vaccines, D5, D53, E28
Valid health information, products, and services. *See also* Life Skills Activity
  accessing, A8–A9
  finding, E13
  sources of, E13, E15
Valid information, E13
Values, A11
  basing decisions on, E48
  friends with similar, A56
Vegetables. *See* Fruits and vegetables
Vein, B12
Verbal communication, A41, *A41*
  developing skills at, A43
  rules for, A43, *A43*
Video games, playing, E10–E11
Violence, A52, C48–C59
  abuse, C50–C51
  alcohol use and, C49, D32, D33
  causes of, C49
  defined, C49
  domestic, C49

family, A52–A53, C49
forms of, C49
preventing, C52–C53
safety in community and, C55
safety in school and, C56–C57
steps to deal with, C58–C59
Viruses, D49, D51
  common communicable diseases caused by, D54
  sexually transmitted diseases caused by, D57
Vision
  caring for eyes, C12–C13, *C12, C13*
  problems, C16–C17
Visual environment, E76–E77
Vitamin C
  for healthy gums, C23
  tobacco use and, D23
Vitamin D, for strong teeth, C23
Vitamins, B37
  evaluating product, E21
Voluntary health organizations, E26–E27
Voluntary muscles, B7
Volunteer, E26–E27, *E26*, E37
  drug-free lifestyle and, D18
  personal benefits of, E27, *E27*
V-sit reach exercise, C35, *C35, C36*

 W

Walking, safety while, C65
  being street smart, C55
  outside in dark, C52, *C52*
Warm-up, C37, *C37*, C39, C42
Washing hair, C8
Washing hands
  avoiding communicable diseases by, D55
  kitchen safety and, C63
  as universal precaution, D61
Washing machine, water conservation in, E62, E70, E71
Wastes, E66–E69
  composting, E69, *E69*
  hazardous, E66
  land pollution from, E66–E67
  precycling, E69, E70

recycling, E68, *E68*, E70
  solid, E66, E67
Wastewater, E58
Water, E56–E63
  conserving, E62–E63, *E62, E70*
  daily use of, in U.S., E60
  drinking plenty of, during physical activity, C39, C40
  floating in, demonstrating, C65
  harmful substances in, E38
  need for clean, E57, *E57*
  as nutrient, B37
  as renewable resource, E65
  supplies for emergency, C82
Water cycle, E57
Water pollution, E57, E58–E61
  food chain and, E59, *E59*
  sources of, E58
  stopping, E60–E61
Water safety, C65
Water supply systems, E35
Water treatment, E60
Weapon(s), C49
  avoiding, C52, E39
  at home, C66
  safety from, C55
  school shootings, C56
  violence and, C49
Weather, E38
  extremes of, C70–C71
  outdoor safety and preparing for, C40
  safety in severe, C68–C72
Web site, health information on, E14–E15
Weed. *See* Marijuana
Weight
  blood alcohol concentration and, D34
  drug effects and, D7
  fitness and, B40
  measuring, C11
  physical activity and, C27
Weight, healthful, B58–B63
  body type and, B63
  defined, B59
  determining, B62–B63
  reasons to maintain, B59
  ways to maintain, B49, B60–B61
Weight gain
  during pregnancy, B28
  tips for, B60

Weight loss
  amphetamines and, D42
  tips for, B61
Wellness, A5
West Nile virus, D54, D55
Wetlands, E57
White blood cells, B12, D52
  as defense against pathogens, D52, *D53*
  helper T cells, D58, *D58*
Whiteout, C69
Whole grains, eating, B40, B44
Wildlife refuges, E74
Wind energy, E65
Withdrawal symptoms
  barbiturates and, D43
  narcotics and, D44
Workout. *See* Exercise; Physical activity
Wound, caring for, C82–C83
Write About It!
  dental care around the world, C24
  emergency guidelines, C75
  function flash cards, B14
  healthful eating habits, B46
  history of health care, E24
  living drug-free, D18
  managing chronic illness, D74
  play about friendship, A56
  self-assessment, A11
  showing affection, A67
  sports and self-esteem, E36
Writing
  about negative peer pressure, A60
  stress management with, A26
  about taking responsibility, A53

 X

X chromosome, B27
X rays, E29
  for broken bones, *C84*
  to treat breast cancer, E28

 Y

Y chromosome, B27
Yeast, B40
Yellowstone National Park, E73, E74
You-message, A42

Credits

Cover and title page photography Dot Box for MMH.

Photography iv: Robert Manella. v: Robert Manella. vi: Photodisc Green/Getty Images. vii: t. Ken Karp; b. Single Image. viii: Robert Manella. ix: t. Robert Manella; b. Comstock/Alamy. x: t. Royalty-Free/Corbis; l. Royalty-Free/Corbis; r. Royalty-Free/Corbis. xi: David Young-Wolff/PhotoEdit. xii: Rob & Sas/Corbis. xiii: Ken Karp. A1: b. Ken Karp; b.l. Photodisc Green/Getty Images; b.r. Ken Karp; c.r. Ken Karp; t.l. Ken Karp; t.r. RubberBall Productions/Alamy. A2: b.c. Photodisc; b.l. Photodisc; c.l. David Young-Wolff/PhotoEdit; t.c. Photodisc; t.l. Imagestopshop/Alamy. A3: b.c. Photodisc; b.r. Hunter/StockFood; c. Photodisc; r. Alamy ; t.l. Photodisc; t.r. SuperStock; t.r. Photodisc. A4: Ken Karp. A5: b. Richard Hutchings/PhotoEdit; c. Richard Hutchings/PhotoEdit; t. Dana White/PhotoEdit. A6: Ken Karp. A7: b. Ken Karp; t. Robert Daly/Stone/Getty Images. A8: Tom Stewart/Corbis. A9: b.l. Ken Karp; b.r. Robert Manella; t. Photodisc; t.l. Ken Karp; t.r. Ken Karp. A10: Richard Hutchings/PhotoEdit. A11: Ariel Skelley/Corbis. A12: b. Dana White/PhotoEdit; t. Bill Aron/PhotoEdit. A13: b. Ken Karp; l. Photodisc; r. Photodisc; t. Ron Chapple/Taxi/Getty Images. A14: Rhoda Sidney/PhotoEdit. A15: Felicia Martinez/PhotoEdit. A16: Robert Manella. A18: Ken Karp. A19: Photodisc Green/Getty Images. A20: Dwayne Newton/PhotoEdit. A21: Ken Karp. A22: c. Ken Karp; l. Photodisc; r. Photodisc; t. Photodisc. A23: LWA-Dann Tardif/Corbis. A25: b. Tony Freeman/PhotoEdit; t. Ken Karp. A26: Dale C. Spartas/Corbis. A27: b. Ken Karp; t. Ken Karp. A28: Ken Karp. A29: Ken Karp. A32: b.l. Photodisc; b.l. Photodisc; c. Photodisc; t.l. Radlund and Associates/Brand X/PictureQuest. A33: b.c. Photodisc; b.r. Comstock/Alamy ; t.c. Alamy; t.r. Alamy . A34: Ken Karp. A35: Ken Karp. A37: Robert Manella. A38: Ken Karp. A39: Robert Manella. A40: Robert Manella. A41: b. Ken Karp; t. Photodisc Green/Getty Images. A42: Courtesy of Nickole Evans. A43: Robert Manella. A44: Robert Manella. A45: Robert Manella. A46: b. Robert Manella; t. Robert Manella. A48: Robert Manella. A49: b. Photodisc; t. Ken Karp. A50: Robert Manella. A51: Don Penny/SuperStock. A52: Ken Karp. A53: Ken Karp. A54: Ken Karp. A56: Tony Anderson/Taxi/Getty Images. A57: Robert Manella. A58: Ken Karp. A59: Robert Manella. A60: Robert Manella. A61: Ken Karp. A62: Robert Manella. A63: Ken Karp. A64: Bob Child/AP Wide World. A65: Robert Manella. A66: Mike Brinson/Image Bank/Getty Images. A67: Digital Vision/Getty Images. A68: Ken Karp. A69: Robert Manella. A72: b.r. Photodisc; t.l. Royalty-Free/Corbis; t.r. Image 100/Alamy. B1: t.l. Ken Karp; b. Ken Karp; b.l. Ken Karp; b.r. Ken Karp; c.r. Ken Karp; t.r. Rob & Sas/Corbis. B2: b. Royalty-Free/Corbis; b. Royalty-Free/Corbis; b.c. Photodisc Green/Getty Images; t.c. Photodisc; t.l. Photodisc; t.l. Royalty-Free/Corbis. B3: b. Royalty-Free/Corbis; b.r. Photodisc; c. Thinkstock/Getty Images; c.r. Photodisc/Getty Images. B4: Reuters New Media, Inc./Corbis. B8: Photodisc. B10: Royalty-Free/Corbis. B12: Courtesy of Amit Bushan. B13: Nancy Sheehan/PhotoEdit. B16: Robert Manella. B17: Photodisc. B19: José Luis Pelaez/Corbis. B22: Ken Karp. B22: Ken Karp. B23: Photodisc. B24: b. Robert Manella; t. Ken Karp. B26: DigitalVison/PictureQuest. B27: Royalty-Free/Corbis. B29: Jiang Jin/SuperStock. B30: Ken Karp. B31: Photodisc. B34: b.l.c. PhotoAlto/PictureQuest; c. Jim Scherer/StockFood ; l.l. Photodisc; l.m Photodisc; t.c. John Svoboda/FoodPix; t.c. Foodcollection/StockFood; t.l. PhotoAlto/PictureQuest. B35: b.c.r. Eising Food/StockFood; b.r. Photodisc; c. Newedel-StockFood Munich/StockFood; c. Photodisc; c. Royalty-Free/Corbis; c.r. Michael Newman/PhotoEdit; t.r. Royalty-Free/Corbis; t.r.c. Iraida Icaza/Taxi/Getty Images. B36: b. Royalty-Free/Corbis; b.r. Photodisc; c. Ken Karp; t. Photodisc; t.c. Royalty-Free/Corbis; t.c. Photodisc; t.l. Photodisc. B37: b. Ken Karp; b.r. Ken Karp; c. Ken Karp; t. Ken Karp; t.l. Ken Karp. B38 (Food Guide Pyramid) Fats Group: t. Photodisc; c.l. Ellen Lieberman/StockFood; b.l. Burke/Triolo/FoodPix/Getty Images; b.r. Spencer Jones/FoodPix. Milk Group: t. Felicia Martinez/PhotoEdit; b.l. David Kelly Crow/PhotoEdit; r. Burke/Triolo/FoodPix/Getty Images. Meat Group: t. Iraida Icaza/Taxi/Getty Images; cl. Eisenhut & Mayer/FoodPix/Getty Images; t.r. Cephas-Rock/StockFood; b.l. Photodisc; c.r. Burke/Triolo/FoodPix/Getty Images; b.cr. David Young-Wolff/PhotoEdit; b.r. Photodisc. Vegetable Group: t.l. Photodisc; t.c. Photodisc; t.r. Corbis; c.l. Photodisc; c. Corbis; b.l. Photodisc; b.c.l. Scott Lanza/FoodPix/Getty Images; b.c.r. Corbis; b.r. Photodisc. Fruit Group: t.l. Photodisc; t. Corbis; t.r. Isabelle Rozenbaum and Frederic Cirou/PhotoAlto/PictureQuest; c. Photodisc; t.c.r. Corbis; b.l. Photodisc; b.c.l. Photodisc; b.c.r. Judd Pilossof/FoodPix/Getty Images; b.r. Isabelle Rozenbaum and Frederic Cirou/PhotoAlto/PictureQuest; b.r. Isabelle Rozenbaum/PhotoAlto/PictureQuest. Bread Group: top row, l. to r.: Brian Hagiwara/FoodPix; Jennifer Durham/FoodPix/Getty Images; Foodcollection/StockFood; Photodisc Blue/Getty Images; Photodisc; Corbis; bottom row, l. to r.: Newedel/StockFood Munich; Jim Scherer/StockFood; Bruce James/FoodPix/Getty Images; Photodisc; Eisenhut & Mayer/FoodPix/Getty Images; Eising Food Photography/StockFood. B39: b. Ken Karp; t. Royalty-Free/Corbis. B40: Ken Karp. B41: Ken Karp. B42: b.l. Ken Karp; b.r. BananaStock/Alamy; c. Ken Karp; t.l. Ken Karp; t.r. Royalty-Free/Corbis. B43: Ken Karp; inset. Christoph Wilhelm/Corbis. B44: Ken Karp. B45: b. Ken Karp; t. Ken Karp. B46: Ken Karp. B48: Ken Karp. B49: l. Ken Karp; r. Spencer Jones/PictureArts/Corbis. B50: Ken Karp. B51: b. Ken Karp; t. Ken Karp. B53: Robert Manella. B54: c. Photodisc; l. Photodisc; r. Photodisc. B55: Ken Karp. B56: b. Ken Karp; t. Ken Karp. B58: Michael Newman/PhotoEdit. B59: Ken Karp. B60: Bob Daemmrich/Image Works. B61: David Young-Wolff/PhotoEdit. B62: Paul Almasy/Corbis. B63: Ken Karp. B64: Ken Karp. B65: Robert Manella. B66: Ken Karp. B67: David Young-Wolff/PhotoEdit. B68: Ken Karp. B69: Photodisc. B72: b.l. Tony Freeman/PhotoEdit; b.r. Michael Newman/PhotoEdit; t.l. Royalty-Free/Corbis; t.r. Nancy Sheehan/PhotoEdit. C1: b. A. Ramey/PhotoEdit; c.l. Robert Manella; c.r. RubberBall Productions/Getty Images; t.l. Robert Manella; t.r. Photodisc. C2: b.c. Photodisc; b.l. Photodisc; b.l. Photodisc; c. Radlunçd & Associates/Brand X/PictureQuest; l.c. Photodisc/Getty Images; t.c. Photodisc Green/Getty Images; t.l. Dennis Gottlieb/FoodPix. C3: b.c. David Young-Wolff/PhotoEdit; c. Photodisc; c.r. Stockbyte/PictureQuest; c.r. Myrleen Ferguson Cate/Photo; c.r. Royalty-Free/Corbis; r. The President's Challenge; t.c.r. Corbis; t.r. Royalty-Free/Corbis; t.r. Amy Etra/PhotoEdit. C4: WS Productions/Brand X/Getty Images. C5: Robert Manella. C7: c. Royalty-Free/Corbis; l. Spencer Grant/PhotoEdit; r. Image Source/Alamy; t. Robert Manella. C8: Robert Manella. C9: Image Source/Alamy. C10: Ken Lax/Photo Researchers. C11: b, b.c. Photodisc; t. Photodisc; t.c. Photodisc. C12: ThinkStock/SuperStock. C13: b. Lisette Le Bon/SuperStock; t. RubberBall Productions/Getty Images. C14: Photodisc/Getty Images. C15: Michael Newman/PhotoEdit. C16: Ken Karp. C17: Michael Newman/PhotoEdit. C18: b. Photodisc; t. Robert Manella. C20: Photodisc. C22: c. Ken Karp; l. Ken Karp; r. Ken Karp. C23: Brand X/Alamy Images. C25: Royalty-Free/Corbis. C26: Tom Cater/PhotoEdit. C28: c. Ken Karp; c.l. David Young-Wolff/PhotoEdit; c.r. John Morgan/Index Stock; l. Robert Manella; r. Photodisc. C29: Photodisc. C30: Richard Hutchings/Corbis. C31: Robert Manella. C32: Bob Hunsicker/Pharos Studios, Inc.; C33: b. Photodisc; l. Brand X/PictureQuest; r. Robert Manella; t.

Credits

C Squared Studios/Photodisc/PictureQuest. C34: b. Robert Manella; t. Robert Manella. C35: Ken Karp. C36: Syracuse Newspapers/ The Image Works. C37: t.l. A. Ramey/PhotoEdit. C37: t.r. Ken Karp. C38: Robert Manella. C39: Robert Manella. C40: Robert Manella. C41: Ken Karp. C42: Robert Manella. C43: Robert Manella. C46: b. Comstock/Alamy; b.c. Jules Frazier/Getty; b.l. Corbis Images/ PictureQuest; c.l. Robin Nelson/PhotoEdit; l. Burke/Triolo/Brand X/PictureQuest; t.c. Royalty-Free/Corbis; t.c.l. Comstock/Alamy; t.l. C Squared Studios/Getty. C47: b.c.r. Corbis Images/Picture- Quest ; c. S. Meltzer/PhotoLink/Getty; c.r. Ryan McVay/Getty; r. David Crausby/Alamy; t.c.r. Erin Garvey/Index Stock Imagery; t.r. Lucidio Studio/SuperStock. C48: Tom Carter/PhotoEdit. C50: Pho- todisc. C51: Mary Kate Denny/PhotoEdit. C52: Ken Karp. C53: Ken Karp. C54: David Young-Wolff/PhotoEdit. C55: Robert Manella. C56: Ken Karp. C57: Geri Engberg/The Image Work. C58: Robert Manella. C59: Michelle D. Bridwell/PhotoEdit. C60: b. Ken Karp; t. Robert Manella. C62: Robert Manella. C63: Robert Manella. C65: Phil Schermeister/Corbis. C66: Robert Manella. C67: Robert Manella. C68: SuperStock. C69: Doug Wilson/Corbis. C70: Robert Manella. C71: Kindra Clineff/Index Stock Imagery. C72: Royalty- Free/Corbis. C73: Courtesy of American Red Cross. C74: Robert Manella. C75: Courtesy of American Red Cross. C76: Ken Karp. C77: Comstock/Alamy. C78: Robert Manella. C80: Royalty-Free/ Corbis. C81: Michael Newman/PhotoEdit. C84: Tony Freeman/ PhotoEdit. C85: John M. Roberts/Corbis. C88: b.l. Ed Reschke/ Peter Arnold; b.r. Najlah Feanny/Corbis Saba; t.l. Bob Daemmrich/ The Image Works; t.r. Felicia Martinez/PhotoEdit. D1: b. David Young-Wolff/PhotoEdit; b.l. SW Productions/Getty Images; b.r. Rubber Ball/Alamy; c.l. Ken Karp; t.l. Comstock/Getty Images; t.r. Arthur Tilley/Taxi/Getty Images. D2: b.c.l. Lon C. Diehl/PhotoEdit; b.l. William Whitehurst/Corbis; c.l. Photodisc; t.c.l._ Comstock/Alamy; t.l. Roy Morsch/Corbis. D3: b.c.r. Royalty- Free/Corbis; b.r. Ken Karp; c. Eric Fowke/PhotoEdit; c.r. Donald Higgs/Index Stock; t.c. Photodisc; t.r. Royalty-Free/Corbis. D4: Bob Hunsicker. D5: Ken Karp. D6: b. Ken Karp; b.c. Photodisc Blue/Getty Images; t. Photodisc; t.c. Royalty-Free/Corbis. D7: Ken Karp. D11: Laura Dwight/Corbis. D12: Ken Karp. D13: Robert Manella. D14: Richard Hutchings/PhotoEdit. D15: David Young- Wolff/PhotoEdit. D16: b. Royalty-Free/Corbis; c. Royalty-Free/Cor- bis; t. Royalty-Free/Corbis. D17: Paul Barton/Corbis. D18: Jiang Jin/SuperStock. D19: Ed Bock/Corbis. D20: DigitalStock. D21: James Leynse/Corbis SABA. D23: Amy Etra/PhotoEdit. D24: HIRB/Index Stock Imagery. D25: Photodisc. D26: Strauss/Curtis/Corbis. D27: Royalty-Free/Corbis. D28: Myrleen Ferguson Cate/PhotoEdit. D30: Mark Peterson/Corbis. D32: Gabe Palmer/Corbis. D33: Kwame Zikomo/SuperStock. D34: Royalty-Free/Corbis. D35: Royalty-Free/Corbis. D36: Courtesy of Lele. D37: Robert Manella. D38: Michael Newman/PhotoEdit. D39: Myrleen Ferguson Cate/PhotoEdit. D40: Janine Wiedel/ Alamy. D41: Photodisc. D43: Photodisc. D44: David Butow/Corbis SABA. D48: b. Photodisc; b.l. Photodisc Blue/Getty Images; c. Photodisc; c.l. Photodisc; l. Corbis Images/PictureQuest; t.c. Pho- todisc; t.l. Single Images. D49: b.c. Photodisc; b.r. Royalty-Free/ Corbis; c.r. Ken Karp; r. Lon C. Diehl/PhotoEdit; t.c.r. Burke/Triolo/ Brand X/PictureQuest; t.r. Photodisc Green/Getty Images. D50: Bryn Colton/Assignments Photographers/Corbis. D52: David Young-Wolff/PhotoEdit. D53: Photodisc. D55: N. Poritz/Photo Re- searchers. D56: Robert Manella. D57: Luis M. de la Maza/Photo- take. D60: Robert Manella. D61: Ken Karp. D62: Robert Manella.

D63: Joseph Sohm/ChromoSohm, Inc./Corbis. D64: Ken Karp. D65: b. Nicolas Russell/Image Bank/Getty Images; t. Larry Mulvehill/ Photo Researchers. D66: b. Single Images; t. Robert Manella. D69: Robert Manella. D70: Ken Karp. D71: Mary Kate Denny/Pho- toEdit. D73: l. Michael P. Gadomski/Photo Researchers; r. David McCarthy/Photo Researchers. D74: Photodisc. D75: Royalty- Free/Corbis. D76: Flash Light/Stock Boston. D80: b.l. Photodisc Green/Getty Images; t.r. James Noble/Corbis. E1: b. Ariel Skel- ley/Corbis; c.l. Ken Karp; c.r. Ken Karp; t. Ken Karp. E2: b.l. Pho- todisc; b.l.c. Photodisc; c. Photodisc; c. Photodisc; l.c. Photodisc; l.c. Photodisc; t.l. Photodisc. E3: b.c. Photodisc; b.c. Francisco Cruz/Superstock; b.r. Photodisc; c.r. Photodisc/PictureQuest; r.c. Photodisc; t.c. Ken Karp; t.c.r. Comstock/Alamy; t.r. Brand X/ Alamy . E4: l. Photodisc; r. Photodisc; t. Brand X/Alamy Images. E5: l. Robert Manella; r. Robert Manella. E6: Ken Karp. E7: David Young-Wolff/PhotoEdit. E8: Rolf Bruderer/Corbis. E9: Studio M/ Stock Connection/Alamy Images. E10: b. Robert Manella; t. Robert Manella. E12: Robert Manella. E14: Photodisc. E15: Charles Gupton/ Corbis. E16: Robert Manella. E17: Myrleen Ferguson Cate/Pho- toEdit. E18: Photodisc Green/Getty Images. E19: Robert Manella. E20: Photodisc Green/Getty Images. E22: Robert Manella. E23: Dennis MacDonald/PhotoEdit. E25: Robert Manella. E26: Jeff Greenberg/PhotoEdit. E27: Robert Manella. E28: Bill Aron/Pho- toEdit. E29: Photodisc. E32: b.l. Photodisc; c. Photodisc Green/ Getty Images; c. Photodisc; l.c. Photodisc; t.l. Joe Atlas/Brand X Pictures/PictureQuest; t.l.c. Joe Atlas/Brand X Pictures/Picture- Quest. E33: b.c. Comstock/Alamy ; b.r. Royalty-Free/Corbis; c.r. Angela Wyant/Stone/Getty Images; c.r. David Young-Wolff/Pho- toEdit; c.r. Photodisc; c.r. Robert Manella; t.r. Bonnie Kamin/ PhotoEdit; t.r.c. John Foxx/Alamy . E34: Royalty-Free/Corbis. E35: Joseph Sohm/ChromoSohm, Inc./Getty Images. E36: Don Mason/Corbis. E37: David Young-Wolff/PhotoEdit. E38: Pho- todisc. E39: Jeff Greenberg/PhotoEdit. E40: b. Royalty-Free/ Corbis; c. Thinkstock/Alamy Images; t.l. Photodisc Green/Getty Images; t.r. MediacolorÕs/Alamy Images. E42: b. Photodisc; b.l. Photodisc; t. Photodisc. E44: David Young-Wolff/PhotoEdit. E45: Myrleen Ferguson Cate/PhotoEdit. E46: Photodisc Green/ Getty Images. E47: Allen Lee Page/Corbis. E48: Gabe Palmer/ Corbis. E49: Bonnie Kamin/PhotoEdit. E50: Image Ideas/Picture- Quest. E51: Royalty-Free/Corbis. E52: Robert Manella. E53: Roy- alty-Free/Corbis. E54: Robert Manella. E55: Mark Gibson/Index Stock Imagery. E56: Cindy Kassab/Corbis. E57: Ariel Skelley/ Corbis. E59: Steven Mark Needham/FoodPix. E60: Jonathan Nourok/PhotoEdit. E61: b. Robert Manella; t. Brandon Cole/ Marine Photography/Alamy Images. E63: David Young-Wolff/ Stone/Getty Images. E64: Rob & Sas/Corbis. E67: Robert Manella. E68: David Young-Wolff/PhotoEdit. E69: Brand X/Getty Images. E70: Myrleen Ferguson Cate/PhotoEdit. E71: l. Tony Freeman/Pho- toEdit; r. USDA/AP Photo. E72: Don Smetzer/PhotoEdit. E73: b. LWA-Dann Tardif/Corbis; t. James A. Sugar/Corbis. E74: Picture Libray Waldhaus/Alamy Images. E75: Tom Stewart/Corbis. E76: Robert Manella. E77: Dorothy Littell Greco/Stock Boston. E80: b.l. Medford Taylor/National Geographic/Getty Images; b.r. Robert Manella; t.l. Robert Manella; t.r. Bill Aron/PhotoEdit.

Illustration Charles Beyl: A19. Joel & Sharon Harris: A24, B5, B6, B7, B9, B11, B12, B15, B18, B21, B28, C6, C12, C14, C21, C24, D6, D22, D31, D51, D53, D58, D72. Joe Kulka: C82, C83. Tadeusz Majewski: B52, C15, D8, D9, E53, E58, E59, E62, E65, E66.